3D Environment Design with Blender 5

Second Edition

Enhance your modeling, texturing, and lighting skills to create realistic 3D scenes

Abdelilah Hamdani

‹packt›

3D Environment Design with Blender

Second Edition

Portfolio Director: Rohit Rajkumar
Relationship Lead: Neha Pande
Project Manager: Sandip Tadge
Content Engineer: Shreya Sarkar
Technical Editor: Sumant Jadhav
Copy Editor: Safis Editing
Indexer: Rekha Nair
Proofreader: Shreya Sarkar
Production Designer: Ganesh Bhadwalkar
Growth Lead: Namita Velgekar

First published: January 2023
Second published: March 2026

Production reference: 1260226

Published by Packt Publishing Ltd.
Grosvenor House
11 St Paul's Square
Birmingham
B3 1RB, UK.

ISBN 978-1-83620-329-2
www.packtpub.com

To my awesome mom and dad, for giving me the advantage and opportunity to succeed. To my two best mentors, MJ Demarco and Jim Rohn, who opened my eyes, guided me, and are still guiding me throughout my entrepreneurial journey.

- Abdelilah Hamdani

Foreword

Environmental art is one of the unsung heroes of the CG world. It doesn't matter whether you're doing a turnaround render of some random 3D prop or building a complete animated film. Those objects and stories exist in a space, an environment. Even if that environment is the void of outer space, it's still an environment.

And that space is more than just the incidental surroundings around some kind of hero object. It has a character of its own, built by millions of tiny stories that contribute to its overall look. That grounding is what makes every other part of the scene believable... makes it feel real. The aesthetic doesn't matter. That environment could be pure fantasy or heavily stylized. Either way, it's the baseline for believability, the scaffolding upon which we suspend our disbelief. And it's the work of you, the designer, to make the audience believe your environment is real.

That's why I'm happy that this book, *3D Environment Design with Blender 5*, exists. Whether you're working in entertainment or doing architectural visualization, all 3D scenes need an environment, and this is exactly the kind of thing I know Blender is really good at. By the end of this book, you'll know it, too.

I don't think I've had the pleasure of meeting Mr. Hamdani personally (though I hope we can remedy that at a BCON in the future), but I have read through the content of this book, and I'm impressed with the clarity and detail that he uses to cover this topic. It can be a lot (I mean, it's the whole environment), but he does a really great job of walking you through all the core processes and tools necessary to make your own environment art. I'm sure you'll be pleased as you work through it.

I can't wait to see what you make!

Jason van Gumster

Professional Blender Consultant and Author

Foreword

In an era defined by the rapid advancement of Artificial Intelligence (AI), it often feels as though the soul of artistry is being sidelined. There is a growing narrative that the "result" is all that matters, regardless of how it was generated. But those of us who live and breathe 3D know the truth: there is an irreplaceable pride and a profound sense of joy in the act of creating.

This book is a testament to that pride. It is an invitation to master the craft of photorealism in Blender, not by taking shortcuts, but by understanding the "why" behind every pixel.

I often use the analogy of a journey. If you need to get from one point to another, you can drive a car. You will arrive quickly, but the world outside will be a blur; you'll miss the texture of the road, the play of light on the leaves, and the subtle details of the path. However, if you choose to *walk*, the journey changes. It takes longer, yes, but you notice everything. You feel the terrain. You understand the landscape in a way a driver never can.

The same is true for 3D environments. Using tools that provide everything "ready-made" might get you to the finish line, but it won't give you the "eyes" of an artist. By learning to build from scratch, as this book teaches, you will develop the awareness to spot the nuances that make a scene feel truly alive.

Within these pages, Abdelilah Hamdani guides you through the entire 3D pipeline. You will dive deep into the mechanics of modeling, the art of preparing object texturing, and the texture creation itself, learning that even a single image can hold the key to a photorealistic surface. From the real-time power of EEVEE to the physical accuracy of Cycles, and through the final touches of lighting and compositing, you are not just learning software, you are mastering a craft.

By the time you reach the final chapter, you won't just have a finished render. You will have the technical confidence to tackle any project and the artistic "background" to know exactly why a scene looks right.

Whether you are just starting or looking to fill the gaps in your knowledge, you have come to the right place. It's time to stop driving past the details and start walking through the world you are about to create.

Be proud of what you build.

Carlos Barreto

Creator of CEB Studios

(Developer of Blender Tools and 3D Animation)

Contributors

About the author

Abdelilah Hamdani is a photorealistic environment designer and 3D animator who is experienced in producing 3D art in a professional environment. Projects he has worked on include the 2020 Kuwait election and the US Gambian bridge construction. Abdelilah is also an online instructor who has taught more than 25,000 students worldwide. He is the founder of Reality Fakers, a platform that teaches 3D photorealism.

About the reviewers

Brent Patterson is an educator and artist, based in New York, with over 30 years of creative design experience. He is an associate professor of art and design at Buffalo State University, where he teaches courses on Blender and digital media. Patterson writes and advocates for the use of free and open source software in education and professional practice and has spoken at the Blender Conference in Amsterdam multiple times. He also works as a creative consultant, art director, and visual effects artist for creative agencies in the United States and Europe.

I would like to say thank you to my dear wife, Stacy, who is always patient and encouraging when I'm tinkering on another Blender project. And a special thank you to my children, Oliver, Avery, Elliot, and London, who continuously amaze me with their creativity, thoughtfulness, and love.

Mohamed Essam El Deen Farouk is a 3D artist from Egypt with nine years of professional experience. Essam has always been passionate about games and bringing ideas to life through 3D modeling. Over the years, he has developed strong expertise in creating a wide range of 3D assets, from characters to environments, with a focus on both creativity and technical precision. His main pipeline includes Blender, ZBrush, Substance Painter, Unreal Engine, and Unity, which are tools he uses daily to design, sculpt, and texture. Essam loves the process of 3D modeling and finds great joy in transforming concepts into detailed, immersive digital art.

Table of Contents

Preface

Creating 3D environments is now more popular than ever. It's a skill that every 3D designer should master. Whether you are or want to be a freelancer or you're simply a hobbyist, this book, *3D Environment Design with Blender 5*, will serve you well.

The second edition of this book will give you a great insight into how 3D works, starting by showing you the mistakes most 3D designers make that prevent people from achieving great results. I have taught more than 25,000 students and responded to hundreds of students' questions. Trust me – I've seen it all. To give you the maximum value, there is no better way to start this book than to show you these mistakes and how you can avoid them. Then, in later chapters, we will dive into the creation of an epic landscape environment in Blender 5.

This book will give you enough knowledge and inspiration to create multiple environments, fill your portfolio, and attract clients and companies.

What makes this book special is that it's sequential; each chapter moves you forward and contributes to the final result. We will only learn the things we need, and anything you learn, you will apply.

Each chapter will upgrade your skills and push you forward toward achieving the final result, which is the creation of realistic landscape environments in Blender.

Who this book is for

This book is for aspiring 3D environment artists, game designers, and CG visualizers who are eager to learn and upgrade their 3D design skills. It is also suitable for hobbyists of Blender who want to fast-track their understanding of 3D environment design and freelancers who want to upgrade their 3D skills, fill their portfolios, and attract clients and companies that require 3D design work. Familiarity with Blender's interface will enable the readers to fully absorb the step-by-step workflows in the book to improve realism for game development, CGI, or visualization projects.

What this book covers

Chapter 1, Most Common Modeling Mistakes That Prevent You from Achieving Photorealism, will cover all the mistakes that designers make in 3D modeling and scale matching, and will show the reader the ways to fix and overcome these challenges by working on a real wood cabin reference.

Chapter 2, The Basics of Realistic Texturing in Blender, will highlight the importance of using different texturing maps to achieve photorealism. We will learn how to create a real wood material from scratch using procedural texturing.

Chapter 3, Efficient Unwrapping and Texturing in Blender, will go through the process of unwrapping the wood cabin and texturing it in Blender – starting by importing materials from one scene into another, understanding how UV mapping works, and using the **Displace** modifier to add random details to the wood geometry.

Chapter 4, Creating and Scattering Realistic Natural Plants, will involve creating a ground under our wood cabin, using the **Proportional Editing** tool to add nice hills to the ground. Then, we will go through the process of creating, unwrapping, and texturing different types of plants and leaves. Next, we will learn how to use Geometry Nodes to scatter objects randomly across a surface, scattering plants and leaves all over the ground.

Chapter 5, Achieving Photorealistic Lighting in Your Environment with Blender, will detail three ways to lighten the wood cabin scene. We will achieve lighting that matches the same lighting we have in the wood cabin reference we're using.

Chapter 6, Creating Realistic Landscapes in Blender, will guide you on how to create realistic snow, rocky mountains, and a river scene. We will learn to install the **A.N.T.Landscape** add-on, create various landscapes, tweak its settings, and change its shape to make it look as realistic as possible.

Chapter 7, Creating and Animating Realistic, Natural-Looking Water, will handle the step of creating a realistic water shader. We will learn to mix between the **Glass BSDF** and **Transparency BSDF** nodes to create a nice reflective and refractive surface. Then we will learn to animate the waves on the surface of the water by inserting keyframes into the Timeline editor.

Chapter 8, Creating Procedural Mud Material, will tap into the unlimited potential of Blender's incredibly powerful node editor. You will learn to create a **Mud** material using procedural texturing by combining many different layers of details, such as adding water puddles and mud details.

Chapter 9, Texturing Landscape with Mud Material, will entail texturing the landscape with the **Mud** material. You will learn how to mix different materials – here, the rocky snow and mud. You will also learn how to optimize and organize your node setup using groups.

Chapter 10, Creating Natural Assets: Rock, will teach you how to create realistic rock assets. These rocks are perfect for giving a realistic and natural feeling to our landscape environment.

Chapter 11, Creating Realistic Flowers in Blender, will describe how to create organic-looking flowers for our landscape environment based on real references.

Chapter 12, Creating Trees Ready for Large Environments, will guide you through creating trees that are optimized to be scattered across large-scale environments.

Chapter 13, Using Geometry Nodes to Scatter Objects in Blender, will outline how to use Geometry Nodes in Blender to scatter trees, flowers, and rocks throughout our landscape and river environments. You will learn how to create a flexible scattering system that places objects in specifically chosen areas, while also adjusting the scale and rotation of assets and controlling their density.

Chapter 14, Finalizing the Landscape and River Scenes – Lighting, Rendering, and Compositing, will sum up our processes and the book by teaching you how to aim your camera to render awesome landscape and river shots. Then, you will learn some compositing tricks to make the final render stand out.

To get the most out of this book

Blender is free software. Throughout this book, we'll be using some techniques that require you to have a decent setup. Anything above an i5 8th gen, 16 GB RAM, and GTX 1060 will do the job.

Software/hardware covered in the book	Operating system requirements
Blender 5 or above	Windows, macOS, or Linux
fSpy	Windows

Once Blender 5 is installed, let's dive in!

Note

Blender is continuously evolving with frequent updates. Because of this rapid development, certain legacy features or third-party add-ons may change, require manual updates, or become deprecated over time. If you encounter interface differences or add-on compatibility issues in future versions, always refer to the official **Blender 5.0 Documentation** for the most up-to-date workflows: https:// docs.blender.org/manual/en/latest/index.html.

This book makes reference to, and includes images of, third-party assets sourced from Pixabay. All such assets have been legally acquired and used in accordance with their respective license agreements. These assets have been incorporated into original projects and demonstrations solely for educational and illustrative purposes as part of this work.

Note that the author acknowledges the use of cutting-edge AI, such as ChatGPT, with the sole aim of enhancing the language and clarity within the book, thereby ensuring a smooth reading experience for readers. It's important to note that the content itself has been crafted by the author and edited by a professional publishing team. Packt does not accept AI-generated content that replaces expert authorship.

Download the assets and resource files

The assets and resource files for the book are hosted on GitHub at `https://github.com/PacktPublishing/3D-Environment-Design-with-Blender-5-Second-Edition`.

We also have other code bundles from our rich catalog of books and videos available at `https://github.com/PacktPublishing`. Check them out!

Download the color images

We also provide a PDF file that has color images of the screenshots used in this book. You can download the PDF file here:`https://packt.link/gbp/9781836203292`

Code in Action

The Code in Action videos for this book can be viewed at `https://packt.link/KKAqz`

Conventions used

There are a number of text conventions used throughout this book.

`CodeInText`: Indicates code words in text, database table names, folder names, filenames, file extensions, pathnames, dummy URLs, user input, and X (formerly, Twitter) handles. For example: "Type `landscape` in the search bar. The list will automatically filter to show relevant extensions."

Bold: Indicates a new term, an important word, or words that you see on the screen. For instance, words in menus or dialog boxes appear in the text like this. For example: "To generate the river, start by changing **Operator Preset** to **River**. This preset is designed to create long, continuous height variations."

Warnings or important notes appear like this.

Tips and tricks appear like this.

Get in touch

Feedback from our readers is always welcome.

General feedback: If you have questions about any aspect of this book or have any general feedback, please email us at customercare@packt.com and mention the book's title in the subject of your message.

Errata: Although we have taken every care to ensure the accuracy of our content, mistakes do happen. If you have found a mistake in this book, we would be grateful if you reported this to us. Please visit http://www.packt.com/submit-errata, click **Submit Errata**, and fill in the form.

Piracy: If you come across any illegal copies of our works in any form on the internet, we would be grateful if you would provide us with the location address or website name. Please contact us at copyright@packt.com with a link to the material.

If you are interested in becoming an author: If there is a topic that you have expertise in and you are interested in either writing or contributing to a book, please visit https://authors.packt.com/login.

Subscribe to Game Dev Assembly Newsletter!

We are excited to introduce **Game Dev Assembly**, our brand-new newsletter dedicated to everything game development. Whether you're a programmer, designer, artist, animator, or studio lead, you'll get exclusive insights, industry trends, and expert tips to help you build better games and grow your skills. Sign up today and become part of a growing community of creators, innovators, and game changers.

https://packt.link/gamedev-newsletter

Scan the QR code to join instantly!

Free benefits with your book

This book comes with free benefits to support your learning. Activate them now for instant access (see the *"How to Unlock"* section for instructions).

Here's a quick overview of what you can instantly unlock with your purchase:

DRM-Free PDF Version

Download DRM-free PDF and ePub copies of this book.

7-Day Packt Library Access

Get 7-day unlimited access to 8,000+ books and videos. No credit card required.

Available for first-time Packt+ trial users only.

Next-Gen Reader Access

Read this book on Packt Reader with progress sync, dark mode and note-taking.

How to Unlock

Scan the QR code (or go to packtpub.com/unlock). Search for this book by name, confirm the edition, and then follow the steps on the page.

Note: Keep your invoice handy. Purchases made directly from Packt don't require one

Share Your Thoughts

Once you've read *3D Environment Design with Blender 5, Second Edition,* we'd love to hear your thoughts! Scan the QR code below to go straight to the Amazon review page for this book and share your feedback.

https://packt.link/r/1836203292

Your review is important to us and the tech community and will help us make sure we're delivering excellent quality content.

Part 1

Turn a Real Reference into a Realistic 3D Scene in Blender 5

Before we can start creating our landscape project, there are some tricks and tools that you need to know about. First, it's important to know the most common modeling mistakes that prevent many 3D designers from achieving photorealism. Next, you will learn the basics of realistic texturing, good UV mapping, scattering with Geometry Nodes, and lighting. Then we will put everything we've learned together to turn a real wood cabin reference into a realistic 3D scene in Blender

This part of the book includes the following chapters:

- *Chapter 1, Most Common Modeling Mistakes That Prevent You from Achieving Photorealism*
- *Chapter 2, The Basics of Realistic Texturing in Blender*
- *Chapter 3, Efficient Unwrapping and Texturing in Blender*
- *Chapter 4, Creating and Scattering Realistic Natural Plants*
- *Chapter 5, Achieving Photorealistic Lighting in Your Environment with Blender*

1

Most Common Modeling Mistakes That Prevent You from Achieving Photorealism

Have you ever tried to create a photorealistic scene in Blender? Are you looking for a step-by-step formula to help you achieve photorealism? Do you find yourself stuck getting the right settings? If so, you're not alone.

In this chapter, we're going to break down the three modeling mistakes that most 3D designers make that prevent them from achieving photorealism in Blender.

Modeling represents the foundation for what's coming next: *texturing*, *UV mapping*, *lighting*, *compositing*, and *rendering*. Getting the foundation wrong will make all your efforts be in vain, so the goal of this chapter is to help you get the modeling foundation right.

The first mistake is relying on only your eyes to estimate the scale of objects you're modeling. When it comes to photorealism, getting the right scale plays a crucial role. So, we'll be discussing the Blender unit system and how to perform research to get the correct, realistic measurements of objects before modeling them.

The second mistake is related to scale matching. Most designers immediately dive into creating a 3D scene based on a real reference without doing any scale matching. This makes it really hard to get the same camera settings (such as position, rotation, and focal length) that an actual photographer would use. This results in an unmatched result to the reference you're working with. To overcome this issue, we will learn how to use **fSpy**, a tool that allows you to replicate the camera settings adopted by a photographer (focal length, camera position, and rotation) when taking a picture of an actual image and export it into Blender.

We will explore how the fSpy interface works, how to use it, and how to install the fSpy add-on into Blender and import fSpy project files.

The third mistake is modeling without the **Bevel** modifier on. By the end of this chapter, you will understand the importance of using the **Bevel** modifier when modeling and the role it plays in achieving photorealism. You will also understand the different beveling settings and how they work inside Blender.

In this chapter, we'll be covering the following topics:

- The importance of using a real-world scale
- Understanding fSpy
- Scale matching in Blender: modeling a wood cabin
- Using the **Bevel** modifier
- Common modeling pitfalls and how to fix them

Your purchase includes a free PDF copy + exclusive extras

Your purchase includes a DRM-free PDF copy of this book, 7-day trial to the Packt+ library (no credit card required), and additional exclusive extras. See the *Free benefits with your book* section in the *Preface* to unlock them instantly and maximize your learning.

Technical requirements

This chapter requires a system capable of running **Blender version 5.0** or above (Windows, macOS, or Linux).

You can download the resources for this chapter from GitHub at: `https://github.com/PacktPublishing/3D-Environment-Design-with-Blender-5-Second-Edition/tree/ab43270b643a41ba8f915f74e3bf78573b10a816/chapter-1`

Visit this link to check out the video of the code being run: `https://packt.link/oBbna`

A note on the second edition

This second edition, *3D Environment Design with Blender 5*, builds on the foundations of the first by updating the workflow to align with the newer Blender 5 version. Several explanations have been refined for clarity, tools and settings have been updated where needed, and common pitfalls observed from real student feedback have been addressed. You can expect clearer step-by-step guidance, more practical context, and improvements that make achieving photorealism faster, more accurate, and more consistent.

Changes in Blender 5 you need to know about before starting

Before we begin modeling, here are the Blender 5 updates that matter for the techniques in this chapter:

- **More accurate Viewport scaling**: Blender 5 has improved the way the Viewport displays real-world units. This makes scale matching easier because *one meter* in the scene now corresponds more precisely to grid spacing and camera depth, reducing distortion when aligning 3D objects to references.
- **Improved camera controls (when using fSpy)**: The camera frame in Blender 5 has clearer borders and improved opacity, making it easier to see your reference image behind the camera. This helps when doing fSpy camera matching, since aligning edges and vanishing points is more readable.
- **Faster modifier performance (including Bevel)**: The **Bevel** modifier is now faster and handles shading more cleanly. This helps when experimenting with small bevel amounts required for photorealism later in the chapter.

Let's get started!

The importance of using a real-world scale

When creating complex scenes in Blender, it's easy to fall into the trap of eyeballing the scale of objects when modeling them, without taking the right measurements. This can lead to multiple problems that will prevent you later on from achieving a photorealistic and eye-pleasing result. We think our eyes are accurate – "*I know how large this window is, it's this size*"; however, we're really bad at estimating measurements simply because we give more emphasis to the things that we pay attention to and neglect the parts we deem unimportant.

This then affects the photorealistic aspect of your scene: you end up wondering what is wrong with your scene. Something just looks off, and you don't know what it is. You start messing around with the materials and the lighting, and maybe those are perfect, but then you realize the foundation was wrong. So, it is important to get this modeling foundation right.

The solution is to always use a real-world scale.

Let's say you're designing a wood cabin (commonly referred to architecturally as a *log cabin*); the first thing you need to do is research on Google: *What is the height of a log cabin?* Here's what I got when I did that search:

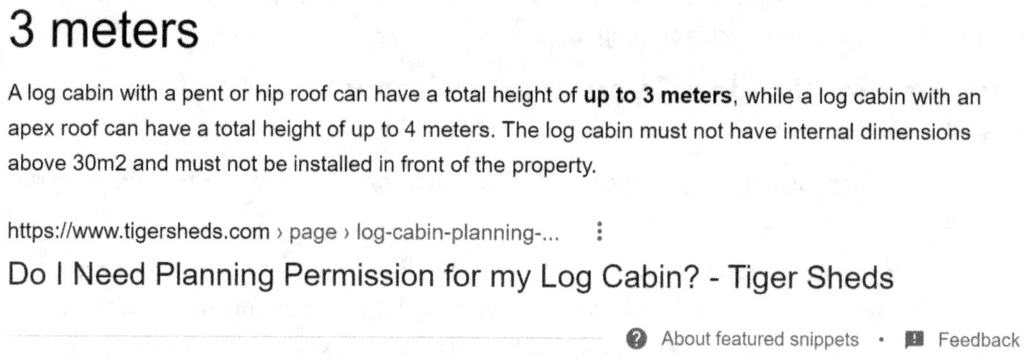

3 meters

A log cabin with a pent or hip roof can have a total height of **up to 3 meters**, while a log cabin with an apex roof can have a total height of up to 4 meters. The log cabin must not have internal dimensions above 30m2 and must not be installed in front of the property.

https://www.tigersheds.com › page › log-cabin-planning-...   ⋮

Do I Need Planning Permission for my Log Cabin? - Tiger Sheds

About featured snippets • 🚩 Feedback

Figure 1.1 – Google search for the height of a log cabin

So, now we understand that a wooden cabin must not exceed 3 meters in height, so everything between 2 and 3 meters should be reasonable. With the apex roof included, another meter is added.

Since we must not exceed 30 m^2, we can give a dimension of 5 m wide and 6 m long (5 m × 6 m = 30 m^2).

Next, we will check the Blender unit scale:

1. Go to **Scene Properties**.
2. Click on the **Units** tab.
3. Then, choose the **Unit System** measurement that suits you.

In *Figure 1.2*, the **Unit System** settings allow you to choose between **Metric** and **Imperial**:

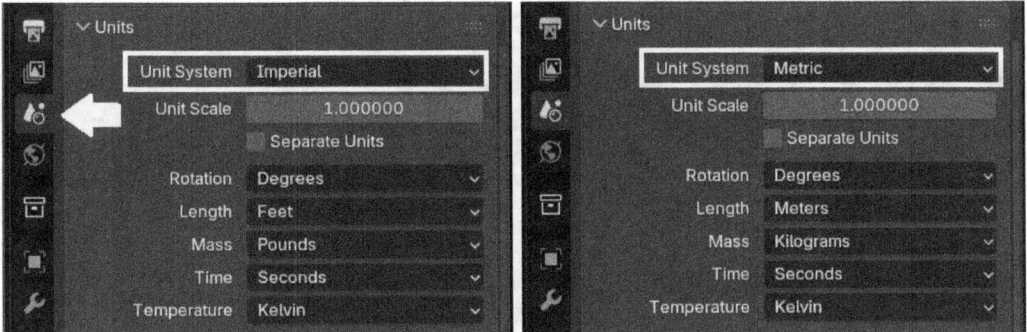

Figure 1.2 – Blender scene properties units system

Choosing **Metric** will measure the length in meters and mass in kilograms, unlike **Imperial**, which will measure the length in feet and mass in pounds. This is the right way to set real-world measurements in Blender.

Another good reason to always use a real-world scale is that it aligns with how physics simulation works in Blender. Physics in Blender, such as gravity, rigid body, and mass, relies on real measurements to function properly.

To emphasize this even more, let's create a sphere; by default, the sphere will be 2 meters in diameter.

Next, we go to **Physics Properties**, and we click on **Rigid Body** while making sure the sphere is selected.

Under the **Settings** tab, you'll see that **Mass** is set to **1 kg** by default. This means that the 2-meter diameter sphere you've just created has a weight of 1 kg.

In *Figure 1.3*, you'll see the **Rigid Body** settings in Blender, where you can adjust the object's mass and dynamics:

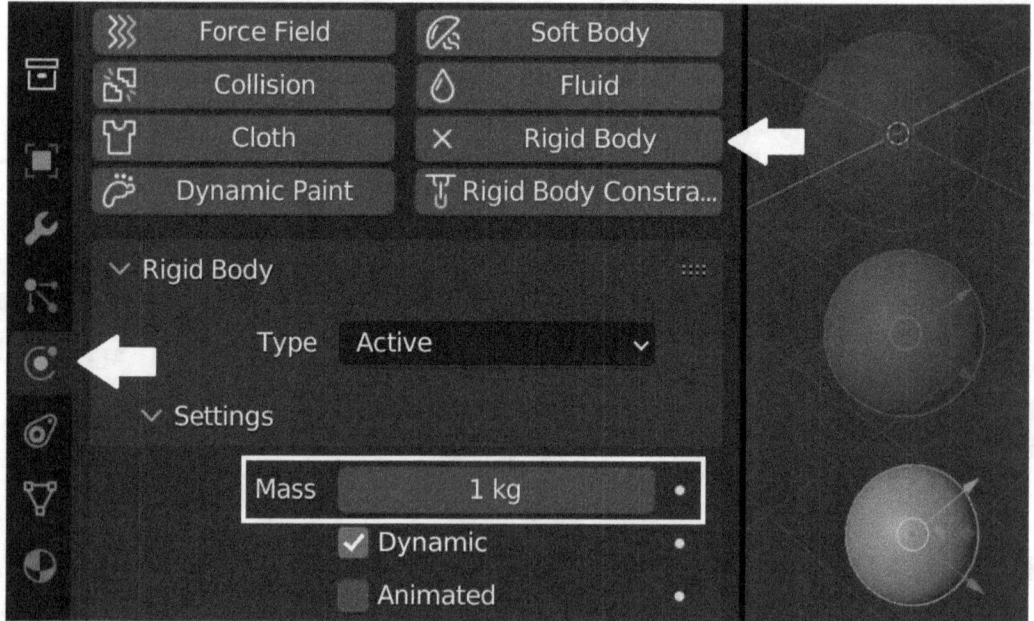

Figure 1.3 – Blender physics properties

Now, if you press the *spacebar*, the physics simulation will start. Our sphere will fall due to the gravitational force. If we change the scale of our sphere to something around 0.2 meters and give it a weight of 4.5 kg, our sphere will behave exactly like a bowling ball. Similarly, if we scale down our sphere diameter to 5 cm and a weight of 170 g, our ball will act like a billiard ball.

The bottom line is to *always* use a real-world scale: it's crucial for achieving photorealistic results that match reality.

Now that we have seen the importance of using real-scale measurements when modeling, let's learn about scale matching. It's an awesome trick that allows us to get almost the exact camera settings from an image reference, so that we can then easily recreate the scene in Blender.

Understanding fSpy

When replicating a real-world reference in 3D, matching the exact camera position, rotation, and focal length can be challenging. For instance, in trying to align the wood cabin reference, these difficulties quickly become apparent. **fSpy** simplifies this process by helping you achieve accurate scale and camera alignment.

Learning about scale matching using fSpy

Next, let's learn about scale matching. To put things in perspective, let's say you have a real reference that you want to replicate as a 3D scene. You can load it as a camera background and start modeling it, but soon enough, you will encounter a big challenge, which is to match the same position, rotation, and focal length of the camera that took the shot.

You can see in this example the difficulties in matching the same wood cabin reference:

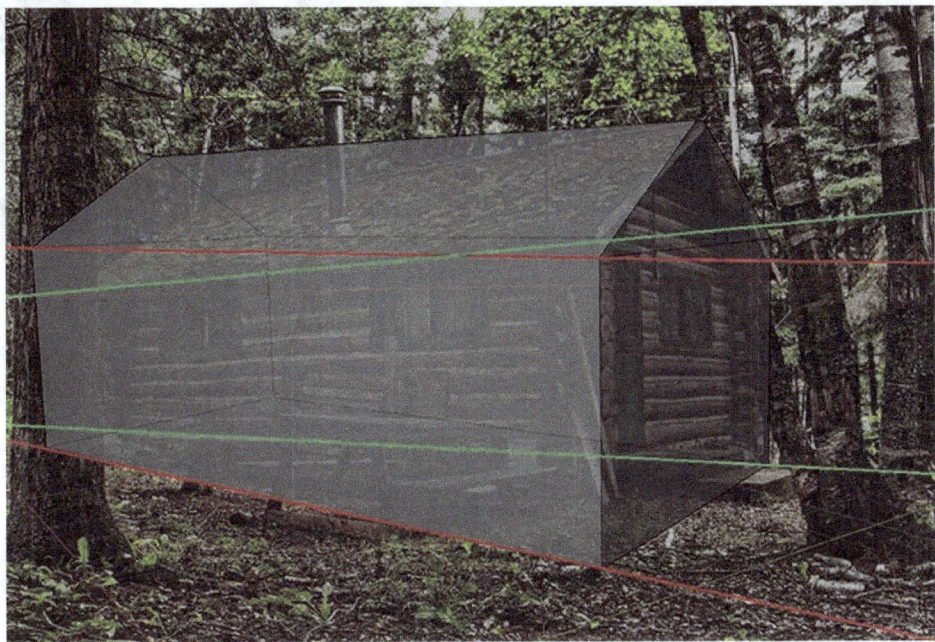

Figure 1.4 – Wood cabin model not matching the reference

Our objective is to place the modeled cube exactly on top of the cabin reference (the *red* lines must be on top of the *green* lines). The corners must match each other in order to have true camera matching; doing it by eye won't cut it, so we need to do it the right way.

Luckily, we have fSpy, which is a free open source software program that allows us to estimate the camera parameters from an image reference and import it into Blender.

The way it works is as follows:

1. Import the reference image whose camera settings you want to match.
2. Choose the number of vanishing points. You will find this feature on the top-left side panel of the fSpy program, as shown in *Figure 1.5*:

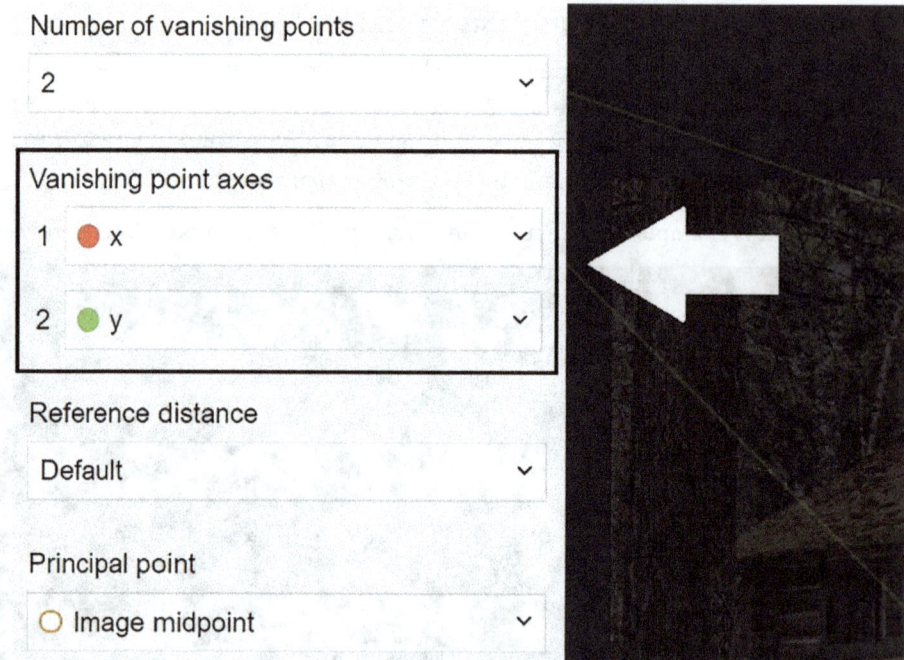

Figure 1.5 – Vanishing point axes in the fSpy interface

Basically, the number of vanishing points depends on the type of reference you're using:

- **One vanishing point**: This means that your reference has a point where all lines meet. If you follow any parallel lines in the reference, they will end up meeting at one point.

Figure 1.6 – Example of one vanishing point reference

- **Two vanishing points**: You can use two vanishing points if there are two kinds of parallel lines in your reference, with each side seemingly slowly fading away into the distance. They will meet at a certain point in the distance. An example would be something like this:

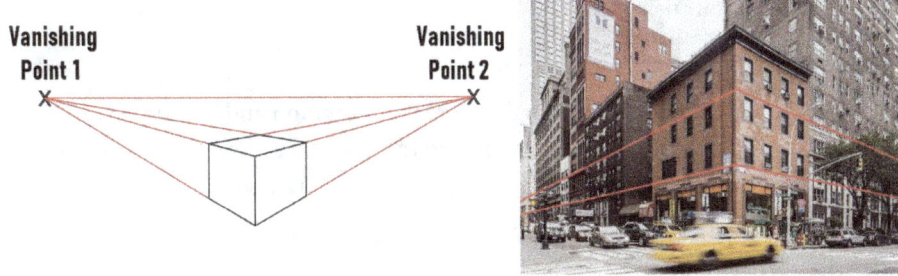

Figure 1.7 – Example of two vanishing points

The camera parameters are as follows: focal length, rotation, and position of the camera.

In our case, we will be using a wood cabin reference that has two vanishing points; you can tell this by following the wood lines on both the *front* and *side* faces of the cabin. You can download this image from GitHub at:

https://github.com/PacktPublishing/3D-Environment-Design-with-Blender-5-Second-Edition/blob/ab43270b643a41ba8f915f74e3bf78573b10a816/chapter-1/Wood-Cabin.png.

Figure 1.8 – Wood cabin reference

Alright, now let's start using fSpy.

Using fSpy

fSpy is a free tool that allows us to analyze a real photograph and extract accurate camera information such as focal length, position, and rotation. By using fSpy, we can match the camera in Blender to a real-world reference image, which is essential for achieving correct scale and realistic results.

Downloading fSpy

First, let's download fSpy. You can Google fSpy or use this official website link:

https://www.fspy.io. Once on the web page, we will do the following:

1. Click the *green* **Download** button.

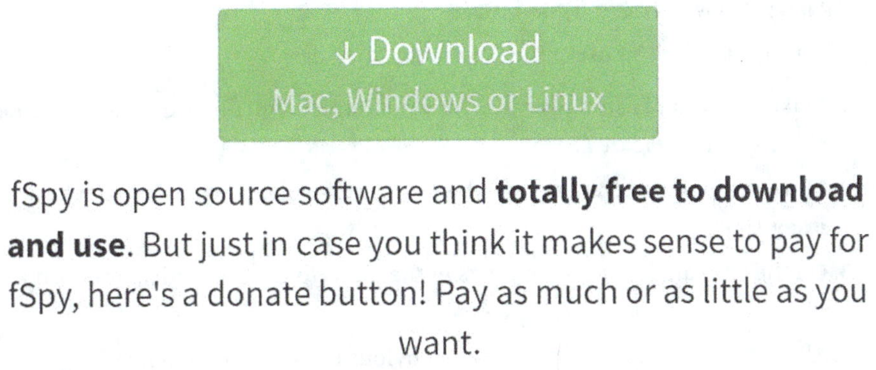

↓ Download
Mac, Windows or Linux

fSpy is open source software and **totally free to download and use**. But just in case you think it makes sense to pay for fSpy, here's a donate button! Pay as much or as little as you want.

Figure 1.9 – fSpy download button

2. You will be directed to GitHub. In GitHub, do the following:

   1. Under **Assets**, we will be downloading the `fSpy-1.0.3-ia32-win.zip` file, which is 47.2 MB. Unzip it and double-click on the **fSpy** icon.

   2. Inside the program interface, on the top bar, go to **File | Open Image**.

   3. Choose the image reference shown in *Figure 1.8*.

If done correctly, this is what you will get:

Figure 1.10 – Wood cabin reference loaded into fSpy

After downloading fSpy, put our image reference into it and set the *X* and *Z* axes to match our reference lines. Now, it's time to understand the fSpy interface and how we can manipulate it to get the best results.

Breaking down the fSpy tools

Alright, let's get to work on using the fSpy tools:

1. Make sure you're using two vanishing points; you will find this feature on the top-left side panel (see *Figure 1.5*).

2. Make the image reference clear, then on the left side, down below, uncheck the **Dim image** box.

3. On the left panel, switch the **y** axis to the **z** axis to get the vertical proportion of your reference.

4. Align the **x** and **z** axes with the most obvious lines in our reference.

In our case, we can rely on the wood lines and the roof. Make sure the lines you choose are far away from each other; this will allow fSpy to calibrate the scene much better.

The final result should be as shown in *Figure 1.11*:

Figure 1.11 – fSpy vanishing point axes aligned with the reference lines

Sometimes, the focal length generated by fSpy won't be accurate, so you have to tweak it a little bit manually – it's really easy to do so.

Adjusting the focal length

To adjust the focal length, perform the following steps:

1. On the left panel, change **Principal point** to **Manual**. By default, **Principal point** will be set to the **Image** midpoint. As soon as you change it to **Manual**, a yellow point will appear in the middle of your reference.

2. If you grab it and move it a little bit, you will change the focal length of your camera. You will see that on the right panel under the **Field of view** tab, beside the **Horizontal** value:

Figure 1.12 – Changing the focal length settings in fSpy

Alright, now let's save this project: go to **File**, click on **Save As**, and save the fSpy file to your desktop.

Exporting the fSpy file

Now, let's export this fSpy file into Blender. To do that, we must install the **Import fSpy project** add-on that allows us to do this.

The add-on is available at this GitHub link for download: https://github.com/PacktPublishing/3D-Environment-Design-with-Blender-5-Second-Edition/blob/ab43270b643a41ba8f915f74e3bf78573b10a816/chapter-1/fSpy-Blender-Addon.zip.

Once you download the fSpy-Blender-Addon.zip file, make sure *not to unzip* this file.

> **Note**
>
> At the time of writing, the **Import fSpy project** add-on works reliably for matching camera settings in Blender 5. Since it's not actively maintained, compatibility may change in future Blender versions.

Once you get the Addon.zip file, we can now jump into Blender and install it. So, in our Blender interface, we'll follow these steps (see *Figure1.13*):

1. Click on **Edit | Preferences**, and click on **Add-ons** on the middle left side.

2. Then, at the top right, click on **Install** and choose the fSpy-Blender-Addon.zip file. Then, you should see a message below saying that the module is installed.

3. Also, make sure that you enabled the fSpy add-on box, **Import-Export: Import fSpy project**.

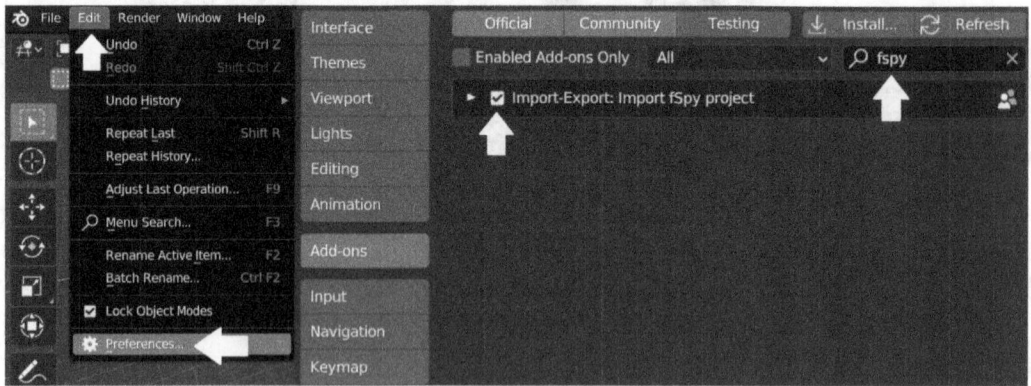

Figure 1.13 – Installing the fSpy add-on in Blender

Alright, now let's import the fSpy file we created with the fSpy program. If you followed the previous steps, when you go to **File** and **Import**, you will see that you have the possibility to import fSpy files into Blender. Just click on **Import** and choose the fSpy file we created earlier. You will then see the following:

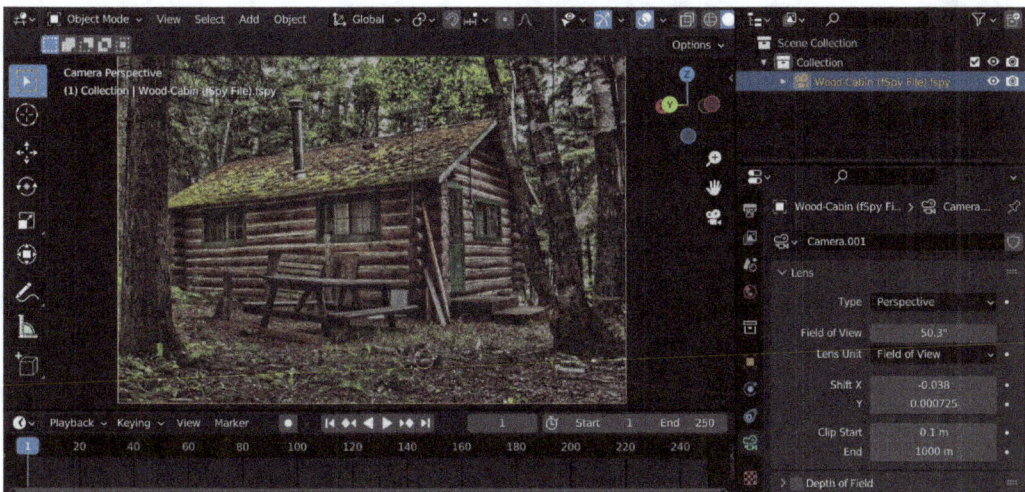

Figure 1.14 – Importing the wood cabin fSpy file into Blender

This is the benefit of using fSpy; now, we have camera settings that match those of the photographer who took this shot. The same camera focal length, camera position, and rotation have been replicated.

From now on, we can start building our scene.

Scale matching in Blender: modeling a wood cabin

In this section, we'll build upon our previous work with fSpy to match a reference of a wood cabin. The goal here is to help you understand and implement scale matching in Blender.

Before we start adding meshes to the scene, it's important to understand how objects are placed in Blender.

New objects are added at the location of the 3D cursor. And since our camera is facing the center grid of the 3D Viewport, we need to ensure that the 3D cursor is at the center of the grid.

Throughout this process of scale matching the wood cabin reference, we'll keep switching between the camera view and the regular 3D Viewport. You can achieve this camera switch by pressing *0* on the numpad or clicking on the **Camera** icon on the right side of the Viewport to enter and exit the camera view.

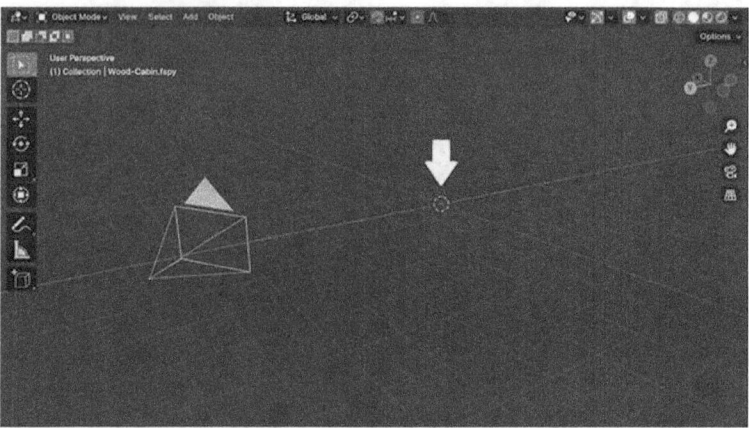

Figure 1.15 – Placing the 3D cursor at the center of the 3D Viewport grid

The 3D cursor is a *red* and *white* circular icon that you'll see in Blender's 3D Viewport. Think of it as a marker that tells Blender where to place new objects.

To center the 3D cursor, follow these steps:

1. Hover your mouse over the 3D Viewport.

2. Press *Shift + S*.

3. Choose **Cursor to World Origin**.

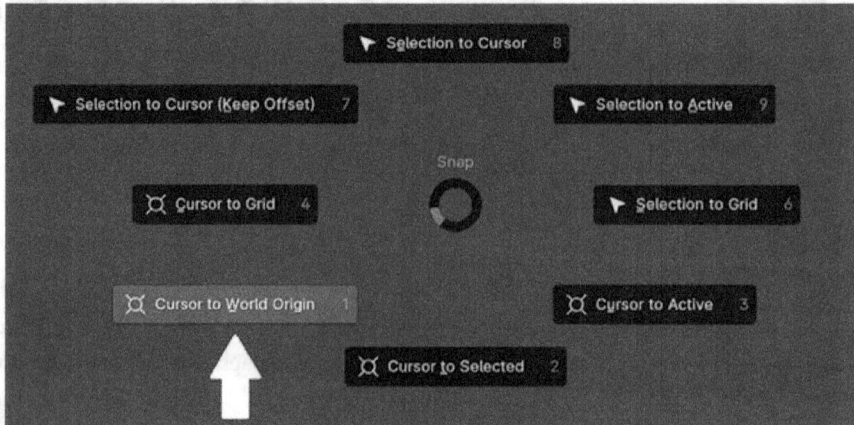

Figure 1.16 – Choosing Cursor to World Origin in the Snap menu

Now that we've set up our camera and 3D cursor, it's time to start building our scene based on the wood cabin reference. We'll begin by creating a ground plane for our cabin to sit on.

Adding the wood cabin ground

With the camera and 3D cursor set up, it's time to start building the scene, beginning with the ground plane where the wood cabin will sit. Follow these steps to add the base:

1. Hover your mouse on the 3D Viewport and press *Shift + A* to open the **Add** menu.

2. From the menu, select **Mesh**, then choose **Plane**.

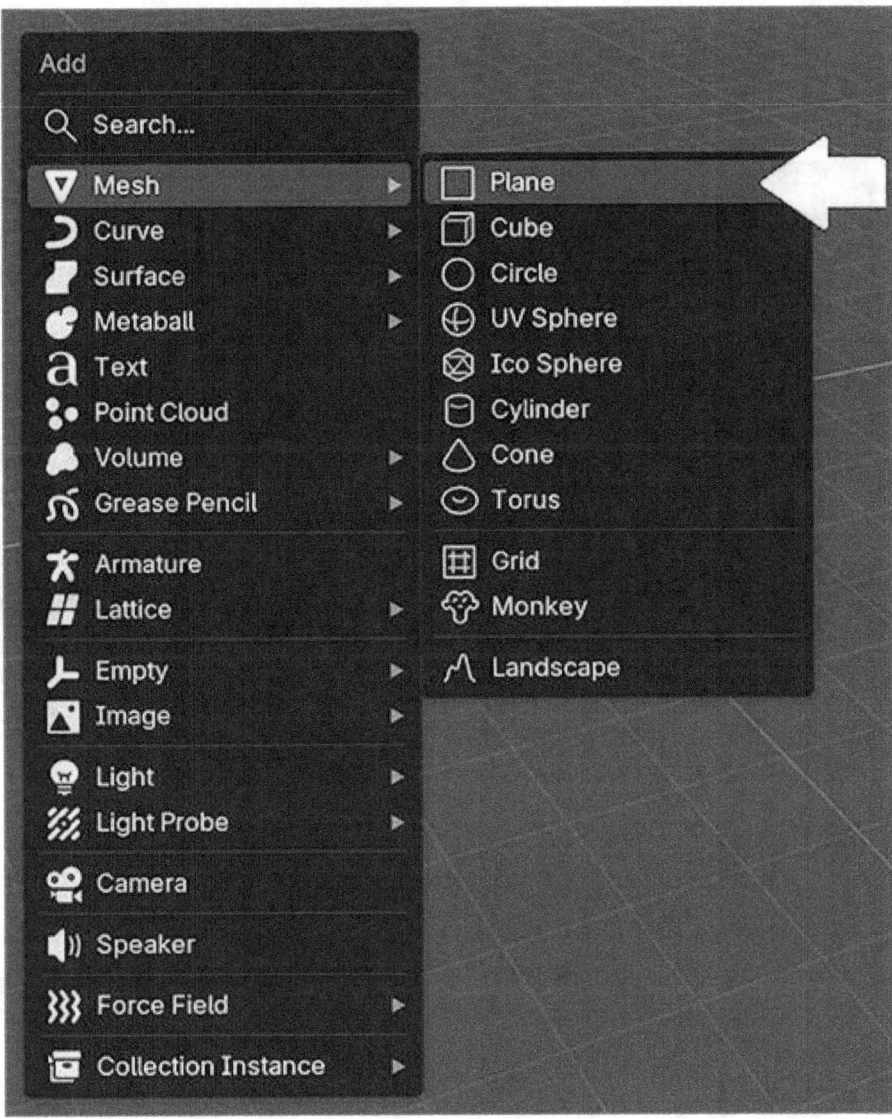

Figure 1.17 – Adding a Plane mesh using the Shift + A shortcut

You should now see a square plane appear in your scene, centered at the 3D cursor's position. The default plane is too small for our needs, so we'll need to scale it up significantly. We want our ground to extend well beyond the boundaries of our cabin, providing a good space for the surrounding environment.

3. Press *N* to open the **Properties** panel on the right side of the 3D Viewport.

4. In the **Properties** panel, locate and click on the **Item** tab.

5. Look for the **Dimensions** section. Here, we'll adjust the size of our plane:

   ◦ Set the **X** axis dimension to 90 meters

   ◦ Set the **Y** axis dimension to 50 meters

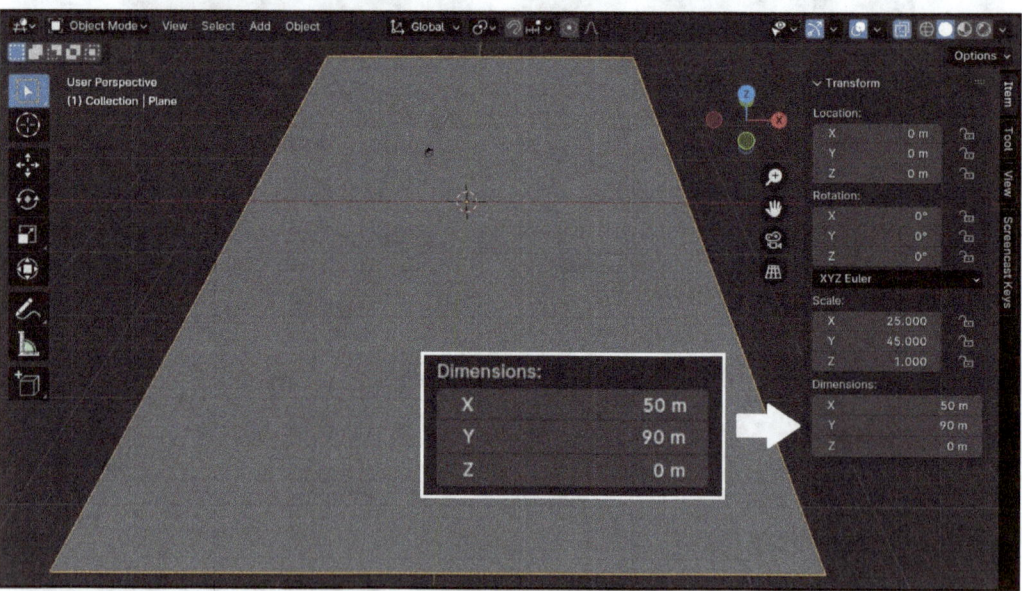

Figure 1.18 – Resizing the ground plane

These dimensions will create a large, rectangular ground plane, as shown in the previous figure, that's appropriate for our wood cabin scene.

Adding the wood cabin base

In the next step, we will add a cube to represent the base of our wood cabin and position it accurately using a reference image. Follow these steps:

1. Add a cube by pressing *Shift* + *A*, and selecting **Mesh** and then **Cube**.

2. Now, let's position the cube. Since the default cube is 2 meters high and half of it is below the ground plane, we need to move it up by 1 meter to rest it on the ground.

3. Press *G* to grab the cube.

4. Press *Z* to constrain the movement to the *Z* axis.

5. Press *1* on the numpad to move it up by 1 meter.

To complete the preceding process manually without shortcuts, select the cube, press *N*, go to the **Transform** panel, then under **Location**, set the **Z** value to 1.0 m.

This places the cube perfectly on top of the ground plane.

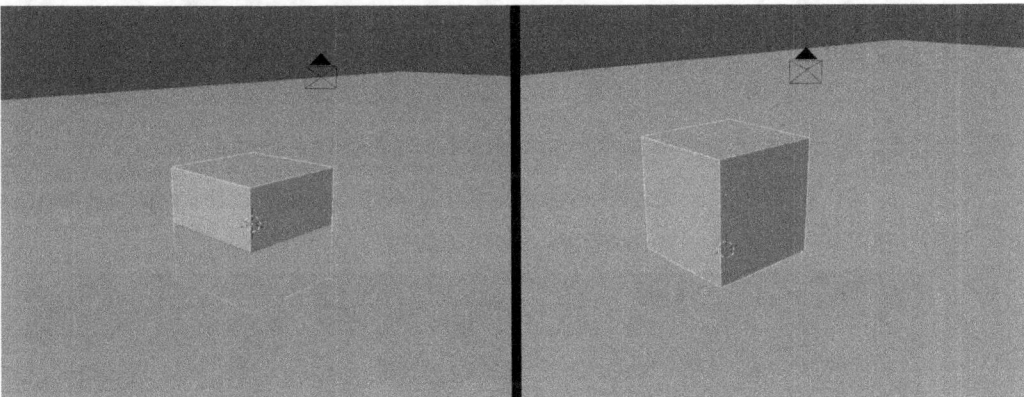

Figure 1.19 – Moving the cube one meter up to match the ground surface

Positioning the cube

Follow these steps to position the cube correctly:

1. Let's return to **Camera View** by pressing *0* on the numpad in order to see the cube related to the wood cabin reference image.

Figure 1.20 – Switching to camera view with the cube and place visible

2. To see through the plane and cube, enable **X-Ray** mode by clicking the **Toggle X-Ray** button at the top of the 3D Viewport, as shown here:

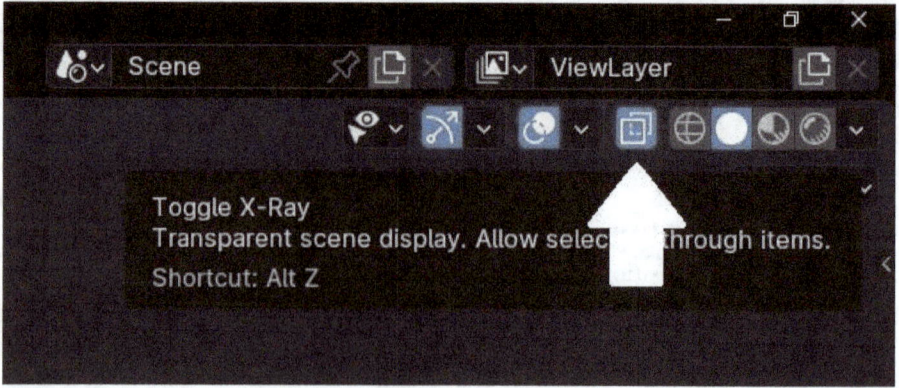

Figure 1.21 – Checking the Toggle X-Ray option

3. This will make the objects semi-transparent, allowing you to view and align them more precisely with the reference image, as illustrated in *Figure 1.22*:

Figure 1.22 – Seeing the reference image through the cube and plane

4. Choose a reference point on the wood cabin reference image, preferably one of the bottom corners. For this example, we will use the bottom-left corner of the wood cabin reference image.

5. Our goal now is to align the cube with the wood cabin, and the best way to do it is by selecting the cube first, then moving it horizontally using the *red* and *green* arrows until the corner of the cube matches the corner of the wood cabin.

   Note that after aligning the cube perfectly on the floor (see *Figure 1.19*), moving it up or down the Z-axis (the *blue* arrow) breaks the 3D perspective. fSpy calculates the vanishing points based on that specific flat ground plane. If you lift or sink the cube, your wood cabin model will float or dig into the ground, and your 3D geometry will no longer align with 2D reference image as you build it.

Figure 1.23 – Putting the modeled cube in the corner of the reference

6. Placing the cube in the corner of the cabin reference will allow you to get the right start. Otherwise, you will be stuck not knowing where to put the initial cube.

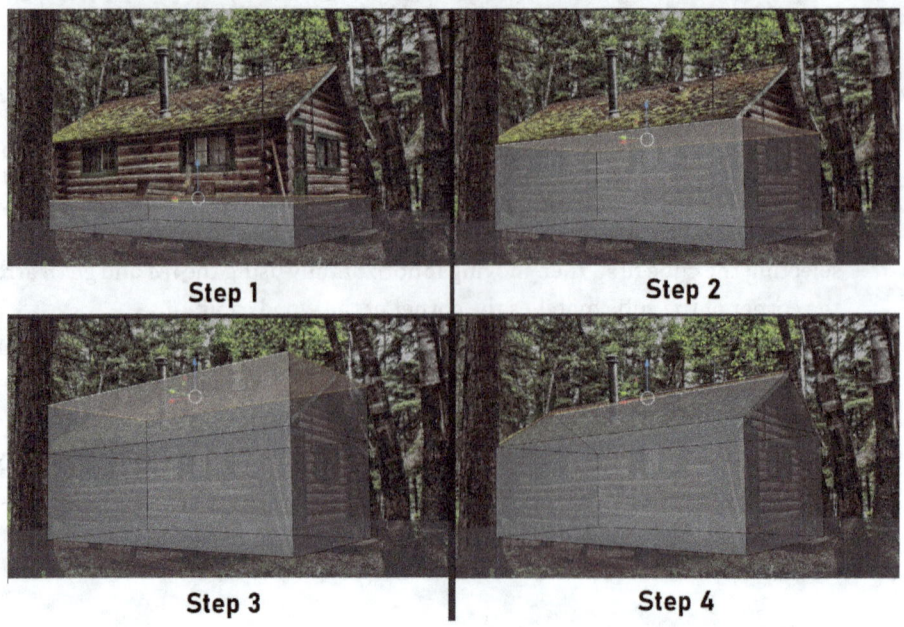

Figure 1.24 – Four steps to model the wood cabin in Blender

Next, we can proceed and create the basic shape of the wood cabin that we have in our reference:

1. Select the cube and enter the **Edit Mode** (press *Tab* to toggle between **Edit** and **Object** modes).

2. In the **Edit Mode**, select the front face, and move it to cover the length of the cabin wood. Also, align the back face with the back of the wood cabin reference.

3. Select the top face and move it upward until it reaches the beginning of the roof.

4. Press *E* to extrude it upward until it reaches the top of the reference.

5. You can scale it on the *Y* axis to make that *A* shape.

As you can see, we will now have a perfect match to our reference image:

Figure 1.25 – Matching the same proportions of the wood cabin

Also, make sure that you are using the measurements we set earlier; to do so without distorting the camera angle, make sure that you scale everything up one at a time, the camera included.

Now that we have finished matching the same scale of our reference and made a simple wood cabin, you can see the beauty of scale matching; our camera settings in Blender now perfectly match the camera settings used to take the reference image. Both have the same focal length and rotation. This is an excellent start to achieving a photorealistic result.

Next, we will cover one of the most fatal mistakes that prevents most 3D designers from achieving photorealism: forgetting the **Bevel** modifier.

Using the Bevel modifier

The **Bevel** modifier gives you the ability to bevel the edges of the mesh it is applied to. Basically, it adds edge lines in between the mesh corners (see *Figure 1.28*). It might seem like a simple step, but the effect that the **Bevel** modifier has is enormous for achieving photorealism; we'll see that later.

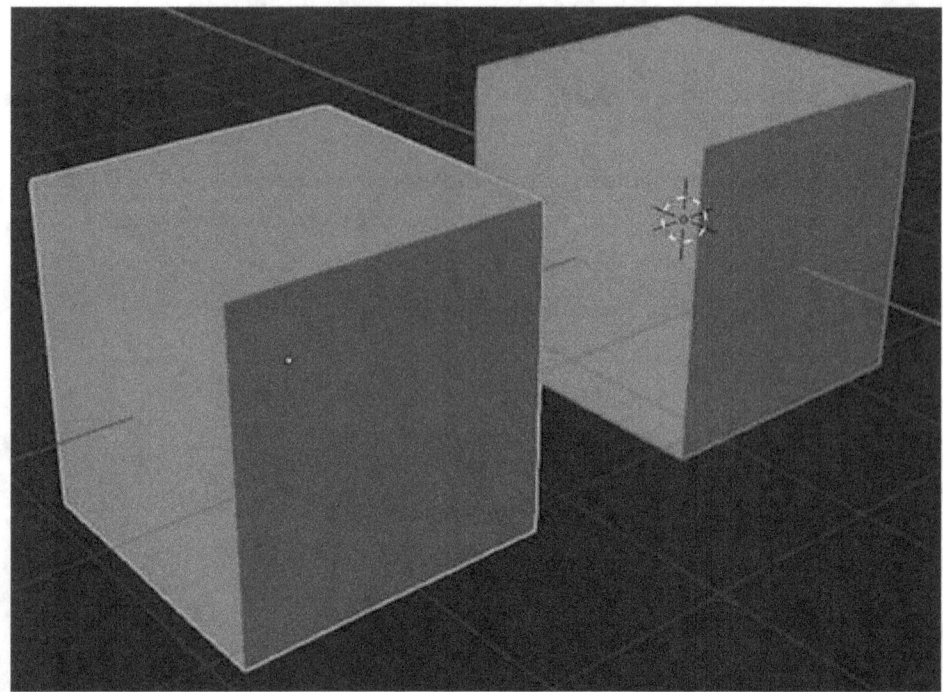

Figure 1.26 – Creation of two cubes

While the **Bevel** modifier is simple to use, its impact on realism is significant.

Importance of using the Bevel modifier when modeling

One of the fatal mistakes that most 3D designers commit that prevents them from achieving photorealistic results is modeling without using the **Bevel** modifier.

Before using the **Bevel** modifier, it's important to make sure the object's scale is applied. Blender evaluates modifiers after object-level transforms, which means that any non-uniform scaling will affect how modifiers behave.

If an object has been scaled in the **Object Mode** (for example, scaled to 2.0 on one axis), the bevel will appear inconsistent or distorted on certain edges. This often results in uneven corner rounding and breaks photorealism.

You can check an object's scale in the **Item Properties** panel in the Viewport or in the **Object Properties** panel. For predictable results, the scale values on all axes should be 1.0 before adding modifiers.

To apply the scale, select the object and press *Ctrl + A*, then choose **Scale**, or use

Object | **Apply** | **Scale** from the Viewport menu. After applying the scale, the object will keep its current size, but the scale values will be reset to **1.0**.

If an object has only been edited in the **Edit Mode**, applying scale is usually not required. However, applying scale is still a good practice, as it helps prevent unexpected issues later when working with modifiers.

Demonstrating the effect of the Bevel modifier

For our example, let's use two cubes, one with the **Bevel** modifier applied to it (*red* cube) and another without any beveling (*blue* cube).

To apply beveling to the *red* cube, let's perform the following steps:

1. Go to **Modifier Properties** (the **wrench** icon), select **Add Modifier**, and choose the **Bevel** modifier, as illustrated in *Figure 1.27*:

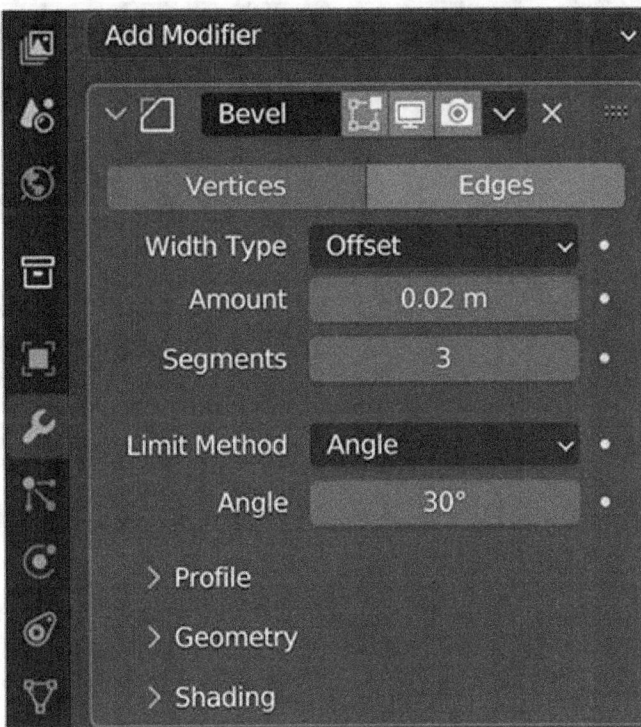

Figure 1.27 – Bevel modifier settings in Blender

2. Set **Amount** to 0.02 m; this represents how large we're going to be affecting the corners of our cube object. Basically, the one corner edge we got by default will be divided into two edges, and the distance between the two edges is the bevel amount.

3. Set **Segments** to 3; this indicates how many face loops there are going to be inside the bevel.

4. Select the beveled cube, then right-click and choose **Smooth**.

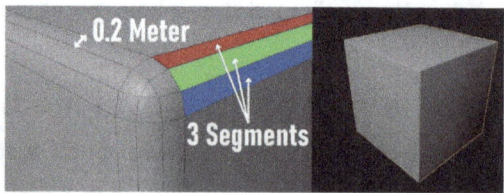

Figure 1.28 – Three cubes demonstrating the Amount, Segments, and Smooth bevel settings

The other cube will remain as default: no beveling will be applied. When you add a source of light to the scene, you will see a big difference between the two cubes:

Figure 1.29 – Final render of the beveled and unbeveled cubes

The *red* beveled cube reflects light on its corners, which makes it more realistic. On the other hand, the *blue* cube looks fake right on the spot: its edges are 100% sharp and non-realistic.

In general, 3D software programs such as Blender make everything perfect by default. When creating a cube, for example, it will come with these sharp 90-degree corners, something that doesn't exist in real life. In nature, you'll never find an object that has completely sharp edges. Even if you zoom in on a sharp knife (zoom really close to its edge), you'll find some sort of beveling.

I've heard a saying that says, "*Imperfection is the CGI perfection*," which means that in order to make objects photorealistic, we have to break the perfection that comes with CGI, and one of the first steps to break it is to always apply the **Bevel** modifier. Now, with the measurements we set earlier and the help of fSpy, we can set the right scale.

Common modeling pitfalls and how to fix them

Before diving into the individual mistakes, it's important to understand that photorealism often fails due to small but fundamental modeling decisions made early in the process.

In this section, we'll look at some of the most common modeling pitfalls that lead to unrealistic results and, more importantly, how to fix them using simple, practical techniques you can apply to any project:

- **Mistake 1**: Eyeballing object scale instead of using real measurements
    - **Symptoms**:
        - The scene *feels wrong*, even with good lighting and materials
        - Physics simulations behave strangely (objects fall too fast/slow or feel weightless)
    - **Fix**:
        - Set **Unit System** to **Metric** (or **Imperial**) under **Scene Properties | Units**
        - Research real-world dimensions of key objects (for example, cabin height, door width, and window size) before modeling
        - Enter those measurements directly in the object dimensions instead of scaling by eye
- **Mistake 2**: Modeling directly on top of a reference image without proper camera matching
    - **Symptoms**:
        - The model never aligns perfectly with the photo, no matter how you move the camera
        - The perspective looks *off* when you compare renders to the reference
    - **Fix**:
        - Use fSpy to estimate camera focal length, position, and rotation from the reference image

- Align vanishing points with clear structural lines (walls, roof edges, and wood planks)

- Export the fSpy project and import it into Blender using the **Import fSpy project** add-on, so your Blender camera matches the photographer's camera before you start serious modeling

- **Mistake 3**: Rescaling the scene after importing the fSpy camera

  - **Symptom**: The model matches the reference at first, but breaks as soon as you scale objects or the camera independently

  - **Fix**:

    - Decide your real-world scale early (for example, cabin dimensions) and stick to it

    - If you need to scale, scale the camera and objects together so the perspective stays correct

    - Avoid uniform *scene-wide* scaling after you've matched the camera

- **Mistake 4**: Modeling with perfectly sharp edges (no bevels)

  - **Symptoms**:

    - Objects look obviously CG, even with good textures and lighting

    - Highlights appear harsh and unnatural; corners are cut into the light instead of catching it

  - **Fix**:

    - Add a **Bevel** modifier to key objects (walls, beams, furniture, and props)

    - Use a small **Amount** value (for example, around 0.01–0.03 m for architectural elements) and a **Segments** value of 2–3 for smooth highlights

    - Enable **Shade Smooth** where appropriate to reinforce the effect

Remember that in reality, almost no edge is perfectly sharp; introducing subtle bevels is essential for photorealism.

Summary

In this chapter, we went through the three main modeling mistakes and how to fix them. Starting with scale matching, we discussed why it's a bad habit to rely on eyes only when modeling, how the Blender unit system works, and how to set the right measurements of objects before modeling them.

Next, we installed and configured the open source fSpy to help us match the same proportions of a real wood cabin reference, following which we learned how to install the fSpy add-on and import the fSpy file into Blender, and built the basic scene that resembles the real reference scale.

Finally, we discussed the importance of using the **Bevel** modifier and why it's crucial to achieving photorealism.

In the next chapter, we will explore the basics of realistic texturing in Blender. We'll break down the different texturing channels: **Base Color**, **Roughness**, **Normal**, and **Displacement**. Understanding these components is vital for achieving realism in your 3D scenes. Finally, we will create an example of realistic wood material in Blender using procedural texturing.

Get this book's PDF version and more

Scan the QR code (or go to packtpub.com/unlock). Search for this book by name, confirm the edition, and then follow the steps on the page.

Note: Keep your invoice handy. Purchases made directly from Packt don't require an invoice.

2

The Basics of Realistic Texturing in Blender

Materials are the holy grail for achieving photorealism. If you have only 10 hours to spend on a scene to make it photorealistic, I would say you need to put at least 5 to 6 hours into materials – that's more than 50% of the work. Yes, materials are *that* important.

We can get away with some modeling mistakes: the scale can be slightly off, and the scene may still work visually. Materials, however, are far less forgiving. The way light scatters when it interacts with a surface immediately communicates important information to the viewer, such as whether a material is rough or smooth, wet or dry, hard or soft, and organic or inorganic. Well-created textures influence how a surface is perceived to the touch, and this tactile impression plays a major role in whether an image is read by the viewer as realistic.

In this chapter, we will highlight the importance of using all texturing channels in achieving photorealism by showing examples of realistic materials and breaking them down into their components: **Base Color**, **Roughness**, **Normal**, and **Displacement**. You will gain an understanding of each one of these maps and how they work inside Blender.

In this chapter, we'll cover the following topics:

- Understanding Blender's node-based material system
- Exploring the components for achieving photorealistic texturing: **Base Color**, **Roughness**, **Normal**, and **Displacement**
- Creating a realistic wood material using procedural texturing

By the end of this chapter, you'll be able to build and evaluate realistic materials in Blender by understanding how each texturing channel works together within a node-based workflow.

Technical requirements

This chapter requires a system capable of running **Blender version 5.0** or above (Windows, macOS, or Linux).

You can download the resources for this chapter from GitHub at: `https://github.com/PacktPublishing/3D-Environment-Design-with-Blender-5-Second-Edition/tree/ab43270b643a41ba8f915f74e3bf78573b10a816/chapter-2`

Visit this link to check out the video of the code being run:`https://packt.link/10023`

Understanding Blender's node-based material system

> If you're new to node-based workflows, this system may feel unfamiliar at first,
> especially if you're coming from layer-based tools. Blender's node system is visual,
> logical, and becomes intuitive with practice. This short overview will give you just
> enough context to follow along with the processes in the book.

Before we start building materials, it's important to understand how Blender's **node-based system** works. In Blender, materials are created by connecting nodes that pass data from left to right. Each node performs a specific task, such as providing color information, modifying surface properties, or defining how the material interacts with light.

Nodes have inputs (on the *left*) and outputs (on the *right*). **Inputs** receive data, while **outputs** send data to the next node in the chain. Different **socket colors** represent different data types, such as colors, values, vectors, and shaders. To create a connection, simply drag from an output socket to a compatible input socket. Nodes can be selected, moved, added, or deleted at any time, making the system flexible and non-destructive.

Once you understand this flow, working with materials in Blender becomes logical and predictable, allowing you to focus on creating realistic textures rather than fighting the interface.

Exploring the components for achieving photorealistic texturing in Blender: Base Color, Roughness, Normal, and Displacement

When we start texturing in Blender, most of us do it the simple way: you search for an image texture, create a simple material, jump into the **Shader Editor**, and assign it to **Base Color** under **Principled BSDF**, and that's it.

The **Principled BSDF** shader in Blender is a physically based, all-in-one shader designed to create realistic materials using a single node. It brings together a wide range of surface properties, including base color, roughness, metallic response, and transparency. In addition, it supports more advanced features such as clear coats, sheen for fabric-like materials, and subsurface scattering, which is especially important for organic surfaces such as skin, wax, and food. By consolidating these properties into one shader, **Principled BSDF** allows you to build physically plausible materials efficiently while maintaining visual consistency.

Figure 2.1 demonstrates how to assign a brick image texture to a plane in Blender using the **Shader Editor**. The texture node is connected to the **Principled BSDF** shader, which allows the brick image to appear on the surface of the plane.

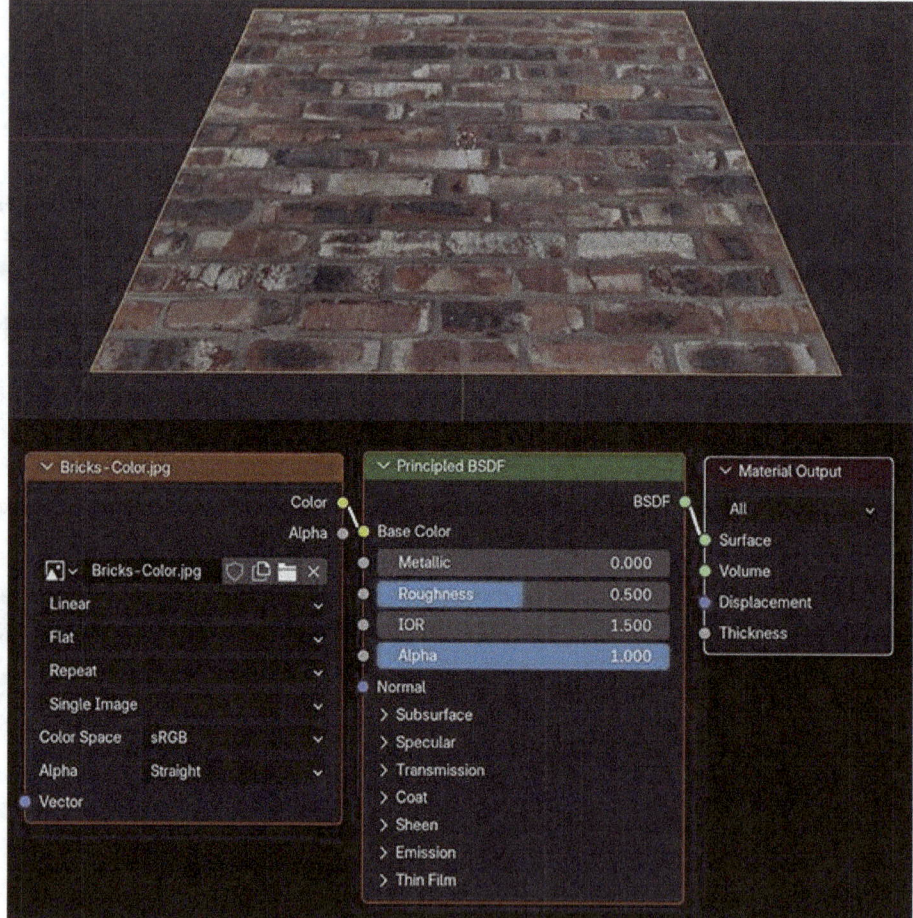

Figure 2.1 – Assigning a brick image texture to a plane in Blender

You can get away with using this method, but it's not the best approach to handling materials.

The simple texturing method illustrated in *Figure 2.1* results in a flat and uninteresting brick surface compared to more advanced techniques, which can make the bricks appear much more realistic and visually appealing. You can see the difference in *Figure 2.2*:

Figure 2.2 – Comparison between flat texturing and realistic texturing in Blender

Back when I started, I always thought that the depth details you see on the bricks shown in the image on the right-hand side of *Figure 2.2* were actually real geometry, but eventually, I figured out that it's just a texturing trick that makes objects look much more realistic.

If we want to achieve photorealistic texturing, we need to provide Blender with multiple pieces of information about the material we're creating. We need to define how it looks, including the following details:

- The color
- Its level of shininess
- The surface quality (whether it is wet, dry, rough, or smooth)
- The amount of surface bumps on the material
- The material's displacement

All these details are represented in images: some call them **maps** or **channels**.

Figure 2.3 – Base Color, Roughness, Normal, and Displacement maps (left to right)

Let me walk you through the different maps available that help in the process of creating photorealistic bricks.

The Base Color map

The first map is the **Base Color** map; this is fairly obvious. It represents the surface color of the material, and it's the first thing we see in our material. When you assign the **Base Color** map in the **Shader Editor**, you will see the same result as on the left-hand side of *Figure 2.2*: flat and boring. It's like printing an image of bricks onto paper! Stopping here is a mistake most of us make in the beginning, and, as you can see in the left sphere of *Figure 2.2*, the brick material is nowhere close to photorealism.

To assign the **Base Color** map to a brand-new Blender scene, do the following:

1. Create a simple plane using *Shift + A* on the 3D Viewport, then choose **Mesh** and **Plane**.
2. From the right panel, click on the **Material Properties** icon.
3. You can change the material name to Bricks.

You can see the same in *Figure 2.4*:

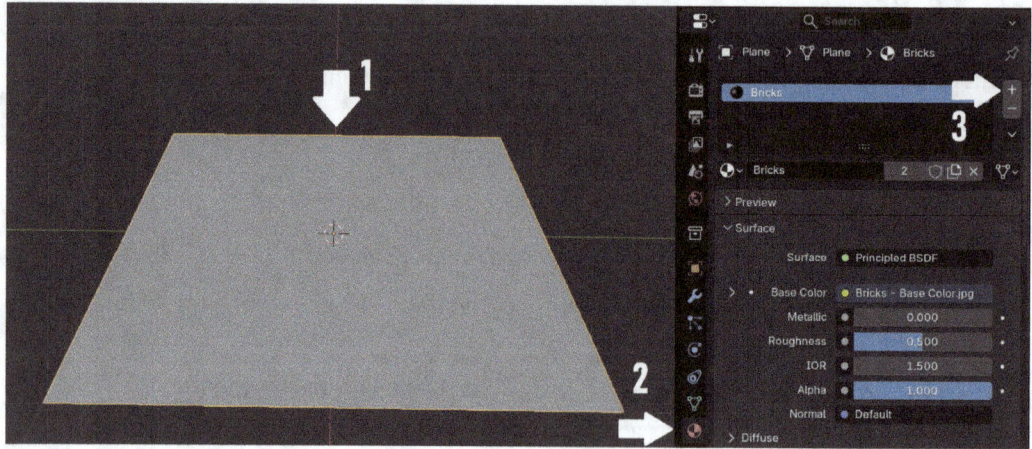

Figure 2.4 – Creating a plane with brick material applied to it

Now, let's jump into **Shader Editor**. We need to switch to **Shader Editor**, where you can work and make changes to your materials by using nodes. At the bottom, by default, we'll have the **Timeline**.

We'll be using the bricks image shown in *Figure 2.3* to texture our plane shown in *Figure 2.4*; this bricks image is available at: `https://github.com/PacktPublishing/3D-Environment-Design-with-Blender-5-Second-Edition/blob/ab43270b643a41ba8f915f74e3bf78573b10a816/chapter-2/Bricks-BaseColor.jpg`.

You can save this image on your desktop.

Now, let's expand the bottom bar to see what's inside; you can do so by grabbing it from the edge and moving it up. Now, if you select the plane, you will see two nodes: **Principled BSDF** and **Material Output**. This means you're on the right track.

Now, we need to switch the view to the **Shader Editor** for more control over the texture. By expanding the bottom bar and selecting the plane, you can access the necessary nodes for editing.

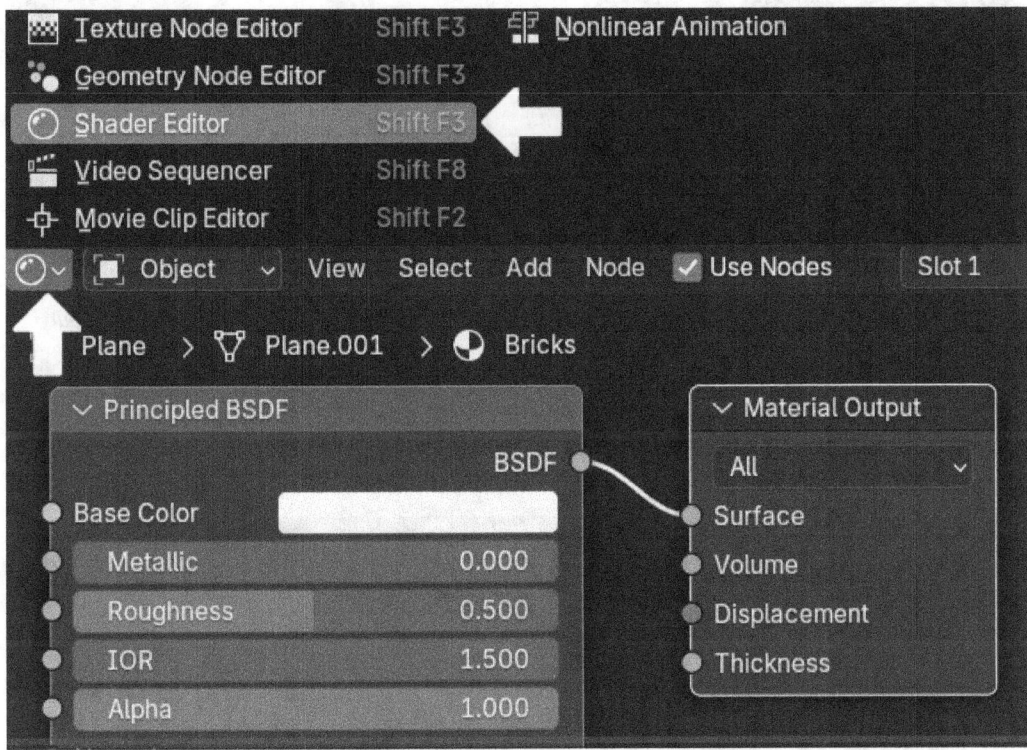

Figure 2.5 – Switching the Timeline to Shader Editor

The first element in the **Principled BSDF** node that is connectable is the **Base Color** map. You can connect the first element in **Principled BSDF** as follows: drag the Bricks - Base Color.jpg texture from your desktop and drop it into **Shader Editor** in Blender. You will see it as an image texture node.

Now, we need to connect the *yellow* **Color** point (as shown in *Figure 2.6*) with **Base Color** on the **Principled BSDF** node:

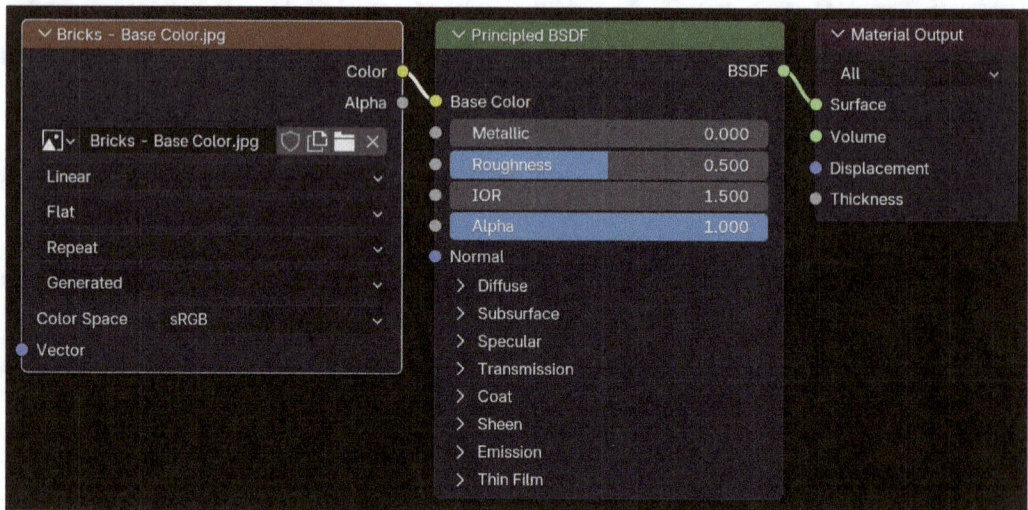

Figure 2.6 – Three nodes in the Shader Editor: brick image texture, Principled BSDF, and Material Output

However, we still do not observe any change. This is because we're in the **Solid** mode by default. This mode shows everything in *gray*. In order to see the materials applied to our object, we need to switch to the **Material Preview** mode. Place your mouse on top of the plane, press Z, and switch to **Material Preview**:

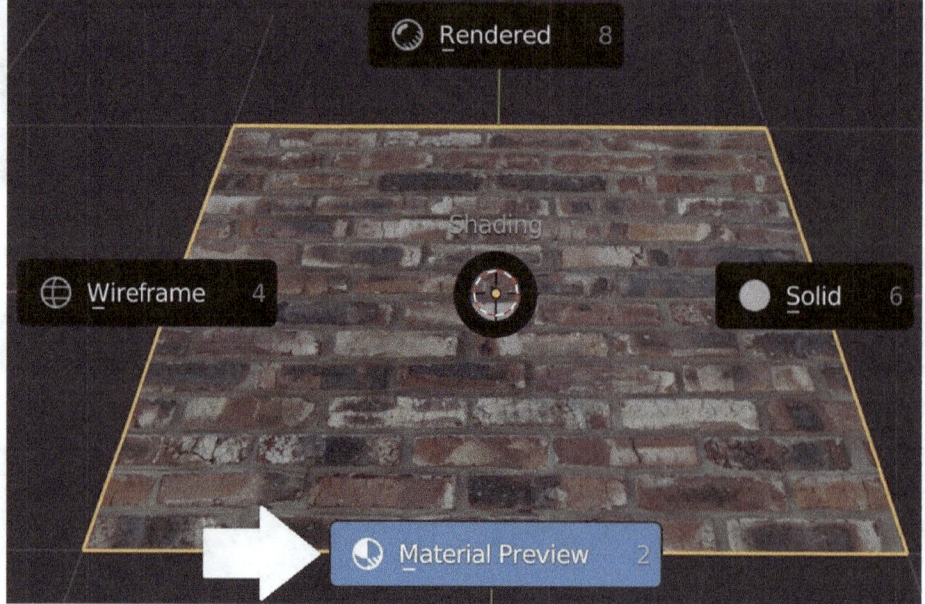

Figure 2.7 – Switching to Material Preview to display the material applied to the plane

Immediately, you will see the texture of the bricks applied to the plane. This is the first step we take to texture an object in Blender, but we should not stop here. We need to give Blender more details about our material in order to achieve photorealism, which brings us to the **Roughness** map.

The Roughness map

The **Roughness** map controls the reflection of the material. It's a *black and white* image that allows us to control how shiny or rough our material is. When we assign the **Roughness** map to our material, any black surface will be displayed as shiny, whereas white surfaces will be translated to rough surfaces.

To explain how Blender handles the **Roughness** map, let's perform this simple experiment:

1. Choose any paint software you have on your computer; I'll be using the **Paint** software on Windows.

2. Try painting some black puddles on a white surface – something like this:

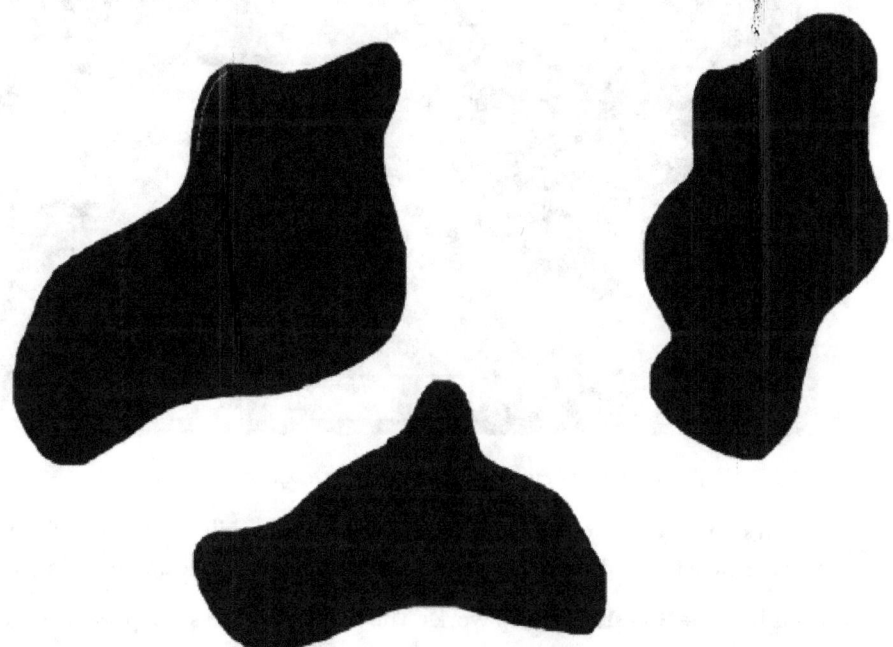

Figure 2.8 – Image with three black puddles used to demonstrate how the Roughness map works

3. Now, back to the Blender scene, we have the brick texture assigned to **Base Color**; let's disconnect it temporarily, and instead, let's drag and drop the black puddles image into

Shader Editor and connect it to **Roughness** in the **Principled BSDF** node (see *Figure 2.9*).

4. Also, to see the effect more clearly, make sure to change the color of the **Base Color** map to black. You'll obtain the following result:

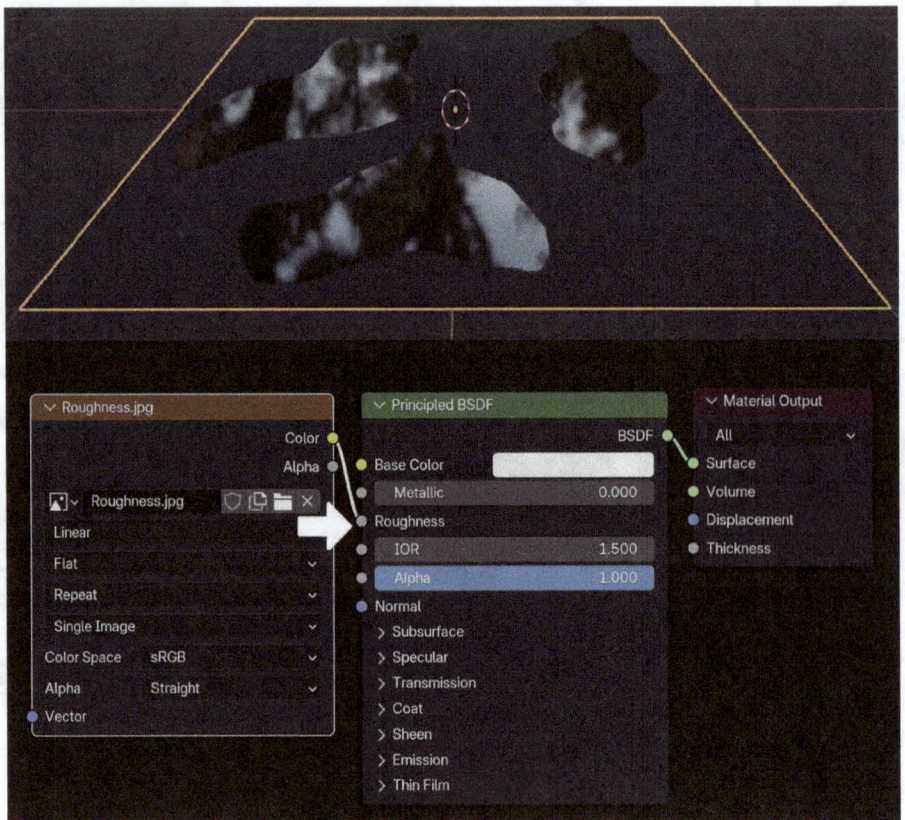

Figure 2.9 – Puddles image used as a roughness map in Blender

You can see that the *black* spots are completely glossy, while the *white* spots are rough. You can delete the puddles image by selecting the image node and pressing *X*.

This is how the **Roughness** map works. The brick **Roughness** map we'll be using can be found here: https://github.com/PacktPublishing/3D-Environment-Design-with-Blender-5-Second-Edition/blob/ab43270b643a41ba8f915f74e3bf78573b10a816/chapter-2/Bricks-Roughness.jpg.

5. After downloading the `Bricks-Roughness.jpg` texture, drop it in the **Shader Editor** and assign it to the **Principled BSDF | Roughness** slot, as the following screenshot shows:

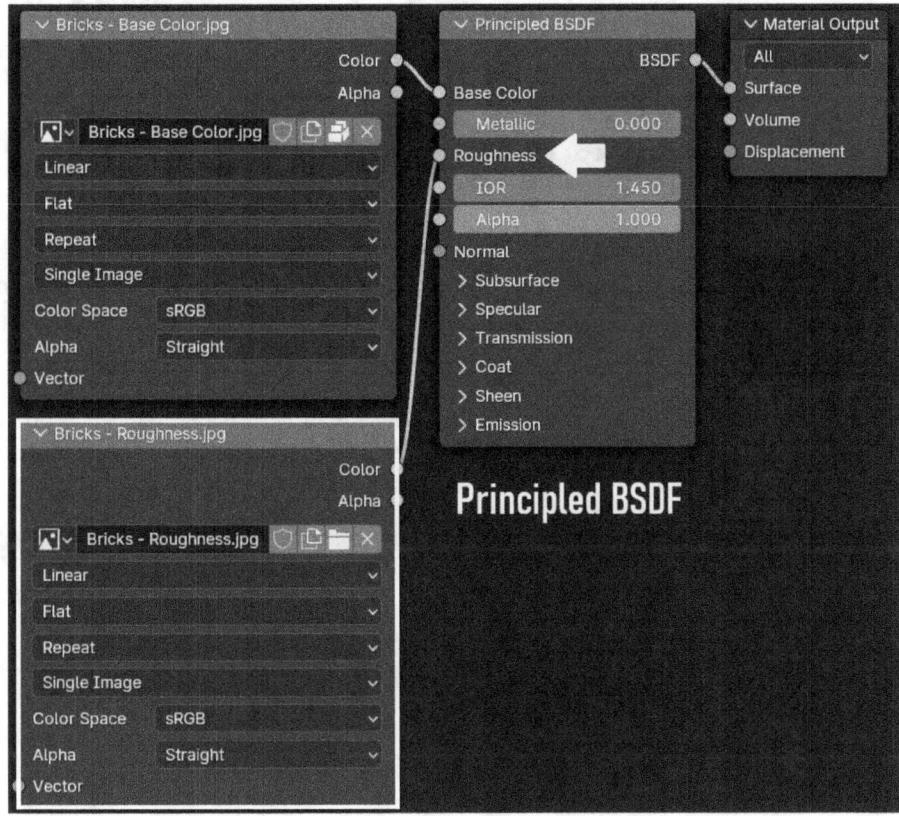

Figure 2.10 – Assigning the Bricks-Roughness image to the Roughness slot of the Principled BSDF

6. After assigning the `Bricks-Roughness.jpg` texture to **Roughness** in the **Principled BSDF** slot, we need to change the **Color Space** type of the roughness texture from **sRGB** to **Non-Color**. The roughness should not be treated as color; we do this to avoid any possible color transforms.

Figure 2.11 – Assigning the Roughness map to the Bricks material

Alright, the preceding screenshot shows the result of the **Bricks** material when we added the **Roughness** map.

Remember that when dealing with the **Roughness** map, *black* means reflective and *white* means rough.

The next step is to apply the **Normal** map.

The Normal map

Have you ever seen bluish images in the texturing process and wondered what their use is? Let's find out.

Figure 2.12 shows a **Normal** map, and when you apply it to a 3D object, it creates the illusion of height.

Figure 2.12 – Example of a Normal map

It adds free detail that costs us nothing in terms of performance; more specifically, it does not affect the render time and adds significant detail and realism to the object it's applied to. Video games heavily use this method to maximize rendering performance while maintaining a photorealistic look.

The following process demonstrates how a simple plane combined with a **Normal** map creates the illusion of depth:

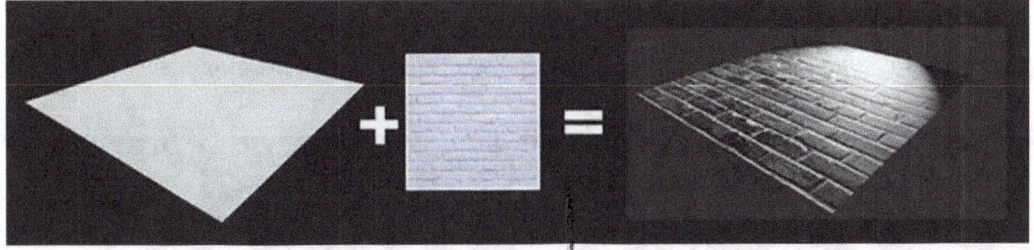

Figure 2.13 – Applying a brick Normal map to a plane

Here's a breakdown of the elements in the preceding figure:

- **Flat plane**: This is the base geometry (zero detail)
- **Normal map**: The RGB data tells Blender how to bounce light
- **Result**: The result is a realistic, tactile surface that reacts dynamically to your lights

Now, let's apply a **Normal** map to our bricks example. To do that, we'll need a new node called **Normal Map**. So, place the cursor on **Shader Editor**, press *Shift + A*, search for **Normal Map**, and press *Enter*. The **Normal Map** node looks like this:

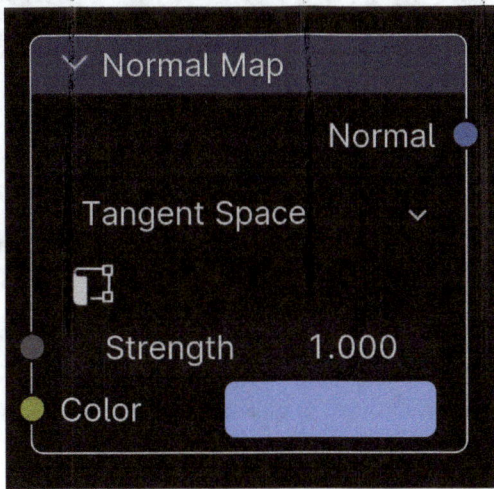

Figure 2.14 – The Normal Map node

To use the **Normal Map** node, we need to connect the **Bricks-Normal** image texture to the **Normal Map Color** slot.

The **Normal** map texture we'll be using is available here for download: `https://github.com/PacktPublishing/3D-Environment-Design-with-Blender-5-Second-Edition/blob/ab43270b643a41ba8f915f74e3bf78573b10a816/chapter-2/Bricks-Normal.jpg`.

Then, on the other side, connect **Normal** to **Normal** on the **Principled BSDF** node. Also, make sure to switch **Color Space** to **Non-Color**, as shown in *Figure 2.15*. This is important because **Normal** maps store vector data, not color information, and using **Non-Color** ensures that the data is interpreted correctly.

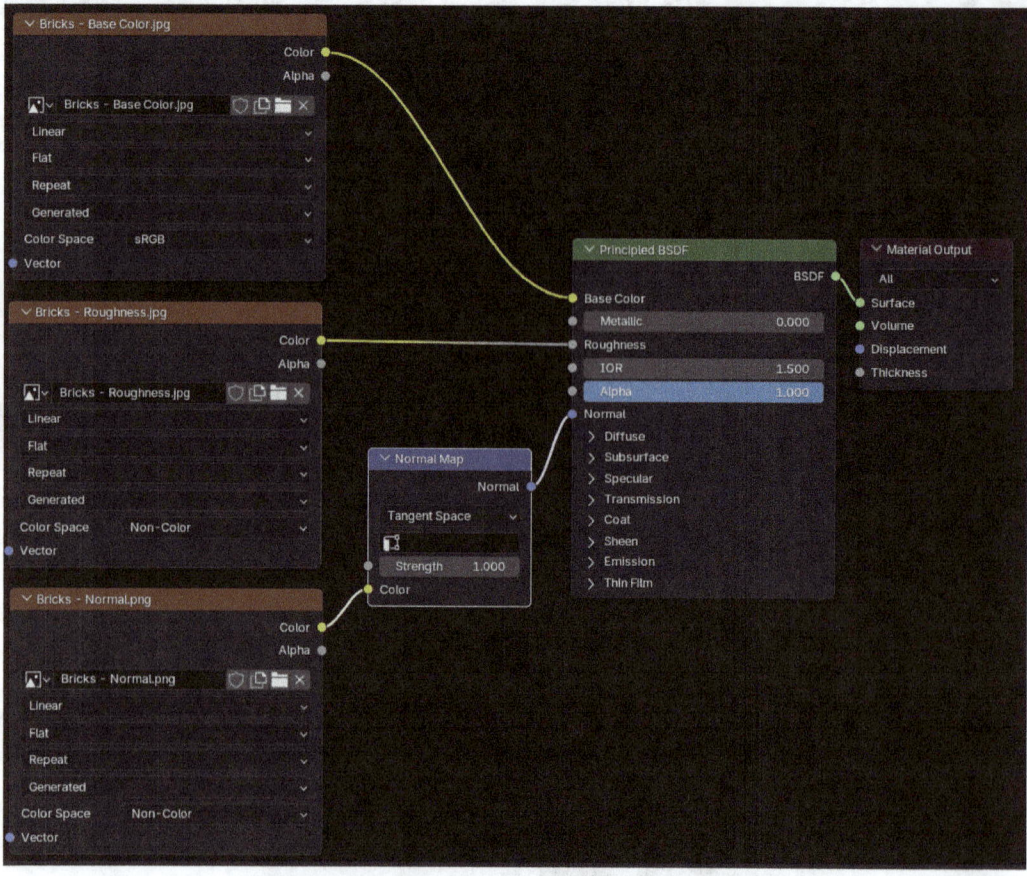

Figure 2.15 – Connecting the Bricks-Normal image texture to the Normal Map node, then to the Principled BSDF Normal slot

Immediately, you'll see the bump effect on the brick's material, as shown in *Figure 2.16*. With the **Normal Map** node applied, our material looks much more realistic. The plane now has free details that do not affect rendering performance:

Figure 2.16 – Bricks texture with Normal Map applied

The next step is to explain the **Displacement** map.

The Displacement map

The **Displacement** map is a *black-and-white* image, similar to the **Roughness** map, but the role it plays is different. Think of it as an alternative way of modeling: we feed Blender a black-and-white image, and it puts it on top of a 3D object. The *white* spots are going to be pushed out or made to extrude, while the *black* spots are going to be pushed inward. The *gray* is neutral; it makes the geometry flat.

There is nothing better than an easy example to understand how the **Displacement** map works. I've created this simple design using Paint:

Figure 2.17 – Simple design created in Paint to demonstrate the Displacement map effect

If we apply this image to a subdivided plane as a **Displacement** map, it will look like this:

Figure 2.18 – Result of applying the Displacement map to a plane in Blender

Note

Note that the plane should be subdivided at least *15 times* for the **Displace** modifier to work properly.

So, as you can see, the **Displacement** map deforms the shape of the mesh it's applied to; this is an actual geometry change. While a **Normal** map only modifies the lighting across the surface of a texture without deforming the geometry, the **Displacement** map goes a step further and actually modifies the shape of the mesh it's applied to.

The amount of extrusion depends on the intensity of white and black colors; *black* in the **Displacement** map represents the lowest point on the plane, *white* represents the highest point on the plane, and gray indicates a **Displacement** value of 0.

Figure 2.19 explains this point:

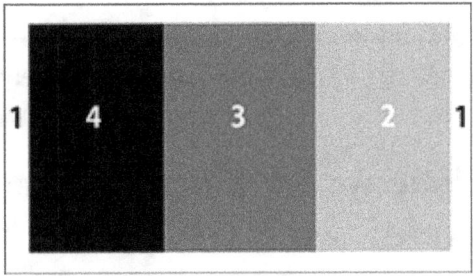

Figure 2.19 - Displacement map with four colors (white, light gray, dark gray, and black)

If we apply this image, which has four colors – *black* (**4**), *gray* (**3**), *light gray* (**2**), and *white* (**1**) – as a **Displacement** map to our plane, we'll get the following result:

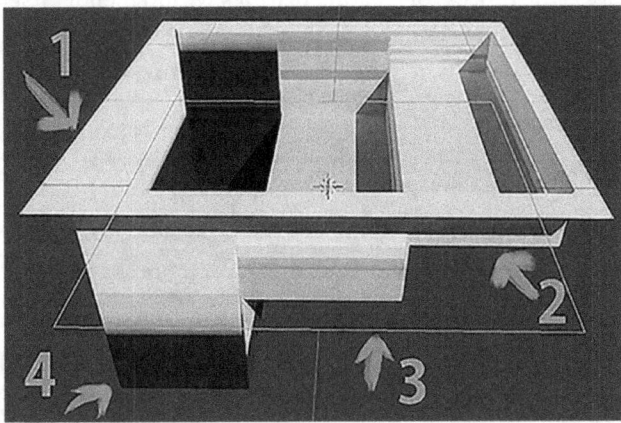

Figure 2.20 – Applying a Displacement map with four colors (white, light gray, dark gray, and black) to illustrate varying extrusion levels on a plane

Let's analyze the image in *Figure 2.20*:

- The *white* borders represented in the **Displacement** map are translated into the highest surface point on our plane
- The second *light-gray* color gives us an extrusion of only 50%
- The third *gray* color gives us a flat 0% **Displacement** detail; it's on the same level as the plane
- The fourth *black* color gives us a 100% extrusion downward

Later, in the coming chapters, we will learn how to apply and use the **Displacement** map.

Now that we have learned how the **Base Color**, **Roughness**, **Normal**, and **Displacement** maps work, let's put everything together and create a realistic wood material to be applied to the wood cabin.

Creating a realistic wood material using procedural texturing in Blender

Let's apply everything we have learned so far to create various wood materials using procedurally generated texturing and apply it to our wooden cabin created in *Chapter 1*.

Let's begin by understanding procedural texturing in Blender.

Procedural texturing is the process of creating textures within Blender itself by using a collection of node textures that are defined mathematically. This is nice because it allows us to create high-quality textures without relying on external textures.

Let's set the Blender scene first:

1. Create a new plane.
2. Assign a new material to the plane and name it Wood.
3. Switch the bottom panel to **Shader Editor** to have more control over the Wood material.
4. On the 3D Viewport, switch to **Material Preview** by pressing *Z* in order to see the progress of our material.

Make sure you're selecting the plane in order to see the **Principled BSDF** and **Material Output** nodes.

Now, we're good to go:

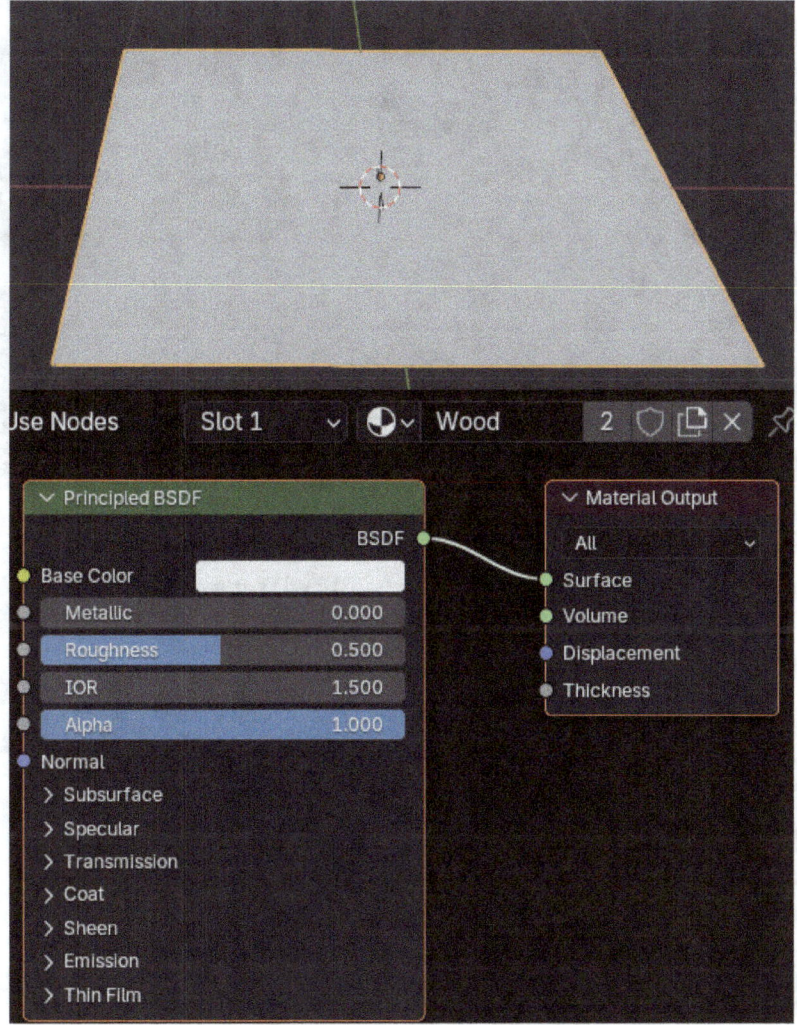

Figure 2.21 – New Blender scene with a plane and the material named Wood applied to it

If we want to create a wood texture, we need to understand the nature of wood itself; this will help us use the right nodes to create the wood texture. *Figure 2.22* shows a real reference to a wood texture:

Figure 2.22 – A real reference to a wood texture

In the preceding figure, if we pay close attention, we'll find that wood is a combination of small layers that are stretched. So, how can we replicate that in Blender?

The node that will allow us to make random layers is called **Noise Texture**. To obtain this node, press *Shift + A* on the **Shader Editor**, click on **Search**, and type `Noise Texture`:

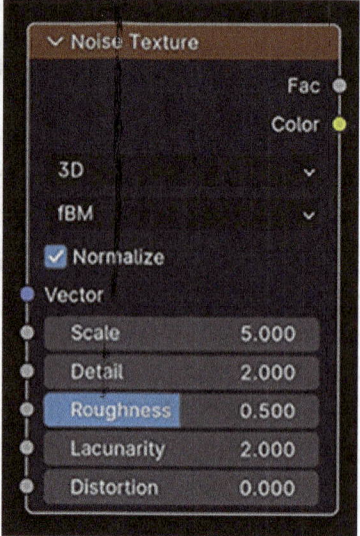

Figure 2.23 – Noise Texture

So, here's the trick to creating a realistic wood material: we'll be combining two **Noise Texture** nodes in a row, one after the other, and connecting them to **Base Color**.

The scale of the first **Noise Texture** node should be set to the default value of **5**, and the scale of the second **Noise Texture** node should be set to **50**. The detail amount should be **0** for both **Noise Texture** nodes. This should obtain the following result:

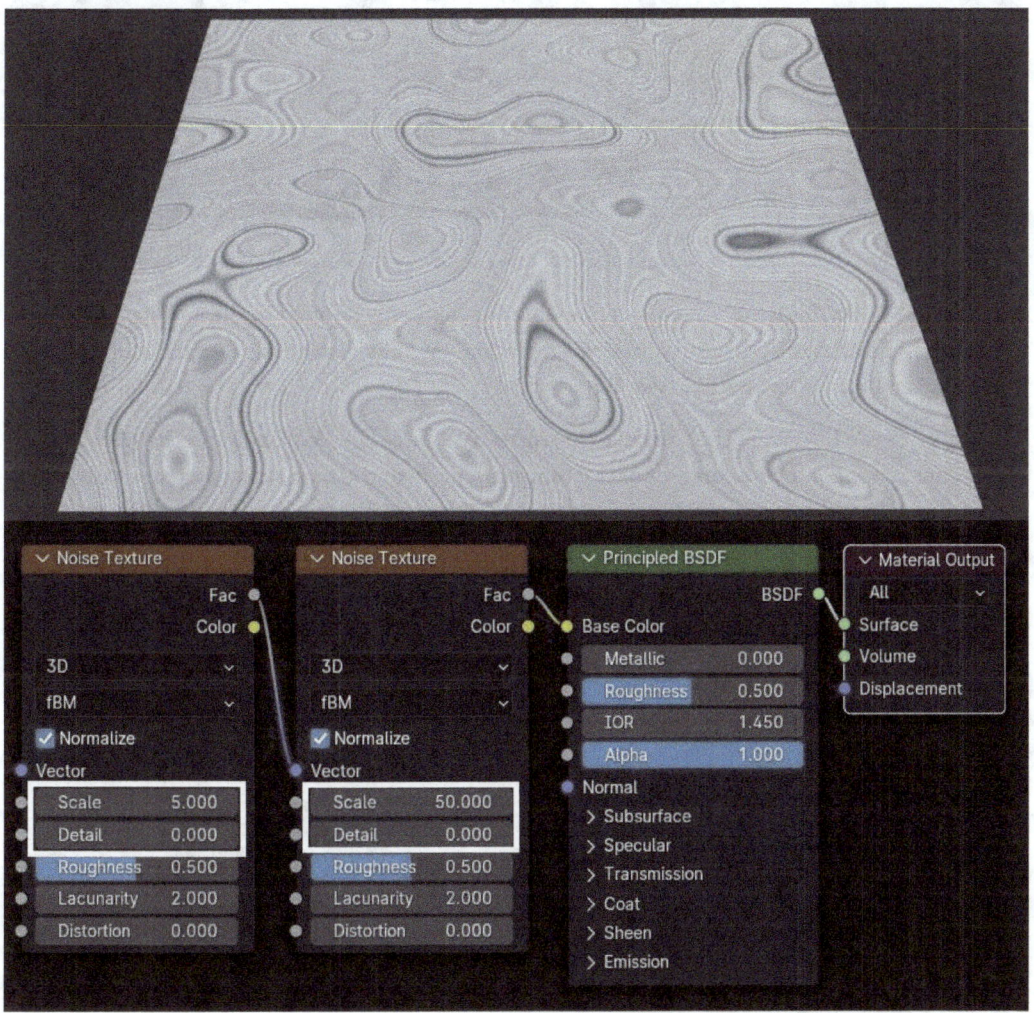

Figure 2.24 – The result of two connected Noise Texture nodes

As you can see, we create layers similar to what you'll see in wood, but we need to add another effect, which is *stretching*. We need to stretch our texture to make it look more like wood. To accomplish this task, we'll be using two nodes, **Mapping** and **Texture Coordinate**:

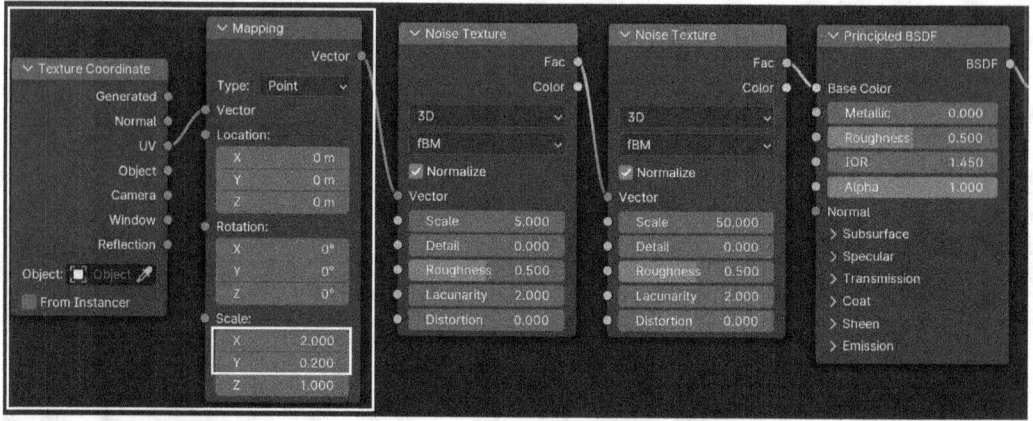

Figure 2.25 – Stretching the wood texture using Mapping and Texture Coordinate nodes

The **Texture Coordinate** node helps define how the texture is applied to the surface, while the **Mapping** node allows us to adjust the scale, rotation, and position of the texture, helping us stretch it to create a more natural wood pattern.

Let's connect the **UV** slot of the **Texture Coordinate** node to the **Vector** slot in the **Mapping** node. Then, connect the **Vector** slot of the **Mapping** node to the first **Noise Texture Vector** slot.

The **Texture Coordinate** and **Mapping** nodes allow us to move, rotate, and scale any texture they are connected to. The **Texture Coordinate** node defines the type of changes you want to make, so we set it to the UVs of the plane. The **Mapping** node gives us three settings to change: the *XYZ* location of our texture, the *XYZ* rotation, and the *XYZ* scale.

The scale settings are on the **X** and **Y** axes. In *Figure 2.25*, **X** is set to 2, and **Y** is set to 0.2. *Figure 2.26* is the result of our wood texture so far:

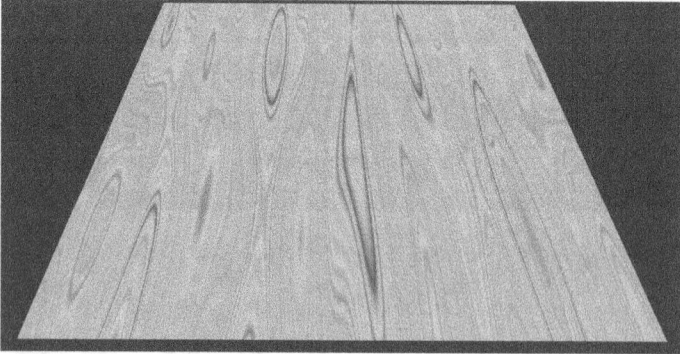

Figure 2.26 – The stretched wood texture

As you can see, our result is starting to resemble actual wood, but the wood texture looks washed out and lacking contrast. How can we enhance the contrast to make the wood texture more vivid and realistic?

We will achieve this goal by using the **Brightness/Contrast** node, as shown in *Figure 2.27*:

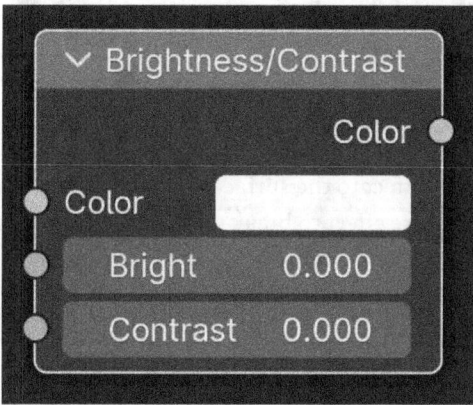

Figure 2.27 – Brightness/Contrast node

Let's drag this node and drop it between **Noise Texture** with a **Scale** value of 50 and **Principled BSDF**. Also, make sure to increase the **Contrast** value up to 2.5, as follows:

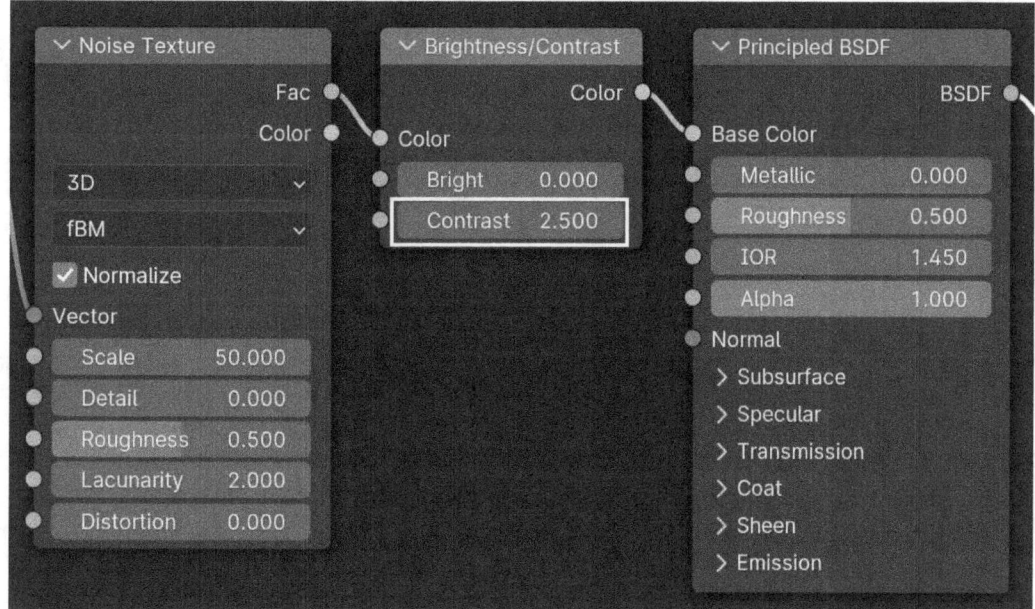

Figure 2.28 – The node setup

Feel free to adjust the **Contrast** value based on how you want the wood to look. Now, the wood layers will look more defined:

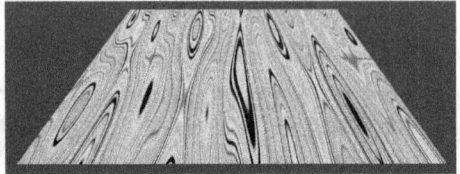

Figure 2.29 – Wood layers look more defined

The next step is to add a noise effect to the surface. If we zoom into the texture, it will look CG-perfect, so we need to add a noise effect to break up the perfection in our wood texture. Hence, we need to add a new **Noise Texture** node.

To obtain the **Noise Texture** node, press *Shift + A* on the **Shader Editor**, click on **Search**, and type Noise Texture:

Figure 2.30 – The Noise Texture node

If we connect the **Noise Texture** node to the **Base Color** slot of **Principled BSDF**, this is how **Noise Texture** looks when applied on its own to a plane:

> **Note**
>
> Note that this action is not needed; it's just to show you how **Noise Texture** appears.

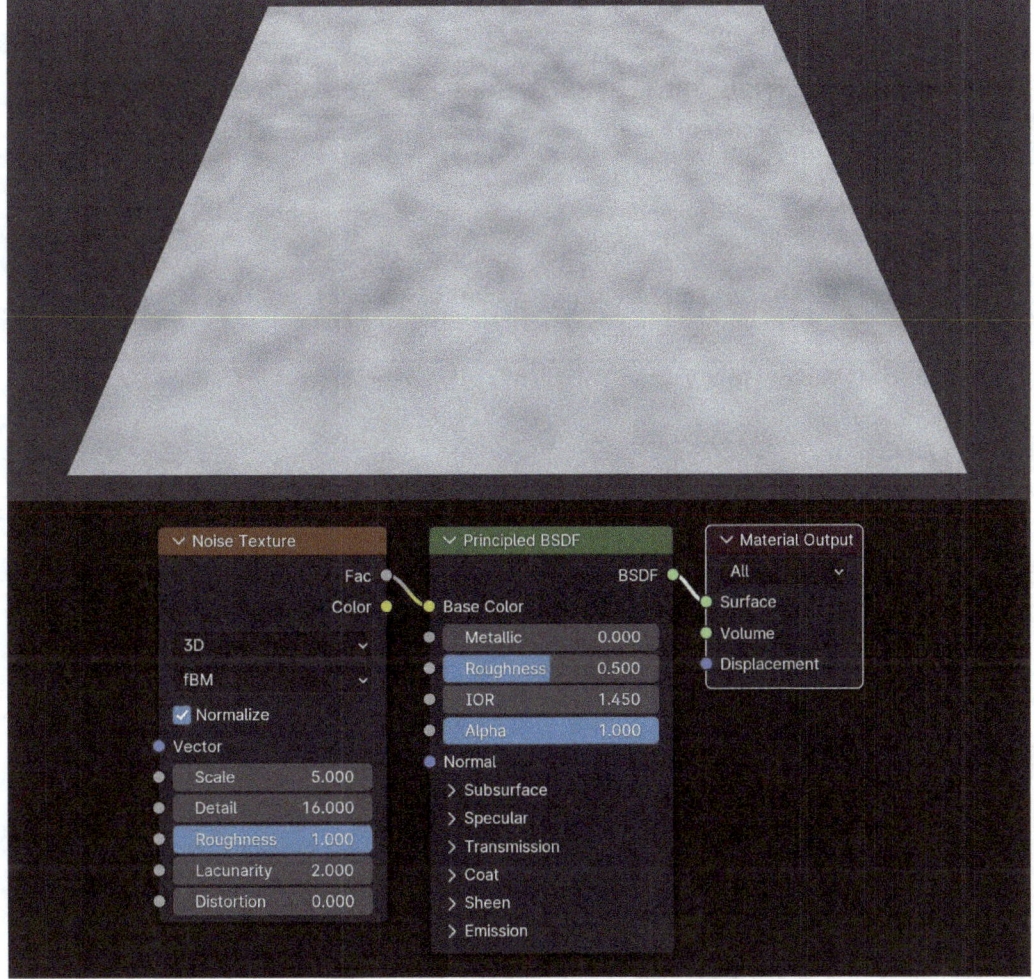

Figure 2.31 – The Noise Texture node applied to a plane

We need to find a way to mix this **Noise Texture** node with the other **Noise Texture** nodes. The way to do it is to use a new node, called the **Mix** node.

Using the Mix node

Imagine you're blending two colors, like mixing paint. The **Mix** node is your tool for this in Blender's world.

To get this node, in **Shader Editor**, press *Shift + A* and search for Mix. In Blender 5, we have five types of **Mix** nodes:

- **Utilities | Math | Mix**: This node blends two number values based on a factor. It is good for procedural effects, such as the wood material we're creating. This is the node we will use later in this section.

- **Color | Mix Color**: This blends two colors using different blend modes (**Mix**, **Add**, and **Multiply**).

- **Shader | Mix Shader**: This blends two shaders based on a factor (for example, **Glossy** and **Diffuse**).

- **Utilities | Vector | Mix Vector**: This blends two vectors smoothly (coordinates and normals).

- **Mix | Math Mix**: This blends two math signals together, acting as a grayscale mixer that supports values below 0 (*super black*) and above 1.0 (*super white*). Unlike **Color Mixer** for **RGB**, this is specialized for single-value data.

Figure 2.32 – Types of Mix nodes in Blender 5

For the procedural wood creation, we need the first option: **Utilities | Math | Mix**. Select **Mix**, press *Enter*, and you'll get the following node:

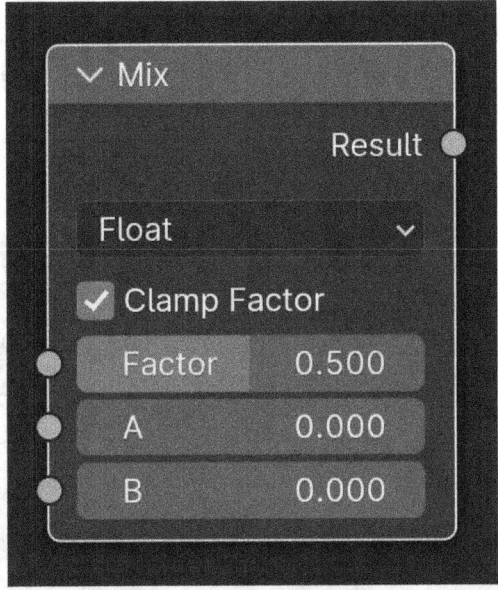

Figure 2.33 – The Mix node

The **Mix** node has three main slots (inputs):

- **Factor** (0 to 1): Think of this as your mixing spoon. It decides how much of each *paint* you get in the final mix. A **Factor** value of 0 means you're getting 100% of **A**, while 1 means you're all-in on **B**. If you're somewhere in between, you'll get a bit of both!

- **A**: This is your first *paint* (or input). It's what you get when the **Factor** value is closer to 0. Here in this slot, we'll connect the **Color** output of the **Brightness/Contrast** node.

- **B**: This is your second *paint*. The closer the **Factor** value is to 1, the more of **B** you'll see in the mix. Here in this slot, we'll connect the **Fac** output of the **Noise Texture** node.

Let's use this **Mix** node to mix the **Noise Texture** node with the **Brightness/Contrast** node.

To set up the **Mix** node connections, follow these steps, as shown in *Figure 2.34*:

1. First, we need to connect the **Color** output of the **Brightness/Contrast** node (on the top) to the **A** input of the **Mix** node. This takes the color data that has been enhanced by the brightness and contrast adjustments, passing it through to be blended.

2. Next, connect the **Fac** (*Factor*) output of the second **Noise Texture** node (on the bottom) to the **B** input of the **Mix** node.

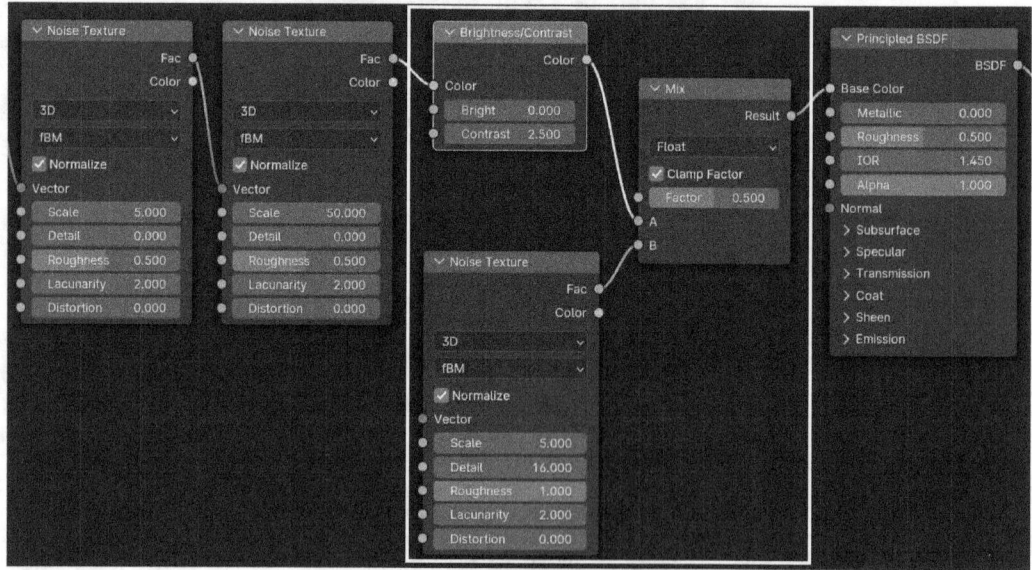

Figure 2.34 – Node setup in the Shader Editor of the wood texture

By connecting these nodes in this manner, the **Mix** node will blend the brightness-adjusted texture (the **A** input) with the noise texture (the **B** input) to give us a nice black and white wood material.

The degree of mixing in the **Mix** node is set to **0.5** by default. A **Factor** value closer to 0 will favor the brightness-contrast adjusted texture, while a **Factor** value closer to 1 will lean toward the noise texture.

I've made the following tweaks to the **Noise Texture** node:

- Increased the **Detail** slot amount to 16
- Set the **Roughness** slot amount to 1

This is how our wood texture will look:

Figure 2.35 – Wood texture with noise effect applied

Now that we have the shape of the wood established, as you might guess, the next step will be to make our wood colorful – and this is actually quite simple. Let's use the **ColorRamp** node.

Adding color to the wood texture using the ColorRamp node

To access the **ColorRamp** node, press *Shift + A* in **Shader Editor**, search for ColorRamp, and drop it between the **Mix** and **Principled BSDF** nodes. It will automatically connect to the node group.

We'll use the **ColorRamp** node to create a gradient effect. This allows us to blend different shades of brown, simulating the natural color variation found in wood.

Now, let's adjust the colors to bring the texture to life:

1. Select the right thumb on the track bar and move it toward a *light brown* color (*1*).
2. Add a new thumb using the **plus (+)** icon at the top of the **ColorRamp** node window (*2*).
3. Change the color of the new thumb to a *darker brown* color (*3*).

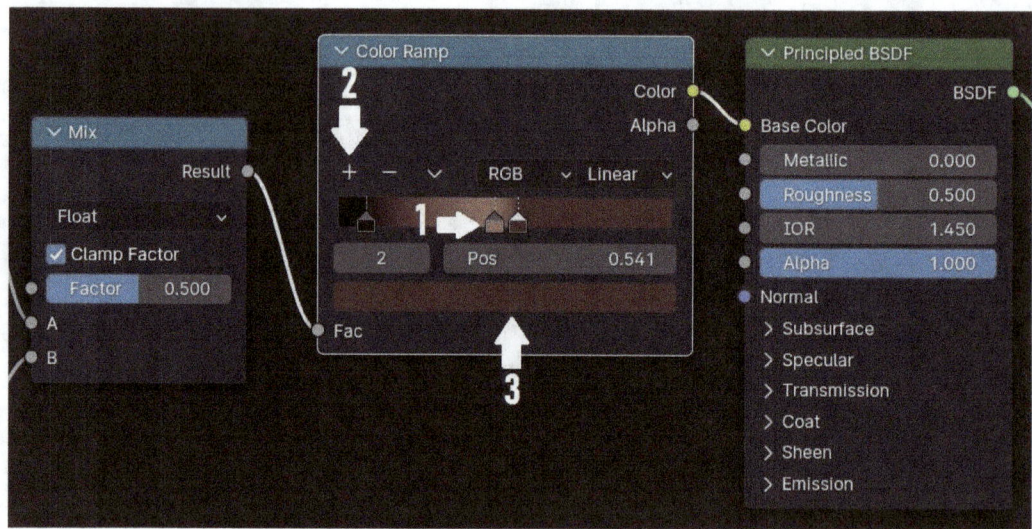

Figure 2.36 – Tweaking the ColorRamp node

I highly suggest you keep playing with this **ColorRamp** node. It will give you excellent control over the color of your material; you can change it to any color you want. This is the beauty of using procedural texturing in Blender: making textures is 100% flexible.

With the tweaks to the **ColorRamp** node, this is what our wood texture now looks like:

Figure 2.37 – Coloring the wood procedural texture using ColorRamp

Now that we have finished working on the first channel of our wood material, **Base Color**, we need other details because, as you know, our wood material is flat and unrealistic right now. We need to add other details, such as **Roughness**, which controls the reflection, and **Normal**, which adds bumps to the surface.

Adding wood reflection using the Roughness map

To work on the wood reflection, we need to add a **ColorRamp** node and connect the output of the **Mix** node to the new **ColorRamp** node and tweak the thumbs on the track bar.

You can see the wood node setup maximized in *Figure 2.38*:

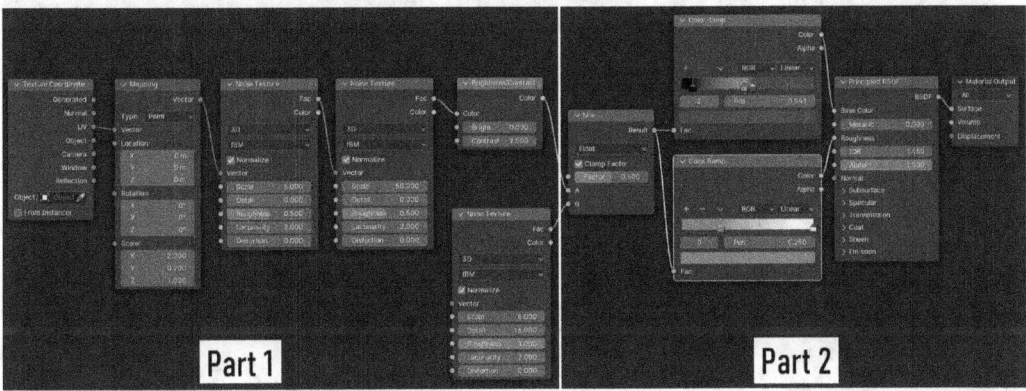

Figure 2.38 – Full node setup for wood material

I've divided the image into two parts so that you can see the minor details. *Figure 2.39* shows **Part 1** and **Part 2** of the wood node setup:

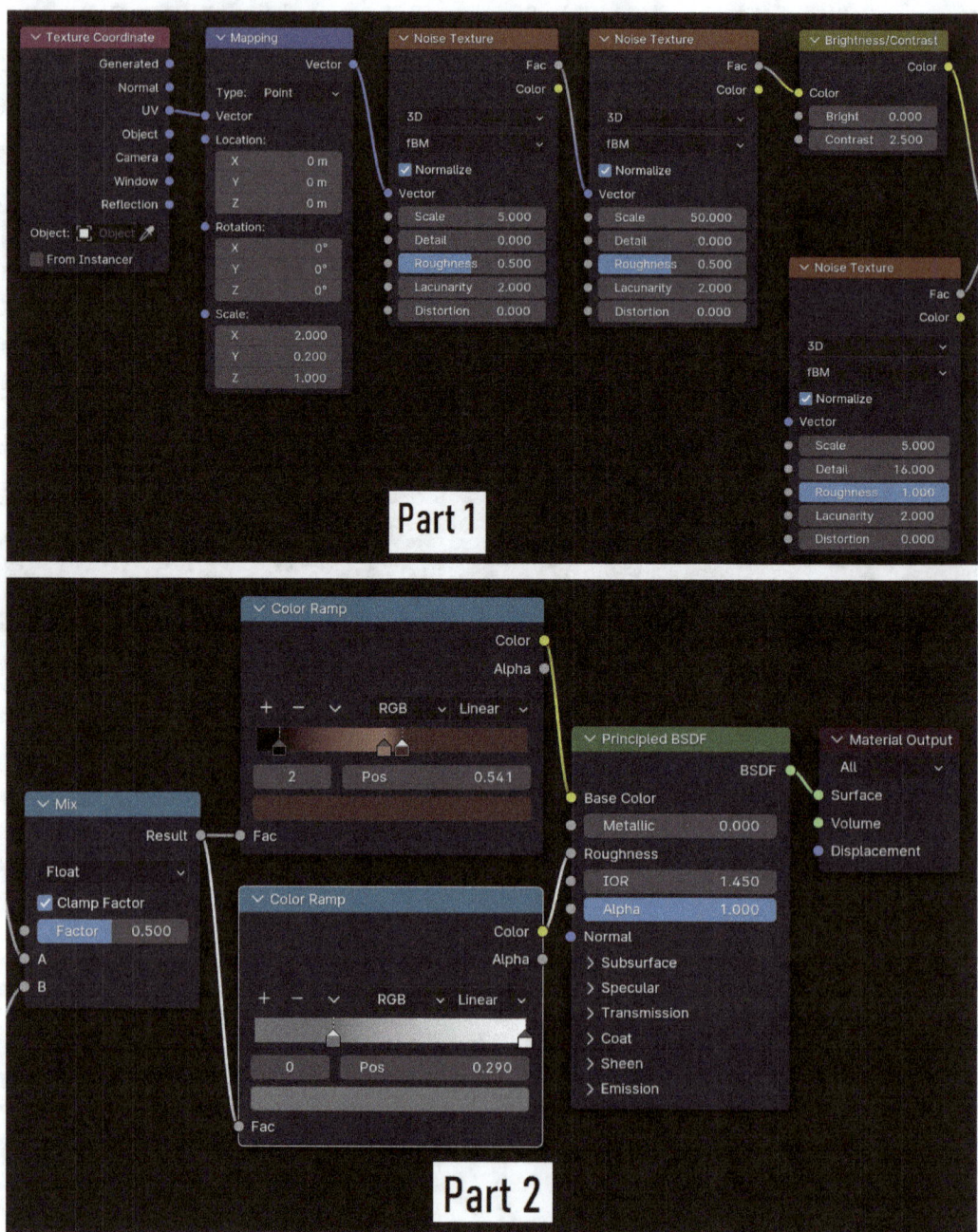

Figure 2.39 – Part 1 and Part 2 of the wood node setup

Here is the final result, showing reflectivity added to the wood:

Figure 2.40 – Adding reflectivity to the wood material

Now, we can see the reflection variation we have in our wood material. The next step is to add bumps to the surface.

Adding bumps to the surface of the wood material

So far, we have the color of wood and a nice reflection on the surface, but our material still looks flat and non-realistic. We need to add the bumps to make it photorealistic.

For this, let's add the **Bump** node and put it between the **Mix** node and **Normal** slot in the **Principled BSDF** node, as shown in *Figure 2.41*:

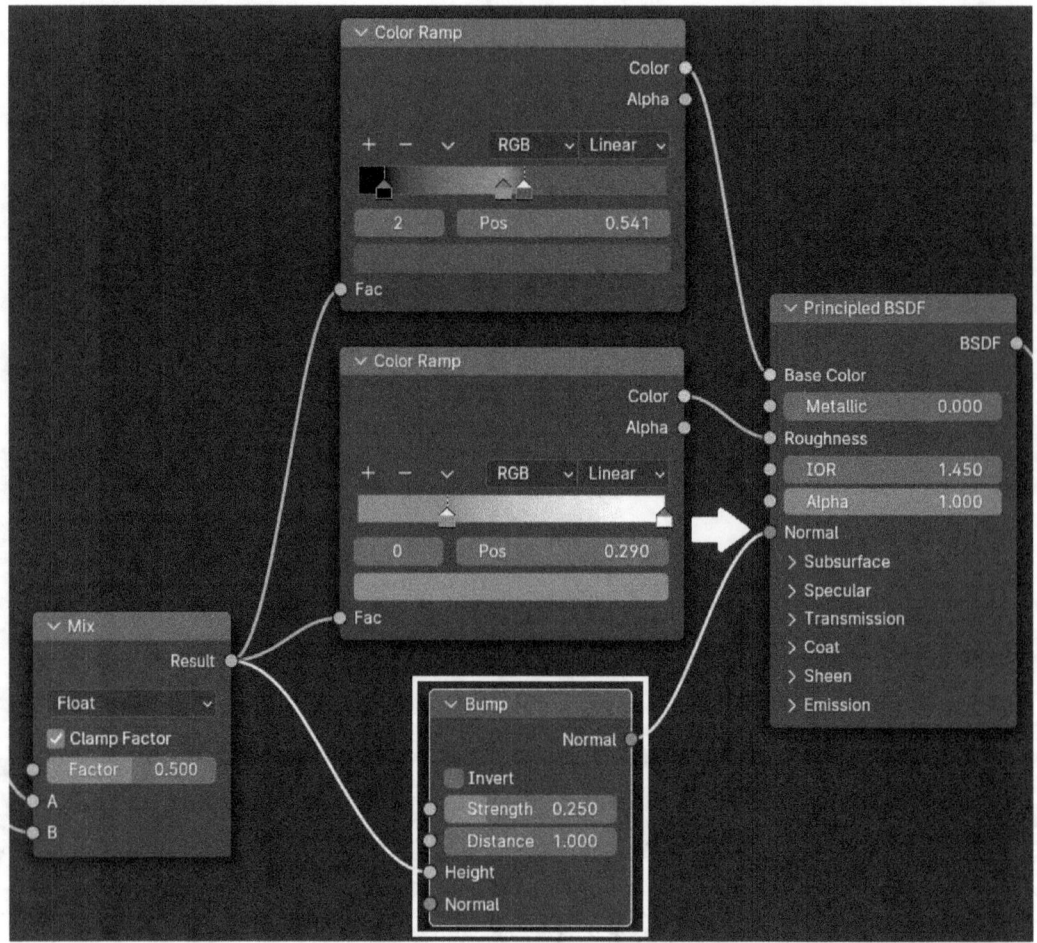

Figure 2.41 – Adding the Bump node to make the wood surface bumpy

Now, we can see the bumps on the surface of our wood material; however, we need to reduce the **Strength** slot of the **Bump** node down to something around 0.25 in order to make our wood look more realistic:

Figure 2.42 – Reducing the strength of the Bump node to 0.25

Before evaluating the wood material, let's switch Blender's color management to **AgX**.

Improving color management for better material preview

AgX handles bright values better and keeps colors from looking washed out, which helps when judging procedural materials such as wood.

Let's perform these steps:

1. Switch to **Render Properties**.

2. In **Color Management**, switch **View** to **AgX**.

3. Set **Look** to **Low Contrast**. We use **Low Contrast** to preserve more wood detail in midtones and highlights, making the wood grain and color variations easier to read.

4. Increase the **Exposure** value to 0.5.

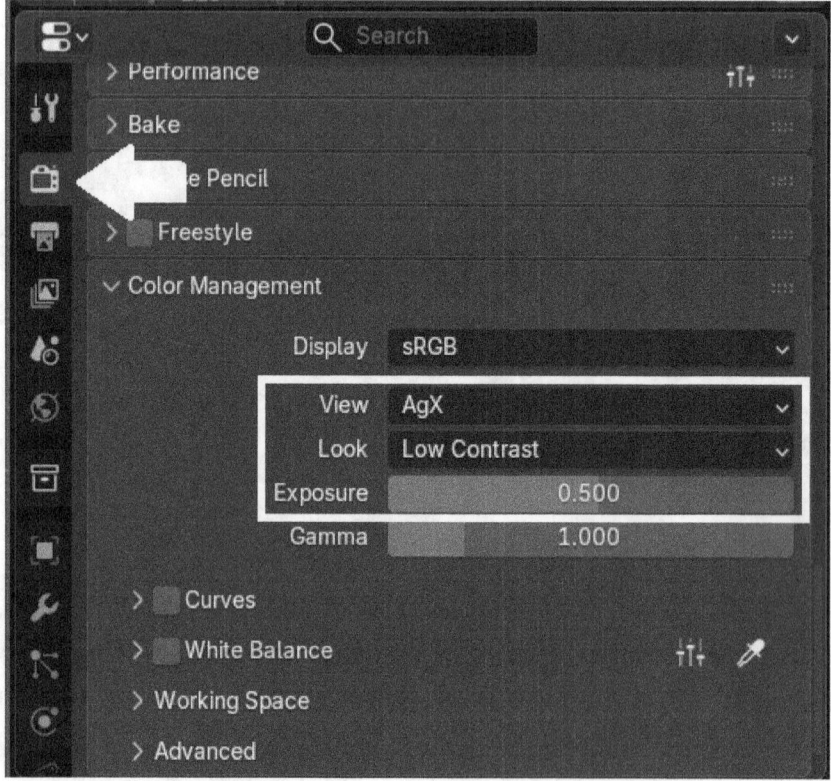

Figure 2.43 – Adjusting Color Management settings using the AgX view transform

We slightly adjust **Exposure** only if the material looks too dark or too bright, and we keep **Gamma** at **1.0** to avoid distorting the midtones.

This setup gives a neutral, realistic preview of the wood material before any final lighting or color grading.

Figure 2.44 – Wood material with Bump and Roughness maps applied (AgX view transform)

Comparing AgX versus ACES

AgX provides a more neutral and predictable image. It preserves highlight detail, keeps colors stable, and is easier to control when working on materials. This makes it better for evaluating surfaces such as wood, where accurate color and roughness are important.

ACES applies a stronger cinematic contrast and color response. Highlights roll off more aggressively, and colors can shift, which is useful for final cinematic renders but less ideal for judging raw materials.

Congratulations! We have created a realistic wood material that can be used later to texture our wood cabin.

Summary

In this chapter, we first went through the basics of realistic texturing in Blender by breaking down the four components of a realistic material: the **Base Color** map, the **Roughness** map for the reflectivity of our material, the **Normal** map for the bumps on the surface, and the **Displacement** map that changes the real shape of the mesh geometry.

Then, we created a wood material using procedural texturing in Blender. We used a combination of nodes, such as **Noise Texture**, **Mix**, **Mapping**, and **Texture Coordinate**, to create a realistic wood material.

In this chapter, we used the **AgX** view transform, which provides more realistic contrast and highlight roll-off compared to the older Filmic view. Proper color management helps materials respond to light in a more natural way and makes it easier to judge roughness, color, and surface detail while working.

In the next chapter, we will focus on UV mapping in Blender and how to do it the right way in order to maximize photorealism. We will apply the wood texture we created to the wood cabin. This will enable you to understand the art of unwrapping 3D objects.

Get this book's PDF version and more

Scan the QR code (or go to `packtpub.com/unlock`). Search for this book by name, confirm the edition, and then follow the steps on the page.

Note: Keep your invoice handy. Purchases made directly from Packt don't require an invoice.

3

Efficient Unwrapping and Texturing in Blender

Unwrapping is an essential skill for applying textures to 3D objects. **UV unwrapping** is the process of flattening a 3D model's surface into a 2D layout so textures can be applied accurately. It defines how an image is mapped onto the geometry without distortion. Therefore, in this chapter, we will understand what exactly unwrapping is and why it is needed, as well as the tools and techniques required to help you efficiently map your 3D objects in Blender.

You will be doing a whole lot of unwrapping of models that have different shapes and sizes, and then texturing them. The goal in this chapter is to unwrap and texture our wood cabin model.

In this chapter, we'll be covering the following topics:

- Importing the wood material
- Texturing our wood cabin
- Unwrapping our wood cabin

By the end of this chapter, you'll have a solid understanding of unwrapping and texturing in Blender. You will have successfully unwrapped and textured a wood cabin, using various techniques. This will enhance your ability to apply realistic materials to your 3D models efficiently.

Technical requirements

This chapter requires a system capable of running **Blender version 5.0** or above (Windows, macOS, or Linux).

You can download the resources for this chapter from GitHub at: `https://github.com/PacktPublishing/3D-Environment-Design-with-Blender-5-Second-Edition/tree/ab43270b643a41ba8f915f74e3bf78573b10a816/chapter-3`.

Importing the wood material

In the previous chapter, we created a wood material using procedural texturing. Now, it's time to apply it to the wood cabin model that you will find in the resources to download, which is available at `https://github.com/PacktPublishing/3D-Environment-Design-with-Blender-5-Second-Edition/tree/ab43270b643a41ba8f915f74e3bf78573b10a816/chapter-3`.

After downloading the wood cabin model, we need to unwrap it first and texture it. To do so, first, let's import the wood material we created in *Chapter 2* and use it inside the `Wood Cabin Model` Blender file. Follow these steps:

1. Click on **File** and choose **Append...**:

Figure 3.1 – Importing files from other scenes using Append

2. Then, select the Blender file (Wood.blend) where you created the wood material. You will see a window asking you what type of folder you want to import from the Blender file you selected:

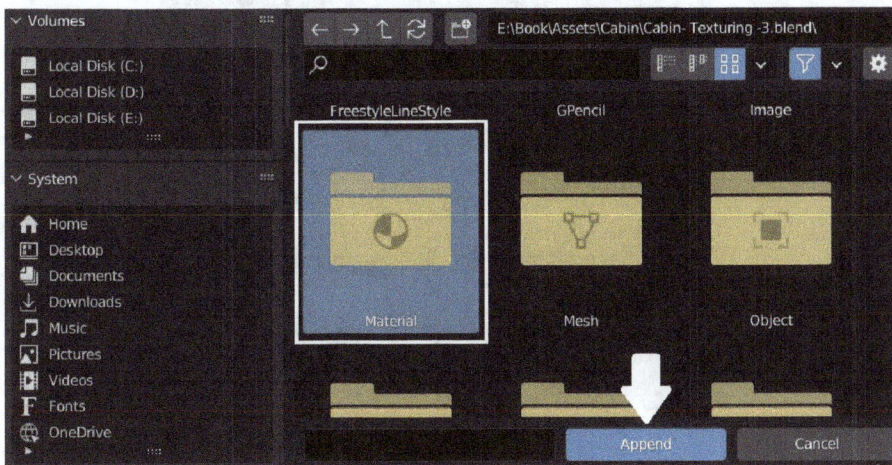

Figure 3.2 – Choosing the type of file to import in Blender

Here, Blender allows us to import anything from the Blender file we chose. In our case, we want a material.

3. Double-click on the **Material** folder (highlighted in *blue* in the preceding figure); you should find the wood material you created.

4. Select it and click on **Append**.

Now, the wood material is appended.

If you want to check that you have the wood material, go to **Material Properties** (*Step 1* in *Figure 3.3*) and then click on the **Materials** repository (*Step 2* in *Figure 3.3*). Here, you will find all the materials you have in the scene, and **Wood Cabin** will be one of them:

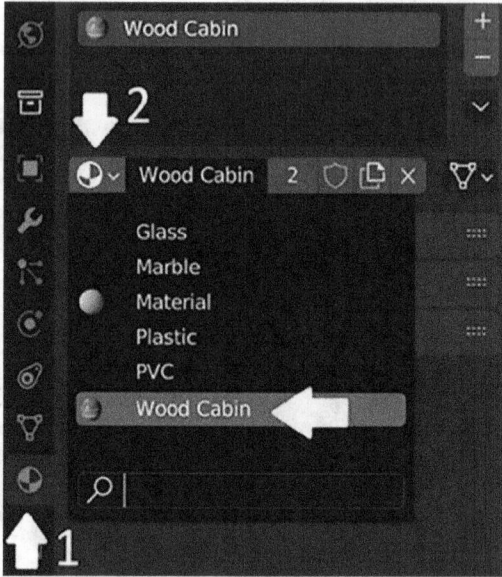

Figure 3.3 – Materials repository in Material Properties

Now that we've imported our wood material into the new wood cabin model Blender scene, let's go ahead and assign it to the wood cabin.

Texturing our wood cabin

Let's texture the wood cabin using the imported wood material:

1. Select the front of the wood cabin.

2. Go to **Material Properties**; you will find it empty. This means that the selected object has no material attached to it.

3. Click on the **Material** repository and select the **Wood Cabin** material we imported into our scene:

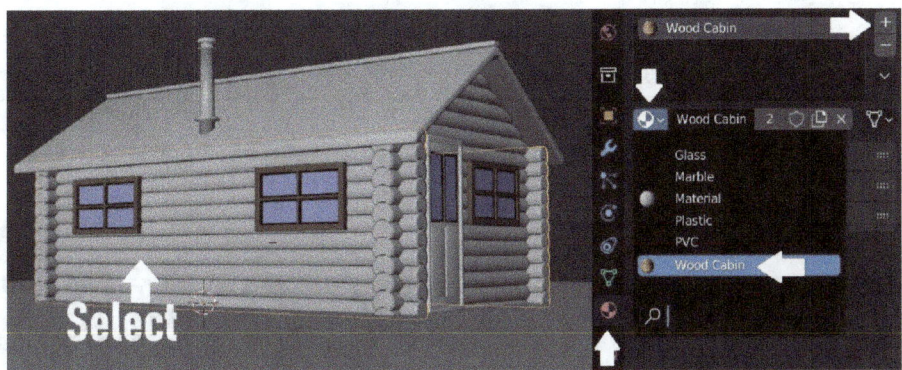

Figure 3.4 – Assigning the wood material to the wood cabin

4. Now, the wood material is applied to the front of the cabin, but we can't see it because the **Viewport Display** is set to **Solid**. **Viewport Display** refers to the overall look of the 3D Viewport. We need to switch **Viewport Display** to **Material Preview** to see the material applied to our objects. So, hover your mouse on the 3D Viewport, press Z, and choose **Material Preview**:

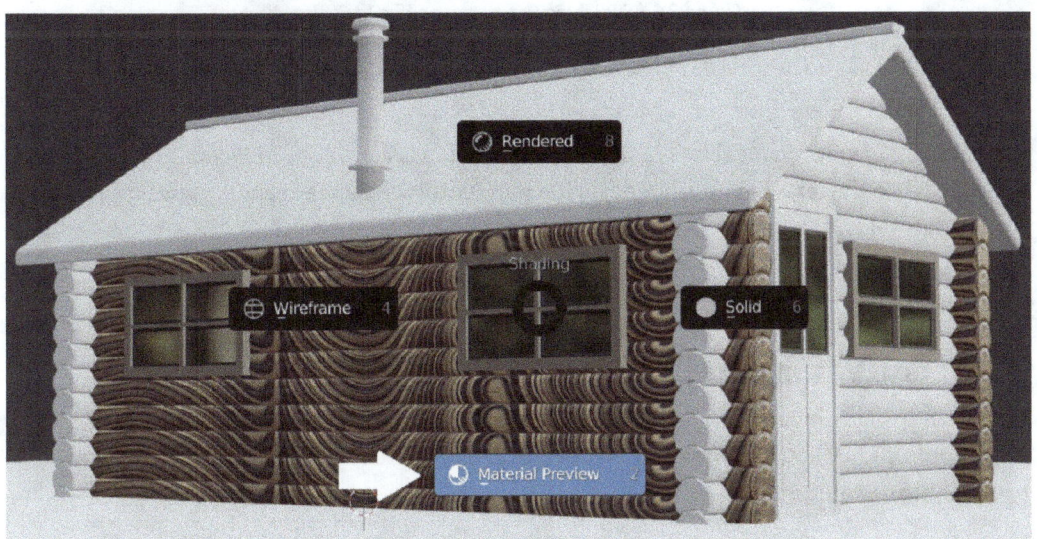

Figure 3.5 – Switching to Material Preview to see the wood material

If you press *Z* and notice that **Material Preview** is missing (showing only **Wireframe**, **Rendered**, and **Solid**), it is because you are currently using the **Workbench** render engine. To access **Material Preview**, make sure your render engine is switched to **EEVEE** or **Cycles**.

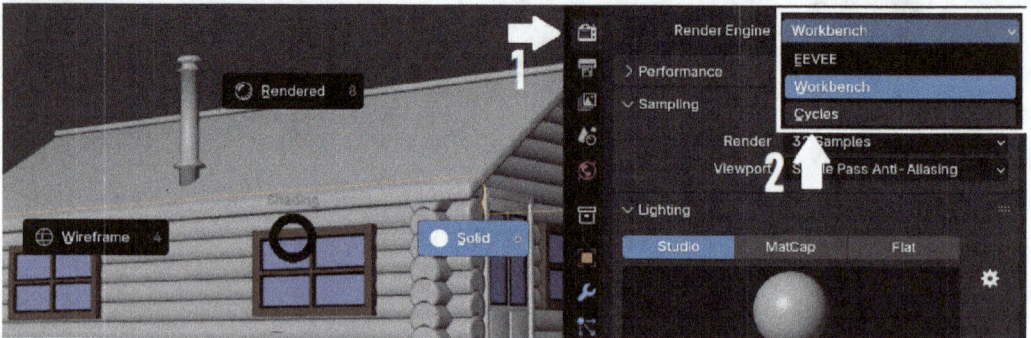

Figure 3.6 – Switching the render engine to Cycles

The current wood texture looks repetitive and non-realistic; this has to do with the bad unwrapping of our cabin.

In our case, *bad unwrapping* refers to the wood repetition issue we see in *Figure 3.5*. This happens when the texture pattern repeats too frequently across the surface, making the wood look unnatural and artificial.

We need to better unwrap our wood cabin to have more control over how we want the wood material to be displayed. To understand what's happening here, let's break down UV mapping.

What is UV mapping?

Before texturing our wood cabin, let's understand what UV mapping is. **UV mapping** or **unwrapping** – both terms refer to the same thing – is the process of wrapping a 2D image texture onto a 3D mesh.

U and **V** are the names of the axes in the **UV Editor**, while *X*, *Y*, and *Z* refer to the coordinates in the 3D Viewport.

By default, meshes are created with UVs, meaning that when you add a mesh, Blender will automatically unwrap it and generate UVs in the **UV Editor**.

The following figure shows a UV-mapped cube, with a horizontal *red* arrow indicating the **U Axis** and a vertical *green* arrow indicating the **V Axis**. This UV map is essential for accurately placing textures on your models, ensuring that they look as intended in the 3D space.

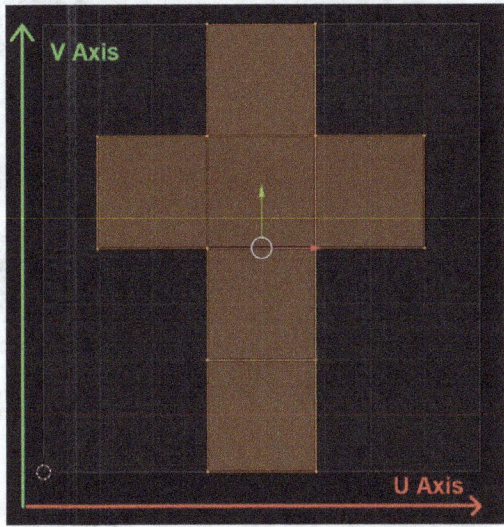

Figure 3.7 – U and V axes displayed in the UV Editor

To understand unwrapping better, let's take an example: I've created a simple cube, as shown in *Figure 3.8*. Imagine you're holding a pair of scissors and cutting the cube along its edges – we've all done this in our childhood.

In order to perfectly unfold the cube and lay it flat, we need to make seven cuts to the edges highlighted in *white*. To achieve this in Blender, follow these steps:

1. Press the *Tab* key to switch to **Edit Mode**, select the highlighted *white* edges, press *Ctrl + E*, and choose **Mark Seam**. This means you're marking the edges for Blender to cut:

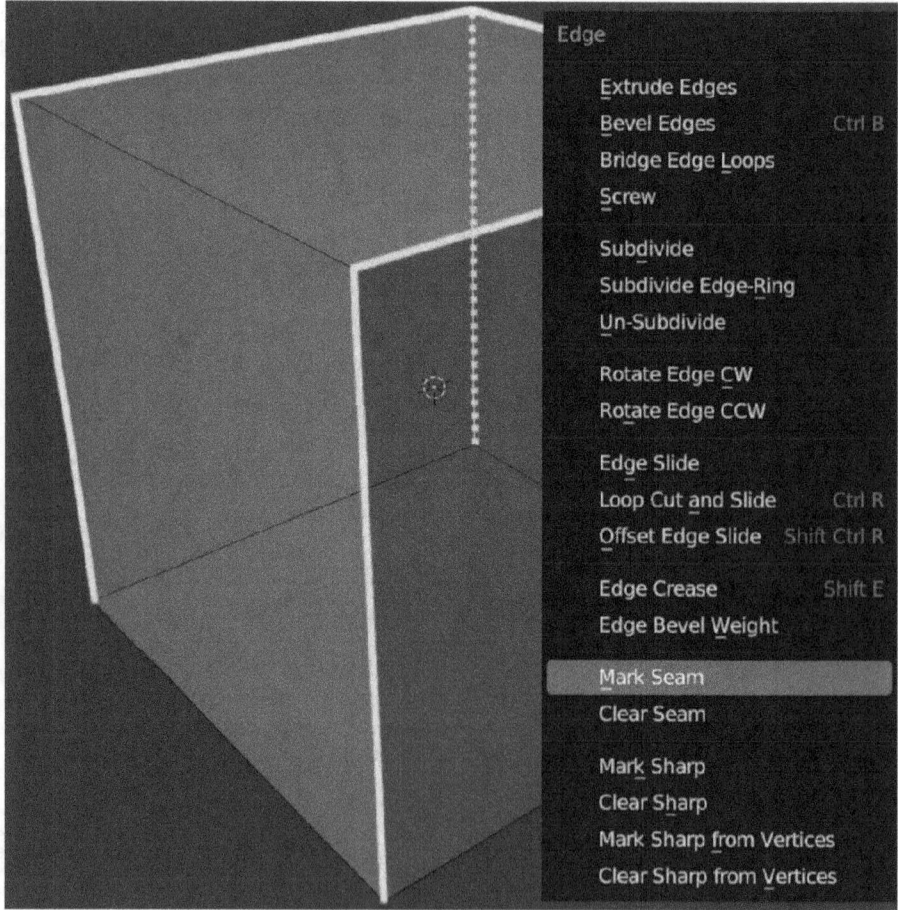

Figure 3.8 – Marking seams of a cube to unwrap it

2. Next, to unwrap our cube, press *U* while selecting the cube in **Edit Mode**. You will get a menu; select **Unwrap**. Let's expand the **Timeline** window and switch it to **UV Editor**, as shown in *Figure 3.9*:

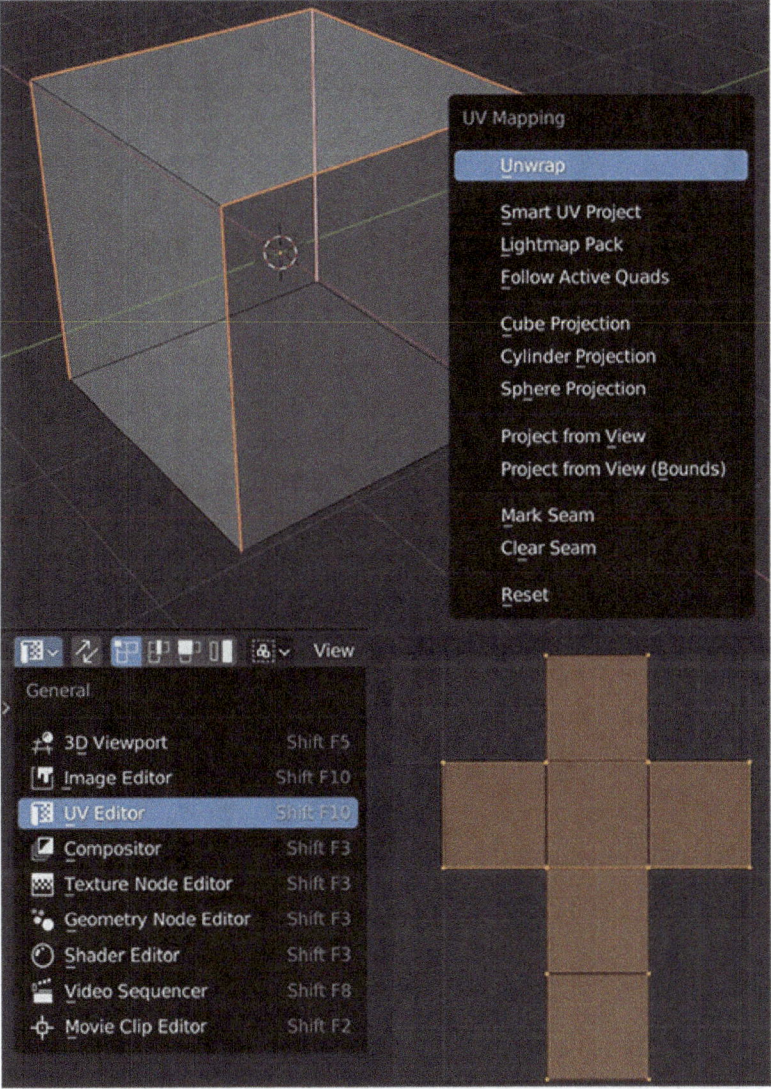

Figure 3.9 – Unwrapping a cube and seeing the UV map in the UV Editor

3. There is a quick alternative to switch to the **UV Editor** instead of manually splitting windows.

   To access the **UV Editing** panel, you can use the **Workspace** tabs located at the top of the Blender interface (e.g., **Layout**, **Modeling**, **UV Editing**, **Shading**), as shown in *Figure 3.10*. Clicking the **UV Editing** tab automatically sets up the perfect layout with the 3D Viewport on one side and the **UV Editor** on the other, saving you time.

Figure 3.10 – Exporting the UV layout of the cube UV map

4. We can see the UV map displayed in the **UV Editor**. The next step is to export the UV map as an image. On the top bar, you will find a **UV** tab (*Step 1* in *Figure 3.11*); click on it and select **Export UV Layout** (*Step 2*):

Figure 3.11 – Exporting the UV layout of the cube UV map

5. Then, you can save the UV layout and open it in any image editor – I'll be using **Paint** in Windows.

6. In the Windows image editor, fill each box with a different color and add numbers, as shown in *Figure 3.12*:

Figure 3.12 – Texturing the cube UV layout

7. In the last box, I've put a wood texture to show you, as an example, that you can put anything you want. Save the UV layout to your desktop; we'll be using it later.

8. Now, back to our Blender scene; let's wrap this texture around our cube by creating a material and assigning it to the cube.

9. Select the cube, click on **Material Properties**, and select **New Material**.

10. Also, make sure to switch the bottom window from **UV Editor** to **Shader Editor** to tweak the cube material.

11. With the cube selected in **Shader Editor**, you will see the **Principled BSDF** node. We need to first drag the texture we have in *Figure 3.12* from your desktop and drop it in the **Shader Editor**. The texture will turn automatically into an image texture node (a **Cube** node), just like in the following figure:

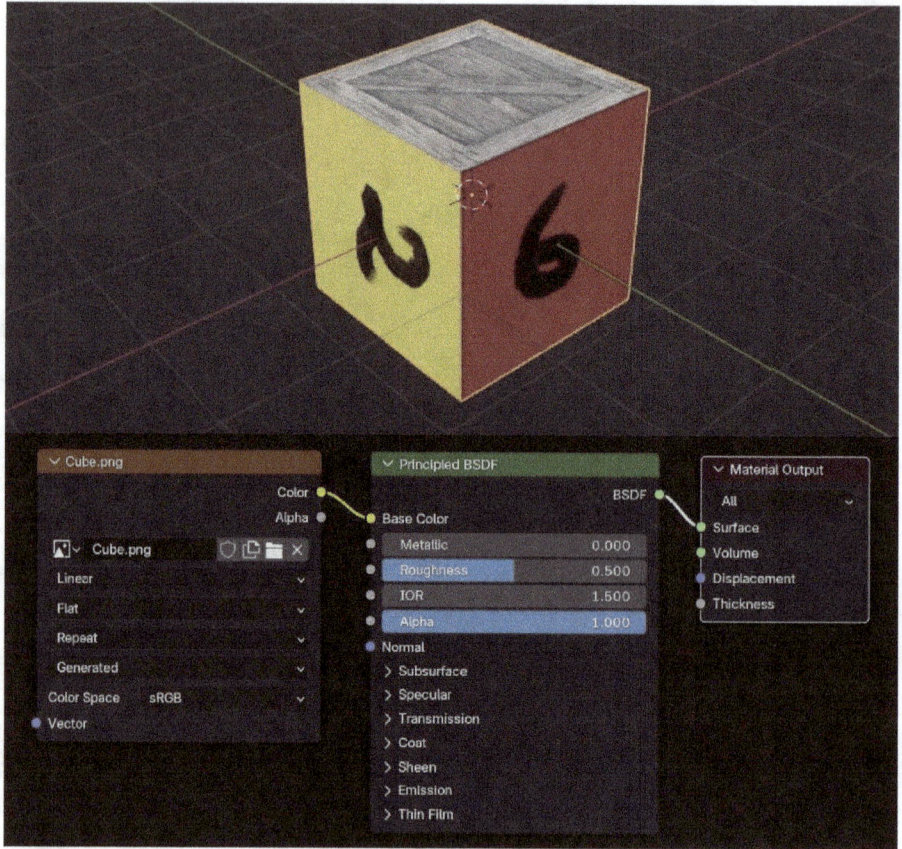

Figure 3.13 – Assigning the textured UV layout to the unwrapped cube

12. Now, to assign the texture shown in *Figure 3.12* to our cube, all we have to do is connect the **Cube** texture node to the **Base Color** of the **Principled BSDF** node and switch the 3D Viewport to **Material Preview** by pressing *Z*. Then, you will see the texture we created in *Figure 3.12* wrapped around the cube, as shown in *Figure 3.13*.

This is the right way to unwrap and texture 3D objects.

Back to our wood cabin, the shape of the wall is multiple cylinders, one on top of the other; let's unwrap them.

Unwrapping our wood cabin

In this section, we'll be doing the same thing we did with the cube to the wood cylinders. Let's unwrap the cylinders!

Unwrapping the cylinders

Unwrapping cylinders is easy. Again, imagine you're holding a pair of scissors to cut a cylinder and then laying it on the floor: we first need to cut the side circles of the cylinder and then make a cut through the cylinder, just like the seams highlighted in red in *Figure 3.14*:

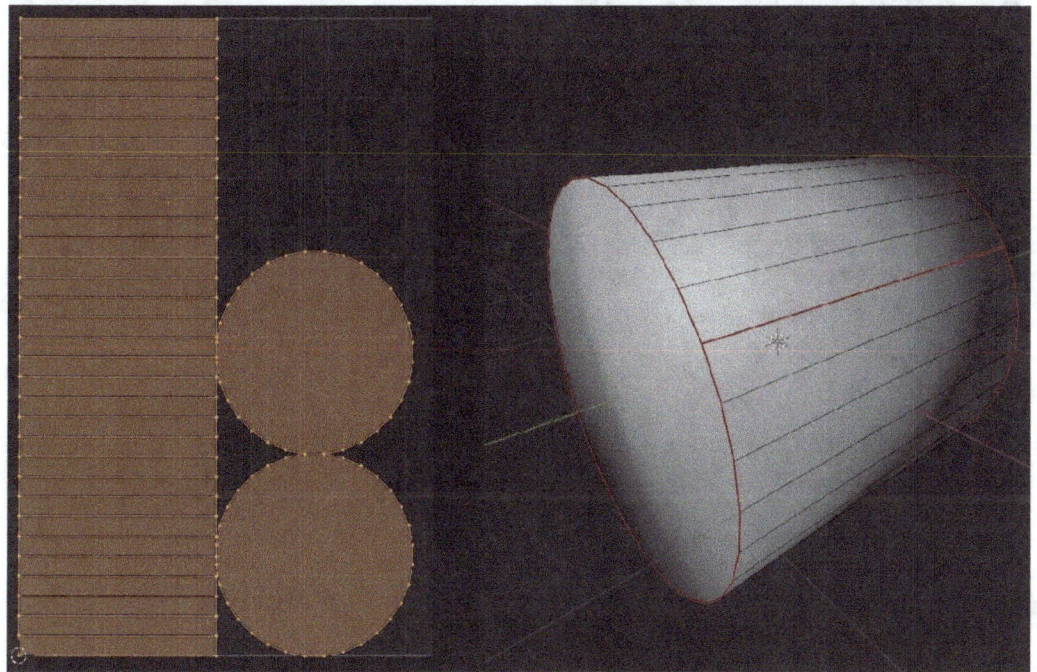

Figure 3.14 – Unwrapping a cylinder

> **Tip**
>
> There is an alternative way to select all the cylinders quickly. To achieve this, we can click on the **Sharp Edges** selection found in the **Select** tab, as shown in *Figure 3.15*.

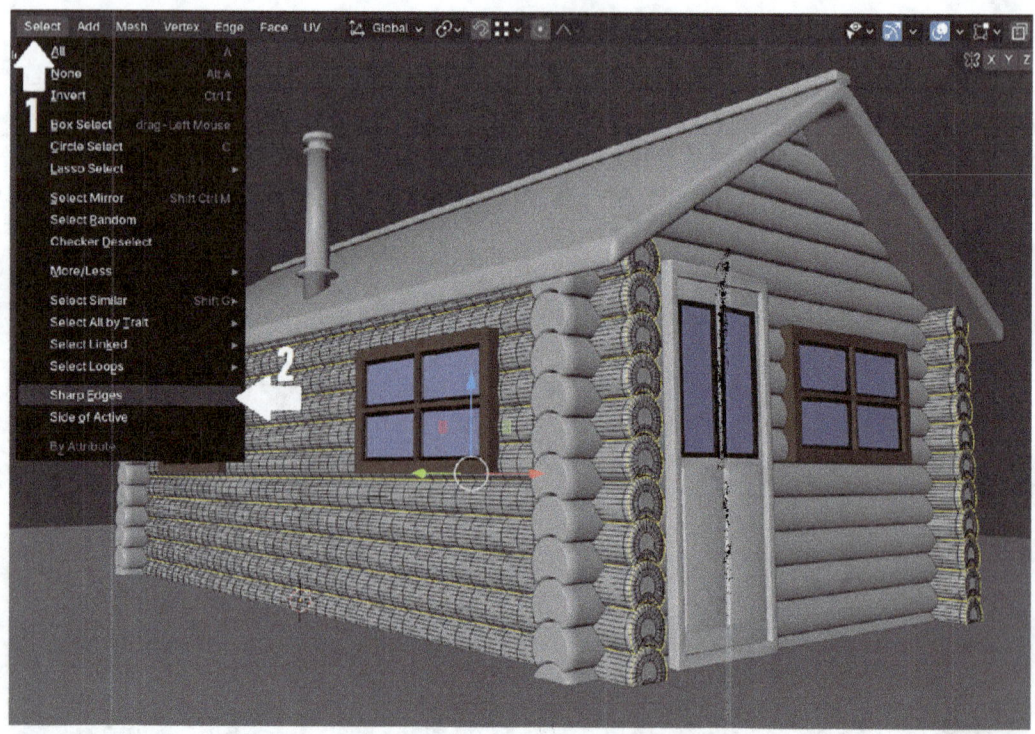

Figure 3.15 – Selecting Sharp Edges of Wood Cabin

Next, press *Ctrl + E* and select **Mark Seam**:

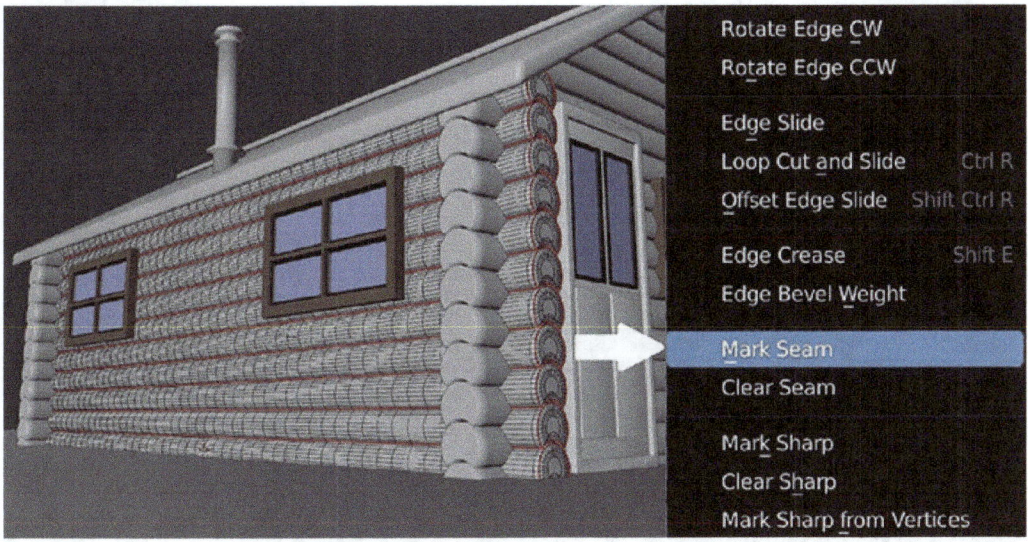

Figure 3.16 – Marking seams of the wood cabin cylinders

After selecting the edges and choosing the **Mark Seam** option, the selected edges' color will turn *red*, indicating that they are now seams. To unwrap the wood cylinders, select them all, press *U*, and choose **Unwrap**.

If you switch to the **Material Preview** mode by pressing *Z*, you will see that the wood looks random, but the texture will appear large, as shown in *Figure 3.17*:

Figure 3.17 – Applying the wood texture to the wood cabin

We need to scale up the UVs to cover a large portion of the texture. To do that, let's go back to the **Shader Editor** and add the **Mapping** node along with the **Texture Coordinate** node, which will control the size of the wood texture.

I have scaled up the wood texture five times. Here, I set the **X** axis to 15 and the **Y** axis to 1:

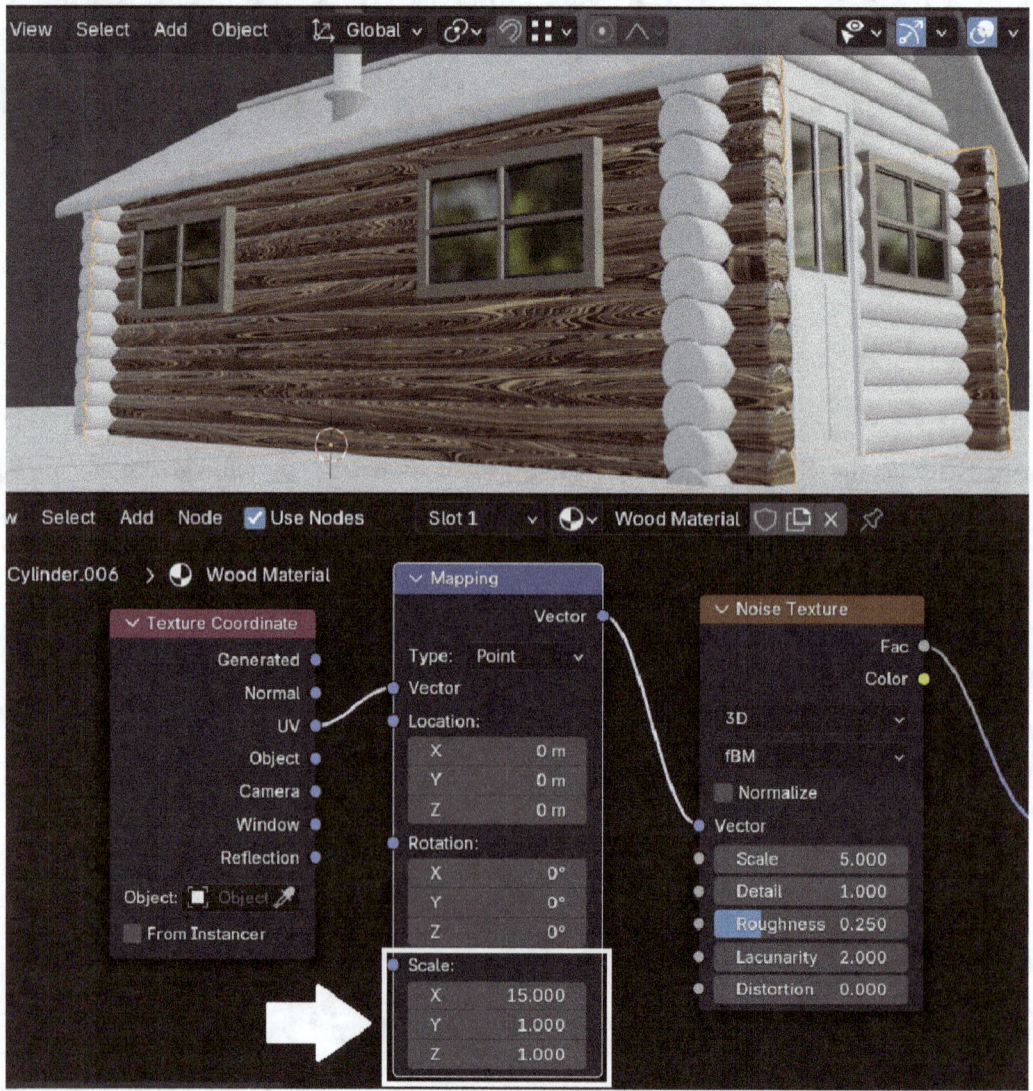

Figure 3.18 – Scaling up the wood texture using the Mapping node

Repeat the same steps for the remaining wooden wall sections: the front, back, and both side walls of the cabin. Once all wall sections are textured, we'll move on to the roof.

Unwrapping and texturing the roof

Next, to texture the roof, let's perform the following steps:

1. Select the roof, go to **Material Properties**, and create a new material called Roof. Save the roof texture on your desktop; it is available in the GitHub repository at https://github.com/PacktPublishing/3D-Environment-Design-with-Blender-5-Second-Edition/blob/ab43270b643a41ba8f915f74e3bf78573b10a816/chapter-3/Roof.jpg.

2. After downloading the roof image texture, Roof.jpg, drag and drop it into **Shader Editor**.

3. Connect the **Color** slot of the **Roof** texture node to the **Base Color** of the **Principled BSDF** node in **Shader Editor**, as shown later in *Figure 3.20*.

If we switch to **Material Preview**, the roof material won't be displayed properly. So, we need a better way to unwrap it. Since the roof is not an important area, there is no need to spend a lot of time marking seams; instead, we will let Blender do it for us by using **Smart UV Project**.

Smart UV Project

Smart UV Project is an automatic method of unwrapping a mesh. If you choose this option, Blender will automatically place new seams and unwrap the mesh for you. While the Smart UV Project might seem like an easy way to unwrap your objects, it often produces results that are less satisfactory than manual unwrapping. We only use it for simple objects, for example, our roof.

To efficiently unwrap your roof using Blender's **Smart UV Project**, follow the steps outlined here:

1. Select the roof, switch to **Edit Mode**, make sure that all the roof geometry is selected, press *U*, and choose **Smart UV Project**. Then, click **OK**.

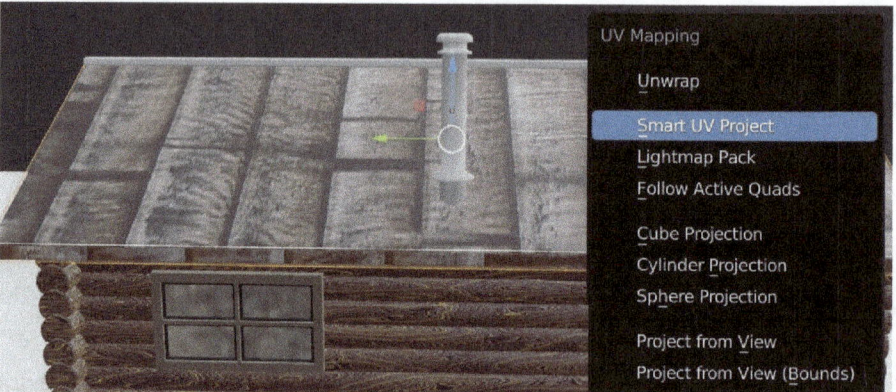

Figure 3.19 – Unwrapping the roof of the wood cabin

Note that this method doesn't work properly all the time, so it needs some tweaking. We have to switch the direction of the top roof texture to horizontal. It often happens that after assigning a texture, the scale may not look correct. We can fix this by adjusting the texture scale using the **Texture Coordinate** and **Mapping** nodes in **Shader Editor**, without changing the UVs. So, let's jump into **Shader Editor** to see the **Roof** material.

2. Next, add the **Mapping** and **Texture Coordinate** nodes:

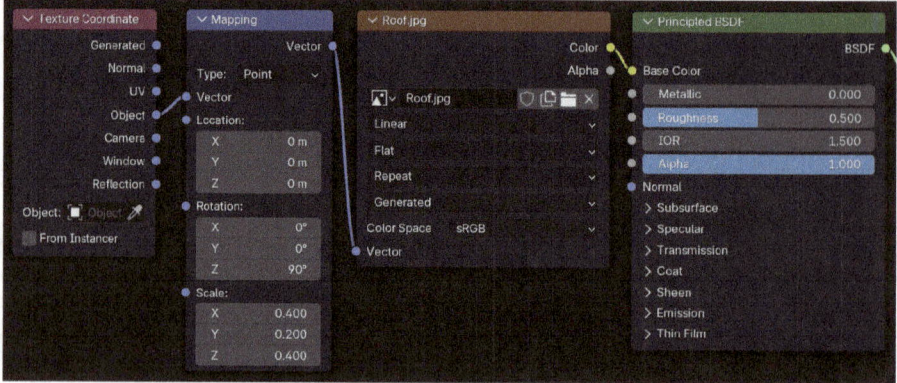

Figure 3.20 – Node setup of the wood cabin material

3. In the **Mapping** node, you might have a different axis to change depending on the texture orientation, **X** or **Y**. Just keep an eye on the roof texture; also, tweak its scale.

4. In my case, I have changed the scale to 0.4 on both the **X** and **Z** axes, with 0.2 on the **Y** axis – I find that this setting works best. I highly advise you to tweak the **Rotation** and **Scale** values while checking the roof to understand how the **Mapping** node works.

Figure 3.21 – Texturing the roof of the wood cabin

Next, we need to tweak the *material reflection* – so far, the roof looks like a flat painting:

1. Let's add the **ColorRamp** node: connect **Color** in the roof texture node to **Fac** in the **ColorRamp** node and place the thumbs in the sliding bars as shown in *Figure 3.22* for better roof reflection.

2. Let's also add the **Bump** node: connect the *yellow* **Color** slot from the roof texture node to the **Height** slot of the **Bump** node with a 0.5 strength to have realistic details on our roof:

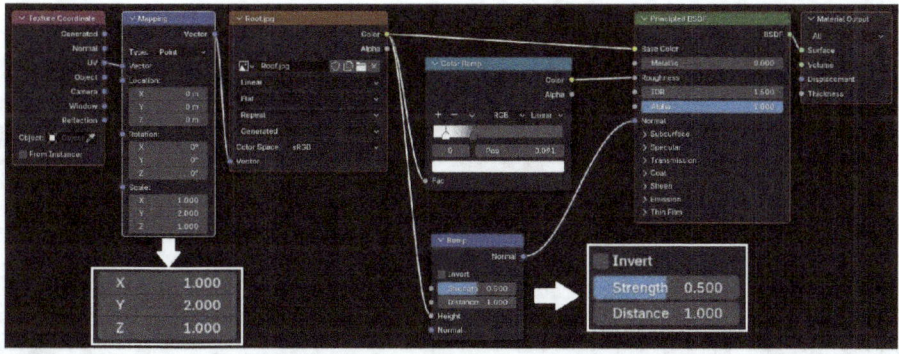

Figure 3.22 – Adding bumps and roughness to the roof material

This is how the roof looks now after applying the roof material we just created:

Figure 3.23 – Roof material texturing completed

Next, let's work on the metal chimney on the roof.

Texturing the chimney

We'll use a metal texture to achieve the look shown in the followng figure:

Figure 3.24 – Texturing the chimney using a metal texture

To texture the chimney and give it a realistic metallic appearance, follow the steps outlined next. This process will guide you through applying a metal texture and refining its properties to achieve a reflective and detailed finish. Here's how to proceed:

1. Select the chimney object, and create a material called `metal`. Save the metal texture to your desktop. You will find it available at `https://github.com/PacktPublishing/3D-Environment-Design-with-Blender-5-Second-Edition/blob/ab43270b643a41ba8f915f74e3bf78573b10a816/chapter-3/Metal.jpeg`.

2. Drag and drop the metal texture in the **Shader Editor**.

3. Connect the **Color** slot of the **Metal** texture node to the **Base Color** of the **Principled BSDF** node.

4. To make the material look like metal, increase the **Metallic** value on **Principled BSDF** to `0.9`.

5. Add a **ColorRamp** node, and place the thumbs in the sliding bars as shown in *Figure 3.25* to make the metal material look reflective.

6. Add a **Bump** node and set **Strength** to a value of `0.1`, as shown in *Figure 3.25*.

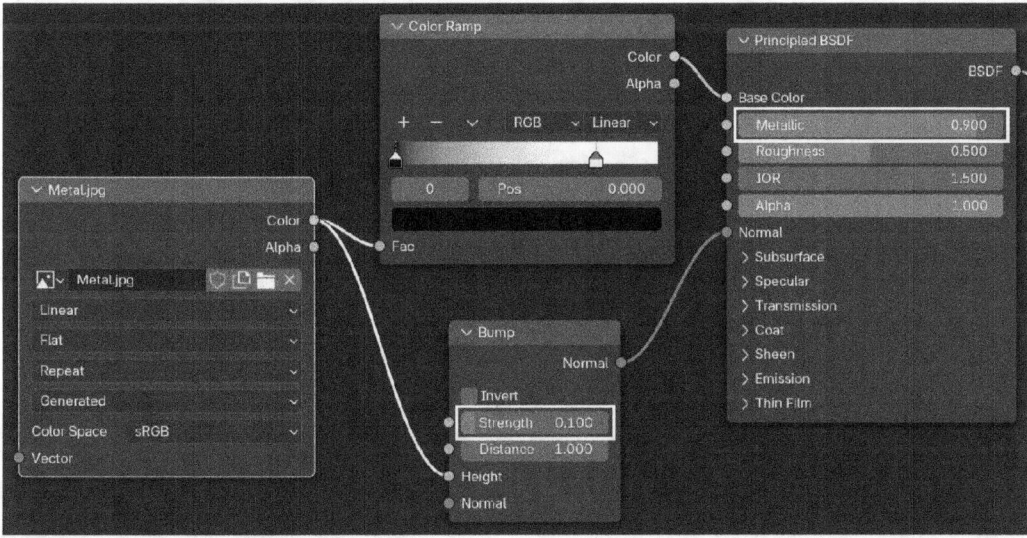

Figure 3.25 – Adding bumps and increasing the Metallic value of the metal material

You can see in *Figure 3.26* that the wood shape is 100% straight and cut too perfectly to be natural. This is impossible unless you cut the wood using a machine, and since the wood used in the cabin is organic, this means that its shape won't be perfect. So, we need to add some sort of imperfections to the shape of our wood to make it look real and similar to the reference.

Figure 3.26 – Metal chimney texturing completed

We can affect the geometry of the wood bars in **Edit Mode**, but it will take a lot of time. Luckily, there is a better way to adjust the geometry using the Displacement map we learned about in *Chapter 2*. We will apply a **Clouds** texture to the geometry, and it will break the CGI perfection.

The **Clouds** texture is a free texture provided by Blender, and it has white and dark spots. It can be used along with the **Displace** modifier to make an object's geometry distorted, similar to what you see in *Figure 3.27*.

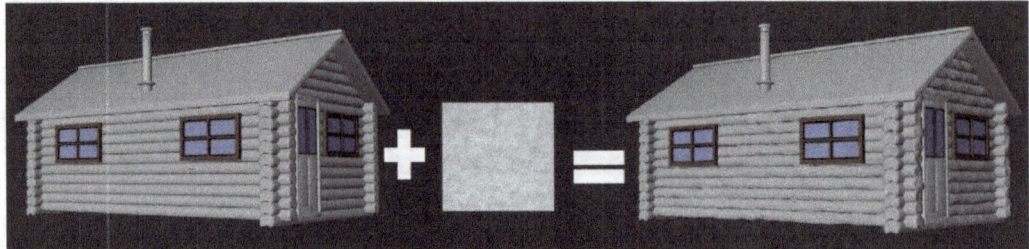

Figure 3.27 – Applying the Clouds texture to the wood cabin model

Figure 3.27 demonstrates the application of a **Clouds** texture to our wood cabin model using the **Displace** modifier. This technique introduces subtle distortions that enhance the realism of the cabin, giving it a more natural, imperfect appearance.

To better understand how the **Displace** modifier works, think of a pin wall.

The object you put through the wall is the displacement map: black areas are pushed while white areas remain flat. The pins represent the **subdivisions**; the more pins you have, the clearer the object will be.

That's why we need to subdivide the wood geometry. The subdivision adds additional geometry, giving the **Displace** modifier enough detail to produce accurate and smooth surface deformation. Follow these steps:

1. Press *Ctrl + E* and choose **Subdivide**. You can also add multiple edge loops using *Ctrl + R* and then scroll your mouse 10 to 15 times.

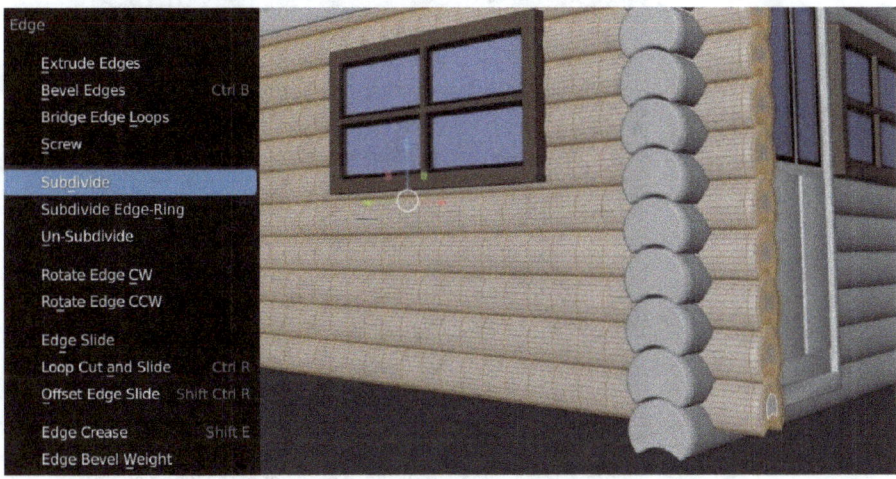

Figure 3.28 – Subdividing the geometry of the wood cabin

2. Now, let's add the **Displace** modifier to our wood cabin. The **Displace** modifier displaces vertices in a mesh based on the intensity of a texture.

3. Make sure you're selecting the wood cabin wall you want to apply the modifier to. On the right bar, you will find a **wrench** icon; click on it and select **Displace**:

Figure 3.29 – Adding the Displace modifier to the wood cabin

4. The next step is to create the **Clouds** texture to use with the **Displace** modifier. Click on **Texture Properties** (the **checkerboard** icon) and select **New**, and for **Type**, choose **Clouds**:

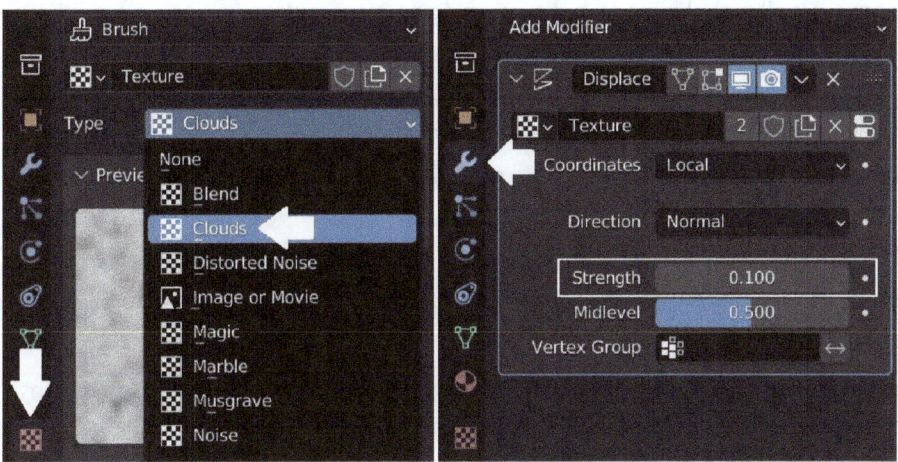

Figure 3.30 – Using the Clouds texture in the Displace modifier while reducing its strength

5. Change the **Strength** value of the **Displace** modifier to a value between 0.1 and 0.5 until you see a good displace effect.

Figure 3.31 – Final render of the wood cabin unwrapped and textured

This completes the process of applying the **Displace** modifier with the **Clouds** texture. By following these steps, you've achieved a more natural appearance to your wood cabin, enhancing its realism. Take a moment to review your work and ensure that the texture integrates well with the model before moving on. Now, we're ready to proceed to the next phase of our project.

Summary

In this chapter, we went through the process of unwrapping our wood cabin and texturing it in Blender.

We started by learning how to import materials from one scene into another, followed by understanding how UV mapping works. We used the **Displace** modifier to add random details to the wood geometry.

Now, with the skills you've learned in this chapter, you can successfully unwrap any 3D object, import and assign materials to that 3D object, tweak the material nodes to make it fit the overall scene, and make the 3D object look realistic by applying displace imperfections.

In the next chapter, we will build on these skills by focusing on creating realistic natural scenes using Blender's Geometry Nodes system. You will learn how to model, texture, and arrange various plants and leaves, as well as how to use Geometry Nodes to scatter these plant assets throughout your scene to achieve natural distribution patterns.

Get this book's PDF version and more

Scan the QR code (or go to packtpub.com/unlock). Search for this book by name, confirm the edition, and then follow the steps on the page.

Note: Keep your invoice handy. Purchases made directly from Packt don't require an invoice.

4

Creating and Scattering Realistic Natural Plants

In this chapter, you will be guided through the advanced process of creating natural, lifelike plants using Blender's latest Geometry Nodes system.

This chapter delves into the procedural modeling of various plant types, including detailed unwrapping and texturing techniques to achieve high realism. You'll learn how to leverage Geometry Nodes to efficiently scatter and arrange these plant assets throughout your scene, ensuring natural distribution patterns that reflect real-world environments.

These methods are crucial for anyone aiming to create lifelike environments in Blender while optimizing both time and resources.

In this chapter, we'll be covering the following topics:

- Introduction to Geometry Nodes
- Modeling realistic natural ground
- Modeling the plants and leaves
- Texturing a realistic natural ground
- Using Geometry Nodes to scatter plants and leaves in our scene

By the end of this chapter, you'll have a strong understanding of how to create and distribute realistic plants, significantly enhancing the realism of your natural scenes in Blender.

Technical requirements

This chapter requires a system capable of running **Blender version 5.0** or above (Windows, macOS, or Linux).

You can download the resources for this chapter from GitHub at:

https://github.com/PacktPublishing/3D-Environment-Design-with-Blender-5-Second-Edition/tree/ab43270b643a41ba8f915f74e3bf78573b10a816/chapter-4.

Visit this link to check out the video of the code being run: https://packt.link/nIPw2

Introduction to Geometry Nodes

Geometry Nodes is a powerful, node-based system introduced in Blender 2.92 that allows for procedural creation, manipulation, and modification of geometry within a 3D scene. Instead of manually editing mesh objects, you can use Geometry Nodes to define a series of operations that automatically generate or alter geometry based on parameters you control.

In this chapter, we will use Geometry Nodes to scatter plants and leaves across the ground. But first, we need to create our plants, leaves, and the ground where we will scatter them.

Modeling realistic natural ground

To create a realistic natural ground, let's follow these steps:

1. Add a plane under the wood cabin by pressing *Shift* + *A* on the 3D Viewport, and scale it 10 times by pressing *S* and typing 10 simultaneously in **Edit Mode**.

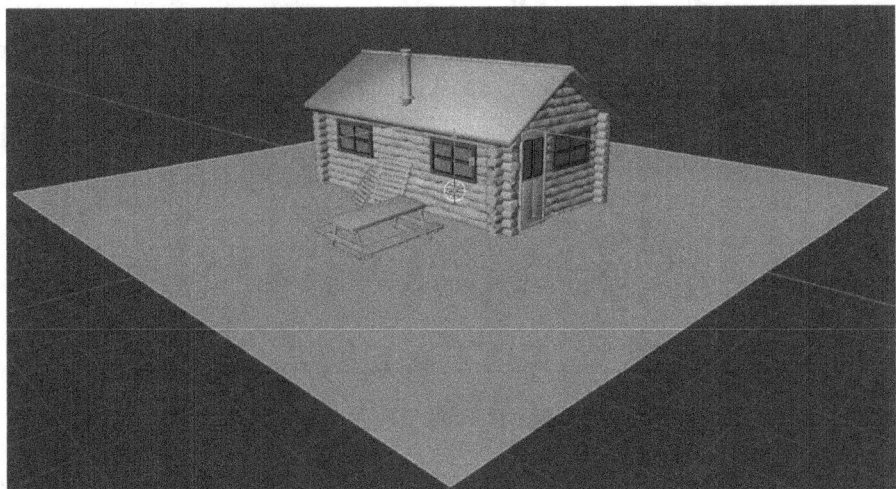

Figure 4.1 – Creating a plane under the wood cabin

Our plane is perfectly flat, but in nature, nothing is ever completely smooth. Let's add some bumps to break its perfection and make the ground more realistic.

2. Select the plane, switch to **Edit Mode**, press *Ctrl + E*, and choose **Subdivide**.

3. In the bottom-left corner, you will find a **Subdivide** tab. Increase the **Number of Cuts** value to 25:

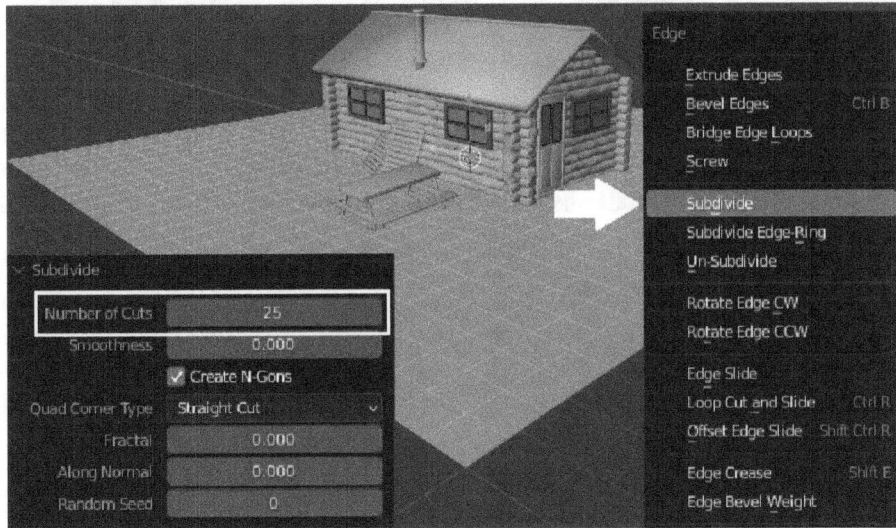

Figure 4.2 – Subdividing the plane 25 times

4. Let's use the **Proportional Editing** tool in the top bar of the 3D Viewport. It has an icon of a **dot surrounded by a circle**. Click on it to activate it, or toggle it by pressing the *O* key as a shortcut. Also, make sure that the mode you're using is **Smooth** because it moves the vertices smoothly, giving you softer and more natural results. This is useful for organic shapes or when you don't want sharp edges.

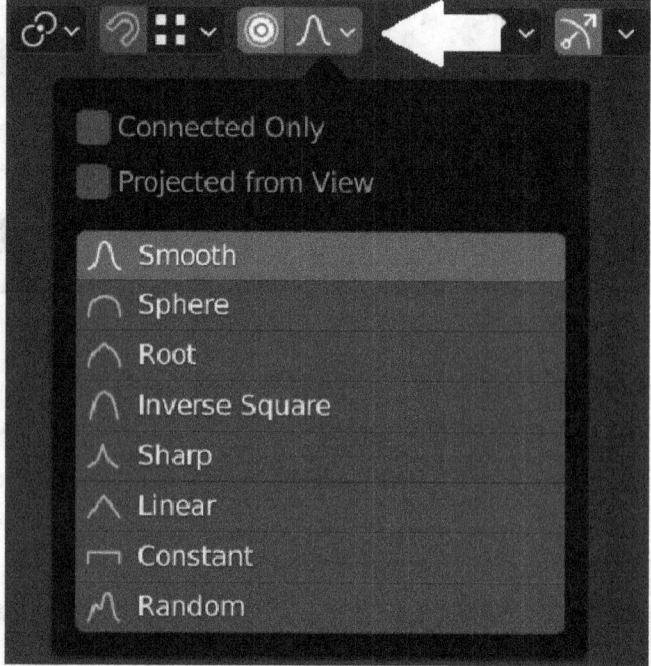

Figure 4.3 – Enabling the Proportional Editing tool

5. Now, if we select three random points from our plane and raise them, we will see that we're making nice hills on our ground. You can change the size of the circle that appears in the middle by scrolling your mouse up or down. This affects the number of vertices around the selected vertices.

> **Note**
>
> I advise you to try different modes, such as **Sharp** and **Linear**, and see the effect they have on the geometry.

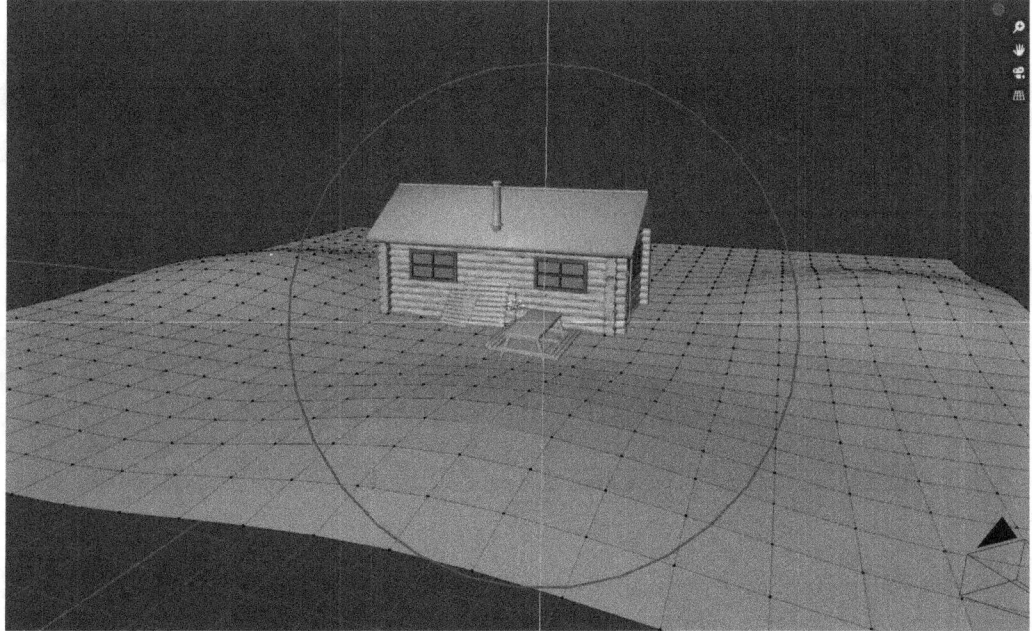

Figure 4.4 – Adding hills to the plane using the Proportional Editing tool

The goal here is to break the perfection of the plane so it's not 100 percent flat anymore. Now, let's go ahead and create plants and leaves to naturally enrich our environment.

Modeling the plants and leaves

Let's begin the process of creating plants and leaves:

1. To create plants, first we need to download the leaves reference, which is available at `https://github.com/PacktPublishing/3D-Environment-Design-with-Blender-5-Second-Edition/blob/ab43270b643a41ba8f915f74e3bf78573b10a816/chapter-4/Leaf-Texture.jpg`, and drop it in the 3D Viewport. It will be dropped as an image plane.

2. Press *N* to get the **Transform** panel on the right side.

3. Set the **Location** and **Rotation** values of the **X**, **Y**, and **Z** axes to 0 to have the plane laid down on the Blender grid.

Figure 4.5 – Leaves reference

With the ground now shaped to be more natural, we have a solid foundation to start populating our environment with realistic plants and leaves.

Creating a green leaf

Now, let's create a green leaf:

1. Press 7 on the numpad to switch to the top view.

2. Create a plane and place it on top of the leaf, as shown in *Figure 4.6*:

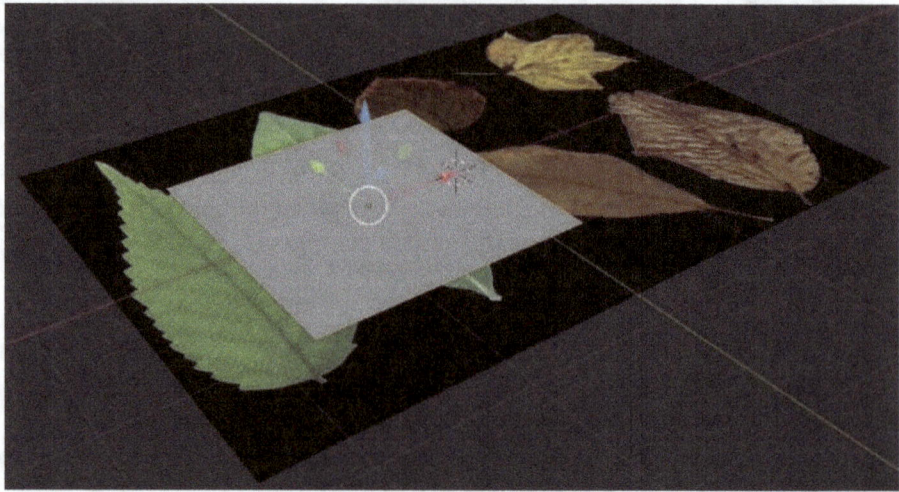

Figure 4.6 – Adding a plane and putting it on top of the leaves reference

3. Select the plane, jump into **Edit Mode**, and insert five edge loops using *Ctrl + R*.

Figure 4.7 – Inserting five edge loops in the plane

4. Press 7 to go to the top view, then make the plane vertices fit the shape of the leaf reference, as shown in *Figure 4.8*:

Figure 4.8 – Aligning the plane with the leaf reference

5. To create the middle vein of the leaf, add three vertical edge loops to the plane using *Ctrl + R*:

Figure 4.9 – Inserting three edge loops inside the plane

6. Select the vertices shown in the following screenshot and move them up. Now, we get the shape of a leaf:

Figure 4.10 – Selecting the middle plane vertices

7. Select the vertices shown in *Figure 4.11* and move them up. Now, we get the shape of another leaf:

Figure 4.11 – Forming the shape of a leaf

8. Let's rotate the leaf using the **Proportional Editing** tool we used earlier with the ground to get a perfect result.

9. We'll select the last point of the leaf and rotate it around the **X** axis. The rotation angle I used here is 40 degrees. This is the result:

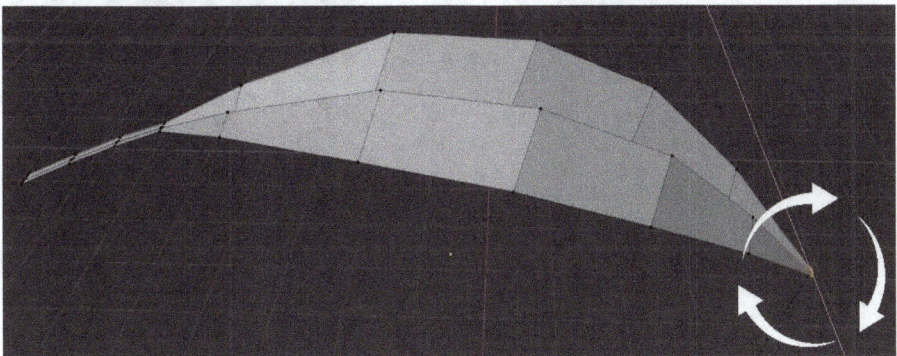

Figure 4.12 – Bending the leaf shape using the Proportional Editing tool

This way of spinning our leaf using the **Proportional Editing** tool gets us a perfect and organic leaf shape. Doing it manually will take time and won't be precise. Now, let's add more details to our leaf.

Applying a Subdivision modifier to the leaf

The leaf still doesn't look good because it has a very small number of vertices. We need to add the **Subdivision** modifier to make it look smoother and more realistic. Let's look at the steps to do just that:

1. Select the leaf.

2. Open the **Modifier Properties** tab, represented by the **wrench** icon.

3. Click on **Add Modifier**, choose **Generate**, and then select **Subdivision Surface**.

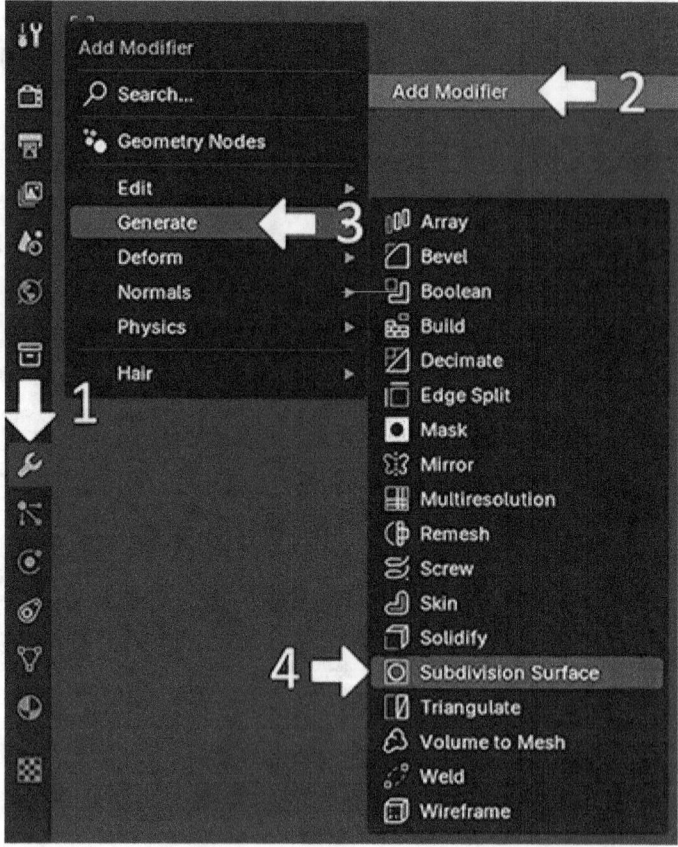

Figure 4.13 – Adding the Subdivision Surface modifier

The **Subdivision Surface** modifier is used to split the faces of a mesh into smaller faces, giving it a smooth appearance. Be careful with this modifier because it doubles the number of vertices exponentially in your object.

Later, we'll be spawning plants hundreds of times, which will heavily affect the performance of Blender. So, I set the number of subdivisions to only 1 for both **Levels Viewport** and **Render**:

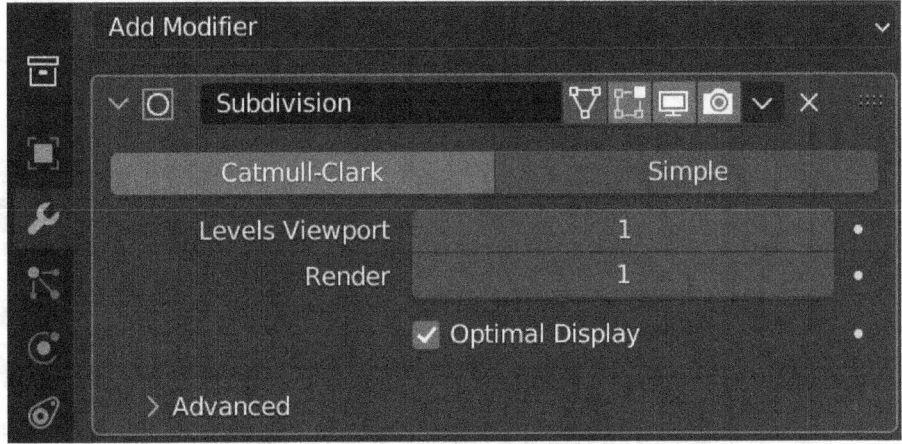

Figure 4.14 – Tweaking the Subdivision Surface modifier settings

4. The last step is to shade-smooth the surface of the leaf. So far, its edges look sharp. To do that, select the leaf, then right-click and choose **Shade Smooth**, as shown in *Figure 4.15*:

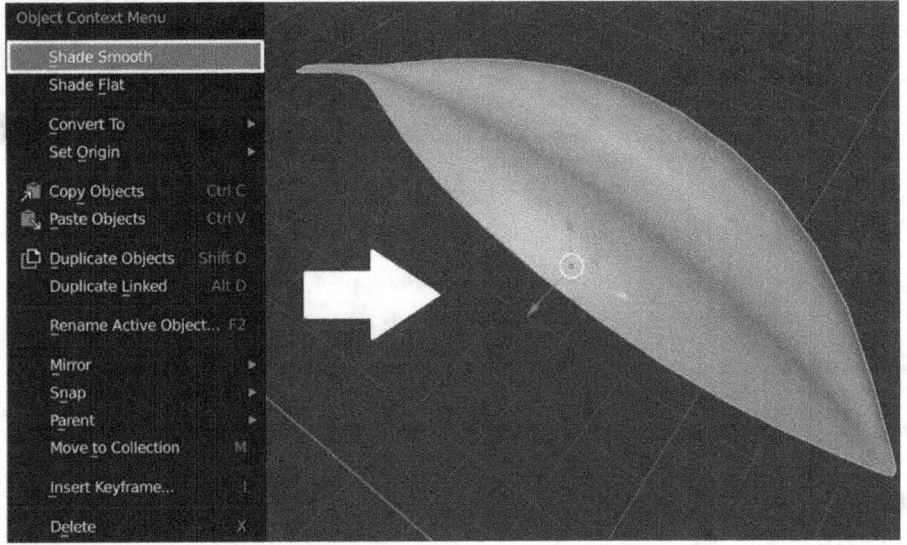

Figure 4.15 – Applying Shade Smooth to the leaf

We have finished creating the shape of the leaf. Now, let's texture it.

Texturing the leaf

Let's look at the steps to texture the leaf:

1. Select the leaf, go to **Material Properties**, and add a new material called Leaf.

2. Switch the bottom window to **Shader Editor**. You will find the **Principled BSDF** node related to the **Leaf** material we have created. Drag the **Leaf** texture we used before as a reference, drop it in **Shader Editor**, and connect it to the **Base Color** input:

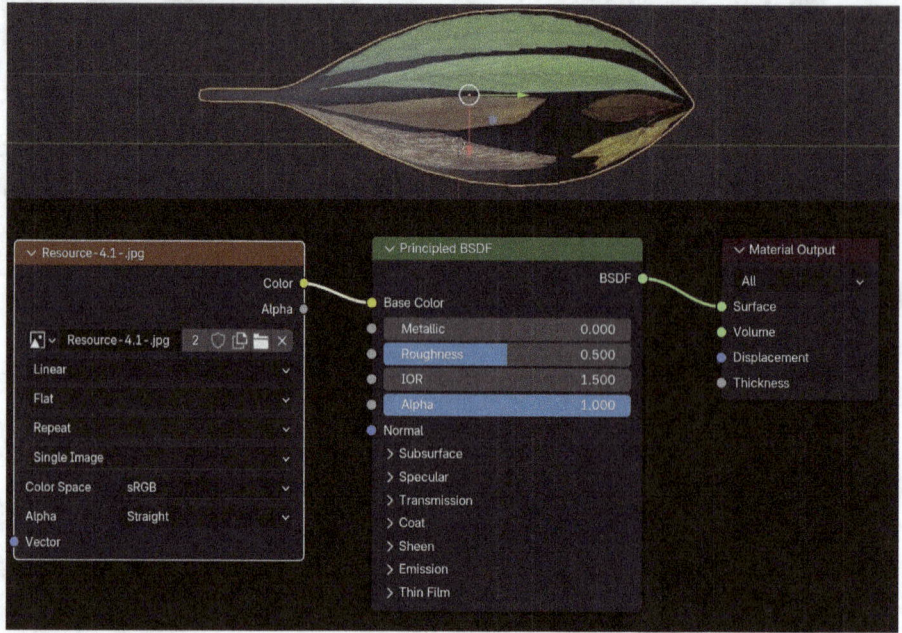

Figure 4.16 – Texturing the leaf

3. Our leaf doesn't look right, so the next step, as you might guess, is to fix the UV map of the leaf. Switch the bottom window from **Shader Editor** to **UV Editor**.

4. Make sure that you're at the top of the leaf. Press *7* to switch to the top view.

5. Select the leaf and press *Tab* to switch to **Edit Mode**.

6. Press *U* and choose **Project from View**. This is a mapping technique that takes the current view in the 3D view and unwraps the mesh as it appears. That's why you need to be at the top, to fully cover the leaf.

7. After unwrapping, make sure to place the leaf vertices you have in **UV Editor** on the green leaf image reference (see *Figure 4.17*). Feel free to tweak the vertices to match the leaf texture.

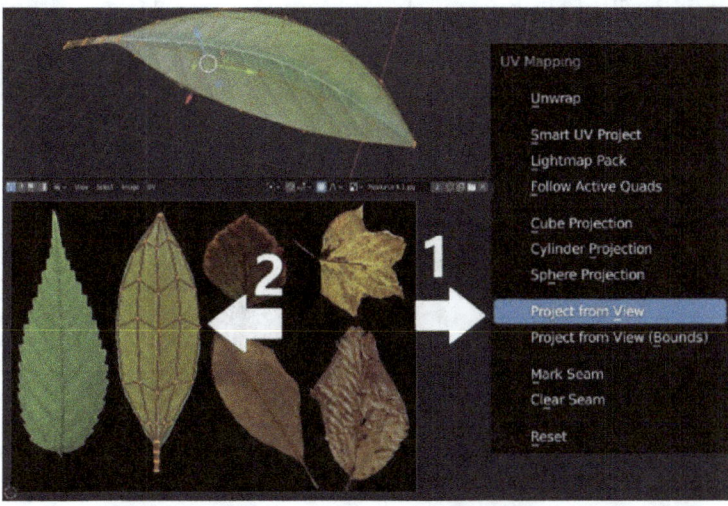

Figure 4.17 – Unwrapping the leaf

8. Next, we need to tweak the roughness and bumps of the **Leaf** material, the same thing we did previously with materials such as wood and metal. *Figure 4.18* shows the node setup of the **Leaf** material:

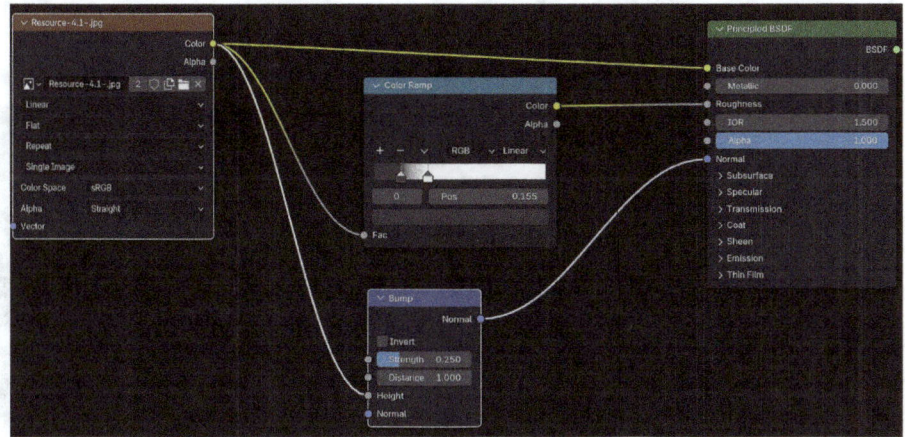

Figure 4.18 – Tweaking the roughness and bumps of the Leaf material

This is what the leaf looks like after applying the roughness and bumps to it:

Figure 4.19 – Final result of the leaf

Now, let's create the stem of the plant; it has a cylindrical shape:

1. Create a cylinder mesh by pressing *Shift + A*.

2. Reduce the geometry of the cylinder to 8 vertices in the bottom-left tab in the 3D Viewport.

3. Set **Radius** to 0.004 m (4 mm) and set **Depth** to 0.4 m (40 cm).

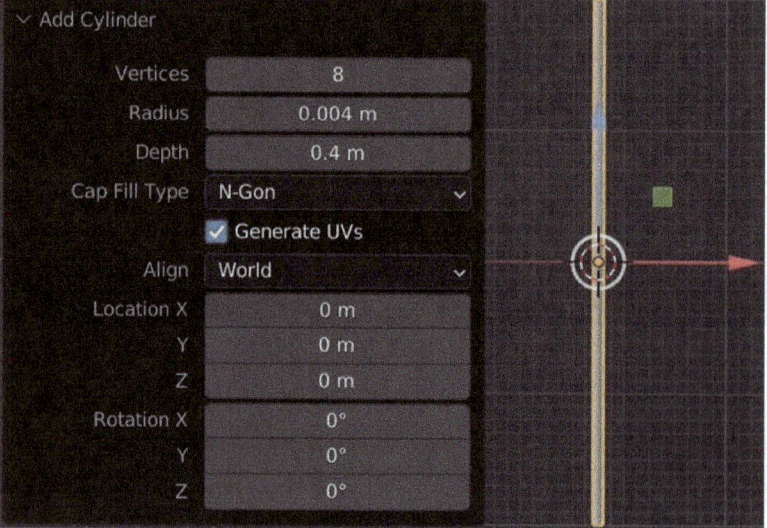

Figure 4.20 – Creating the stem of the plant

4. Select the cylinder, switch to **Edit Mode**, and add edge loops vertically by pressing *Ctrl + R*. You can insert up to five edge loops. We need to keep our geometry low.

5. Scale down the top of the cylinder while enabling the **Proportional Editing** tool. In nature, stems get narrower toward the top. You need to scale down the top only on the **X** and **Y** axes. To do that, press *S + Shift + Z*. This way, you'll be excluding scaling on the **Z** axis.

6. Enable the **Proportional Editing** tool with the **Sharp** mode applied to slightly move the top of the stem sideways. This will allow all the rest of the edge loops to follow smoothly.

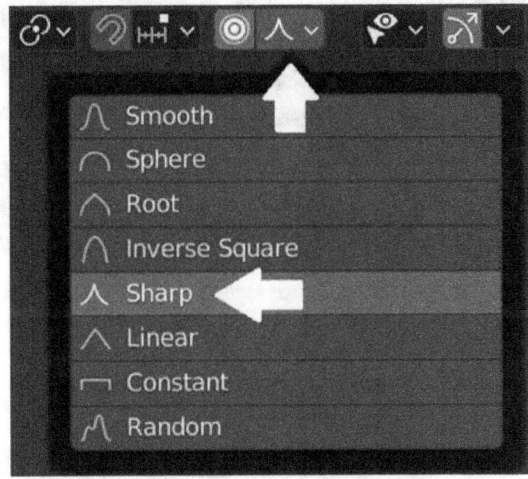

Figure 4.21 – Enabling the Sharp Proportional Editing tool

Figure 4.22 illustrates *steps 4, 5,* and *6* from the previous instructions:

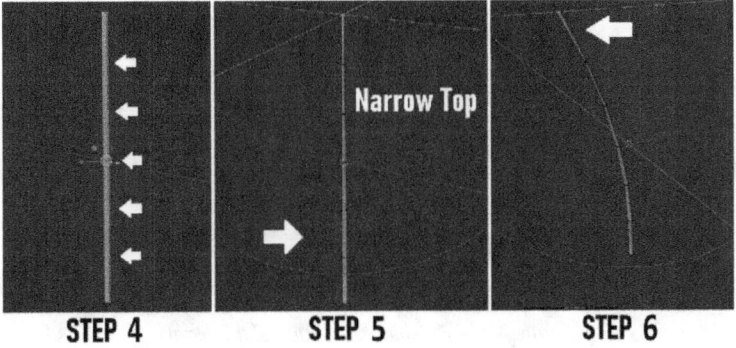

Figure 4.22 – Three steps to create a plant's stem

Next, we'll, let's connect the leaves to the stem (see *Figure 4.23*):

1. For the base, duplicate the six leaves we created for the plant base and place them randomly at the bottom of the stem. They must be connected to the stem.

2. Add more layers of leaves as you go up.

3. With each level, scale down the size of the leaves:

Figure 4.23 – Connecting leaves to the stem, illustrating the steps from left to right

This is what the final shape of the plant looks like:

Figure 4.24 – Finishing the shape of the plant

Make sure to combine all the parts of the plant, leaves, and stem into a single object. To do that, select all the parts and press *Ctrl + J* to join them.

With our first plant fully modeled and textured, we can now move on to creating a different type of plant to add variety to our scene.

Creating the second type of plant

Let's use the same leaf reference to create the second green leaf. This one's shape is different. It has a wavy edge, and it is longer than the previous one. We need that differentiation in shape between the two plants. So, repeat the same steps we did with the previous leaf to create this new one (see the *Modeling the plants and leaves* and *Texturing the leaf* sections). Feel free to make some changes to the shape as you like:

Figure 4.25 – Creating a different type of leaf

All leaves have the same center. Unlike the previous plant, this plant has no stem, so it will be easier to create. This is what the second plant looks like:

Figure 4.26 – Connecting the leaves to the center

We can create grass by scaling down on the **X** axis to make the leaf narrower, then expanding it to make it look tall (see *Figure 4.27*). Then, we can use the **Proportional Editing** tool to make it look wavy:

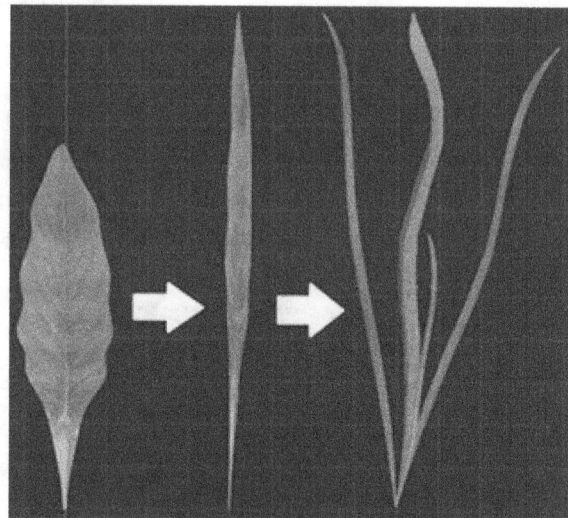

Figure 4.27 – Scaling down the leaf on the X axis

The last step is to create some dry leaves, as we'll see in the next section.

Creating the dry leaves

To create the dry leaves, use the reference again and follow the same process we used for the other leaves. This time, add as many loop cuts as needed based on the shape of the dry leaves. These leaves will be smaller and more irregular, so adjust the geometry accordingly.

When modeling, make sure to keep the geometry as low as possible. These dead leaves will be small objects thrown on the ground:

Figure 4.28 – Creating dry leaves

Now, we have to put the leaves inside a collection, which will help us later with scattering these assets across our environment. Follow these steps:

1. Select any plant and press *M* and choose **New Collection**; name it Plants.

Figure 4.29 – New Collection

2. For the other assets, you can select them one by one and press *M*, and choose the collection you've created:

Figure 4.30 – Repeating the process for other assets

This way, we will have all the plants we created inside the **Plants** collection, as shown here in the **Outliner** panel:

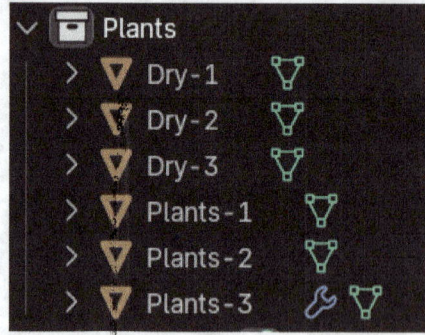

Figure 4.31 – The Plants collection in the Outliner

Now that we have created plants and leaves, as well as moved them into a collection, let's go ahead and texture our ground.

Texturing a realistic natural ground

Let's texture the ground using the forest texture available at this GitHub link: `https://github.com/PacktPublishing/3D-Environment-Design-with-Blender-5-Second-Edition/blob/ab43270b643a41ba8f915f74e3bf78573b10a816/chapter-4/Ground-Texture.jpg`.

Here are the steps:

1. Select the plane.

2. Go to **Material Properties** and add a new material.

3. Drag and drop the **Ground** texture and drop it in **Shader Editor**.

4. Connect it to the **Base Color** input.

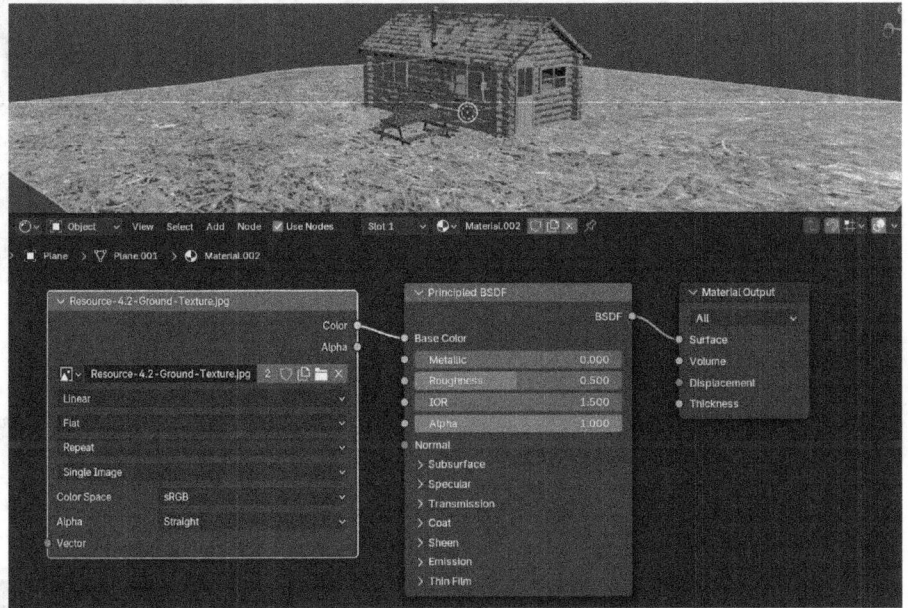

Figure 4.32 – Texturing the ground

5. As you can see, the texture size is small. We need to scale it up. To do that, let's add **Mapping** and **Texture Coordinate** nodes and connect them to the **Ground Texture** node. I set the **X** and **Y** scale of the texture to 5.

6. Add a **Bump** node with a 0.250 strength and add a **ColorRamp** node to tweak the material's roughness. The nodes' setup should look like this:

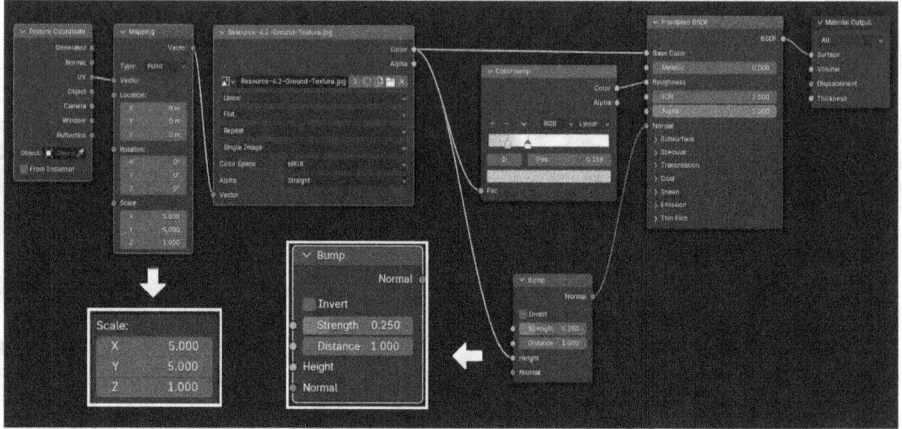

Figure 4.33 – Tweaking the Ground material settings

7. Also, I would like to show you a cool trick to enhance the **Ground** material's appearance and make it look better. Let's search for the node called **Bright/Contrast** using *Shift + A* in **Shader Editor**.

8. Next, put it in between the **Ground Texture** and **Base Color** nodes, and set the **Bright** value to -0.200:

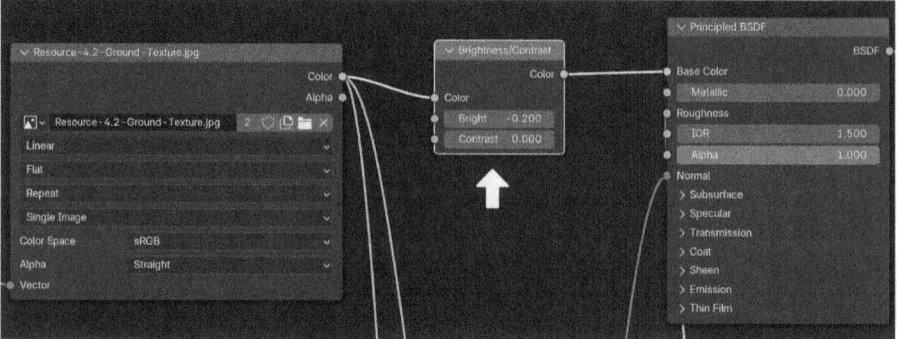

Figure 4.34 – Adding the Bright/Contrast node

Figure 4.35 shows what the ground looks like before and after applying the brightness to it:

Figure 4.35 – The effect of the Bright/Contrast node applied to the ground

You can see that the colors look more vivid and fit the scene better.

Now that our ground texture is complete and the environment looks more vivid, it's time to populate the scene with natural elements. We'll use Geometry Nodes to efficiently scatter plants and leaves across the ground, creating a natural and cohesive look.

Using Geometry Nodes to scatter plants and leaves in our scene

Now that we have plants and leaves, the next step is to scatter them all over the ground. You can do it manually by duplicating plants, scaling and spinning them around to make them look different, but this method will take a lot of time and effort and won't be efficient.

Luckily, there is a better way: using Geometry Nodes in Blender. This system allows you to procedurally scatter objects across a surface.

Now, let's see how we can use Geometry Nodes to scatter plants and leaves across the ground:

1. Select the ground object, which will be used to scatter the plants.

2. Change **Shader Editor** to **Geometry Node Editor**.

3. Click on the **New** button in the **Geometry Node Editor** header to create a new node tree. This will add a **Geometry Nodes** modifier to your ground object and allow you to start building the node setup:

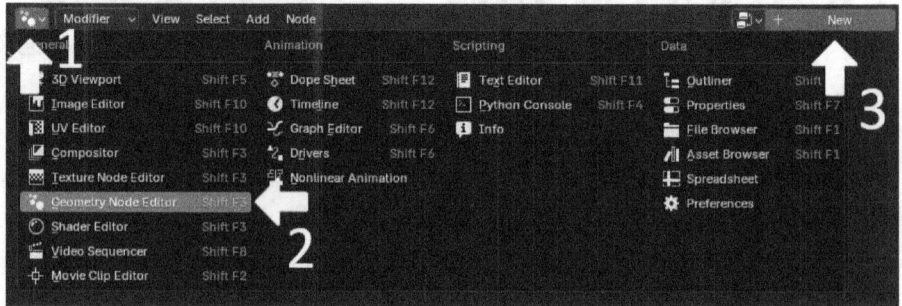

Figure 4.36 – Adding a new Geometry Nodes tree

Immediately, you will see two nodes: **Group Input** and **Group Output**. The **Group Input** node is where your object, such as the ground, enters the Geometry Nodes setup. The **Group Output** node is where your final result comes out, showing what your object looks like after all the changes.

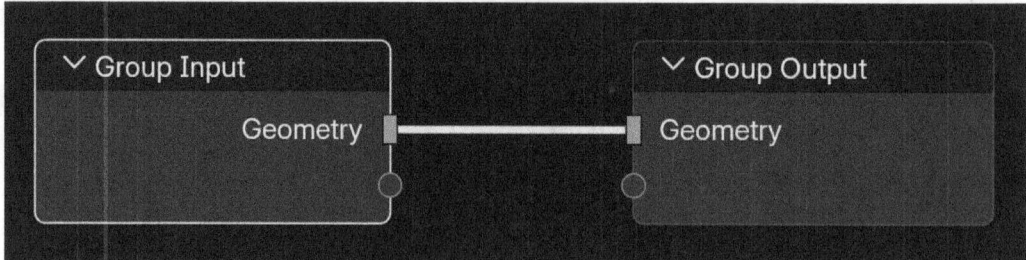

Figure 4.37 – Starting our nodes tree

Now, we'll scatter points across the surface of the ground object.

Using the Scatter on Surface node

To begin with, press *Shift + A* and search for Scatter on Surface. Drop the **Scatter on Surface** node on the line between **Group Input** and **Group Output**.

The **Scatter on Surface** node simplifies the process of scattering objects on planes. Instead of manually wiring multiple nodes, it combines the logic into one easy-to-use geometry node.

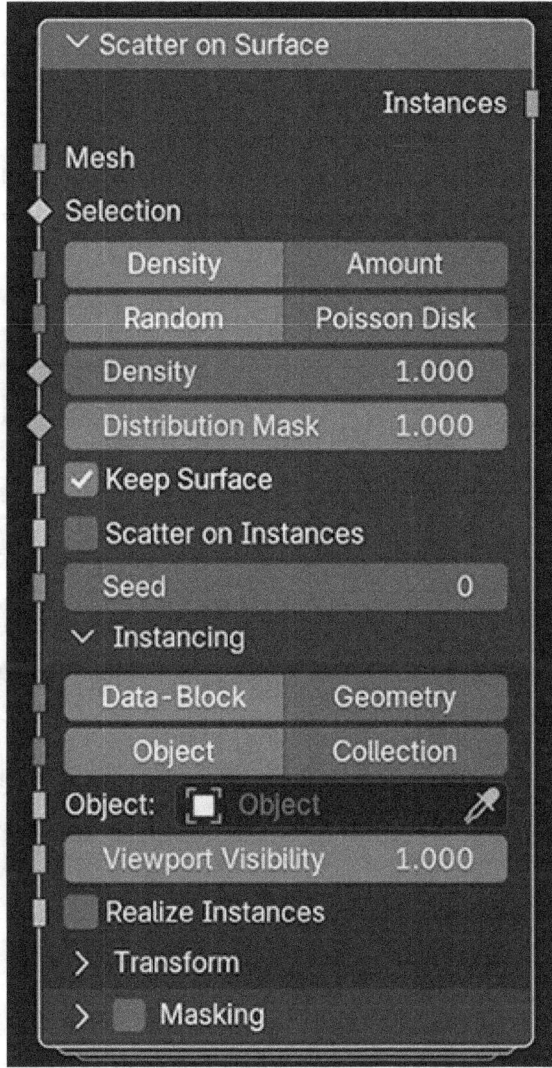

Figure 4.38 – Preview of the Scatter on Surface node

Let's use this **Scatter on Surface** node to scatter plants on the ground. Follow these steps:

1. Change the **Instancing** mode from **Object** to **Collection** and select your **Plants** collection.

2. Make sure to check the **Pick Instance** option. Without this option checked, Blender will spawn the entire collection at every single point (so, you would get five plants stacked on top of each other at every spot). Checking this tells Blender to *pick one random flower* for each point.

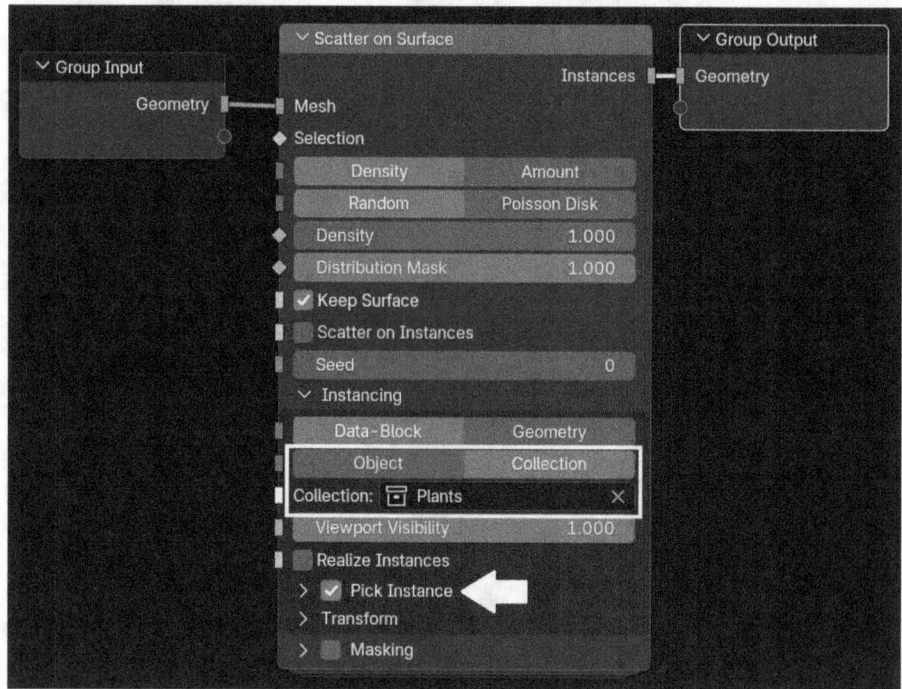

Figure 4.39 – Selecting the Plants collection in the Scatter on Surface node

Right now, your plants will look too big, too uniform, and point in the same direction, as shown in *Figure 4.40*:

Figure 4.40 – Plants scattering first iteration

Let's fix that to make them look organic.

3. Expand the **Transform** section of the node. Lower the **Scale** value to 0.05 (or whatever fits your scene).

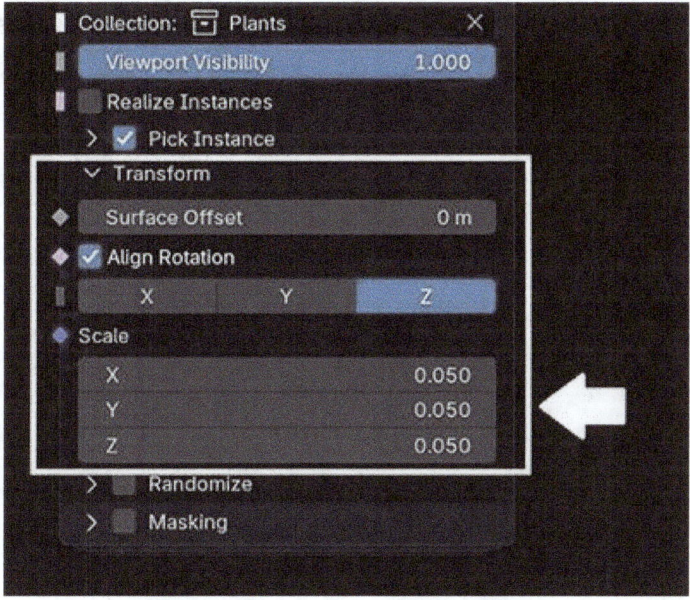

Figure 4.41 – Adjusting the Scale of Plants

This is how the plants will be scattered on the ground:

Figure 4.42 – Lowering the scale of plants

In nature, plants don't grow facing the same compass direction. We need to spin each plant randomly. To achieve this, let's follow these steps:

1. Check **Randomize Rotation**. Increase the **Z** maximum rotation to 360°.

2. Increase the **Scale** value to 0.500; this will make sure that some plants are small, and some are big, breaking up the repetitive visual pattern.

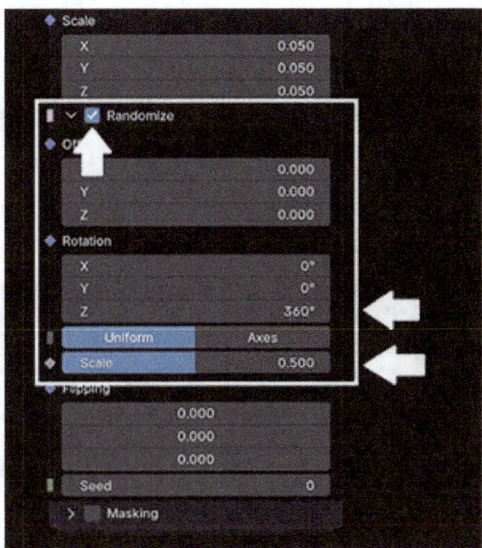

Figure 4.43 – Randomizing the rotation and scale of scattered plants

Now, the plants are random in rotation on the **Z** axis and on **Scale**, as shown in *Figure 4.44*:

Figure 4.44 – Preview of randomized rotation and scale of plants

Next, we need to define the map where we want to scatter these plants.

Creating a density map (weight painting)

We want plants on the grass, but not on the path where people walk. So, we will use **weight painting** to tell Blender where the path is. Now, let's follow these steps:

1. Select your plane.

2. Go to the **Object Data Properties (green triangle** icon) panel. Under **Vertex Groups**, click the plus (**+**) sign and name the new group Plants.

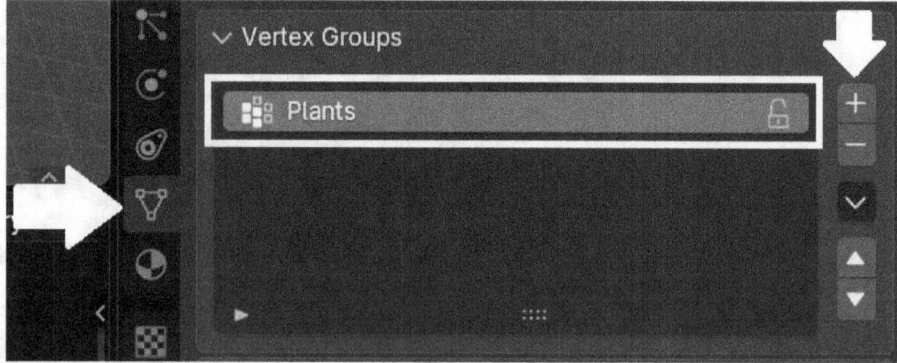

Figure 4.45 – Adding a Plants vertex group

3. Switch **Viewport** mode from **Object Mode** to **Weight Paint** and make sure to reduce **Weight** to 0 to be able to paint with *blue*:

   - **Blue (Weight** 0.0): Means "No plants here"

   - **Red (Weight** 1.0): Means "Max plants here"

4. Use the brush to paint your walking path *blue* and the grassy areas *red*, as shown in *Figure 4.46*:

Figure 4.46 – Painting the walk path using Weight Paint

Finally, we need to send this painted data into the **Scatter** node. We'll execute these steps:

1. In the **Geometry Node Editor**, add a **Named Attribute** node. Make the following adjustments:

   ◦ Keep the type as **Float**.

   ◦ Change the **Name** value to Plants.

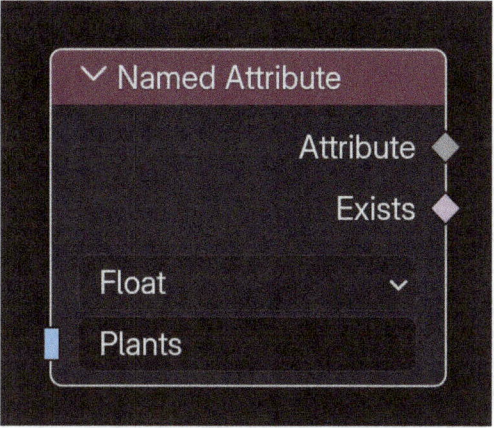

Figure 4.47 – Preview of the Named Attribute node

2. Plug the **Attribute** output into the **Distribution Mask** input of the **Scatter on Surface** node.

3. Now that we have hidden the plants on the path, the number of plants might look low. Increase the **Density** value to 10.0 to fill the *red* areas nicely.

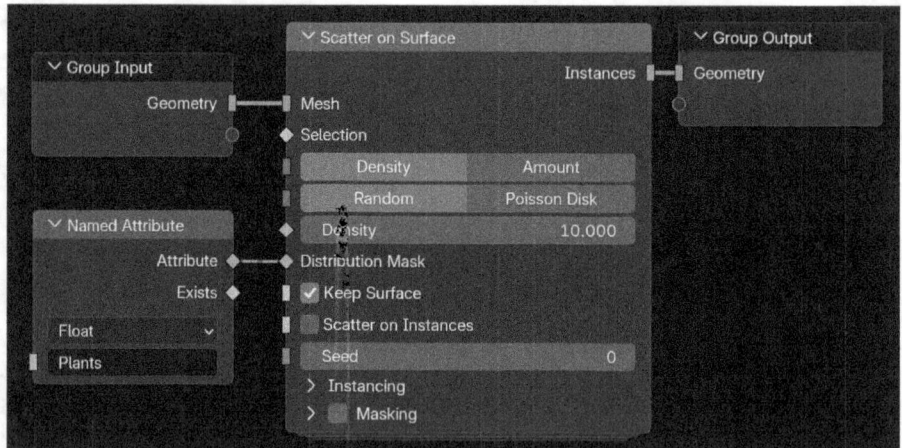

Figure 4.48 – Connecting Named Attribute to Distribution Mask of the Scatter on Surface node

This way, we will have scattered the plants on the ground, except for the *blue* part:

Figure 4.49 – Ignoring the walk path when scattering plants

The final step is to add the tree and bench assets, which you can find in the downloadable resources at https://github.com/PacktPublishing/3D-Environment-Design-with-Blender-5-Second-Edition/blob/ab43270b643a41ba8f915f74e3bf78573b10a816/

chapter-4/Wood-Cabin-Resources.blend. Apply the **Append** method we used in *Chapter 3* (see *Figure 3.1* in the chapter).

Figure 4.50 – Rendering the wood cabin scene in the 3D Viewport

This wraps up our work on adding plants and leaves to the scene. With our environment now populated, we can move on to refining the lighting in the next chapter.

Summary

In the first part of this chapter, we created a realistic ground under our wood cabin, and we learned how to use the **Proportional Editing** tool to add nice undulation to the ground. Then, we went through the process of creating, unwrapping, and texturing different types of plants and leaves.

Next, we learned how to use Geometry Nodes to scatter objects on a surface. In this case, we scattered plants and leaves all over the ground. We explored how to adjust the Geometry Nodes settings, such as randomizing the scale and rotation of plants and controlling their distribution.

In this chapter, you've learned how to create a realistic natural scene with various plants and leaves in Blender. You've also learned how to model, texture, and place different types of plants in your environment using Geometry Nodes.

In the next chapter, we will learn how to get better lighting in Blender. We will look at different ways to apply realistic lighting to our wood cabin.

Get this book's PDF version and more

Scan the QR code (or go to packtpub.com/unlock). Search for this book by name, confirm the edition, and then follow the steps on the page.

UNLOCK NOW

Note: Keep your invoice handy. Purchases made directly from Packt don't require an invoice.

5

Achieving Photorealistic Lighting in Your Environment with Blender

Lighting can make or break any 3D project. In this chapter, we will explore the basics of lighting in Blender. We will look at three different ways to apply realistic lighting to our wood cabin scene, the different properties those three lighting methods offer, and how we can configure them.

The objective of this chapter is to achieve realistic lighting in our wood cabin scene that matches the color, direction, and intensity seen in the wood cabin reference image we're using.

First, we will break down the three Blender rendering engines to understand the difference between them and the role each one plays in achieving photorealism.

Then, we will learn how to use the sun to emit realistic lighting based on the Kelvin temperature scale, add a background to our scene, and then render it. We will also make use of the Blender **Sky Texture** node to light our environment, exploring the differences between **Single** and **Multiple Scattering** for accurate sky simulation. Additionally, we will cover the new **AgX** color management to improve the dynamic range of our renders. Finally, we'll show how to achieve realistic lighting using HDRI maps.

In this chapter, we'll be covering the following topics:

- Differences between the three render engines of Blender
- Using the sun to emit realistic lighting
- Using the **Sky Texture** node to light our environment

- Lighting our wood cabin with lamp objects
- Improving color management for better material preview

By the end of this chapter, you will have the skills to professionally light your 3D scenes, transforming flat models into photorealistic environments that capture the mood and atmosphere of the real world.

Technical requirements

This chapter requires a system capable of running **Blender version 5.0** or above (Windows, macOS, or Linux).

You can download the resources for this chapter from GitHub at: `https://github.com/PacktPublishing/3D-Environment-Design-with-Blender-5-Second-Edition/tree/main/chapter-5`.

Differences between the three render engines of Blender

We will need to render our scene at some point. **Rendering** is the process of turning a 3D scene into a 2D image. Blender includes three rendering engines that you can use; each one has its own strengths and weaknesses:

- The **EEVEE** render engine
- The **Workbench** render engine
- The **Cycles** render engine

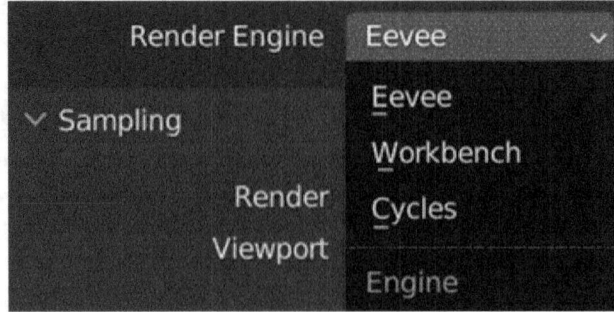

Figure 5.1 – Blender rendering engines

Let's explore each of these render engines in more detail.

The EEVEE render engine

EEVEE is a real-time renderer. It uses some clever, speedy tricks to render your scene really quickly, but it sacrifices some aspects of realism. However, with the help of the newly introduced feature of ray-traced shadows, EEVEE can now achieve more realistic lighting and shadows, making it a better option when you need a balance between speed and realism.

The Workbench render engine

The **Workbench** render engine is a modeling preview rendering engine optimized for fast rendering. This engine renders images similar to the **Solid** mode of the 3D Viewport. It is not intended for rendering final images. Personally, I use this engine when making animations as it helps me render the animation much faster in **Solid** mode. This allows you to check the flow of your animation without spending hours rendering it in the **Cycles** engine.

The Cycles render engine

Cycles works by tracing light rays from each pixel of a designated camera onto a scene; these rays are then reflected and absorbed by objects until they hit a light source or reach their bounce limit, which you can define in light paths. **Cycles** uses multiple rays or samples from a pixel and slowly calculates the result. In terms of accuracy, it's the closest you can get to true photorealism. However, rendering using this process is very time-consuming.

Cycles is a ray-tracing engine, meaning that when rendering a scene, Blender sends rays from the camera, and when a ray hits a reflective surface, it repeats the process until it reaches a light source. It computes many different effects including shadows, mirrors, glossy reflections, and refractions.

With the ongoing optimizations introduced in recent updates, **Cycles** now renders faster and reduces noise more effectively, particularly in scenes with complex lighting. This makes it more efficient while maintaining its high level of realism.

A downside to path tracing is *noise*. However, noise vanishes as more paths accumulate, which is why we need to check the **Denoise** box when using **Cycles**.

We'll be using the **Cycles** render engine heavily in our project.

Next, let's take a look at the first method we'll be following to add lighting to our scene.

Using the sun to emit realistic lighting

The first method we'll be using to add lighting to our scene is to create a sunlight source. So, let's add it using the following steps:

1. In the 3D Viewport, press *Shift + A*.

2. Go to the **Light** tab and choose **Sun**:

Figure 5.2 – Adding sunlight to the scene

> **Note**
>
> Make sure you're on the **Cycles** rendering engine, although this lighting
> method works well on both **EEVEE** and **Cycles**.

3. Now, let's go ahead and switch the shading mode to **Rendered** in order to see how the
   lighting looks:

Figure 5.3 – Switching to Rendered view

The lighting currently looks dark and creepy, so the first setting we need to adjust is the
sunlight's strength.

4. While selecting the **Sun** object, jump into the **Object Data Properties** pane represented by the **light bulb** icon and find the **Strength** value set to 1 by default. Increase it by 10 times to 10:

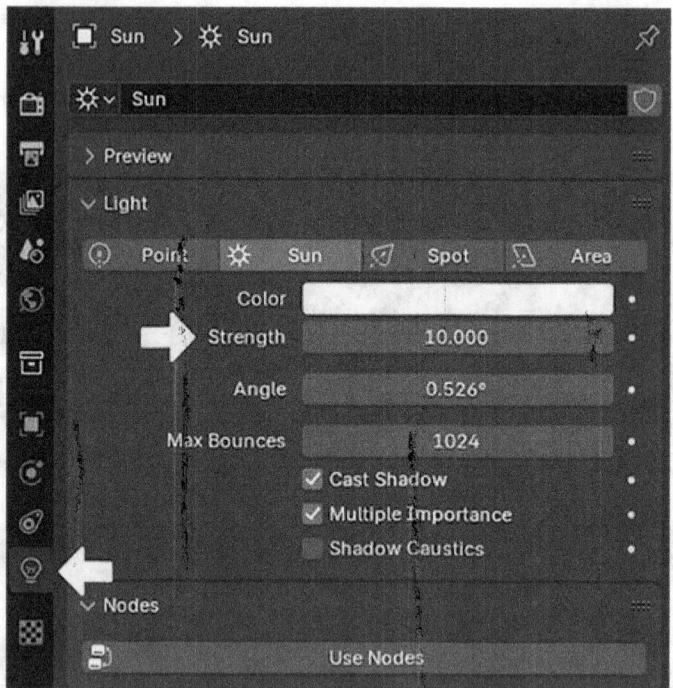

Figure 5.4 – Adjusting the strength of the sunlight

5. Now, let's switch the shading mode one more time to Rendered to see the lighting effect of increasing the sun strength 10 times:

Figure 5.5 – Switching to Rendered view

We're getting better. Now we need to adjust the rotation of the sun to make it match the lighting in our wood cabin reference image. Follow these steps:

1. Select the **Sun** object and press *N* to access the **Transform** panel.

2. Change **Rotation** on the **Y** axis to -30.

3. Set the **Z** axis rotation to 50.

4. Check the **Rendered** mode again to see this:

Figure 5.6 – Rotating the sun object on the Y and Z axes

But here we can see that the shadow cast onto the cabin is too strong. We need to fade it a bit to match the same lighting as in our wood cabin reference.

To do that, select the **Sun** object from the 3D Viewport and in the **Object Data Properties** pane, increase the **Angle** to a higher number: 60 degrees will be fine. This will reduce the strength of the shadow around our wood cabin:

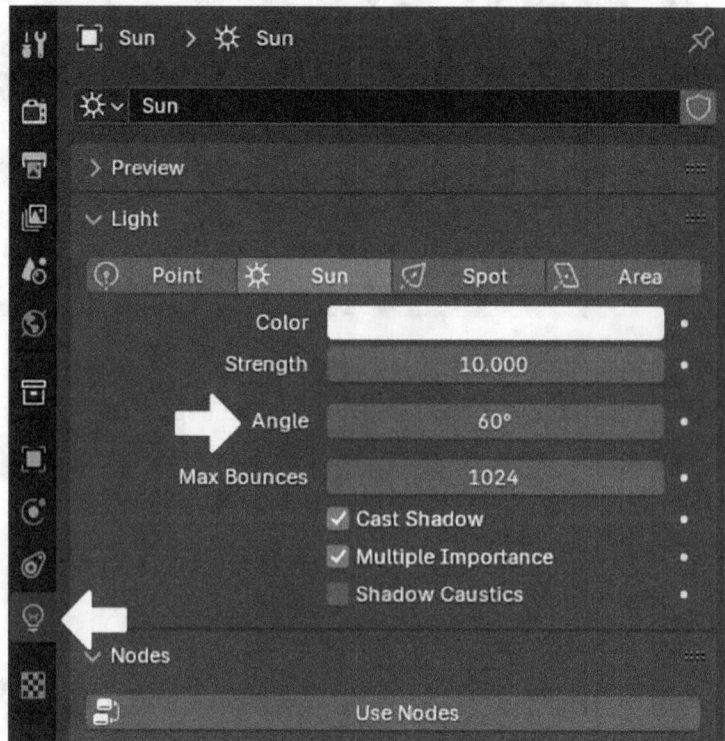

Figure 5.7 – Tweaking the sun shadow angle

This is how the lighting looks now:

Figure 5.8 – Rendering the scene on the 3D Viewport

Now the lighting looks better and is starting to resemble our reference, but it's still not 100% accurate. The reason it's not accurate is because of the color of the sunlight. The default color setting for the sunlight is *white*, which is unrealistic. As you know, when the sun's rays pass through the Earth's atmosphere, they look *yellowish*. So, let's change it to a warmer color:

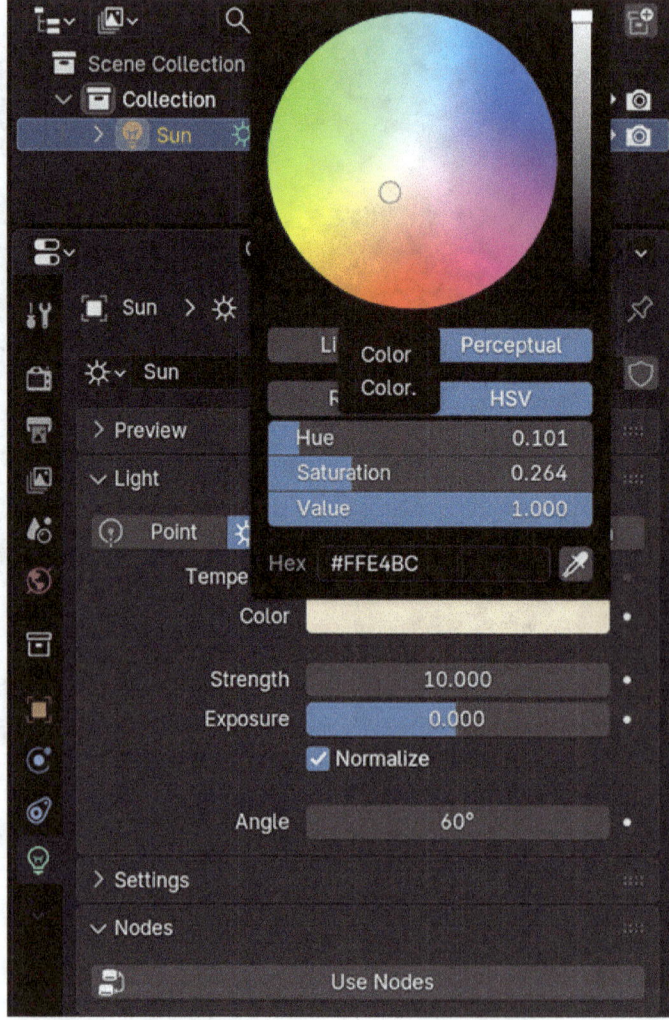

Figure 5.9 – Changing the sunlight color manually

As you can see, we can tweak the sunlight color, but this is not the right method of coloring the sun. You can change the sunlight color manually, but you will never make it as accurate as real life. To fix this, let me introduce you to the Kelvin scale.

The Kelvin scale

The **Kelvin scale** is a series of temperature units that can be used to create realistic natural lighting emissions in our scene. As you can see in the following diagram, if we set the Kelvin value for our sun to 5500, it will emit daylight:

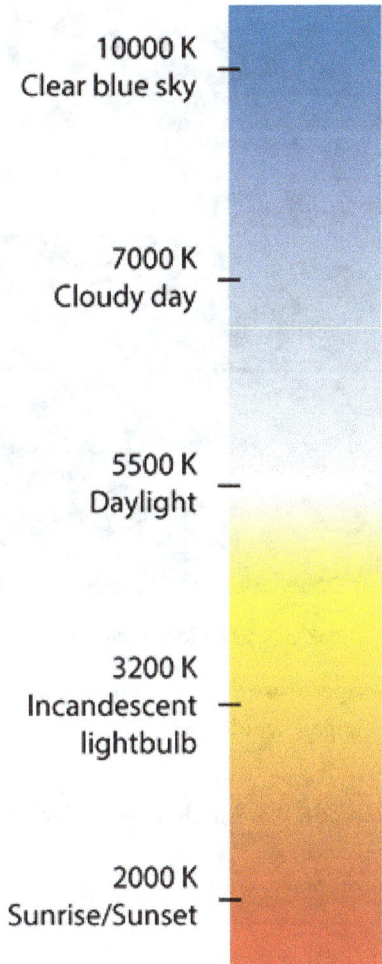

Figure 5.10 – Kelvin temperature scale

But how can we use this scale with our sun? This is where the **Blackbody** node comes to play.

Applying the Kelvin temperature scale to the sun using the Blackbody node

The **Blackbody node** converts the Kelvin temperature value to an RGB value. We can apply it to our sun by doing the following:

1. Select the **Sun** object and jump into the **Object Data Properties** pane.

2. Check the **Temperature** checkbox and adjust the value as follows:

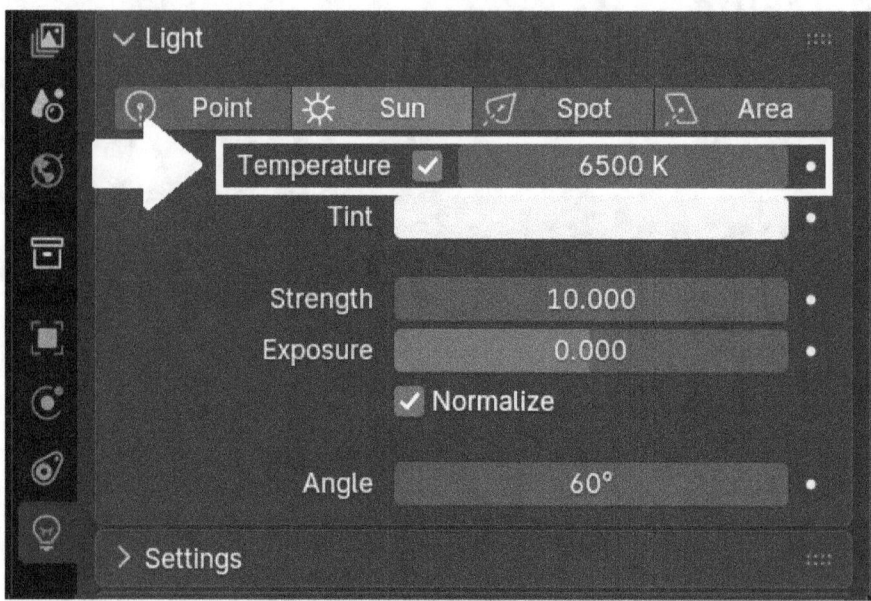

Figure 5.11 – Temperature checkbox

3. Now you will see the **Temperature** setting. This is where we will use the Kelvin scale. Based on our reference image, I would go with 5500 K up to 6500 K, which is the daylight temperature:

If you now jump into **Rendered** mode, you should have perfect, realistic lighting:

Figure 5.12 – Rendering the scene with the Blackbody node applied to the Sun object

Now that we have the lighting right, we need to fill the background of our rendered scene. The next step is to work on the background, which we will do in **Compositing** mode, but before that, we need to render our scene. For this, we will be using the **Cycles** render engine; we'll be using this heavily in our project.

Rendering our scene

Before rendering our scene, we need to check some rendering settings. So, jump into the **Render Properties** tab represented by a **camera** icon and follow these steps:

1. To achieve maximum photorealism, we need first to opt for the **Cycles** render engine. Light behaves more realistically with this engine.

2. On the **Render** tab shown in the screenshot in *Figure 5.13*, you will find the **Max Samples** setting.
   Samples are the noisy boxes that appear as your scene is rendering. The more samples, the clearer your render is, but the longer it takes. In our case, we're still experimenting with the lighting, so we'll go with 64 samples to allow the rendering to process quickly.

Once we're satisfied with the lighting, we can increase the samples to a higher number, between 200 and 500. Keep in mind that a higher number of samples is generally better, but there comes a point where more samples do almost nothing to your render – I'm talking about higher numbers, such as 10,000 samples.

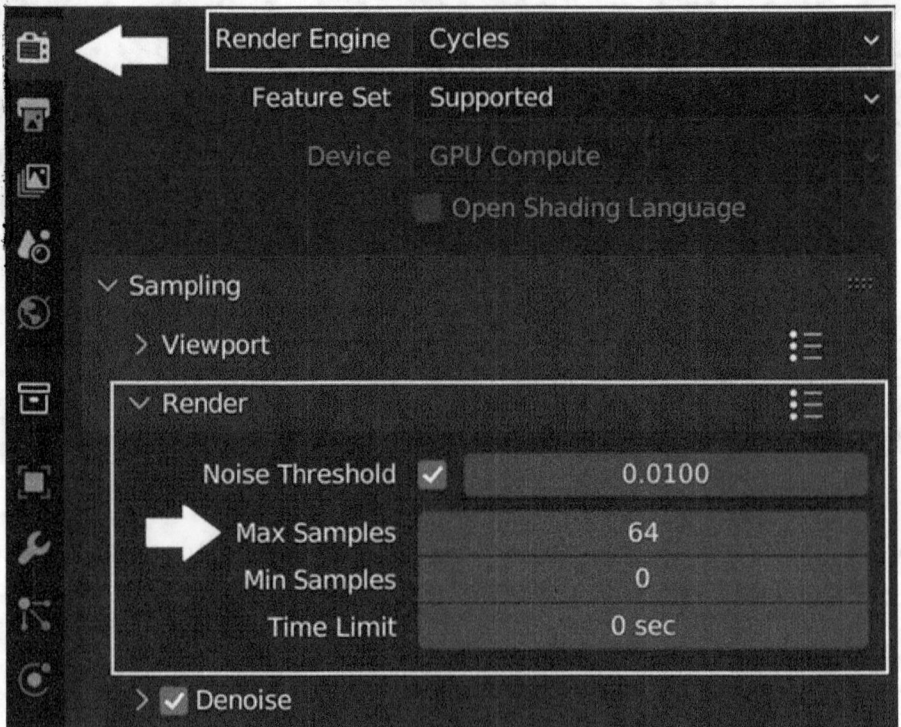

Figure 5.13 – Tweaking the rendering settings

3. Also, since we want to add a custom background to our render to fill the dark areas in the back, we need to make our render transparent. To do that, let's check the **Transparent** box under the **Film** dropdown:

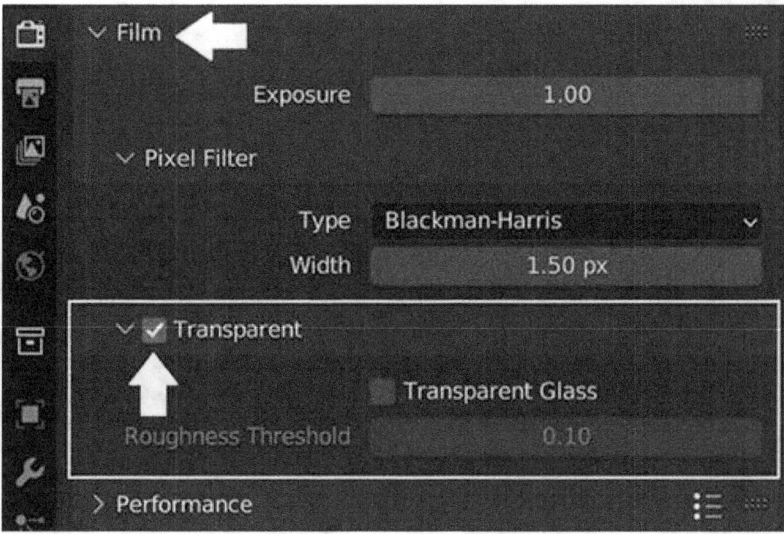

Figure 5.14 – Configuring the Transparent feature in our render settings

4. Alright, now let's go ahead and render our scene. So, on the top bar, click on **Render** and choose **Render Image**. The shortcut key is *F12*:

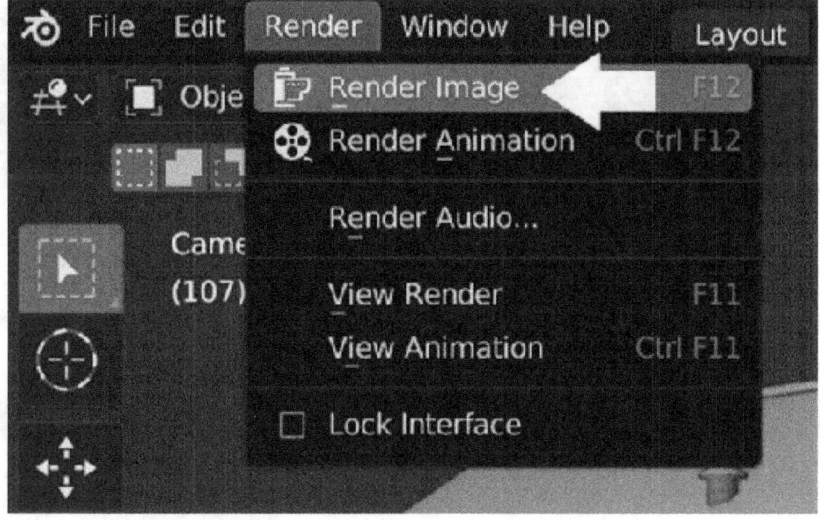

Figure 5.15 – Rendering the image

Now, let's see how we can add a background image to our render in the **Compositing** mode.

Adding a background to your render

Now the rendering process will begin. In the meantime, let's perform these steps:

1. Jump into the **Compositing** tab found on the top bar and click on **New**.

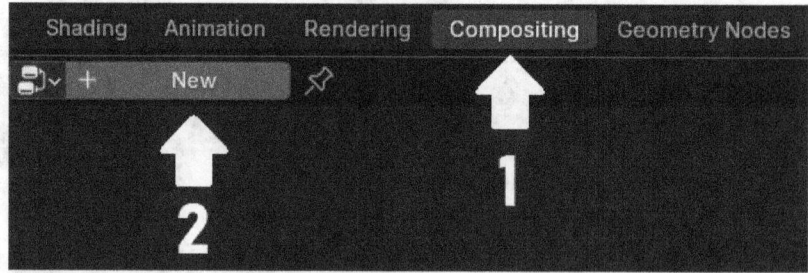

Figure 5.16 – Switching to Compositing

2. By default, you get three nodes: **Render Layers** connected to **Group Output** and **Viewer**. This makes the render image visible in the background.

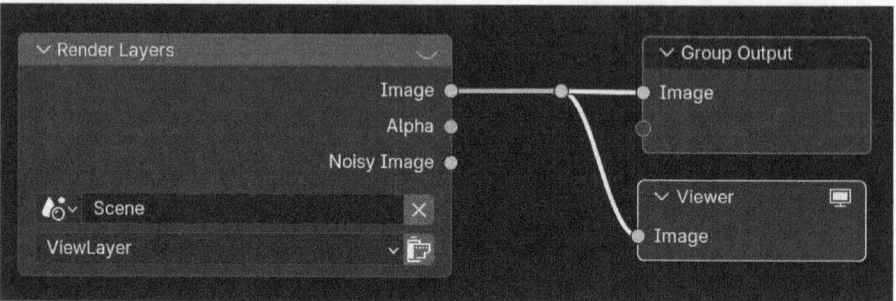

Figure 5.17 – Switching to Compositing

The next step will be to add a background image to our render. This is the background that we'll be using:

Figure 5.18 – Reference of the background used to fill the transparent areas in our render

It's a nature scene that fits our wood cabin reference. You can find the image in the book's GitHub repository (see the *Technical requirements* section).

You can drag and drop the image file onto the **Composite** node setup. This will create a **Single Image** node:

Figure 5.19 – The Single Image node in Compositing

Now, let's connect it to the node setup. Follow these steps:

1. To begin with, we will need an **Alpha Over** node. Search for it by pressing *Shift + A*. Basically, this **Alpha Over** node will fill the alpha space in our render.

2. Connect the **Alpha Over** node with the **Background** node **Image** output as follows:

    ○ The **Background Image** node output goes to the **Alpha Over Background** slot.
    ○ The **Render Layers Image** slot goes to the **Foreground** slot of the **Alpha Over** node.

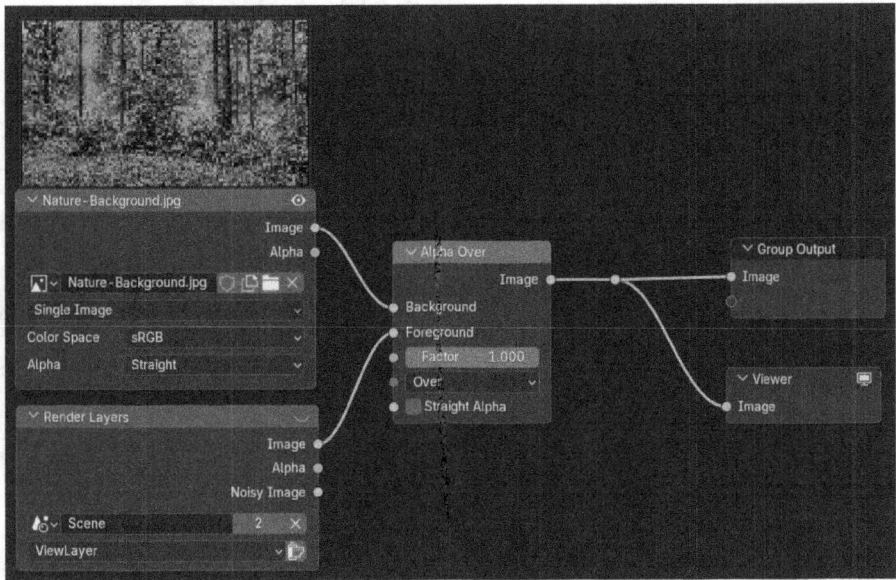

Figure 5.20 – Mixing the nature background with the render using an Alpha Over node

The **Alpha Over** node has two inputs on the left side:

1. Connect the **Background Image** node to the **Background** input of the **Alpha Over** node, and the **Render Layers** node to the **Foreground** input.

2. Connect the **Alpha Over** right-hand **Image** output to both the **Group Output** and **Viewer** nodes' **Image** inputs.

Now we have the background image replacing the alpha space in our render:

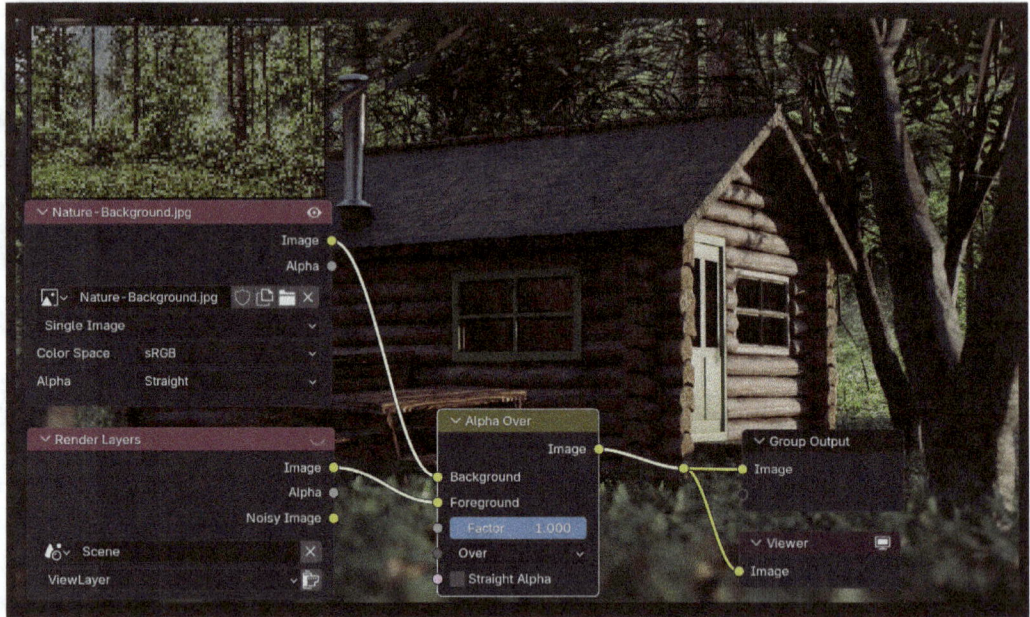

Figure 5.21 – Adjusting the scale of the background using a Scale node

You can see that the background perfectly fits the wood cabin. It looks like the background is part of the render.

Now that we've discussed the first lighting method using our sun, let's discover the second method of lighting: using a Blender **Sky Texture** node.

Using the Sky Texture node to light our environment

The **Sky Texture** or **Sky Box** is a node provided by Blender that adds procedural sky lighting to our scene. To set it up, let's perform these actions:

1. Go to the **World Properties** panel, represented by a **globe** icon.

2. Click on the dot next to **Color**.

3. Choose **Sky Texture** from the **Texture** list:

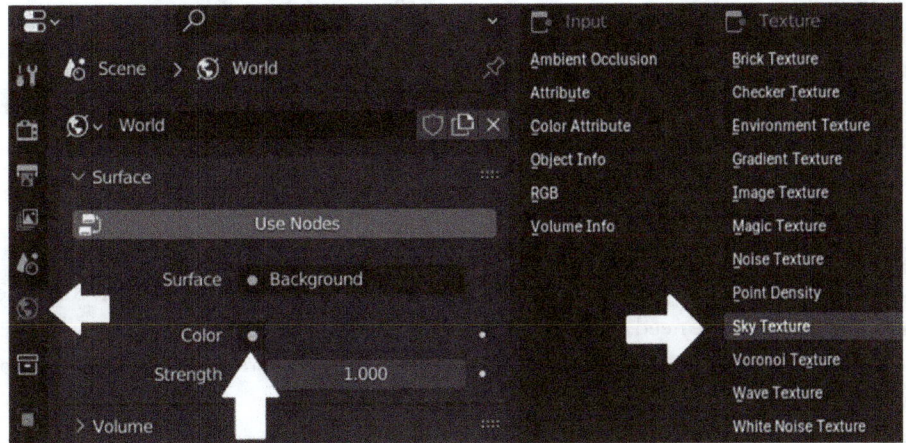

Figure 5.22 – Adding Sky Texture to apply lighting to our environment

4. Turn off the **Transparent** feature in **Render Properties** that we enabled earlier.

Now, if you jump into the **Rendered** mode, you will see some nice lighting with a beautiful *blue* sky in the background:

Figure 5.23 – Rendering our scene by using a Sky Texture node as a light source

> **Note**
>
> Keep in mind that **Sky Texture** node comes with its own sun, so if you already have sunlight in the scene, just delete it. The **Sun Disc** feature is currently supported only in **Cycles**. In **EEVEE**, you will get the lighting and sky colors; however, the actual sun itself will not be visible in the sky.

In order to tweak the **Sky Texture** lighting, let's jump into the **Shader Editor**. But to see the **Sky Texture** node, we need to switch from **Object** to **World**, as shown in *Figure 5.24*. Basically, in **Object** mode, we tweak objects' materials, but in **World** mode, we get the chance to tweak the overall lighting of our scene:

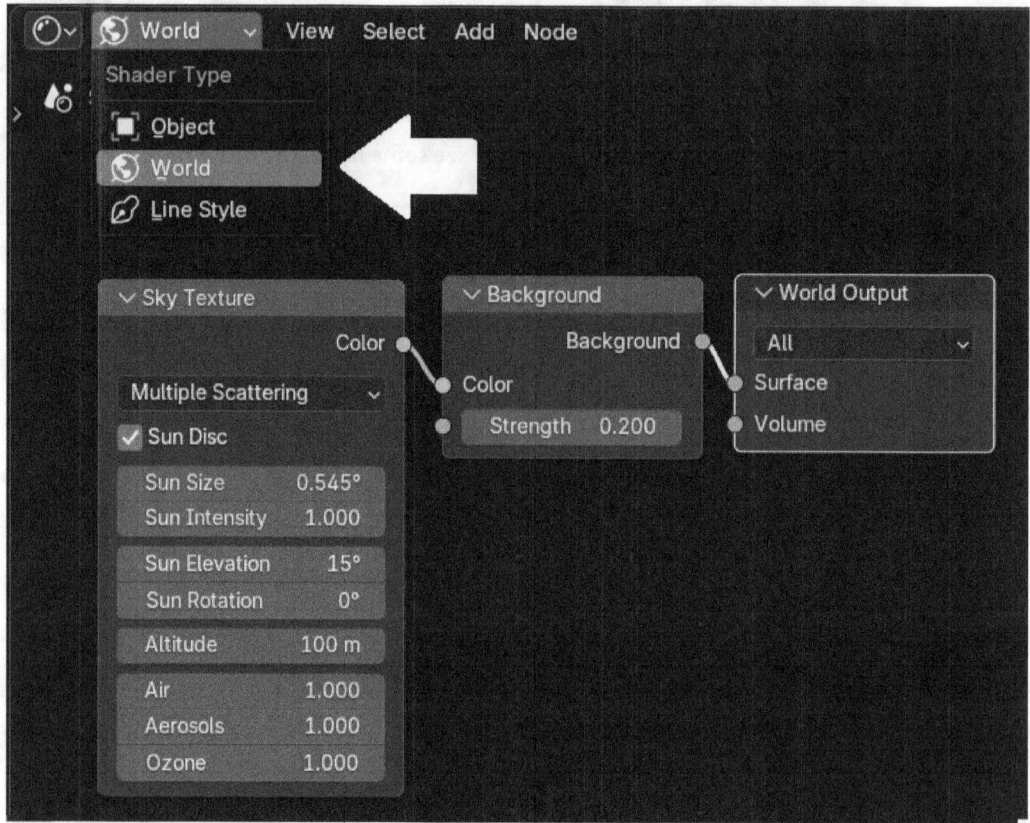

Figure 5.24 – Switching from Object to World mode in the Shader Editor

The **Sky Texture** will be connected to a **Background** node. This node is used to add background light emission, and it also helps us to control the brightness of our environment. If the lighting in your scene is too bright, you can reduce it to a value of 0.2, just like in our example.

Let's look at the values we need to adjust:

- **Single versus Multiple Scattering (Sky Texturing)**:

  - **Single Scattering**: Light is scattered only once before reaching the camera. This produces a clearer, higher-contrast sky with sharper gradients, suitable for simple or stylized looks.

  - **Multiple Scattering**: Light bounces and scatters several times in the atmosphere. This results in a softer, more realistic sky with brighter horizons and smoother color transitions, closer to real-world lighting (this is the option to keep).

- **Sun Size**: If you increase the angle, the sun's diameter will get bigger:

Figure 5.25 – Tweaking the size of the sun

- **Sun Intensity**: This controls how intensely the sun will emit light.

- **Sun Elevation**: This changes the location of the sun. 0 degrees will put the sun on the horizon just like the sunset, while 90 degrees will position the sun vertically in the sky, just like in the middle of the day:

Figure 5.26 – Changing the location of the sun in the sky

The other settings are as follows:

- **Altitude** is the distance from the sea level to the location of the camera: 0 meters means that you will get the lighting at sea level. Increasing this value to something such as 30000 meters will give you the lighting you see when you see a satellite.

Figure 5.27 – Sky Texture with Altitude set to 30000 m

- **Air** controls the density of air molecules.

- **Aerosols** controls the density of dust and water droplets.
- **Ozone** controls the density of ozone molecules and is used to make the sky appear bluer.

Now, we will experiment with another way of lighting our wood cabin by using lamp objects.

Lighting our wood cabin with lamp objects

I've also added some lamps around the wood cabin. To add light points in your scene, use the following steps:

1. Press *Shift + A*, go to the **Light** tab, and choose **Point**.
2. Create multiple points and place them around the wood cabin where you might hang lamps in real life:

Figure 5.28 – Adding lamp objects to the scene

Next, we need to adjust the color of the point light. To do that, we'll repeat the same process we did with the sun previously:

1. Select the **Point** object.
2. Jump into the **Object Data Properties** pane and click on **Use Nodes**.
3. Add the **Blackbody** node and set **Temperature** to 2.500.

Based on the Kelvin scale, we will get a warm lighting color similar to an incandescent light source, which fits the wood cabin theme perfectly:

Figure 5.29 – Rendering the scene while applying the Blackbody node to the lamps

Now that we've learned how to use the **Sky Texture** node along with point lights to apply lighting to our scene, let's examine the final method to apply realistic lighting to our scene: using HDRI maps.

Setting up realistic lighting using HDRI maps

HDRI stands for **high dynamic range image**. Think of this as a large image that covers 360 degrees of the surroundings. They are created by combining several pictures of the same scene.

When we assign an HDRI map to our environment, Blender will wrap it around an invisible sphere that will surround our 3D scene from all angles:

Figure 5.30 – Demonstration of how Blender deals with HDRI maps

An **environment light** surrounds all of the objects in your 3D scene and will light and reflect off all surfaces. This makes HDRI maps very powerful for environment lighting.

Setting up an HDRI environment background for our scene

In order to set up the HDRI map, let's switch the **Shader Editor** from **Object** mode to **World** mode, just as we did earlier in *Figure 5.24*.

Next, in the **Shader Editor**, press *Shift + A* and search for `Environment Texture`. Connect its **Color** output to the **Color** input of **Background**:

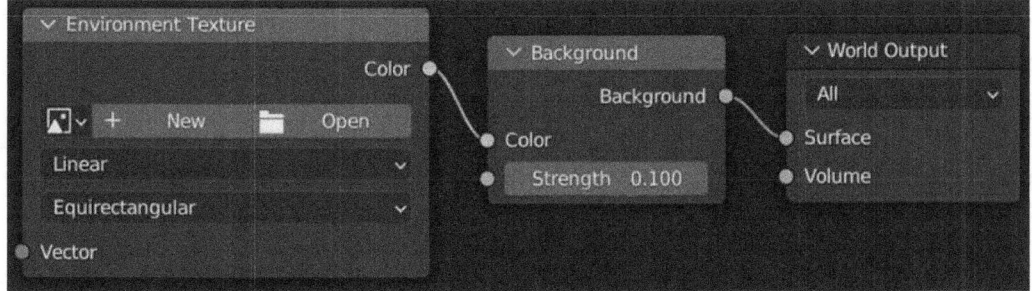

Figure 5.31 – Adding an Environment Texture node in the Shader Editor

Now let's download the HDRI map; you will find it at this GitHub link: `https://github.com/ PacktPublishing/3D-Environment-Design-with-Blender-5-Second-Edition/blob/main/ chapter-5/Nature-HDRI-Map.exr`

Once you download the HDRI map, click on **Open** on the **Environment Texture** node and choose it from there.

> **Note**
>
> Make sure to adjust the **Background** node's **Strength** to 1 to get the default lighting of the HDRI map.

Now, straight out of the box, we have realistic lighting projected in our scene. In order to tweak the **Environment Texture** node, we will need two additional nodes: **Mapping** and **Texture Coordinate**. Search for them and add them to the **Shader Editor**, then connect them as shown in *Figure 5.32*:

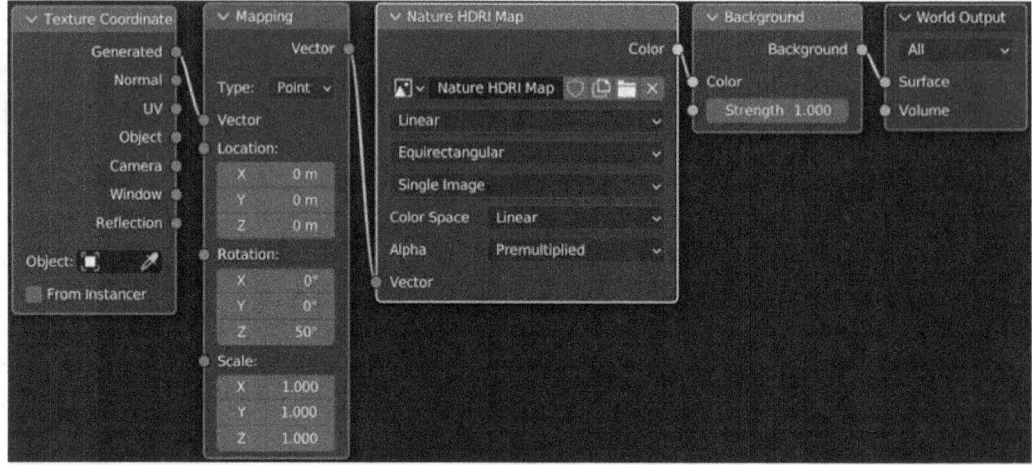

Figure 5.32 – Tweaking the HDRI map rotation by using the Mapping and Texture Coordinate nodes

Now, using the **Mapping** node, we can rotate the HDRI map around the scene to produce different lighting effects. In my case, I set it to 50 degrees and rendered the scene.

Improving color management for better material preview

As we discussed in *Chapter 2*, we can use **AgX** again here to handle bright values better and keep colors from looking washed out. Follow these steps to implement it:

1. Inside **Render Properties**, scroll down to **Color Management**.

2. Switch **View** to **AgX**.

3. Set the look to **High Contrast** because our reference image is high contrast.

4. Tweak **Exposure**. In my case, I set it up to 0.750.

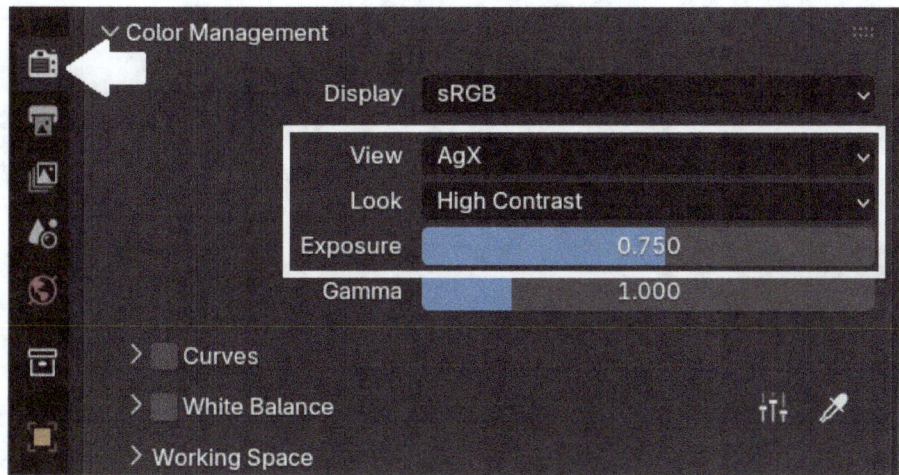

Figure 5.33 – Using AgX in Color Management

This is the result I got:

Figure 5.34 – Final render of the wood cabin scene

Now, compare it to this wood cabin reference image we've been using:

Figure 5.35 – Reference used to create the wood cabin scene

And there you have it. We finished our first objective, which is to turn our reference image into a realistic 3D scene in Blender. In the next chapter, we'll be expanding our environment by creating landscapes.

Summary

In this chapter, first, we broke down the differences between the three Blender rendering engines, understanding the role each one plays in achieving photorealism. We then covered three ways to apply lighting to our wood cabin scene. We achieved our objective, which was to make our scene match the wood cabin reference image we're using.

Next, we explored the basics of lighting in Blender by taking a look at the different ways we can add light to a scene, the properties that those different light sources offer, and how we can configure them.

In the next chapter, we will zoom out and expand our environment. We will learn to create large, natural, and realistic landscapes in Blender.

Get this book's PDF version and more

Scan the QR code (or go to packtpub.com/unlock). Search for this book by name, confirm the edition, and then follow the steps on the page.

Note: Keep your invoice handy. Purchases made directly from Packt don't require an invoice.

Part 2

Creating Realistic Landscapes in Blender 5

This is the main topic of our book, where we will build two separate environments: a mountain landscape and a river scene. First, we will learn how to generate realistic snow and rocky mountains for our landscape. Then, we will create a nice-looking mud texture using procedural texturing and apply it to the terrain. Finally, we will dive into creating realistic, natural-looking water and animating it for our river and landscape environment.

This part of the book includes the following chapters:

- *Chapter 6, Creating Realistic Landscapes in Blender*
- *Chapter 7, Creating and Animating Realistic, Natural-Looking Water*
- *Chapter 8, Creating Procedural Mud Material*
- *Chapter 9, Texturing Landscape with Mud Material*

6

Creating Realistic Landscapes in Blender

In this chapter, you will learn how to create realistic landscapes with snow and rocks in Blender. Modeling landscapes by hand is a tedious process. This is where the **Another Noise Tool (A.N.T.) Landscape extension** comes in handy. It can help us generate terrain for our scenes way quicker than it would be to model terrain by hand. This is an essential technique that will be a great addition to any 3D artist's arsenal.

In this chapter, we will cover the following topics:

- Enabling the **A.N.T.Landscape** extension
- Creating landscapes using the **A.N.T.Landscape** extension
- Creating a river environment using the **A.N.T.Landscape** extension
- Creating a realistic snowy mountain

By the end of this chapter, you will have successfully created a realistic mountain range ready for a river. You will master the **A.N.T.Landscape** tool to generate complex terrain in seconds, and you will also learn a powerful procedural texturing workflow that automatically creates snow on peaks and rocks on cliffs.

Technical requirements

This chapter requires a system capable of running **Blender version 5.0** or above (Windows, macOS, or Linux).

You can download the resources for this chapter from GitHub at: https://github.com/PacktPublishing/3D-Environment-Design-with-Blender-5-Second-Edition/tree/ab43270b643a41ba8f915f74e3bf78573b10a816/chapter-6

Visit this link to check out the video of the code being run: `https://packt.link/flQE0`

Enabling the A.N.T.Landscape extension

A.N.T. uses different procedural noises to generate various landscapes. The first thing to do is to enable it. Let's jump into a brand-new scene and do the following:

1. Click on **Edit** on the top bar and choose **Preferences...**:

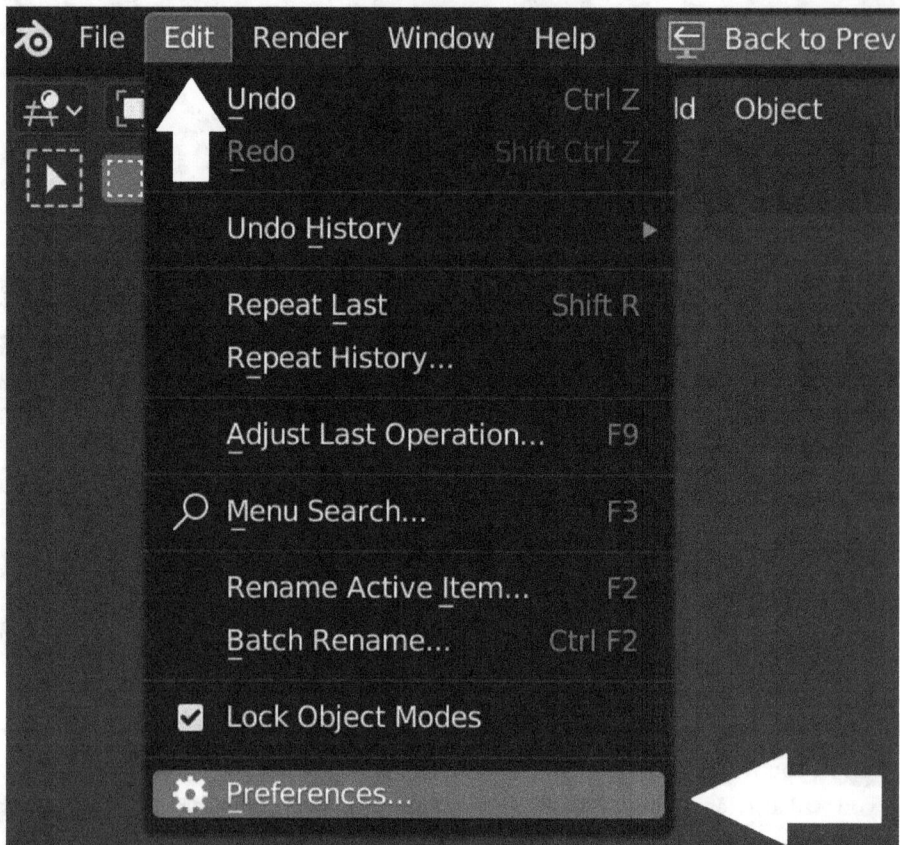

Figure 6.1 – Accessing Blender preferences

2. Select the **Get Extensions** option.

3. Type `landscape` in the search bar. The list will automatically filter to show relevant extensions.

4. Simply click on the **Install** button next to **A.N.T.Landscape**:

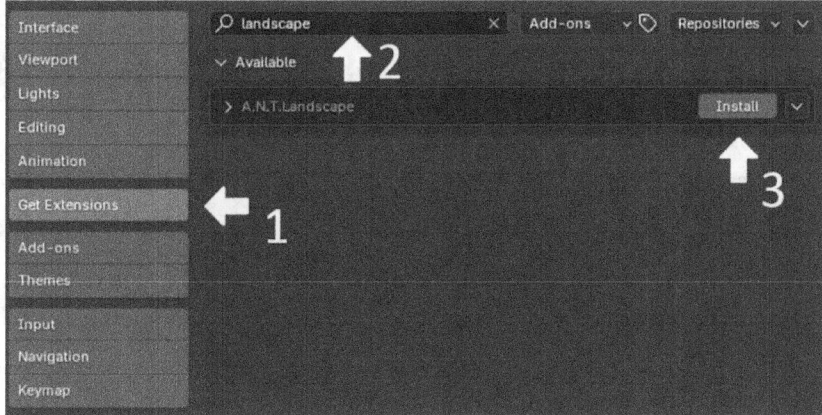

Figure 6.2 – Searching for the A.N.T.Landscape extension

And voilà, you have successfully installed the **A.N.T.Landscape** extension. To check whether it's installed properly, you can go back to the 3D Viewport, press *Shift + A*, and go to **Mesh**, and you should see **Landscape** in the bottom list:

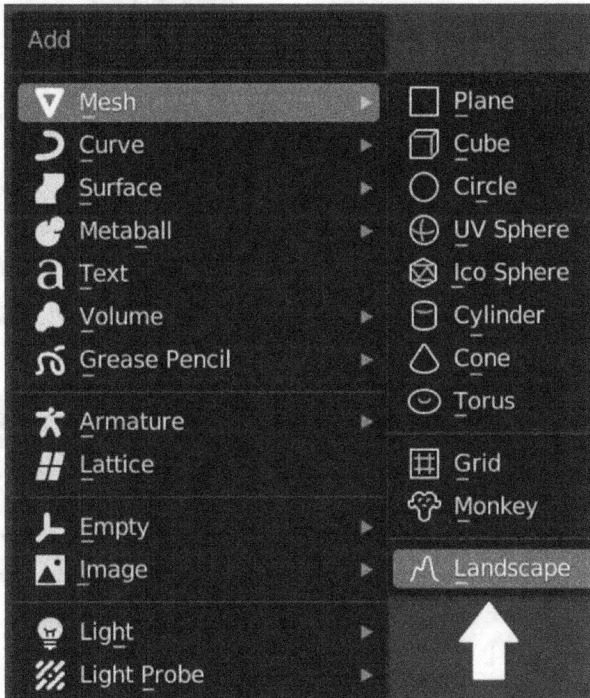

Figure 6.3 – Searching for a Landscape 3D object using Shift + A

Now that the extension has been successfully installed, we can go ahead and use it in our scene.

Creating landscapes using the A.N.T.Landscape extension

To add landscapes, let's press *Shift + A*, choose **Mesh**, and at the bottom, click on **Landscape**; voilà – we have a landscape in our scene:

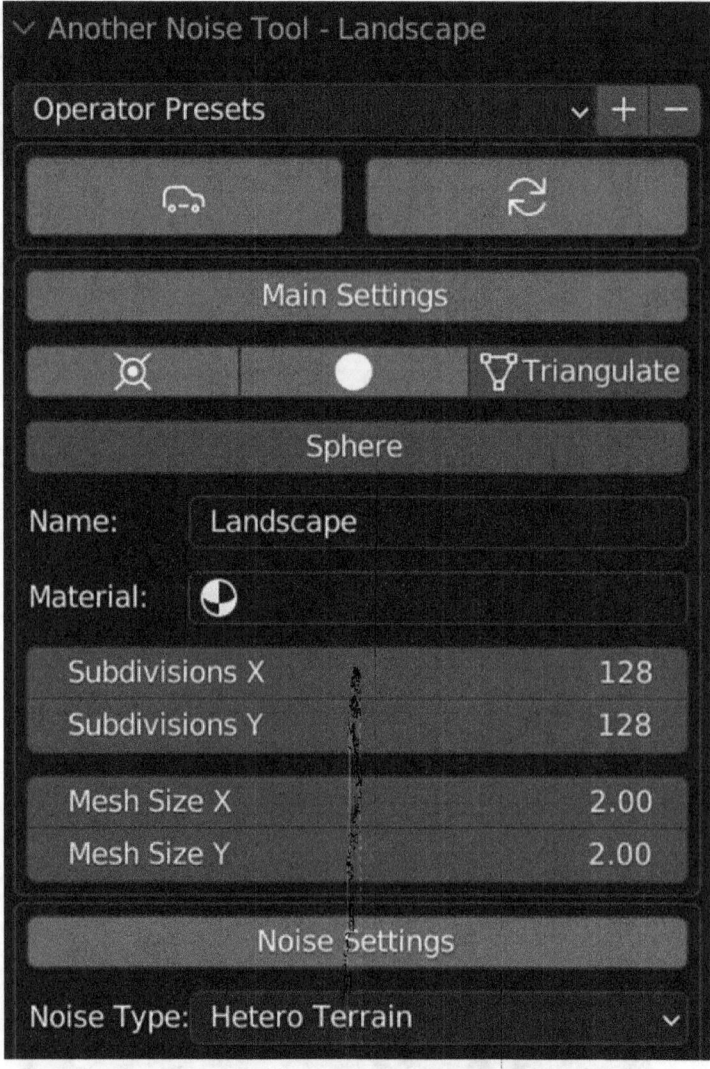

Figure 6.4 – Adding a 3D landscape object

Adding a landscape using A.N.T. should open a menu on the left-hand side of the 3D Viewport; you can press *F9* to maximize it. We will use this menu to customize the landscape shape.

Make sure not to click anywhere else in the Viewport – if you click away, you will lose your settings. Be careful to only click once you're satisfied with the shape of the landscape you're building.

Tweaking the shape of the landscape

Let's look at the steps to change the shape of the landscape:

1. The first setting to change is **Mesh Size** to 5.00 on both the *X* and *Y* axes:

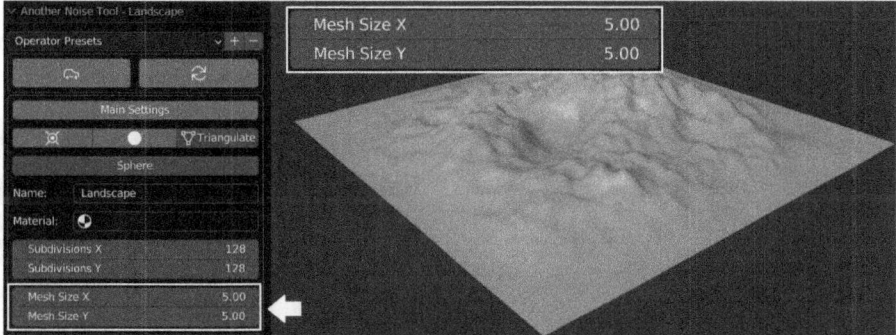

Figure 6.5 – Tweaking the landscape mesh size

2. Next, we'll move to the **Noise Type** setting. Let's change it from the default **Hetero Terrain** to **Slick Rock**, and switch **Noise Basis** from the default **Blender** to **Voronoi F2**:

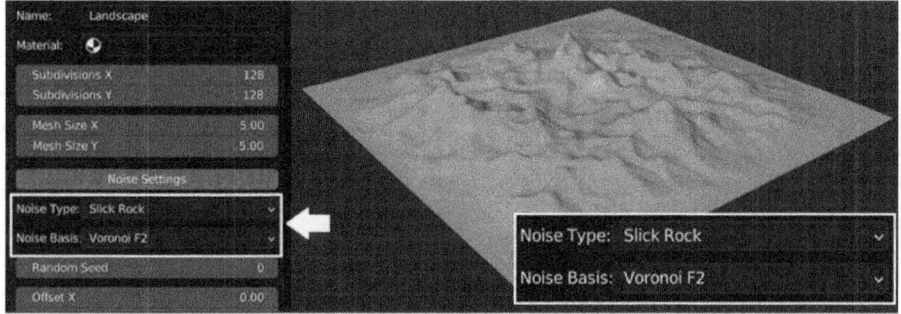

Figure 6.6 – Changing Noise Type for the landscape to Slick Rock

3. At the bottom, we will set **Falloff** to **Y** to make it continuous on the *X* axis and set the **Falloff Y** value to only 1.00:

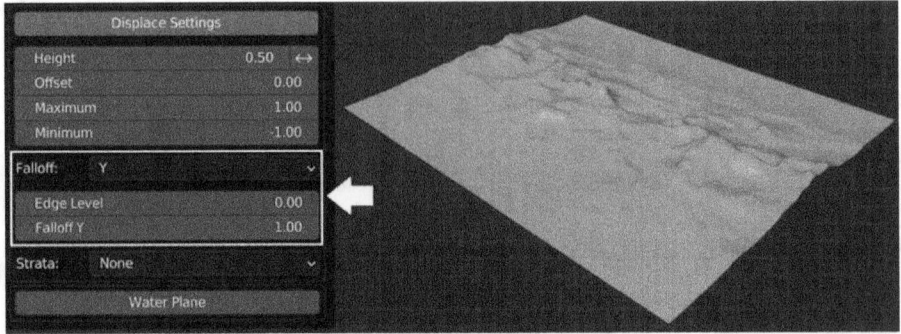

Figure 6.7 – Setting Falloff Y of the landscape to 1.00

4. Next, let's change **Size X** to 2.00 to expand the landscape and tweak the **Height** setting – we need to increase it from 0.50 to 0.75, and change **Offset** to 0.10:

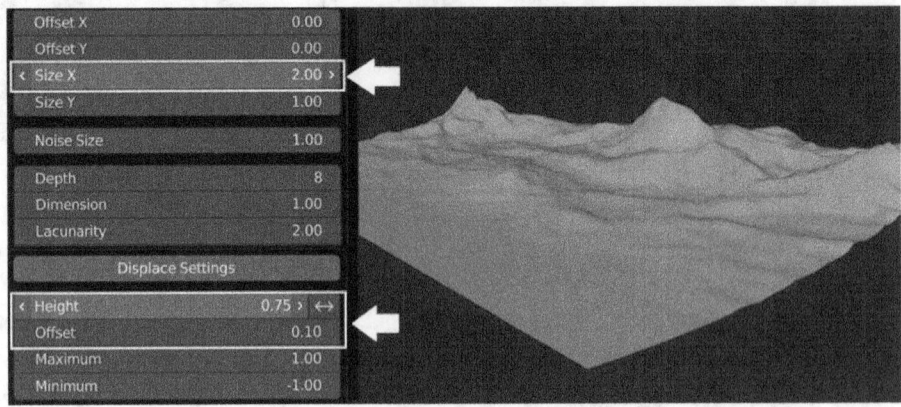

Figure 6.8 – Tweaking the size, height, and offset of the landscape

5. Finally, let's increase **Subdivisions X** and **Subdivisions Y** to 512 to get more detail in our landscape:

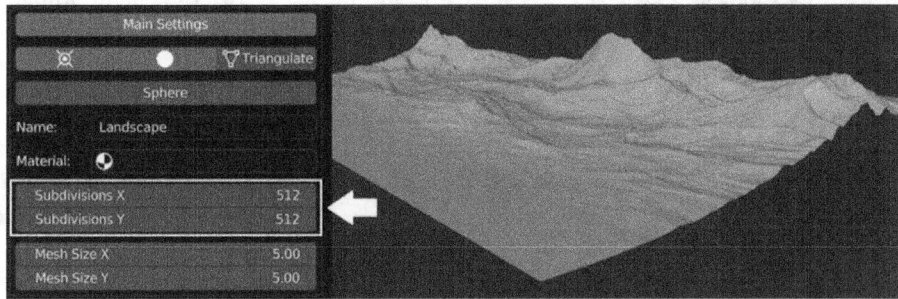

Figure 6.9 – Changing the landscape X and Y subdivisions

We now have the shape of the landscape, but we need to make sure it has the right realistic scale.

Giving the landscape a real-scale measurement

Before scaling our landscape, we need to research to get the scale right. I found that the average landscapes rise at least 300 meters above the surrounding land, so anything in the 300-meter height range should look believable.

Let's scale up our landscape:

1. Select the landscape object and switch to **Edit Mode**.

2. Press *N* to access the right panel where the object dimensions are displayed.

3. Scale the landscape by pressing *S* while keeping an eye on the **Z** dimension value:

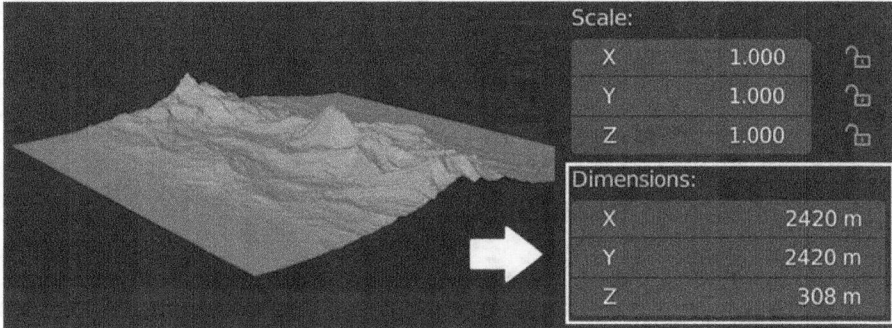

Figure 6.10 – Scaling up the landscape object to 308 meters in height

And there we go – we have an excellent start to a realistic landscape. However, the **A.N.T.Landscape** add-on is capable of much more than just elevation. Before we move on to texturing, let's look at how we can use it to procedurally generate a river environment.

Creating a river environment using the A.N.T.Landscape extension

Creating a river that looks accurate can be difficult to sculpt by hand. By using the **A.N.T. Landscape** add-on, we can procedurally generate natural-looking channels and banks in seconds.

To generate the river, start by changing **Operator Preset** to **River**. This preset is designed to create long, continuous height variations.

Next, set **Subdivision X** and **Subdivision Y** to 512. A *high subdivision level* is important because rivers rely on smooth, detailed elevation changes. With more geometry, the river can curve naturally, avoid blocky edges, and blend better into the surrounding terrain. This is shown in *Figure 6.11*.

Then, set **Noise Basis** to **Voronoi F4**. This noise type produces broken, organic patterns with clear separation between shapes. When used for a river, it helps create more realistic banks and variations in width.

These settings together ensure the river has enough detail, smooth flow, and natural irregularity to feel believable within the landscape.

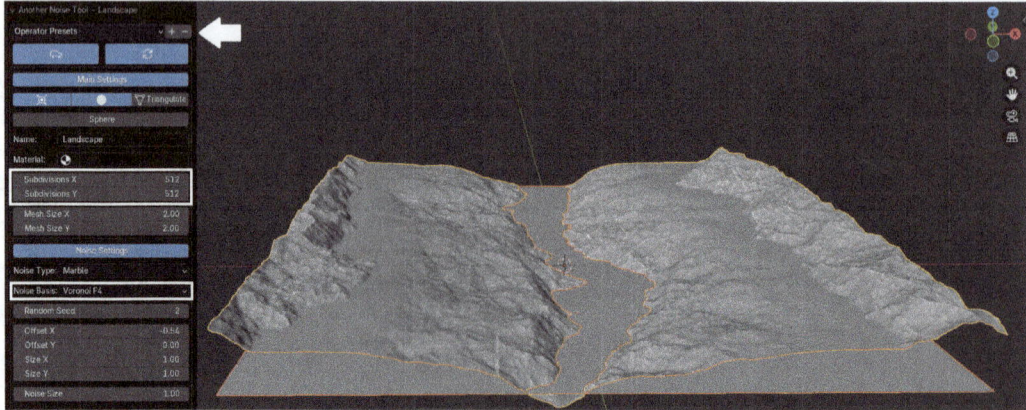

Figure 6.11 – Creating a river using the A.N.T.Landscape add-on

Now that we understand how to use the **A.N.T.Landscape** add-on to generate landscapes and river environments, we can move on to the texturing stage and create the snow material.

Creating a realistic snowy mountain

Select the **Mountain** object, jump into **Material Properties**, and create a new material called Mountain:

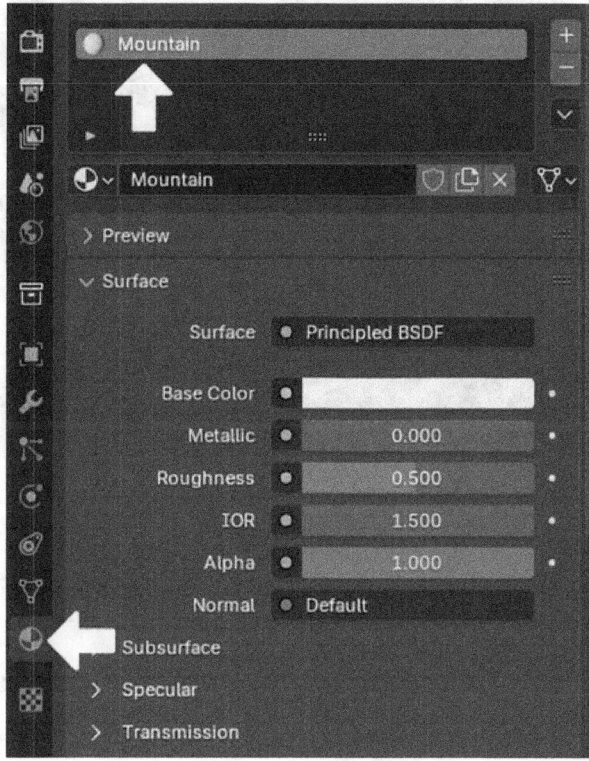

Figure 6.12 – Adding a material called Mountain

Switch the bottom window of Blender to the **Shader Editor** window, and let's start tweaking the **Mountain** material:

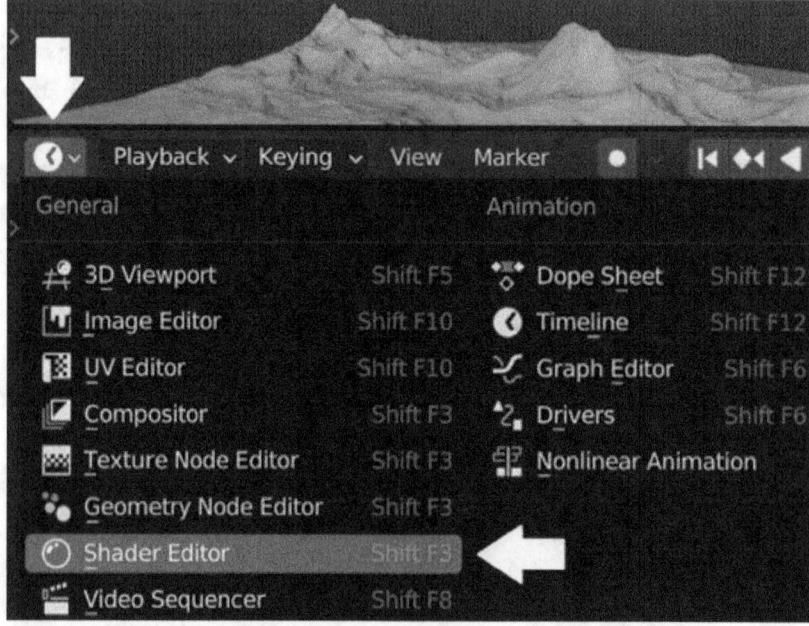

Figure 6.13 – Switching the bottom window to Shader Editor

Now, we want to create a snow mask, which is a black and white mask that will tell Blender what portions of the mountains we want to be rock and what portions of the mountain we want to be snow.

To explain further, we need to highlight only the flat surfaces that are facing the Z axis in our landscape because these are the areas where the snow will gather.

To do that, let's add the following nodes:

    1. Add a **Geometry** node:

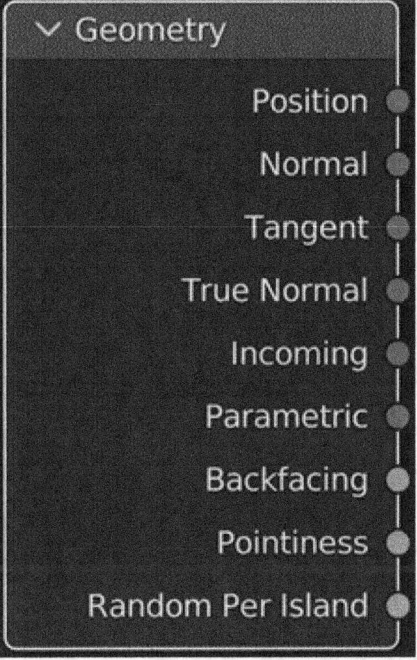

Figure 6.14 – Adding a Geometry node

This node gives us geometric information about the object it's assigned to. In our case, the information we need here is **Normal**.

2. Let's first assign the **Normal** slot of the **Geometry** node to the **Base Color** slot of the **Principled BSDF** node:

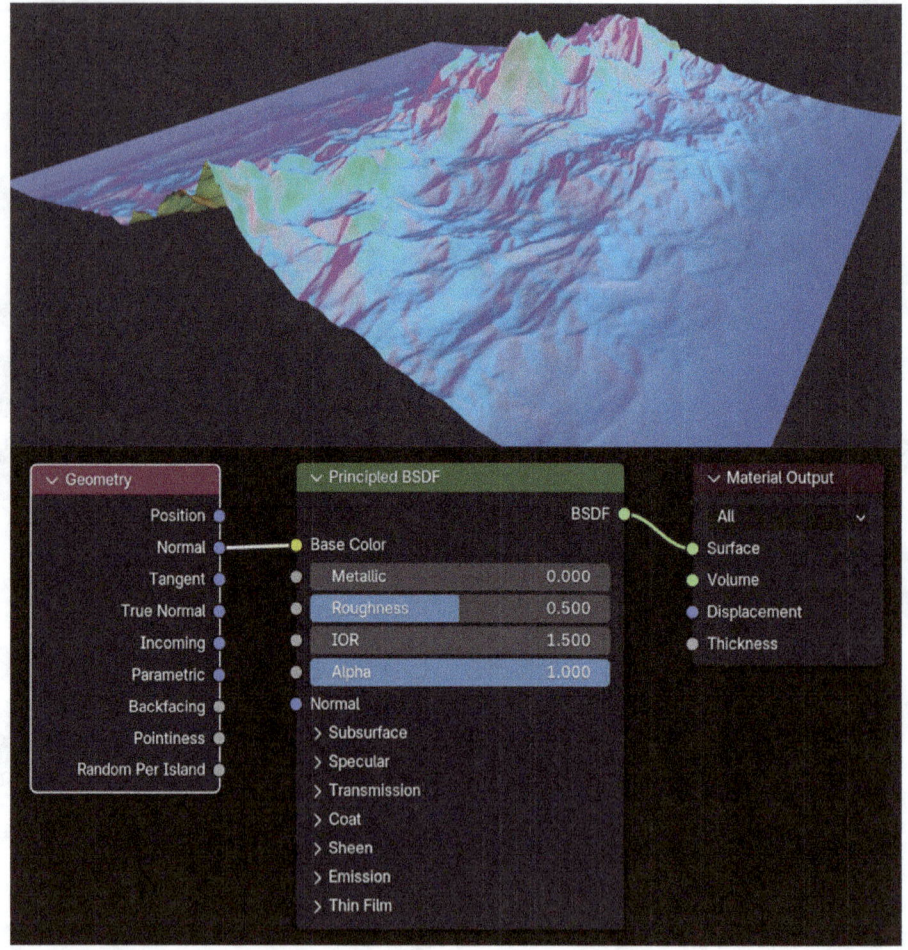

Figure 6.15 – Assigning the Normal slot to the Base Color slot

This is how our landscape appears now:

Figure 6.16 – Displaying the landscape with normal geometry

The **Normal** slot of the **Geometry** node is coloring our object in three colors: *red*, *green*, and *blue*. These RGB colors translate to *x*, *y*, and *z* coordinates:

- Surfaces that are aligned with the Y axis will be *green*
- Flat surfaces will be *blue*
- Surfaces that are aligned with the X axis will be *red*

Since there is no 100% flat surface, we're not seeing 100% of the *blue*, *green*, or *red* colors.

In the cube example here, you can see the three colors displayed clearly because the faces of the cube are perfectly aligned with the *X*, *Y*, and *Z* axes:

Figure 6.17 – Displaying normal geometry of a cube

Now, you might wonder how this normal *X*, *Y*, and *Z* axes will be useful to us. Basically, this is where the **Separate XYZ** node comes into play.

Using the Separate XYZ node

The **Separate XYZ** node will allow us to separate the normal *X*, *Y*, and *Z* colors and pick any axis we want – *X*, *Y*, or *Z*:

1. Let's add the **Separate XYZ** node to our node setup:

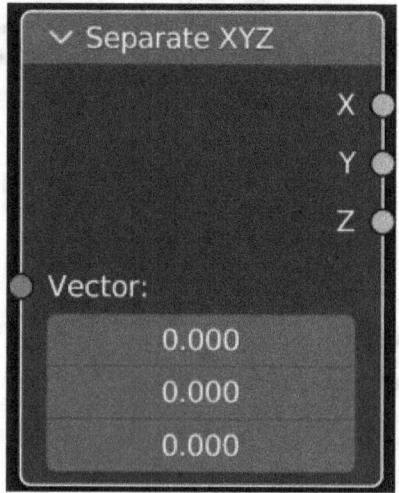

Figure 6.18 – Adding a Separate XYZ node

2. Let's connect the **Normal** slot of the **Geometry** node to the **Vector** slot of **Separate XYZ**.

3. On the right side of **Separate XYZ**, connect the **X** slot to **Base Color** on **Principled BSDF**:

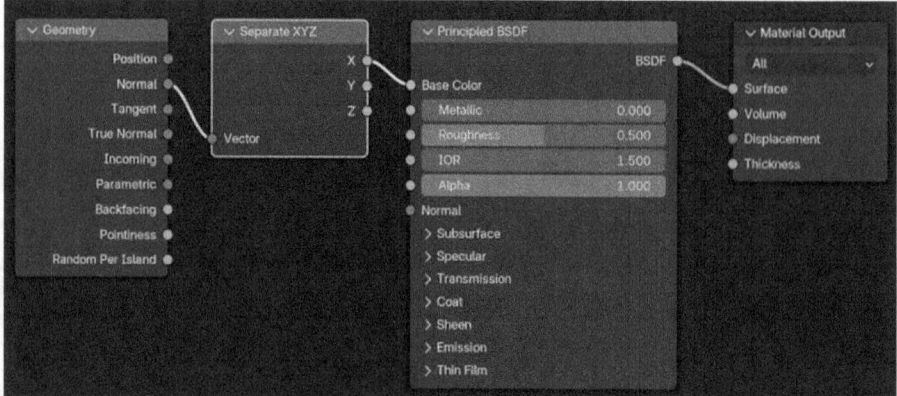

Figure 6.19 – Connecting the Geometry node to Separate XYZ, then to the Principled BSDF node

This way, we'll only be seeing the faces that are aligned with the red **X** axis.

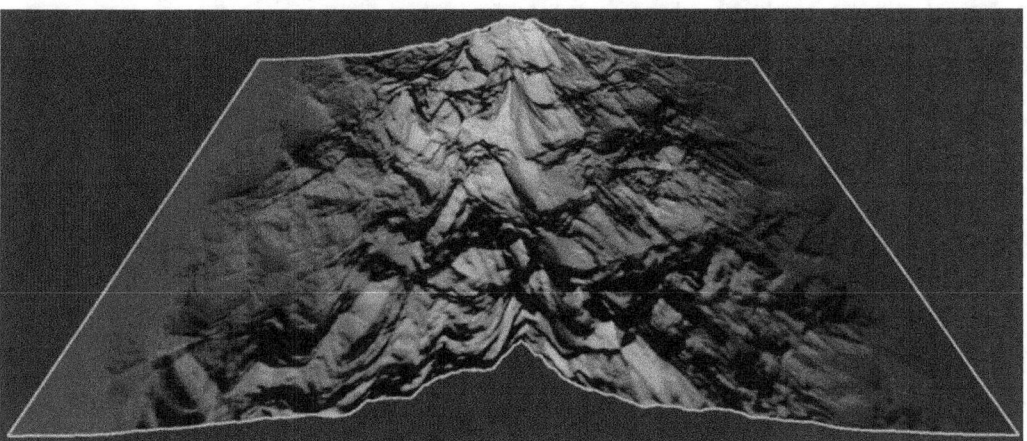

Figure 6.20 – Switching to Material Preview to check the landscape

I just want you to see this nice effect, but actually, we're looking to highlight the top faces that are aligned with the **Z** axis.

To have more control over the mask we're creating, we need to add a **ColorRamp** node and connect all three nodes as follows:

1. Move the *white* handle to the left until you see the **Pos** value set to 0.850.

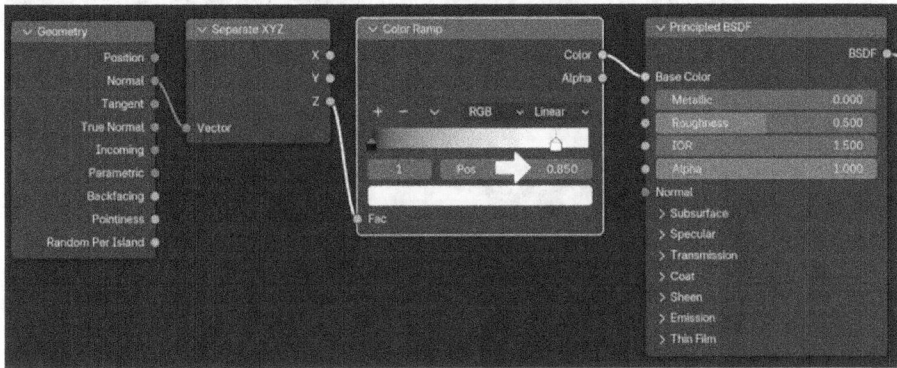

Figure 6.21 – Connecting the mask node setup to Base Color

2. Switch the **Interpolation** type of **ColorRamp** from **Linear** to **Constant**; this will make the black and white mask edges sharp:

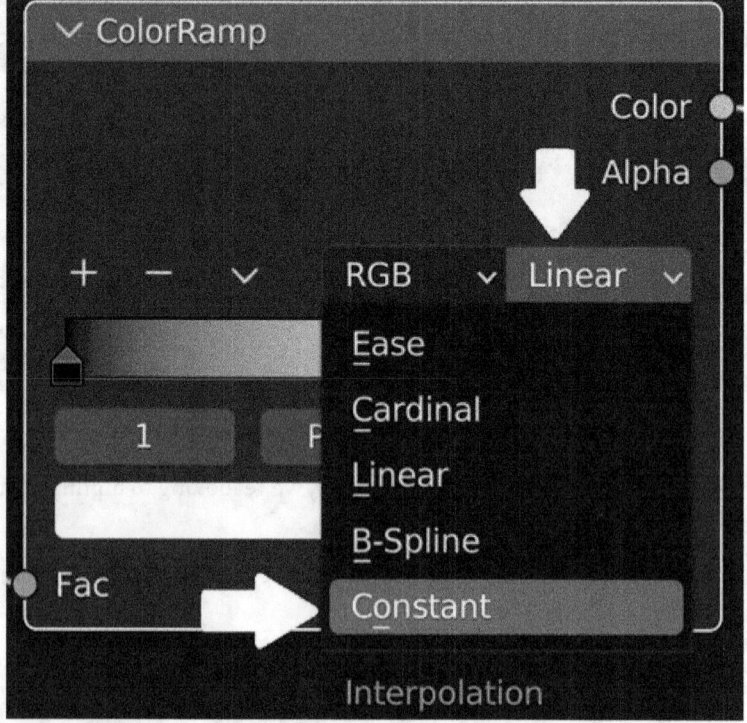

Figure 6.22 – Switching the ColorRamp type from Linear to Constant

This is what our landscape snow mask looks like:

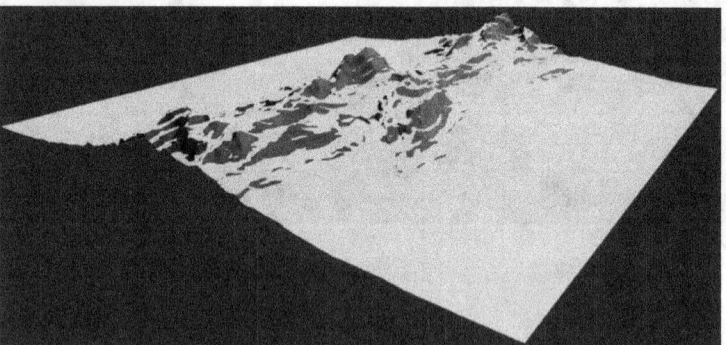

Figure 6.23 – Landscape in Material Preview with the mask node setup applied

When working with nodes, you might want to preview a particular node to see the effect it has on the whole material you're working on.

Using Node Wrangler to display nodes

In order to preview any node, we can press *Ctrl + Shift* and left-click on the node we want to preview. But this shortcut won't work unless you enable the **Node Wrangler add-on**.

You can see how to enable the **Node Wrangler** add-on in the *The fastest way to set up PBR materials in Blender* section of *Chapter 10*.

For example, I pressed *Ctrl + Shift* and left-clicked on the **Geometry** node:

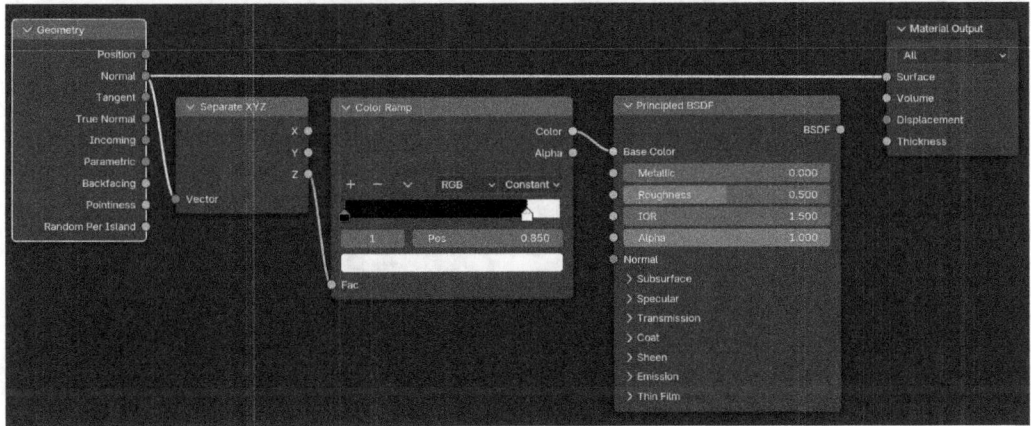

Figure 6.24 – Displaying the Geometry node using the Ctrl + Shift + left-click Node Wrangler shortcut

Blender will connect the node you want to preview directly to the **Material Output** node. This way, you will only see the **Geometry** node's output exactly as shown in *Figure 6.14*.

To preview the entire node setup, press *Ctrl + Shift* and left-click on **Principled BSDF**.

Now that we have the snow mask applied, the next step is to replace the *black* areas with rocks.

Adding the Rocks texture to our mountain

We'll be using the Rocks texture, which you can find at this GitHub link: https://github.com/
PacktPublishing/3D-Environment-Design-with-Blender-5-Second-Edition/blob/
ab43270b643a41ba8f915f74e3bf78573b10a816/chapter-6/Rocks.jpg.

Drag and drop this Rocks image texture into the **Shader Editor**:

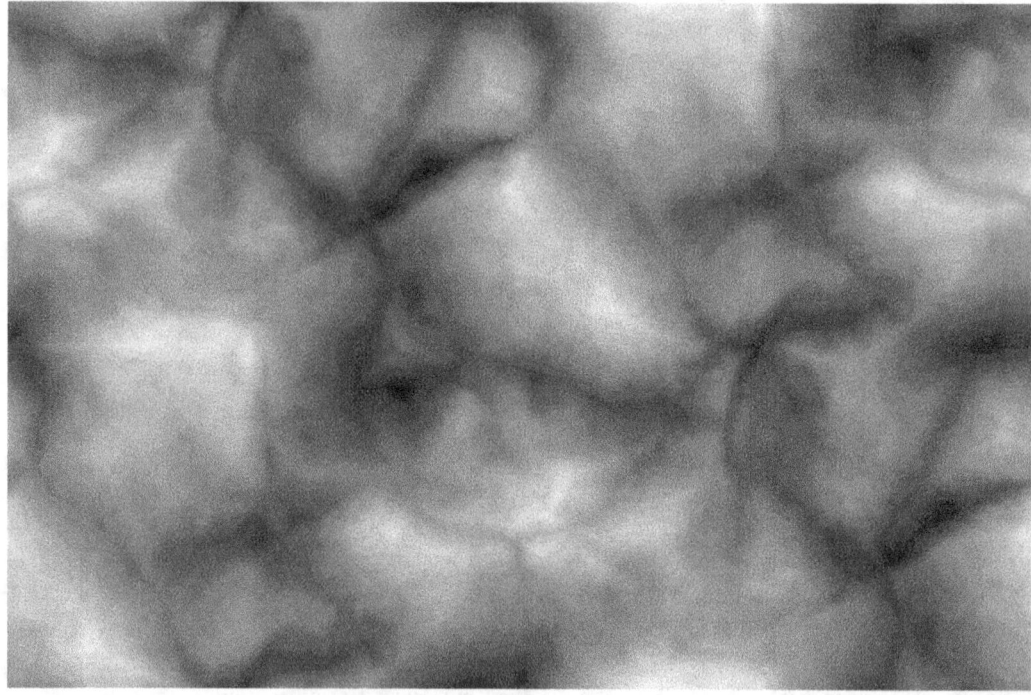

Figure 6.25 – Rocks height map texture

We need to mix it with our mask. Let's look at how we can do this:

1. Add a **Mix** node.

2. Change the **Mix** node type from **Float** to **Color**.

3. Connect the **Color** output of the **ColorRamp** node to the **Factor** input of the **Mix** node.

4. Connect the **Rocks** image texture to the **Color B** input of the **Mix** node.

5. Add a **Displacement** node.

6. Connect the **Color** output of the **Mix** node to the **Height** input of the **Displacement** node.

7. Connect the **Displacement** node's output to the **Displacement** input of the **Material Output** node.

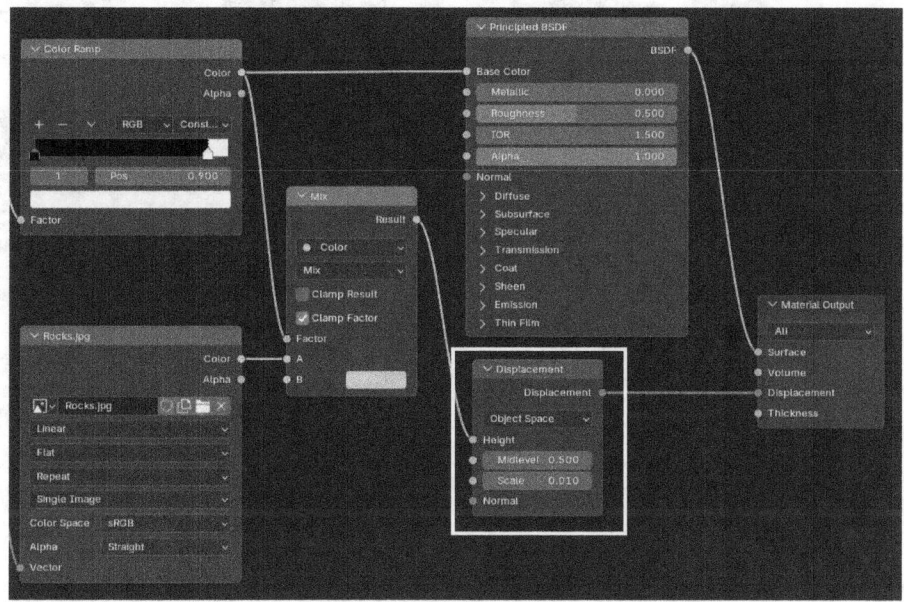

Figure 6.26 – Adding the Rocks height map texture to the node setup

8. The last step is to scale up the Rocks image texture 10 times – to do that, let's add two additional nodes, **Mapping** and **Texture Coordinate**, and connect them as shown in *Figure 6.27*.

You can quickly add these two nodes by selecting the **Rocks** image texture node and pressing *Ctrl + T*. This shortcut will automatically insert the **Mapping** and **Texture Coordinate** nodes and connect them appropriately.

9. Make sure to scale up the **X** and **Y** values on the **Mapping** node to `10.000`:

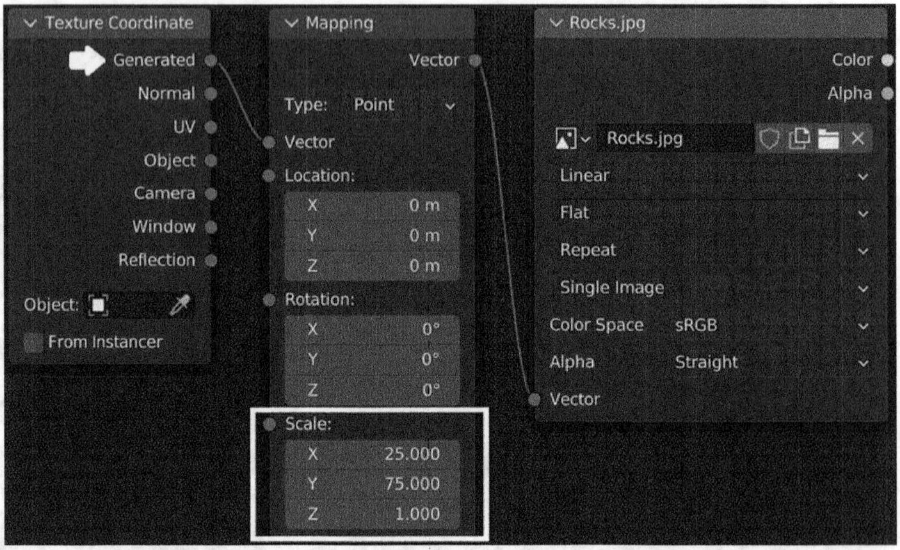

Figure 6.27 – Changing the Scale settings of the Rocks height map texture

In order to see the mountain texture even better, let's set **Sky Texture**.

Adding Sky Texture to lighten our world

In the **Shader Editor**, let's switch its type from **Object** to **World** – this way, we'll be able to adjust the lighting of our environment:

1. Press *Shift + A* and search for Sky Texture. Select it.

2. Connect it to the **Background** node:

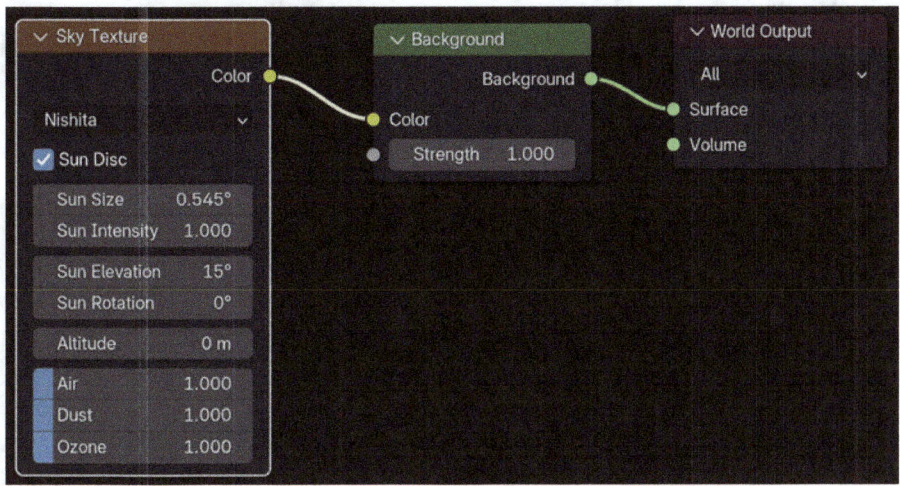

Figure 6.28 – Adding Sky Texture to lighten the scene

Now that we have decent lighting in our scene, let's do a quick render of our environment to see the landscape with the displacement map applied.

If we jump back to the 3D Viewport and switch to the **Rendered** view, this is what our mountain will look like:

Figure 6.29 – Rendering the landscape on the 3D Viewport with the snow mask node setup applied

It has this nice effect of snow melting from the top to the bottom. It looks beautiful!

Changing the shape of the mountain

We're planning to add a river to our scene, and as you know, rivers are always at the bottom (water always reaches the bottom) of a mountain. Let's look at the steps to add the river:

1. Select the **Mountain** object.

2. Switch to **Edit Mode** by pressing *Tab*.

3. Press *7* to switch to the top view.

4. Press *Z* and switch to **Wireframe** (this way, our geometry will be transparent, and if we select a portion of our object, we won't miss any vertices).

5. Select either the right half or the left half of the bridge. In our example, we will select the left side:

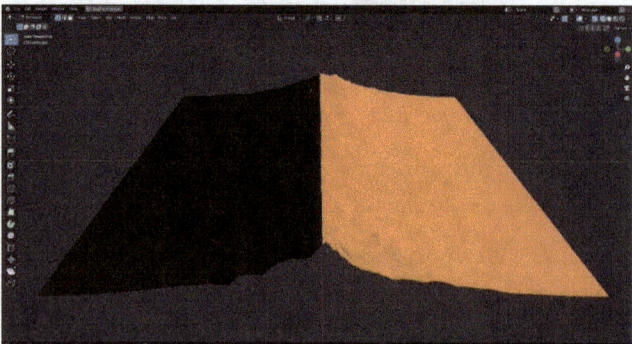

Figure 6.30 – Example showing the left half of the landscape selected in Edit Mode

It's *black* because it's heavy with details. We have around 262,000 vertices to work with on this mountain; the density of the vertices makes the entire mountain look black on **Wireframe**.

Remember that this density is directly controlled by the **Subdivisions X** and **Subdivisions Y** settings we increased to 512 earlier (see *Figure 6.9*). Higher subdivision values create more geometry, resulting in a denser, more detailed mesh.

As a new user, it is easy to accidentally create too much geometry, which causes Blender to lag or freeze. If your Viewport starts slowing down, check your **Statistics**:

- **Laptop users**: Try to keep your scene under 1,000,000 (1 million) vertices.

- **Desktop users**: You can generally push up to 5,000,000 (5 million) vertices before experiencing major slowdowns.

If you exceed these limits, consider lowering your **X** and **Y** subdivision levels (see *Figure 6.9*).

If you want to see the number of vertices you have in a particular object, you can click on **Show Overlay**, which you will find at the top right of the 3D Viewport, and enable **Statistics**.

6. Select **Statistics** in **Show Overlay**, and you will get access to the **Objects** and **Vertices** data:

- **Objects**: This shows the number of objects you are selecting.
- **Vertices**: The first number shows the number of vertices selected, and after the slash, you have the total number of vertices that the selected object has. The same thing goes for **Edges**, **Faces**, and **Triangles**:

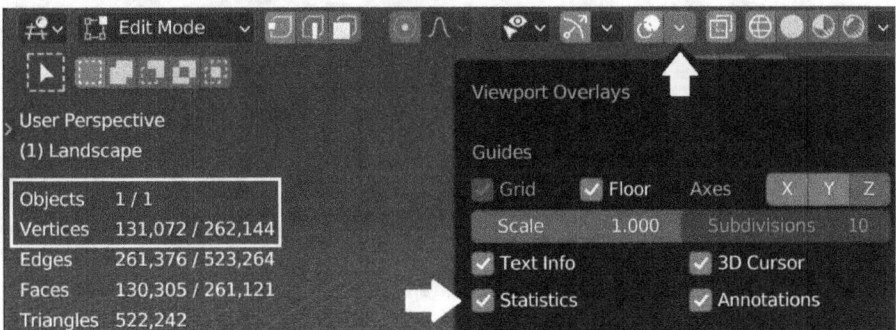

Figure 6.31 – Enabling the Statistics feature

7. With the left side of the mountain selected, press *P* to separate it from the rest.

8. Press *Tab* to exit **Edit Mode**.

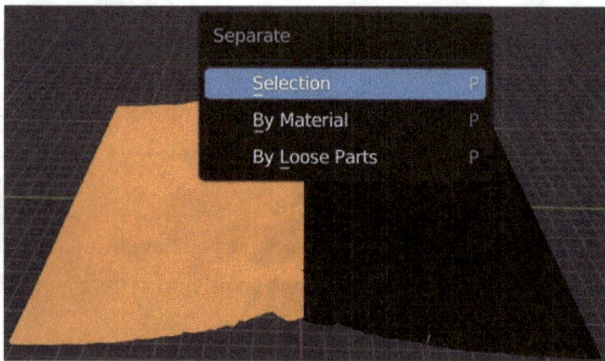

Figure 6.32 – Separating the half-selected part of the landscape

9. Move the separated part of the mountain to the right-hand side until both mountain parts match perfectly:

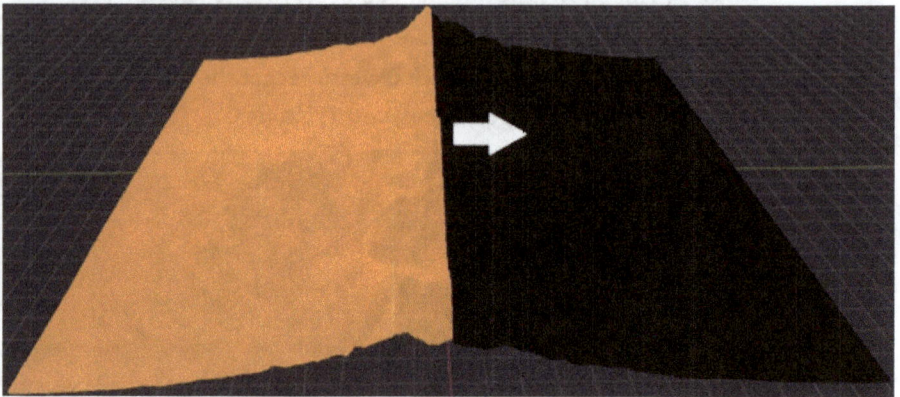

Figure 6.33 – Preparing the half-separated part of the landscape on the left side

10. Move it to the right until it matches the left:

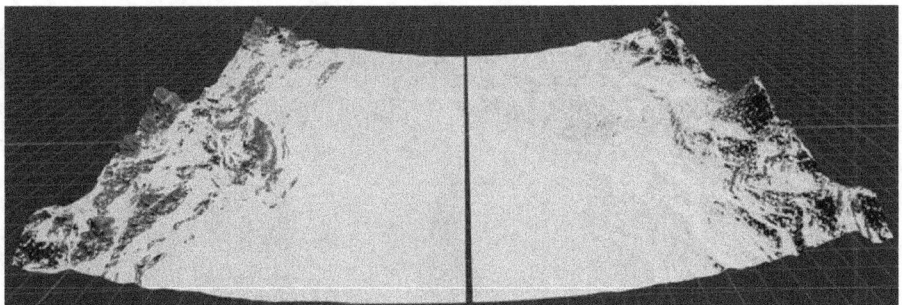

Figure 6.34 – Moving the half-separated part of the landscape to the right side

11. Now, we need to connect both parts of the mountain, so select both parts and press *Ctrl + J* to join both parts into a single part.

12. Next, we need to fill the gap between these two parts. Select the mountain and switch to **Edit Mode**.

13. Zoom into the intersection between the two sides of the mountain:

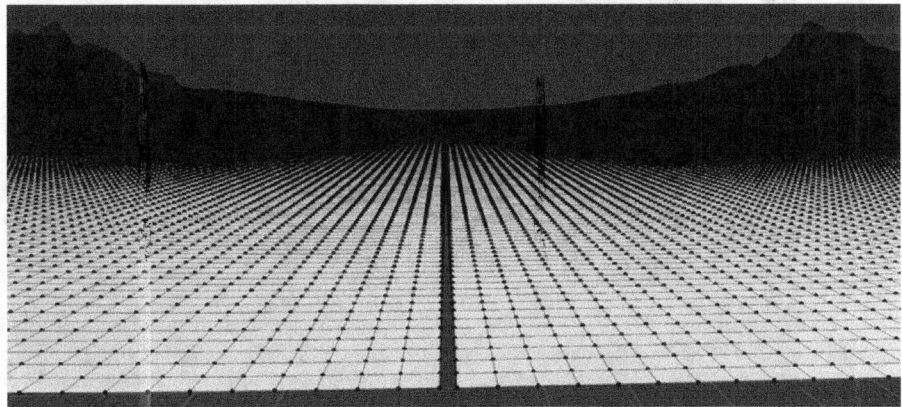

Figure 6.35 – Zooming into the intersection between the two sides of the mountain

To fill the gap shown in *Figure 6.35*, we'll be using the **Bridge Edge Loops** feature. In order to do that, we need to select both mountain edges first:

1. Press *Alt* and left-click on the first side of the mountain.

2. Hold *Shift* to keep the first selection active.

3. Press *Alt* and left-click on the second side of the mountain.

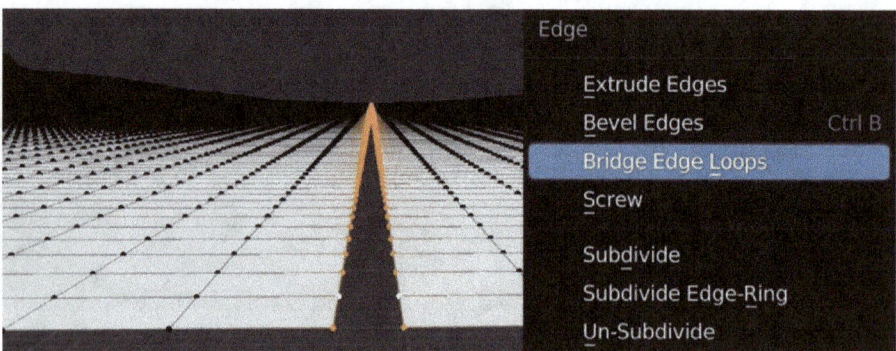

Figure 6.36 – Selecting both edges of the side parts of the mountain

4. Now, in order to fill that gap shown in *Figure 6.36*, you can press *Ctrl + E* and choose **Bridge Edge Loops**. This way, we will fill the gap between the two mountain parts and make it a single large, beautiful mountain like this:

Figure 6.37 – Joining both landscape parts

5. Now, if we jump into **Object Mode** and press *Z* to switch to **Rendered**, we will have an excellent mountain curve that will be perfect for adding a river at the bottom:

Figure 6.38 – Rendered scene of the landscape

To demonstrate that, I've added a plane and put it at the lowest point of the mountain.

I've added a new material to the plane and changed its color to a sky-bluish color. I've also reduced **Roughness** to 0 in order to have a completely glossy and reflective river material:

Figure 6.39 – Adding a basic river to the landscape

The river water looks fake right now, but don't worry – this is just a demonstration of where the river will be placed. In the next chapter, we'll be focusing on creating a photorealistic river that makes your scene stand out.

Summary

In this chapter, we went through the process of creating a realistic snow and rocky mountain. We started by installing the **A.N.T.Landscape** built-in extension, and then added a landscape, tweaked its settings, and changed its shape to make it look as realistic as possible.

In the second part of the chapter, we focused on texturing the landscape by creating a snow and rock mask using procedural texturing.

In the next chapter, we'll create and animate a realistic river, adding natural water movement to our landscape scene.

Get this book's PDF version and more

Scan the QR code (or go to packtpub.com/unlock). Search for this book by name, confirm the edition, and then follow the steps on the page.

Note: Keep your invoice handy. Purchases made directly from Packt don't require an invoice.

7

Creating and Animating Realistic, Natural-Looking Water

Water is such a complex material, with specific features such as reflection and refraction. In this chapter, we will take a look at creating an animated and realistic river from scratch.

We will learn how to use **Glass BSDF** and **Transparent BSDF** to achieve the kind of reflection and refraction that real water has. We will learn how to create and switch between shaders, and change the colors of shaders to achieve a nice-looking water surface.

Then, we will add a wave effect to the surface of the water using **Noise Texture**. Finally, we will learn how to animate the waves on the surface by inserting keyframes into the Timeline editor.

In this chapter, we'll be covering the following topics:

- Creating a realistic, natural river
- Creating a continuously looping animation

By the end, you'll be able to create and animate a realistic, natural-looking river with a flowing wave and a looping water animation inside your landscape scene.

Technical requirements

This chapter requires a system capable of running **Blender version 5.0** or above (Windows, macOS, or Linux).

Creating a realistic, natural river

In the previous scene, we created a snowy and rocky landscape. Now, let's fill it with details, starting by adding a river to our scene.

Let's add a plane that's going to represent the water in our scene:

1. In the 3D Viewport, press *Shift + A* and create a plane object.

2. Scale the plane object by pressing *S* to make it fit the landscape size.

3. Move the plane object down until it collides perfectly with the bottom curve of the landscape. We just need to show a little bit of the plane on the surface.

Take a look at *Figure 7.1* here, which shows where to place the plane object that we have created:

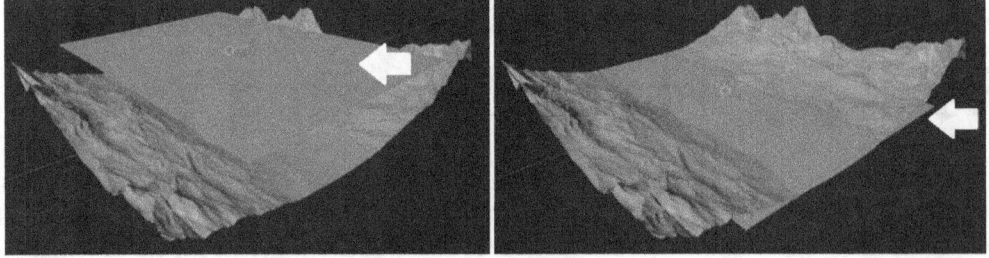

Figure 7.1 – Fitting the plane to the bottom curve of the landscape

Now that we have placed the plane object at the bottom of the landscape, we need to create a water material and assign it to this plane.

Creating a water material

Now that we have our plane, let's add a material called **Water** to it:

1. Select the plane object.

2. Go to **Material Properties**.

3. Add a material called **Water** to the plane object.

4. Switch the bottom menu of Blender to **Shader Editor** so that we can edit our material. Here are the preceding steps shown in our Blender scene:

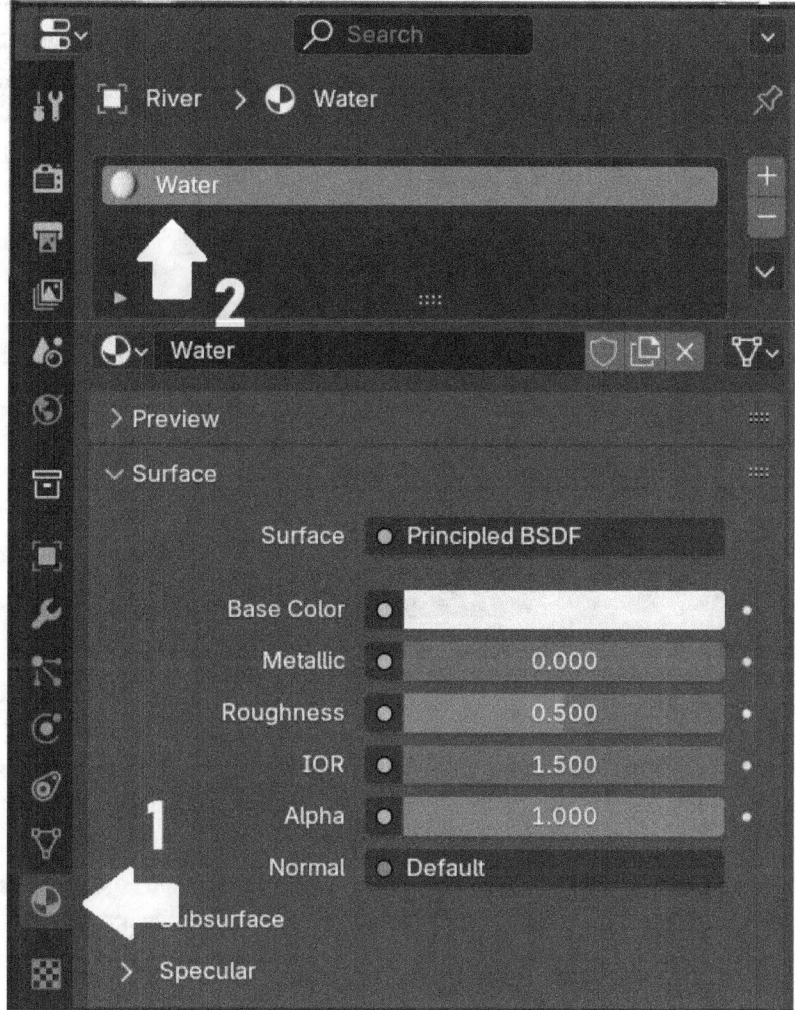

Figure 7.2 – Adding a water material to the river plane

5. Now, the first thing to do is to delete the **Principled BSDF** node, as we don't need it to create our water material. For water, we don't need the full feature set of **Principled BSDF**. Using only **Transparent** and **Glossy** shaders gives more direct control over reflection and transparency, which better suits this specific material. So, we'll select the **Principled BSDF** node, press *X*, and it will be deleted. We'll be left with the **Material Output** node alone:

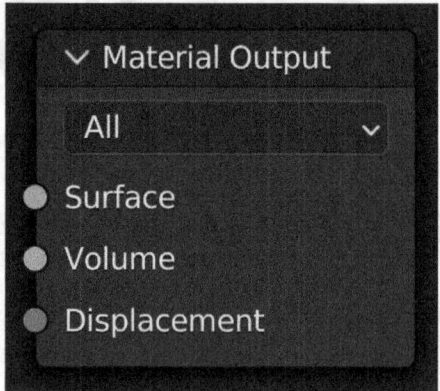

Figure 7.3 – The Material Output node

Next, to create water, we will need to mix two effects – *reflectivity* and *transparency*:

1. Let's add a **Glass BSDF** node. Search for it by hitting *Shift + A* in the **Shader Editor**. This node works like a glass shader. It is used for creating materials that refract and reflect light passing through them at certain angles.

2. For transparency, we'll search for a node called `Transparent BSDF`. **Transparent BSDF** is used to add transparency without refraction, passing straight through the surface as if there were no geometry there.

   Figure 7.4 shows the **Glass BSDF** node, the **Transparent BSDF** node, and the **Material Output** node:

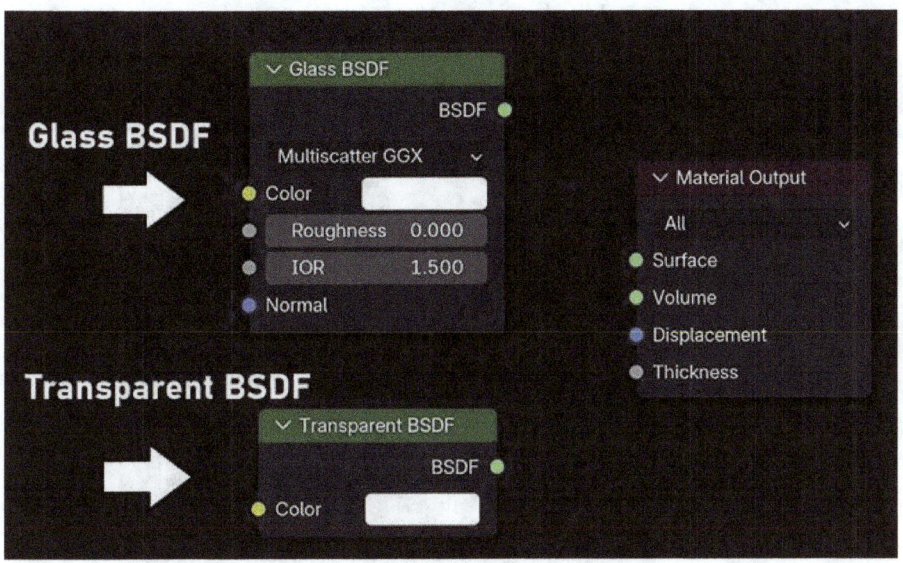

Figure 7.4 – Glass BSDF and Transparent BSDF

Notice that in **Glass BSDF**, we have a value called **IOR**, which stands for **index of refraction**. The IOR is a measure of how much a ray of light bends when passing from one medium to another. Each material has its own IOR (water, glass, plastic, and so on). If you do a Google search on the IOR of water, you will find that it's equal to 1.33:

Figure 7.5 – Search that shows the IOR for water

3. Let's replace the **IOR** default value, **1.450**, with the IOR of water, 1.330:

Figure 7.6 – The Glass BSDF node

Now, the next step is to *merge the transparency and the reflection*. Follow these steps:

1. Let's search for a node called Mix Shader:

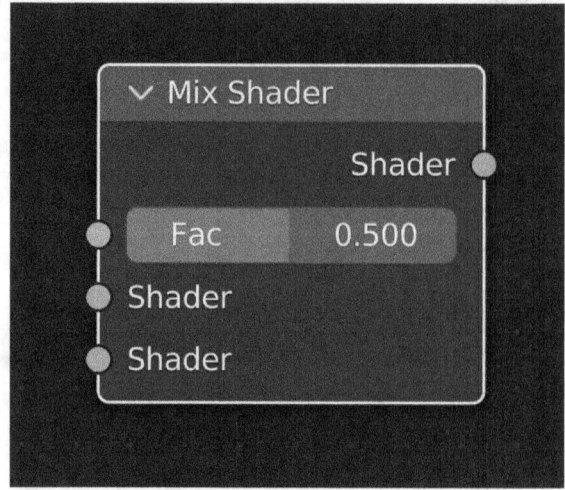

Figure 7.7 – The Mix Shader node

The **Mix Shader** node is used to mix two shaders. You can connect the first shader to the top slot and the second shader to the bottom slot.

Fac controls how you want the mixture to go. The **0.5** default value means that the mixture will be even, meaning that the output shader will have 50% of the first shader and 50% of the second shader. If you set it to 0.25, it means that the output shader will have 75% of the first shader and only 25% of the second, and so on.

2. Let's connect **Glass BSDF** to the top of **Mix Shader** and **Transparent BSDF** to the bottom. Then, we will connect the right-hand slot of **Mix Shader** to **Material Output** (see *Figure 7.8*).

3. For the **Fac** amount, we'll go with 0.25, meaning that we'll be using 25% of **Transparent BSDF** and 75% of **Glass BSDF**.

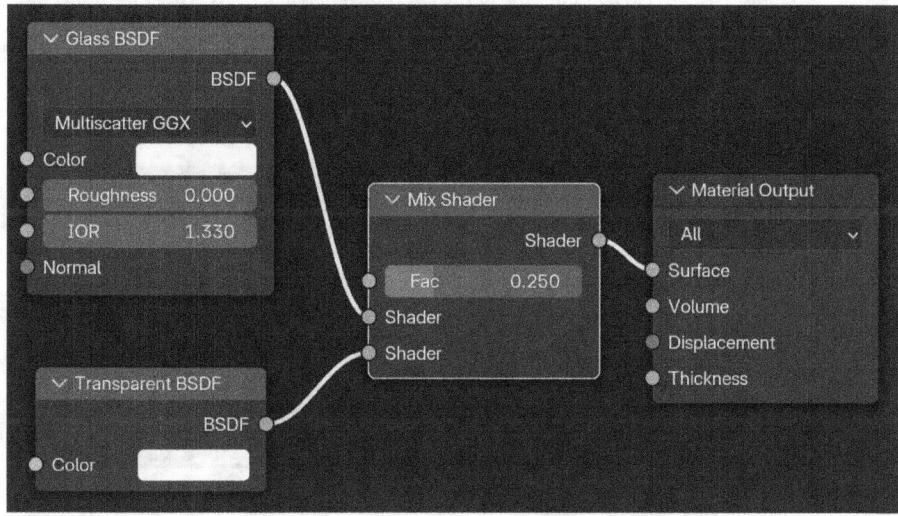

Figure 7.8 – Mixing Glass BSDF and Transparent BSDF using Mix Shader

Next, we need to *tweak the color of our water material*. To do that, let's perform these actions:

1. Add a **ColorRamp** node.

2. Connect the right-hand **Color** slot of **ColorRamp** to both **Glass BSDF** and **Transparent BSDF**:

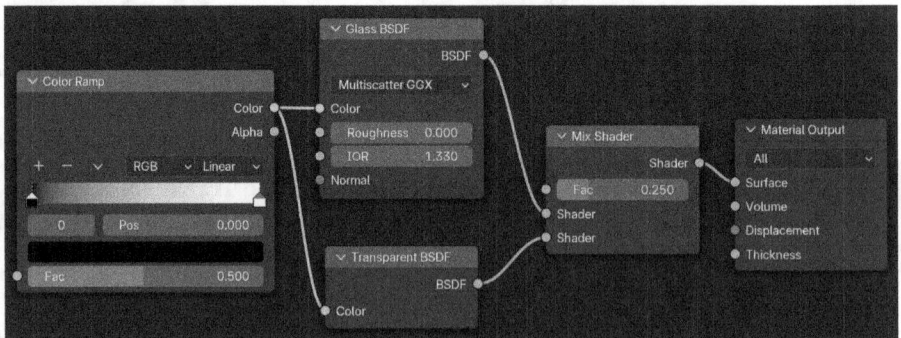

Figure 7.9 – Adding a ColorRamp node and connecting it to Glass BSDF and Transparent BSDF

3. In **ColorRamp**, we need to have *four handles* to work with, so let's add two additional handles by clicking on the **plus (+)** icon. These four handles will be used to match the *ocean blue* color palette shown in *Figure 7.11*.

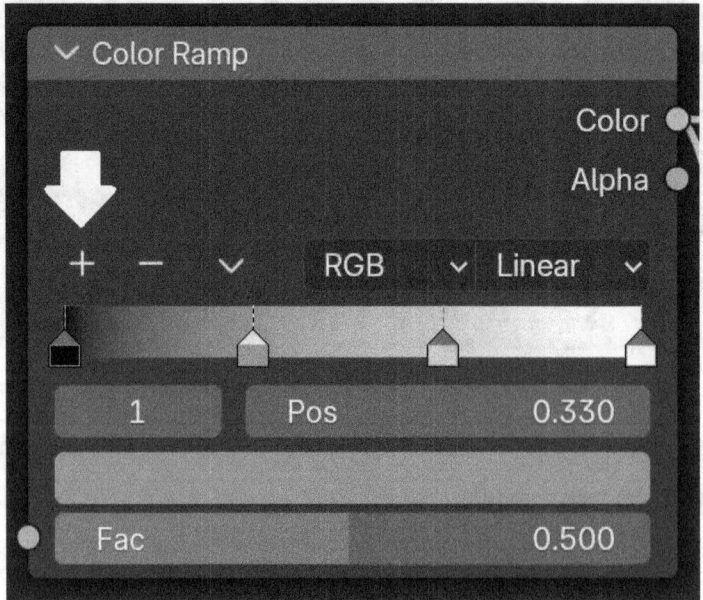

Figure 7.10 – Adding two additional handles to the ColorRamp node

4. Make sure that the distance between the four handles is the same, as shown in *Figure 7.10*.

The next step is to *color our water*. To do that, follow these steps:

1. We'll be using the watercolor palette shown in *Figure 7.11*, which gives us a variety of ocean colors based on how deep the water is.

Figure 7.11 – Ocean blue palette used to create river water

This ocean blue color palette is made up of multiple shades of blue, which include ocean colors, from *dark blue*, which is how the deepest points of the ocean look, to *light gray-blue*, which we see on the surface of the ocean.

We need to feed this ocean blue color palette to our **ColorRamp** node to achieve a photorealistic water shader. So, let's add four blue shades with the color hex codes to our **ColorRamp** node.

> **Note**
>
> Keep in mind that this method is not a real representation of how water works in real life. In fact, the perceived color of water is a complex mix of both refracted and reflected light from the environment. Here, we're just trying to create a nice water shade that looks as realistic as possible in our landscape environment.

2. Select the first handle on the right, click on the bottom *white* color space, and switch to **Hex**, as shown in *Figure 7.12*:

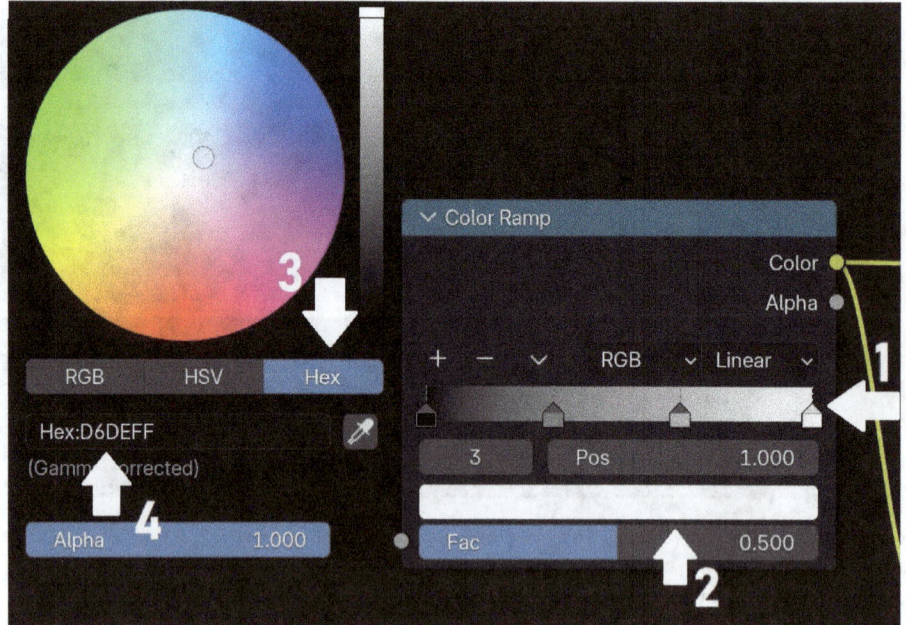

Figure 7.12 – Changing the Hex color code

3. Enter the following **Hex** codes for each of the four handles' colors:

   ○ **Color 1**: Dark blue – #D6DEFF

   ○ **Color 2**: Yale blue – #5E6F82

   ○ **Color 3**: Turquoise blue – #4C6381

   ○ **Color 4**: Light blue – #112945

4. After coloring each of the four handles, this is how the **ColorRamp** node will look:

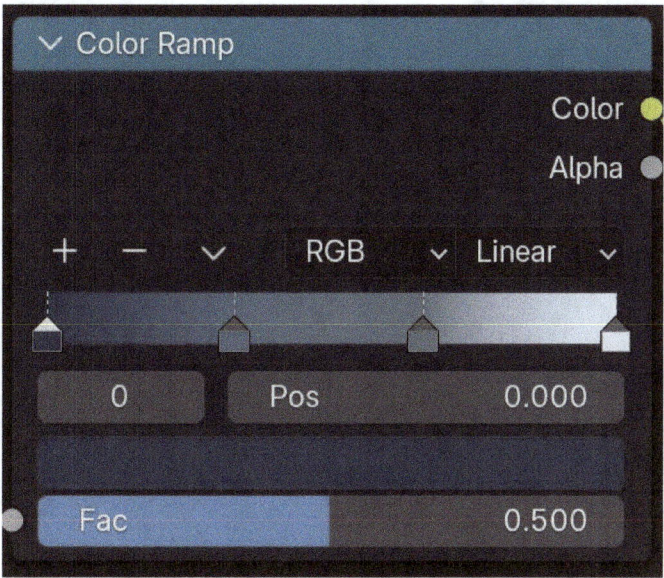

Figure 7.13 – Adding four colors to ColorRamp

5. Now, if we jump into the **Rendered** view by pressing *Z* on the 3D Viewport, we'll see those colors applied to the surface of our water.

Figure 7.14 – A rendered preview of the landscape scene with a river

However, notice that the surface of the water looks 100% flat and smooth. So, now we need to add small waves to make it look like real river water.

Adding waves to the water's surface

To add waves to our water, we need to use the **Noise Texture** node, and here's why. **Noise Texture** provides natural, non-uniform variation, which makes it ideal for breaking up a perfectly flat surface. When used with a **Displace** modifier, it creates organic, wave-like height variation that closely resembles the randomness found in real water surfaces.

Here are the steps:

1. Press *Shift + A* in the **Shader Editor** and search for Noise Texture.

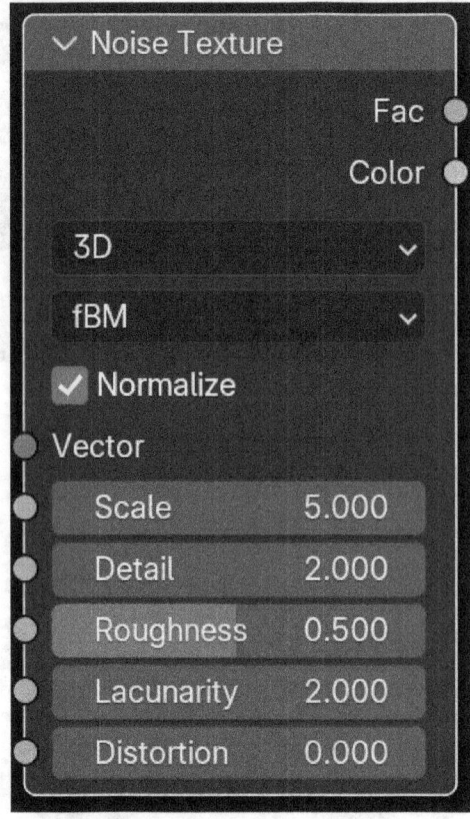

Figure 7.15 – Noise Texture

2. To connect **Noise Texture** to a **Displacement** node, let's search for the Displacement node. The **Displacement** node is used here to control surface shading variation, allowing us to simulate wave depth without actually modifying the mesh geometry.

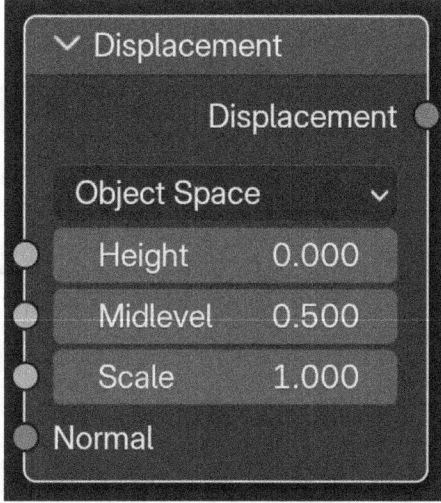

Figure 7.16 – Displacement node

3. Connect the **Fac** slot of **Noise Texture** to the **Height** slot for **Displacement**.

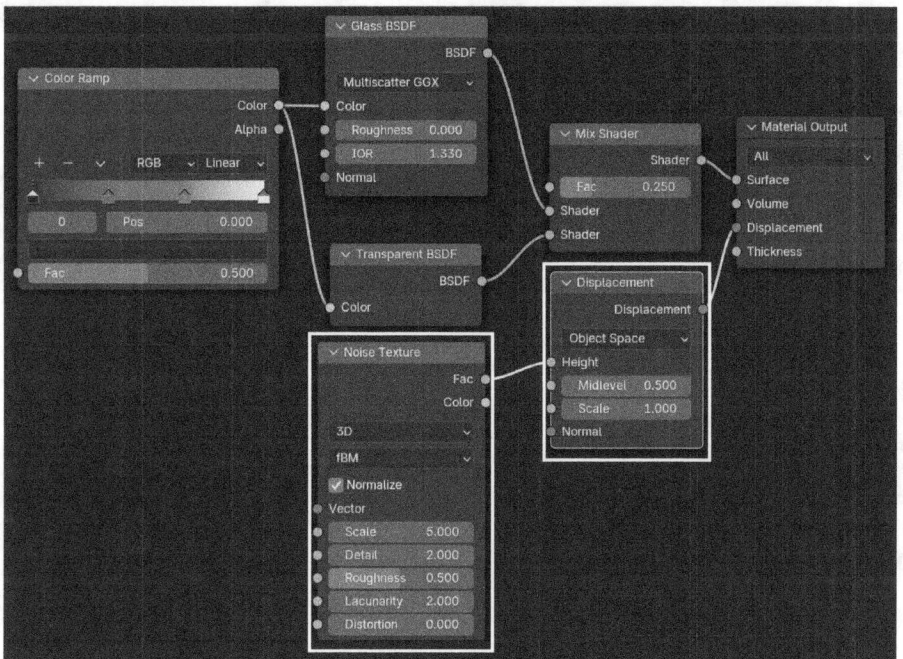

Figure 7.17 – Connecting Noise Texture to the Displacement slot

4. This is the effect the **Noise Texture** node is applying to our water; note that it's strangely warping the surface.

Figure 7.18 – A rendered preview of the landscape scene with a river

The reason the river water looks like in *Figure 7.18* is because of the low noise scale under **Scale** on **Noise Texture**, so we need to increase **Scale** to around 200.000. It might be a different value based on your own setup, so just adjust it accordingly until you have a nice-looking wave effect.

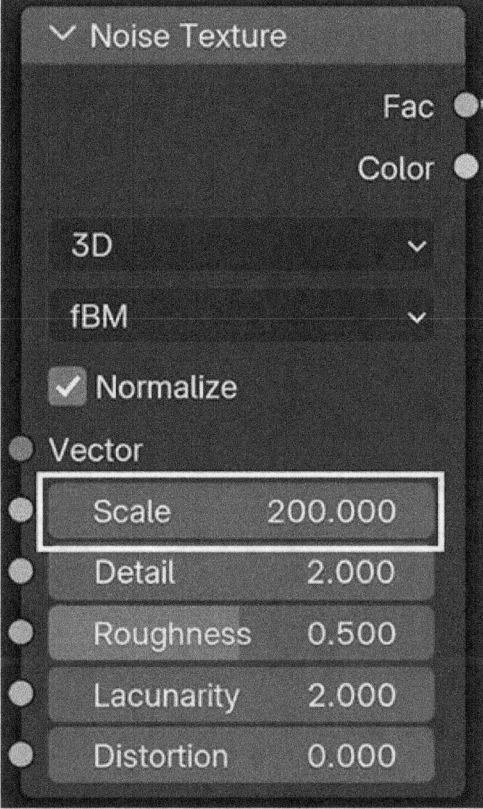

Figure 7.19 – Increasing Scale for Noise Texture

However, the problem is that this noise effect on the surface of the water is too strong; we need to reduce its strength. You can see in *Figure 7.20* that the water waves don't give us a good reflection of the landscape on the water.

Figure 7.20 – A rendered preview of the landscape scene with a river

5. In order to fix this problem, let's reduce the **Scale** value of the **Displacement** node to
`0.100`:

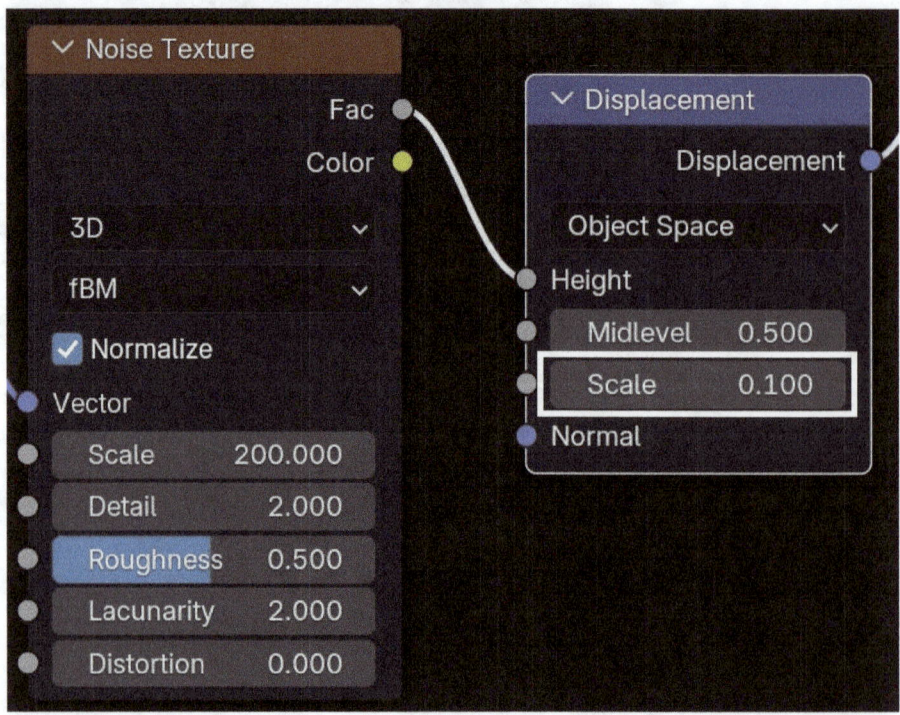

Figure 7.21 – Dropping the Displacement node between Noise Texture and Material Output

> **Note**
>
> In Blender 5, the displacement effect is more pronounced compared to Blender 3, so you may need to lower the scale even further if you're working in Blender 5. Adjust the value gradually until you reach the desired look.

6. Now, let's jump into the Rendered view by pressing *Z* on the 3D Viewport. We'll see those nice waves applied to the surface of our water.

Figure 7.22 – A rendered preview of the landscape scene with a river

Now, this is how our water material looks; it has a subtle wave effect on the surface of it that looks great. However, if we pay attention to the water surface when animating it, the wave effect will be fixed with no water surface movement, which looks unnatural, so we need to animate the waves.

Animating the water flow

We will have a look at a cool trick that will allow us to animate our water surface, making the waves move. The trick is to animate the **Z** value in the **Mapping** node, which moves the texture coordinates over time and creates the illusion of flowing water.

Now, follow these steps:

1. Add **Mapping** and **Texture Coordinate** nodes.
2. Connect the **Generated** slot on the **Texture Coordinate** node to **Vector** on the left side of the **Mapping** node.
3. Connect the right-hand **Vector** slot of the **Mapping** node to **Vector** on **Noise Texture**.

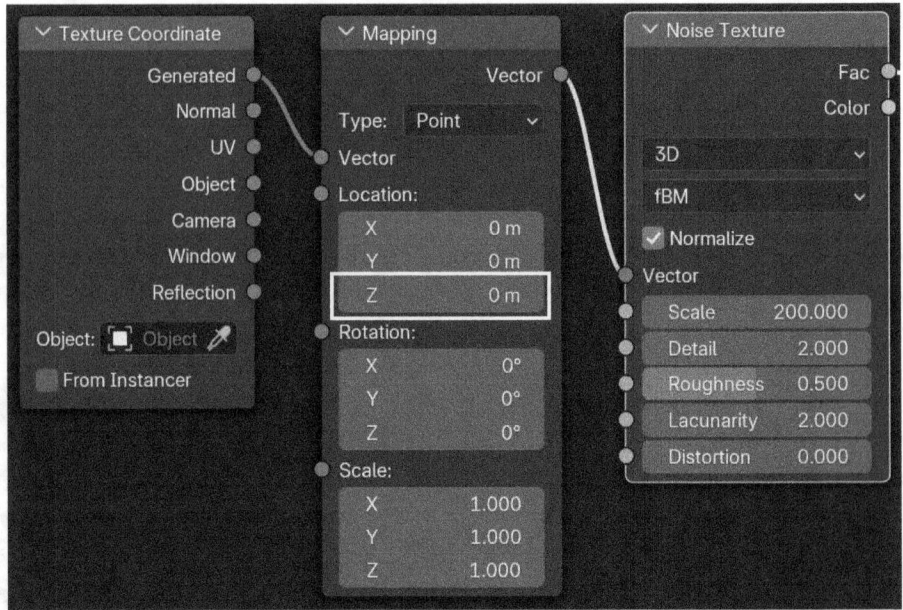

Figure 7.23 – Adding the Mapping and Texture Coordinate nodes to Noise Texture

4. Now, if you change the value of the **Z** location on the **Mapping** node, you will notice that **Noise Texture** is moving.

5. To animate the **Z** location value on **Mapping**, we need access to the Timeline editor, so hover your mouse over the bottom-right window, left-click, and drag upward.

6. This will give you a new duplicated window of the **Shader Editor**. Let's switch it to the Timeline editor and jump into the first frame.

> **Note**
>
> **Timeline** is identified by a **clock** icon; it is used for manipulating keyframes.
> **Keyframes** give specific information about a certain object at a certain time.
> Think of this like a person holding a GPS device and going from place to place,
> from a coffee shop to a restaurant and then to the car parking lot. At each time,
> we can locate their position and write down the time that the person was there.

7. In the Timeline editor, you can see the keyframes as *diamond* shapes. We're not seeing them because we haven't inserted any details about any object. Let's switch from the **Shader Editor** window to **Timeline**, as shown in *Figure 7.24*:

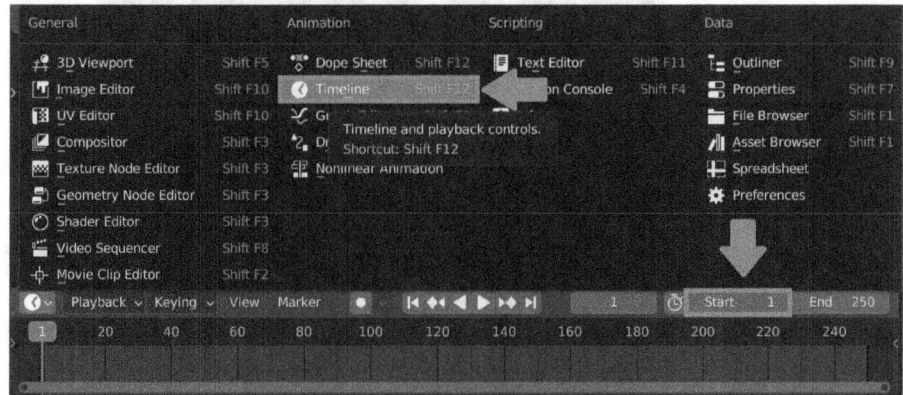

Figure 7.24 – Switching to Timeline

8. Now, go to the **Shader Editor** window, find the **Mapping** node, and right-click on the **Z** location value:

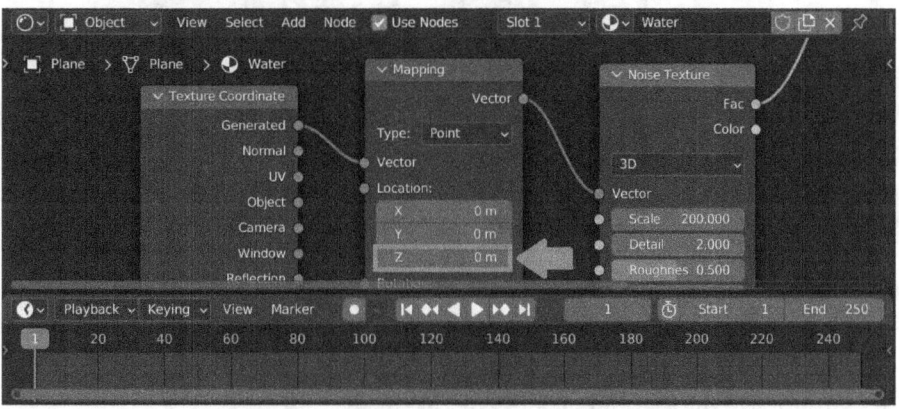

Figure 7.25 – Highlighting the Z location of the Mapping node

9. By right-clicking on the **Z** location value, you will get access to this menu:

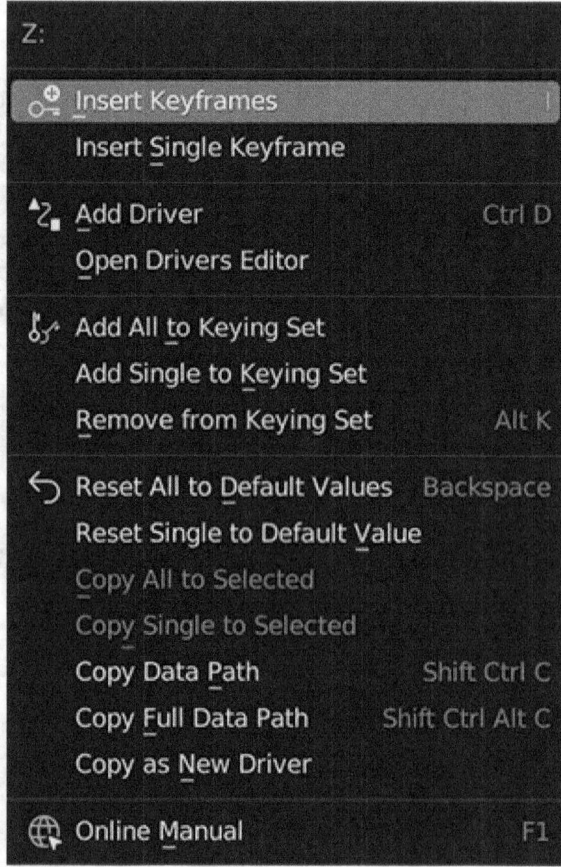

Figure 7.26 – Inserting the keyframes of the Mapping node's Z location

10. Click on **Insert Keyframes** and you will have a new keyframe inserted into the first frame of the Timeline editor. This means that, in the first frame of our animation, the **Z** location of the **Mapping** node is set to **0** m.

11. Immediately, a keyframe will show in the Timeline editor in the form of a *yellow diamond* shape:

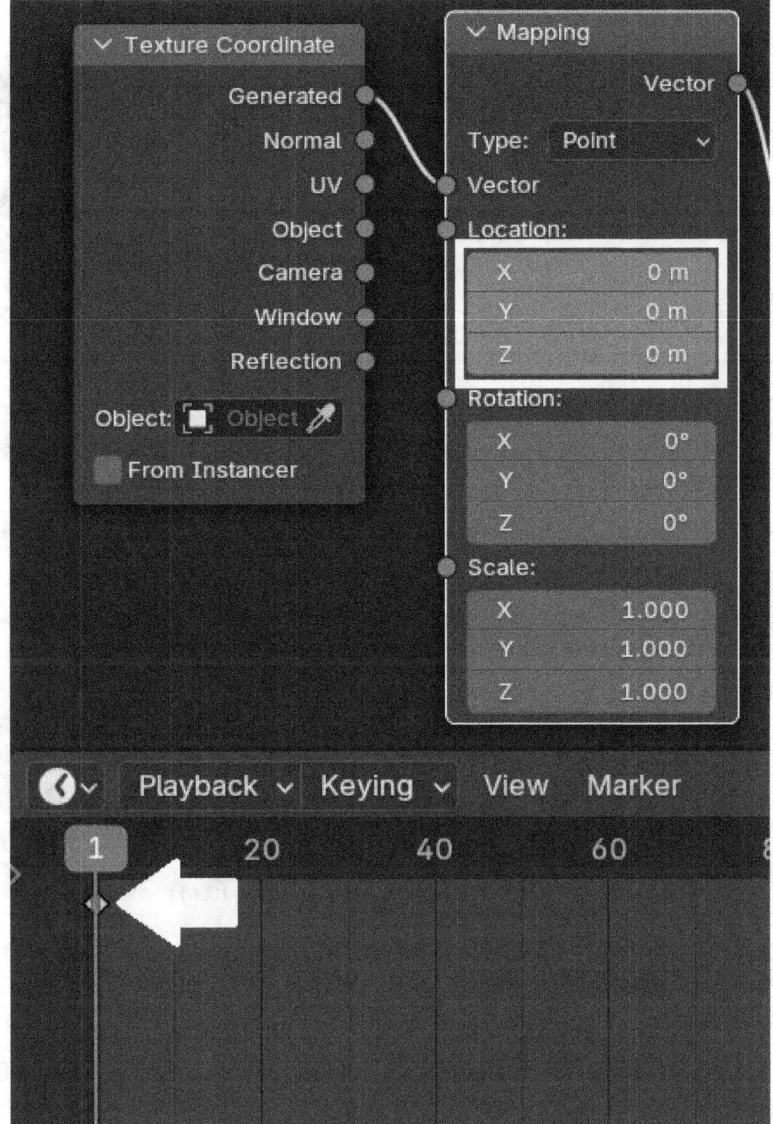

Figure 7.27 – Inserting one keyframe in the first frame on the Timeline editor

If you're not seeing this diamond shape, it means that the plane with the water material isn't selected. Make sure first to select the plane with the water material assigned to it to be able to see the keyframe diamond shape in the Timeline editor.

12. Now, let's jump to frame **100**.

Figure 7.28 – Jumping to frame 100 on the Timeline editor

13. Let's increase the **Z** location of **Mapping** to 1 m by right-clicking on the **Z** location and selecting **Insert Keyframes**.

14. Now, we have inserted two keyframes:

    ○ The *first keyframe* is on frame **1**; it has the **Z** value of the **Mapping** node set to **0** meters

    ○ The *second keyframe* is on frame **100**; it has the **Z** value of the **Mapping** node set to **1** meter

15. Once you have inserted both keyframes, the Timeline editor will have *two diamond shapes* for keyframes **1** and **100**, as shown in *Figure 7.29*:

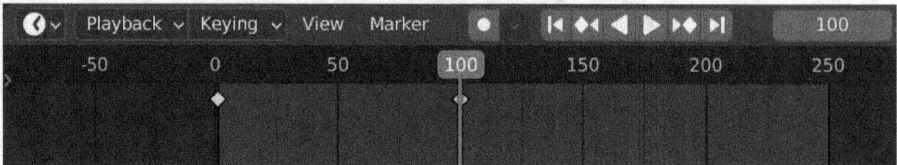

Figure 7.29 – Inserting the second keyframe into the 100th frame on the Timeline editor

In general, the keyframes contribute to the actual time. In the **Output Properties** tab, we have a setting called **Frame Rate** – this controls how timeline frame numbers relate to actual time.

By default, we have **Frame Rate** set to **24 fps**, meaning that we have 24 frames per second.

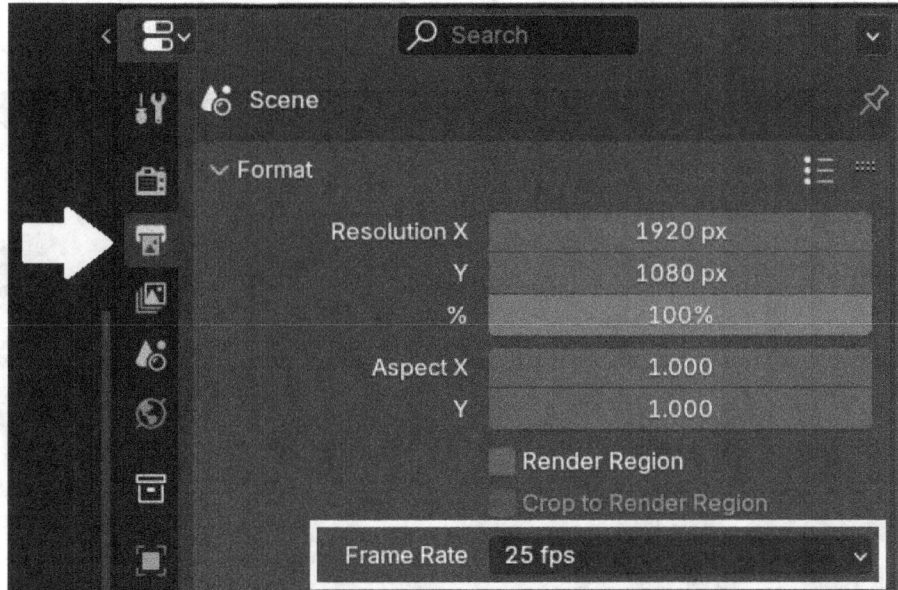

Figure 7.30 – Checking Frame Rate under Output Properties

So, in our example, we're moving the water surface waves by 1 meter at a time interval of 4 seconds (100 frames divided by 25 fps). The water animation will stop at frame **100**, but how can we make it cyclic and continuous? Let's figure that out in the next section.

Creating a continuously looping animation

The last thing to do is to make our wave movement continuous. So far, it stops at frame **100**, which means that at frame **100**, or 4 seconds after playing the animation, the water will freeze again.

To make this animation cyclic, press *Shift + E* on the Timeline editor and select **Make Cyclic (F-Modifier)**:

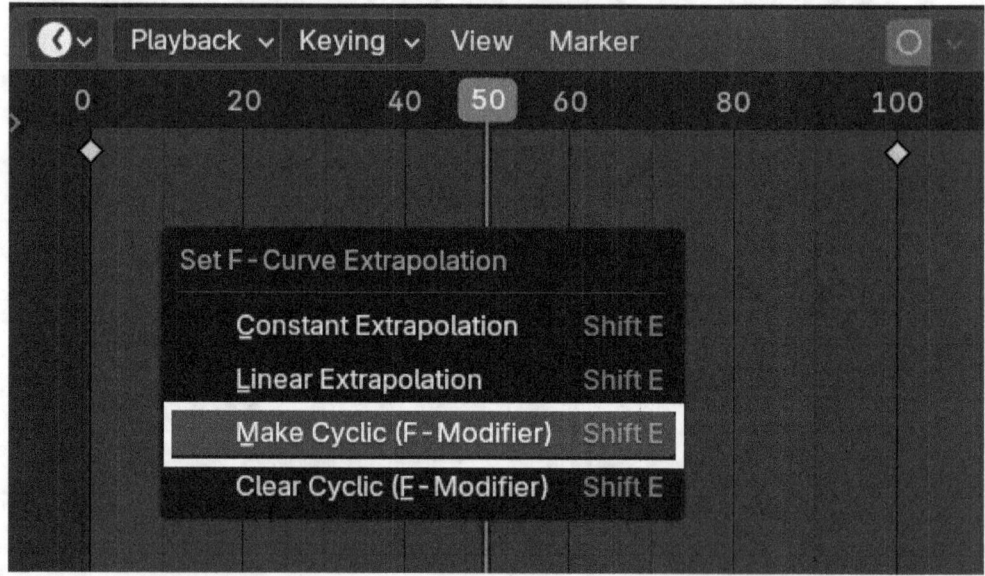

Figure 7.31 – Making the animation cyclic by pressing Shift + E on the Timeline editor

Basically, that's it. Our animation is now cyclic. We can press the **play** icon at the top right of the Timeline editor to play the animation.

Summary

In this chapter, we went through the process of creating a realistic water shader and applying it to our river. We learned how to mix between the **Glass BSDF** and **Transparent BSDF** nodes to create a nice reflective and refractive surface. Then, we added a subtle wave effect on the surface of the water using **Noise Texture**. Finally, we learned how to animate the waves on the surface by inserting keyframes into the Timeline editor.

In the next chapter, we'll improve the texture of our landscape by using the mud texture. We will learn to use Blender's node editor to create customizable procedural textures from scratch.

Get this book's PDF version and more

Scan the QR code (or go to packtpub.com/unlock). Search for this book by name, confirm the edition, and then follow the steps on the page.

Note: Keep your invoice handy. Purchases made directly from Packt don't require an invoice.

8

Creating Procedural Mud Material

In this chapter, we will be creating a realistic mud material using procedural texturing and using it to texture the bottom of the landscape that we created in *Chapter 6*. You will learn how to create and combine many different layers of details, such as adding water puddles and mud details, and combining all these details into one complex, realistic result.

Gaining proficiency in procedural texturing is a crucial skill for any environment artist. Unlike traditional image textures, which can suffer from resolution limits and visible repetition, procedural materials are mathematically generated. This means they are seamless, infinitely scalable, and fully customizable. By learning how to layer these nodes effectively, you are not just creating mud; you are understanding the logic behind Blender's shader system, building materials from scratch.

We will tap into the unlimited potential of Blender's powerful node editor and learn how to create advanced and highly customizable procedural textures from scratch. We will learn how to keep our node setup organized and easy to use.

In this chapter, we'll be covering the following topics:

- Creating a realistic mud material using procedural texturing in Blender
- Organizing the node setup using the **Frame** node
- Creating procedural soil for the mud material
- Mixing soil with water puddles
- Adding mud details
- Setting good lighting in our scene

Technical requirements

This chapter requires a system capable of running **Blender version 5.0** or above (Windows, macOS, or Linux).

If you want to skip the mud material creation workflow, you can download the final material from the GitHub repository: `https://github.com/PacktPublishing/3D-Environment-Design-with-Blender-5-Second-Edition/blob/main/chapter-8/Procedural-Mud-Material.blend`.

Creating a realistic mud material using procedural texturing in Blender

We'll create the mud material using procedural texturing in Blender – but first, we need to understand the nature of mud. If we break down mud, we will find that it is a combination of soil and stones, and everything is mixed with water. So, these are the elements that we will be creating procedurally in Blender:

- Water puddles
- Soil

To keep you motivated, *Figure 8.1* shows the final result that you'll have by the end of this chapter:

Figure 8.1 – The final result of the mud material that you will achieve

I promise you'll master handling nodes by the end of this chapter, but if procedural texturing doesn't spark your interest, feel free to grab the final Blender file from this GitHub link and jump ahead to the next chapter:

https://github.com/PacktPublishing/3D-Environment-Design-with-Blender-5-Second-Edition/blob/main/chapter-8/Procedural-Mud-Material.blend

If you've chosen to stick around, let's dive in and create our mud material together!

Creating the mud material

To create the mud material, let's launch a new Blender scene and add a sphere object by pressing *Shift + A* and choosing **Sphere**.

The **Sphere** object itself is not part of our landscape project; it's simply used to showcase the mud material. We'll remove it later once we apply the mud to the landscape.

By default, the **Sphere** object's edges will be visible, so we need to smooth the object out. To smooth the mesh and hide the edge lines, right-click on the sphere and choose **Shade Smooth**, as you can see in *Figure 8.2*.

With the **Sphere** object selected, go to **Material Properties** and add a new material and name it Mud:

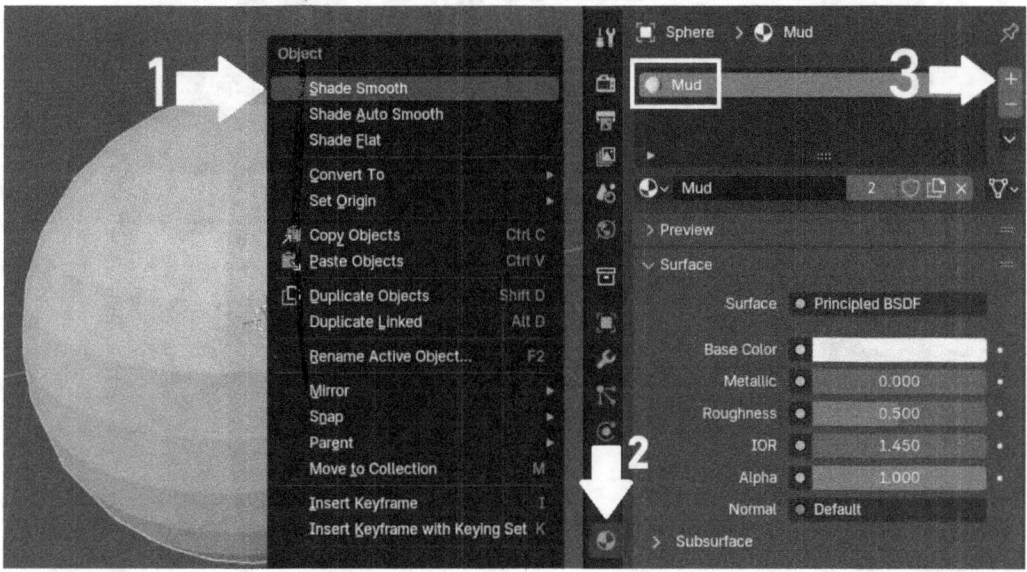

Figure 8.2 – Using Shade Smooth on the Sphere object and adding a material called Mud

Next, let's start working on the mud material. With the **Sphere** object selected, click on the **Shading** tab at the top of the Blender interface (see *Figure 8.3*). This workspace is pre-configured for texturing and automatically gives us a large **Shader Editor** window.

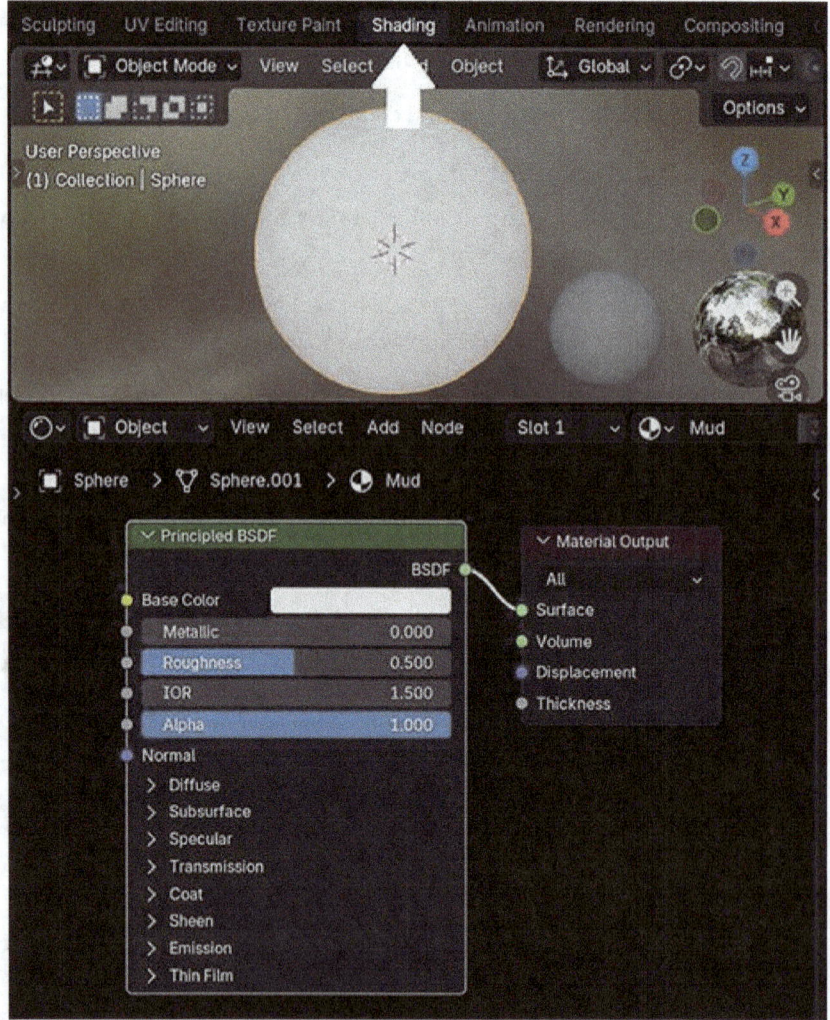

Figure 8.3 – The Principled BSDF and Material Output nodes

By default, you will have the **Principled BSDF** node connected to **Material Output**, as shown in *Figure 8.3*.

Now that we have created our material and assigned it to the **Sphere** object, let's start with the first step of creating the mud material, which is adding water puddles.

Creating water puddles for the mud material

To create water puddles, we will use a combination of procedural Blender nodes to simulate the natural appearance of water puddles. Here's how we can achieve this water puddles effect step by step:

1. Add **Noise Texture**. This node will serve as the base for creating the puddle surface:

    1. In the **Shader Editor**, press *Shift + A* and search for Noise Texture.

    2. Increase the **Detail** value of **Noise Texture** to 7.5. This adds finer details, making the texture look more realistic.

2. Add a **ColorRamp** node. The **ColorRamp** node is a converter that will help us control the contrast of **Noise Texture** and define the puddle areas more precisely:

    1. Press *Shift + A* and search for ColorRamp.

    2. Connect **Noise Texture**'s left **Fac** slot to **ColorRamp**'s right **Fac** slot, as shown in *Figure 8.4*.

3. Adjust the **ColorRamp** node handles. By default, we have two handles in the **ColorRamp** node. Adjusting the position of the handles will allow us to control the contrast between the water and the surrounding surface:

    1. Select the *white* handle, which represents the lighter areas in the **Noise Texture** node, and set its position (the **Pos** value) to 0.4.

    2. Select the *black* handle, which represents the darker areas in **Noise Texture**, and set its position value to 0.6.

    This is how the node setup will look:

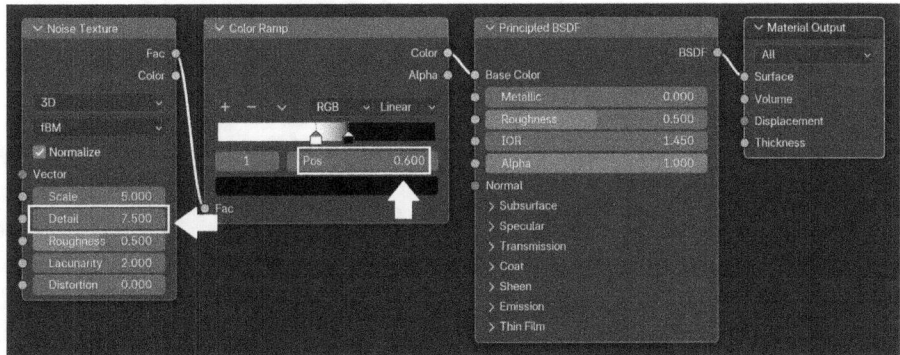

Figure 8.4 – Connecting Noise Texture to the ColorRamp node

4. Change the color of the *black* handle to *light gray* by setting the **V** value to 0.18.

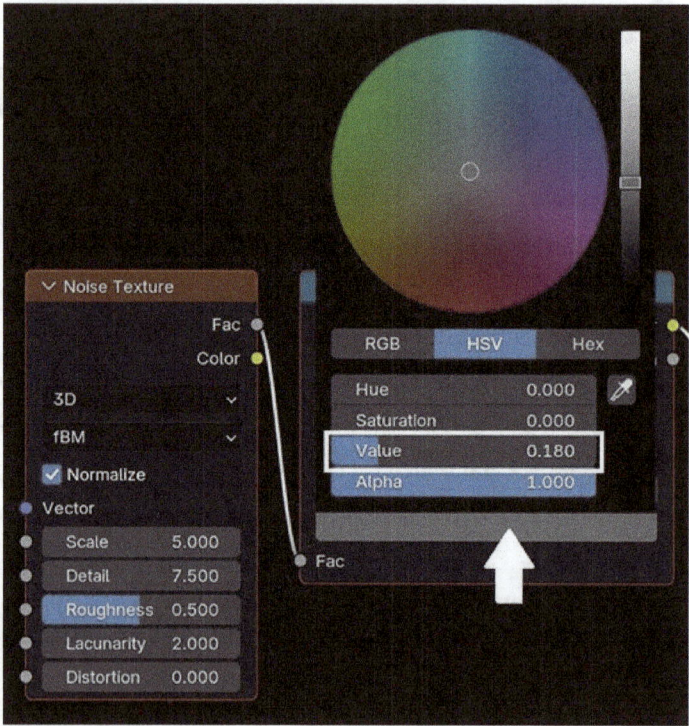

Figure 8.5 – Changing the color of the ColorRamp handles

To help you understand the role of the **ColorRamp** node that we added, let's look at *Figure 8.6*:

- On the left side, you'll see the **Noise Texture** node applied alone, without **ColorRamp**, which is just irregular noisy patterns

- On the right, we have the **Noise Texture** node with **ColorRamp** applied; it darkens the areas where the water will form

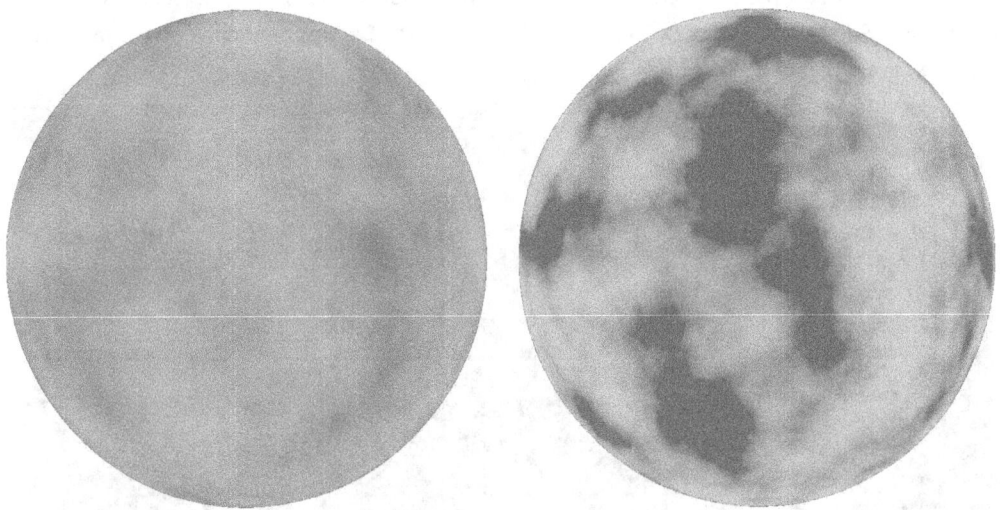

Figure 8.6 – Difference between using and not using the ColorRamp node

As you can see, the **ColorRamp** node is crucial for defining the puddles. I recommend experimenting with the **ColorRamp** handles to better understand how they affect the contrast. The *black* spots that appear represent the water surfaces in the final result.

For now, before we proceed with more details and make our node setup large and *seemingly* confusing, we need to find a way to organize our node setup. So, let's learn about the **Frame** node.

Organizing the node setup using the Frame node

Frame is used for organizing nodes by collecting related nodes together in a common area. You can give this area a specific name and a particular color to make it different from the other frames.

To keep our node setup organized, we'll put the water puddle nodes that we created inside a **Frame** node. So, in the **Shader Editor**, press *Shift + A*, go to **Layout**, and click on **Frame**. You will get a small, empty *black* frame:

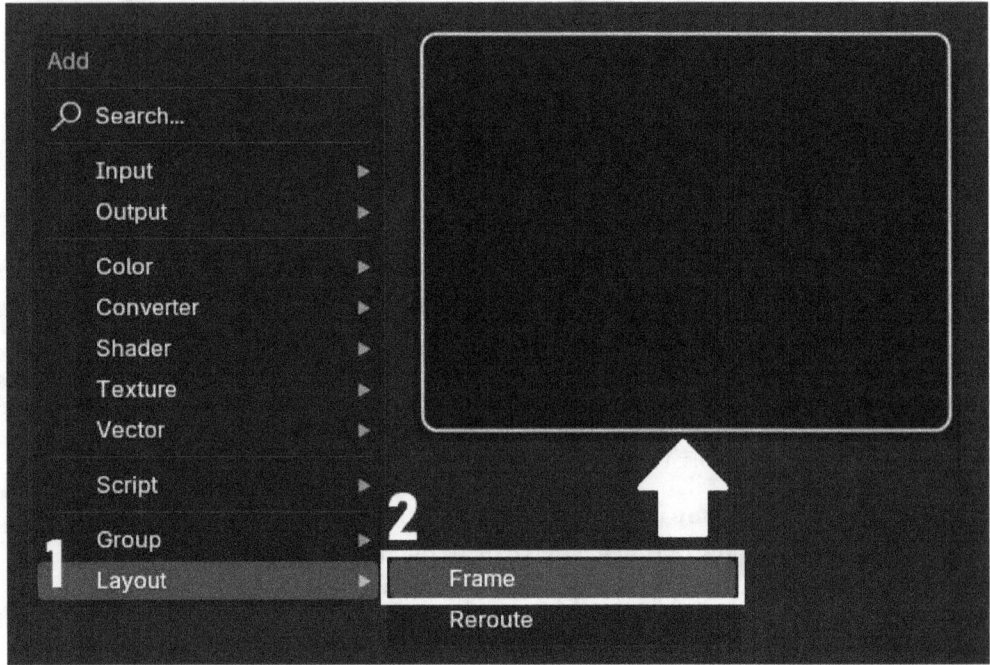

Figure 8.7 – Adding a Frame node to organize the mud node setup

Now, let's select the **Noise Texture** and **ColorRamp** nodes and drag them inside the frame by pressing *G*.

We can also change the label name on the top of our frame by pressing *N* to access the left panel and changing the **Label** text to Water Puddles, or anything you want:

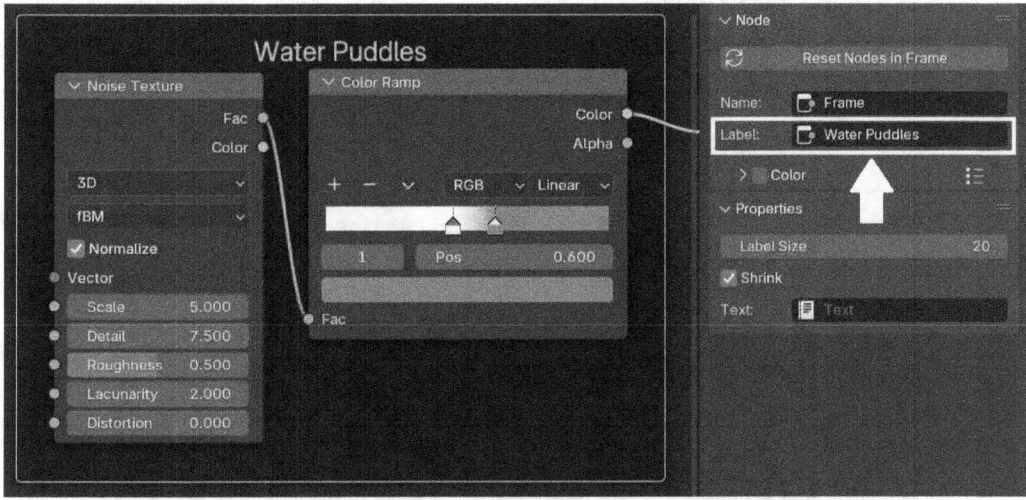

Figure 8.8 – Putting Noise Texture and ColorRamp inside a frame and calling it "Water Puddles"

By default, the **Shrink** option is enabled (see the right panel in *Figure 8.8*), which forces the frame to wrap tightly around your nodes. If you plan to add more nodes later, uncheck **Shrink**. This allows you to manually resize the frame and organize your nodes more freely.

Now that we have organized the water puddle nodes inside a **Frame** node, let's add soil details to our mud material.

Creating procedural soil for the mud material

To add soil to the mud material, we'll follow a similar approach to the water puddles, but with different settings:

1. Start by adding a new **Noise Texture** node.

2. Increase the **Scale** value to 5 and set **Detail** to 7 for a more complex texture.

3. Adjust the **Roughness** value to 1 for sharper variations, which will help define the stone shapes more clearly.

4. Next, connect this **Noise Texture** node to a new **ColorRamp** node and apply these settings to the **ColorRamp** node:

   ○ Change the *black* handle's position (**Pos**) to 0.250.

   ○ Reduce its **Value** strength to 0.135. This adjustment will control the contrast and intensity of the soil's appearance.

5. Finally, group these nodes into a new frame and label it Soil (see *Figure 8.9*). This will help organize your workspace and keep the setup clear.

Figure 8.9 – Putting Noise Texture and ColorRamp inside a frame and calling it "Soil"

Now, let's bring together the **Water Puddles** and **Soil** frames by blending them with a **Mix Color** node to create a seamless transition between the two textures.

Mixing soil with water puddles

To combine the water puddles and soil, we'll use a **Mix Color** node in the **Shader Editor**. Follow these steps:

1. Start by adding the **Mix Color** node (it may appear as **Mix** in the node search). This is how the **Mix Color** node looks:

Figure 8.10 – Mix Color (Mix) node

The **Mix Color** node blends two colors or textures based on a selected mix type. It has two inputs, **A** and **B**, and a **Factor** (**Fac**) option that controls the blending ratio.

2. To mix the water puddles and soil, connect the **ColorRamp** node for the water puddles to input **A** of the **Mix Color** node. Then, connect the **ColorRamp** node for the soil to input **B**, as shown in *Figure 8.11*.

   This will allow the two textures to blend, with the water puddles and soil combining based on their respective settings. The **Mix Color** node will control how they interact, allowing us to achieve a seamless transition between the two.

3. Set the mixing type of the **Mix Color** node to **Multiply** to blend the two textures effectively.

4. Adjust the mixing amount to 0.85. This setting ensures that 85% of the texture will consist of water puddles, while 15% will be made up of soil, creating a natural combination of both elements.

You can see the node setup in *Figure 8.11*:

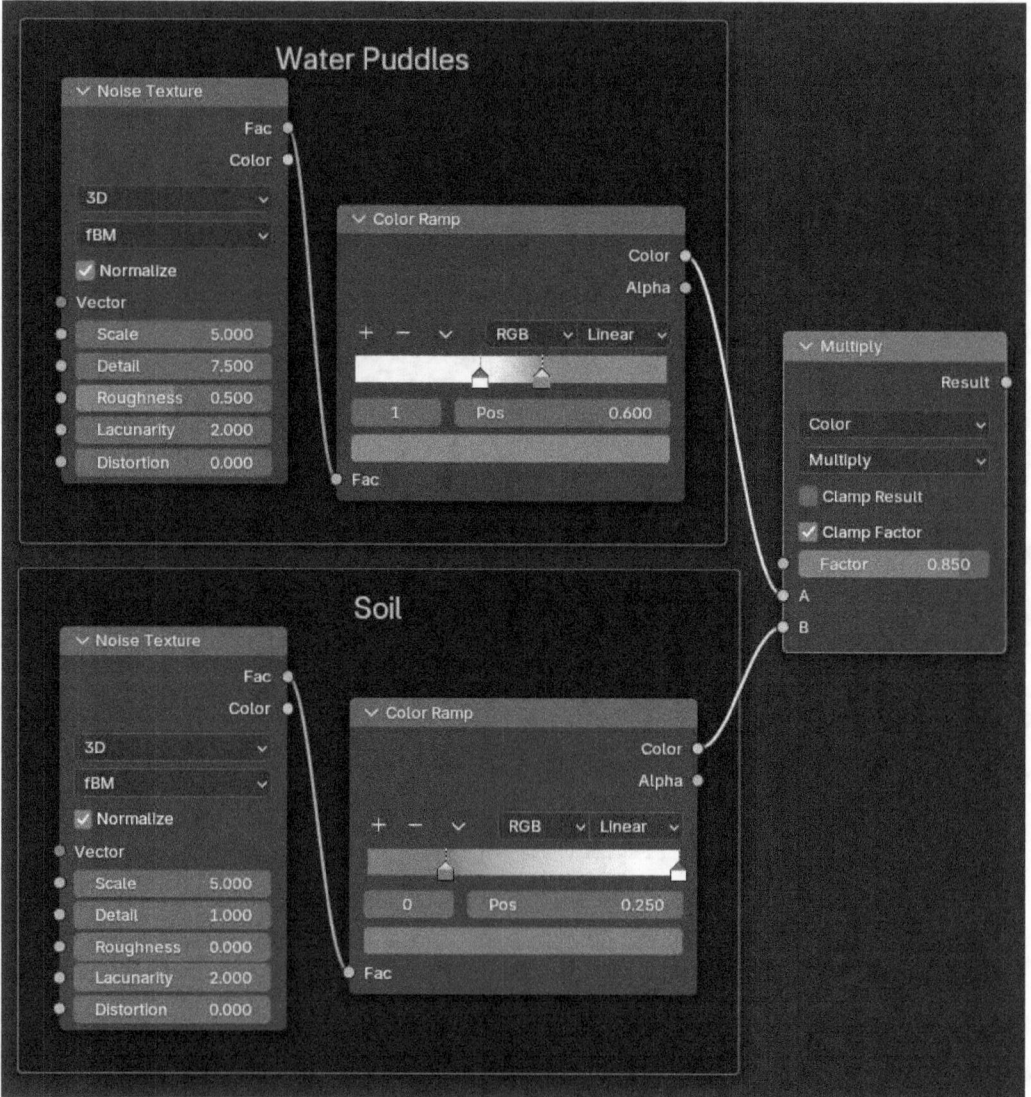

Figure 8.11 – Mixing water puddles with soil using the Mix Color node

Now that we've combined the water puddles and soil elements, we're ready to add more details to our mud material to enhance its natural look.

Adding mud details

If we check the current material in the 3D Viewport, we'll notice some smooth, empty areas that lack texture. This is annotated in the following figure:

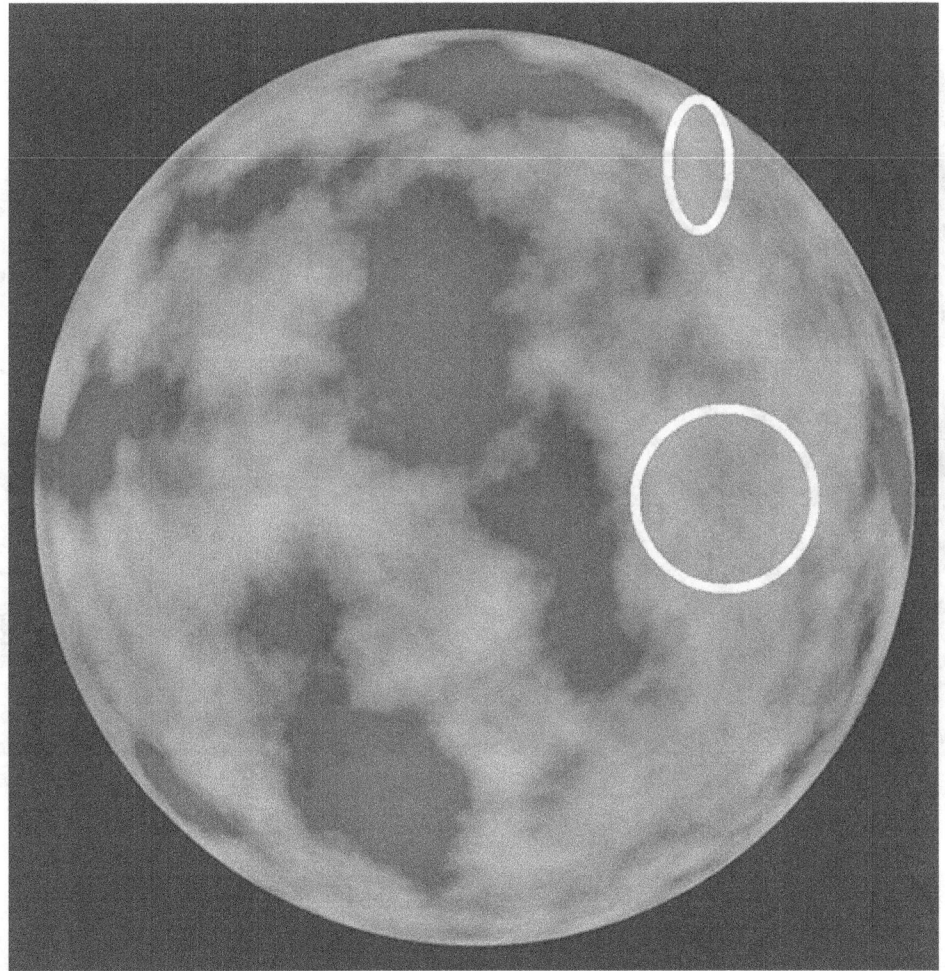

Figure 8.12 – Highlighting empty surfaces in the mud material

But in real mud, there are no smooth, featureless surfaces; everything has some level of detail. We need to fill these areas with some noisy details. To do that, we'll be using a new **Noise Texture** node, so press *Shift + A* and add **Noise Texture**. Then, follow these steps:

1. Set the **Noise Texture** node to the following:

   ○ Change **Scale** to 1.5

- Increase the **Detail** value to 7.5

- Increase **Roughness** to 0.7

2. Now, we need to mix the **Water Puddles** and **Soil** node setup with this new **Noise Texture** node. So, let's add a new **Mix Color** node and set it to the following:

- Keep the mixing type as **Multiply**

- Set the mixing value to 0.85

You can see the node setup in the following figure:

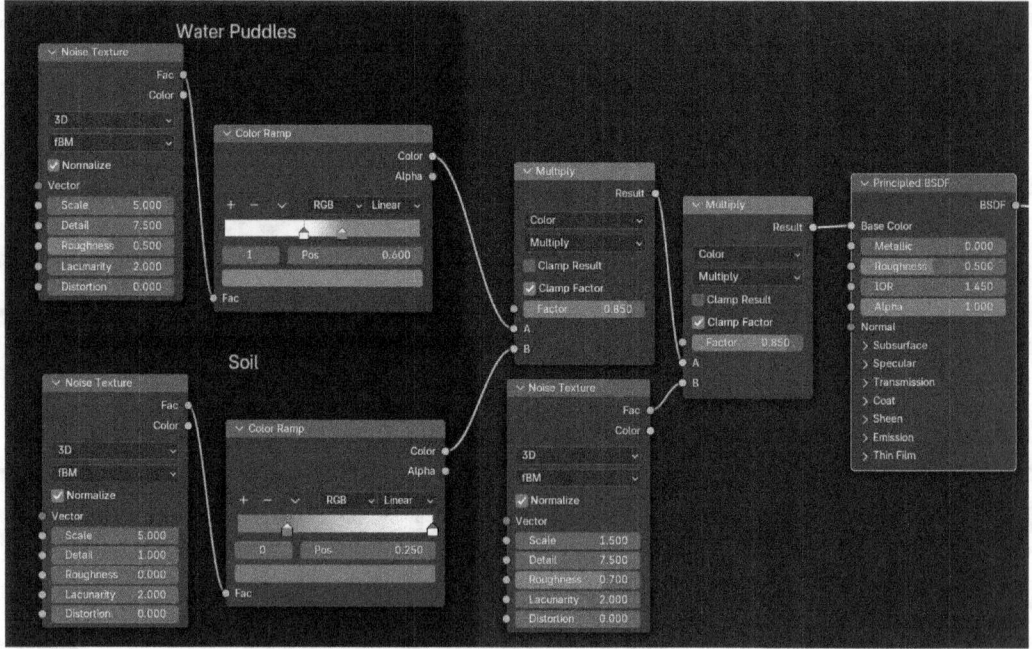

Figure 8.13 – Water puddles node setup applied to the sphere

This step may seem like it does nothing to the mud at first, but it actually plays a crucial role in adding subtle details (noise details that help remove empty flat surfaces) that significantly enhance the realism of the final result. You'll see the difference later when the details start to come together.

At this stage, our node setup represents the core structure of the mud material. We'll now build upon this foundation to add essential details such as the mud color, reflections, roughness, and displacement. Let's begin by focusing on the mud color to establish a strong base for the material.

Adding color to the mud material

To create the mud color, we need to understand its nature. Mud isn't just a flat brown color. It's made up of various shades due to different soil types, moisture content, and lighting.

To simulate the brownish mud color more realistically, let's add a **ColorRamp** node and use three colors instead of just two. By incorporating a third color, we can introduce more variation into the mud's appearance, which makes it look more natural.

To add the third handle to **ColorRamp**, you can click on the plus (**+**) sign, as shown in *Figure 8.14*:

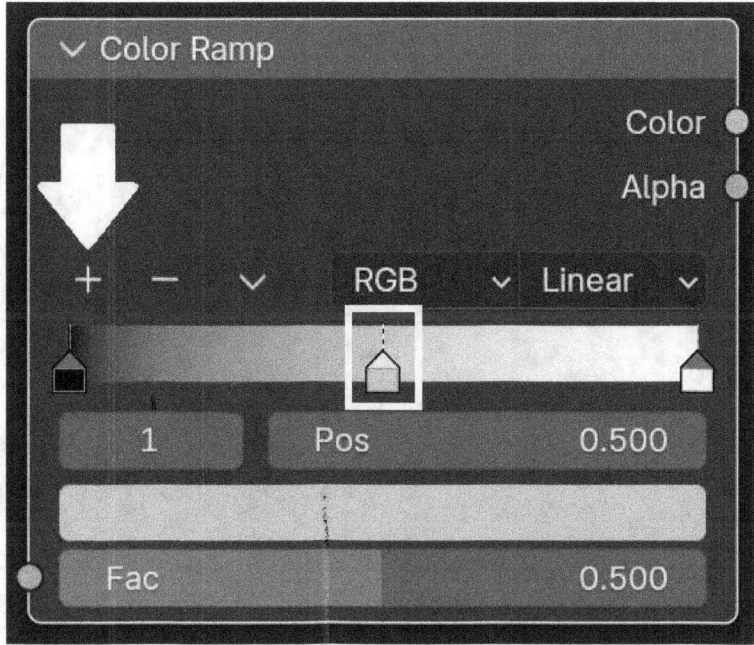

Figure 8.14 – Adding a third handle to the ColorRamp node

Now, follow these steps, shown in *Figure 8.15*:

1. Select the first handle on the left side of **ColorRamp**. Click on the handle color, as shown on the right side of *Figure 8.15*, and change the following values:

    ◦ **Hue**: 0.15

    ◦ **Saturation**: 0.2

    ◦ **Value**: 0.1

2. Next, select the second handle, change the **Pos** value to 0.225, and set the handle color to the following values:

- **Hue**: 0.03
- **Saturation**: 0.6
- **Value**: 0.03

3. For the third handle, set the **Pos** value to 0.3, and the handle color details to the following:

- **Hue**: 0.1
- **Saturation**: 0.3
- **Value**: 0.1

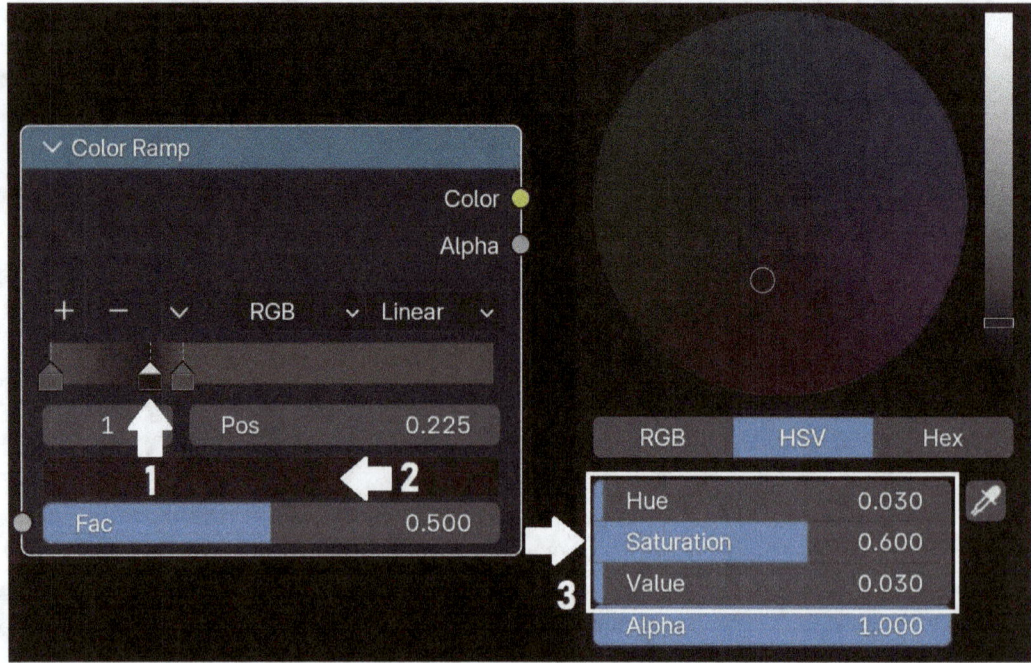

Figure 8.15 – Changing ColorRamp node handle colors

We adjusted the **Hue**, **Saturation**, **Value** (HSV), and **Pos** (position) values of the **ColorRamp** handles to create realistic variations in mud color. Let's understand these parameters in more detail:

- **Hue** changes the color itself, such as brown or reddish tones
- **Saturation** controls the intensity of the color, with lower values for more muted shades
- **Value** adjusts the brightness, with darker values for a more earthy look
- **Pos** sets the handle's position along **ColorRamp**, controlling color transitions

These adjustments give the mud a natural, varied appearance by simulating different shades found in real-world mud.

Now, let's connect the last **Mix Color (Multiply)** node to the left slot of the **Fac** slot of the **ColorRamp** node we created in *Figure 8.15*, and connect the right **Color** slot of the **ColorRamp** node to **Principled BDSF**'s **Base Color** slot, as follows:

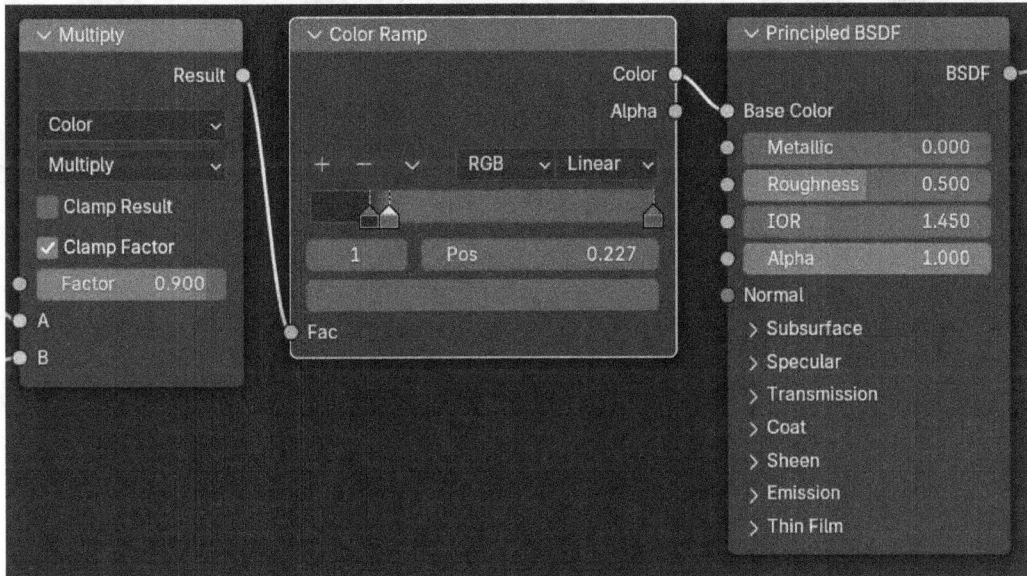

Figure 8.16 – Connecting MixColor (Multiply) to the ColorRamp node

If you want to see the entire node setup, this is how it looks:

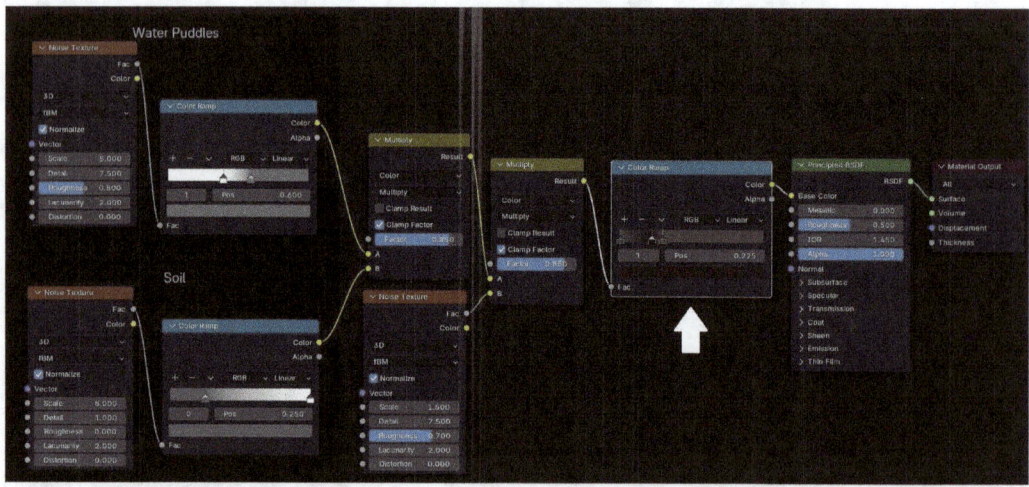

Figure 8.17 – Full mud material node setup shown for reference (the node text is not intended to be read)

This is how our material will look when we connect **ColorRamp** to the **Base Color** slot of **Principled BSDF**:

Figure 8.18 – Adding color to the mud material

Now that we have the mud material color, the next step is to work on the material reflection, which involves the roughness map.

Adding reflection to the mud material

We need to make the water puddles reflective to light, while the mud spots need to be less reflective. To achieve this goal, let's add another **ColorRamp** node and set it to the following:

1. Select the first *black* handle and set the **Pos** value to 0.1.

2. For the second *white* handle, change its **Pos** value to 0.2, click on its color, and change the **V** value to 0.6 to make the *white* color look *gray*. This is how the **ColorRamp** node should look:

Figure 8.19 – ColorRamp node used for adding reflection to the mud material

Here, we're handling **ColorRamp** to control the roughness of the mud material. Roughness determines how shiny or rough a surface appears when it interacts with light. Since water puddles are typically reflective and smooth, we want them to have low roughness (the *black* handle), while the mud spots should appear rougher and less shiny (the *gray* handle).

Now, let's connect the last **Mix Color** node to the left slot of this **ColorRamp** node, and connect the right **Color** slot of the **ColorRamp** node to **Principled BDSF's Roughness** slot, as follows:

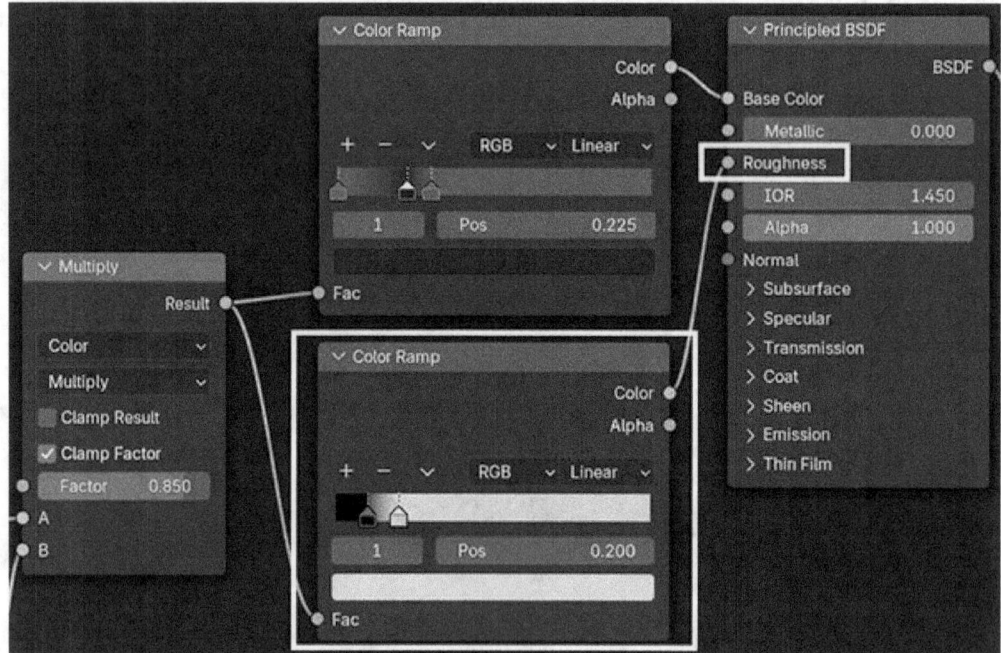

Figure 8.20 – Connecting ColorRamp to the Roughness slot of Principled BSDF

This is how our material will look once we've applied the roughness adjustments. By controlling the roughness with **ColorRamp**, we've created a surface that better represents the realistic behavior of mud and water.

We now have the mud color with the right reflection (roughness), distinguishing the water puddles from the mud. But the surface of the mud material is smooth.

Figure 8.21 – Adding reflection to the mud material

Hence, the next step is to add bump details, which will make the material look more three-dimensional without using real geometry.

Adding bumps to the mud material

Bump mapping simulates surface detail without adding extra geometry. It works by altering how light interacts with the surface, creating the illusion of bumps and wrinkles.

To add mud bumps, we'll be using a new node called **Bump**. Let's search for this **Bump** node in the **Shader Editor**. This is how it looks:

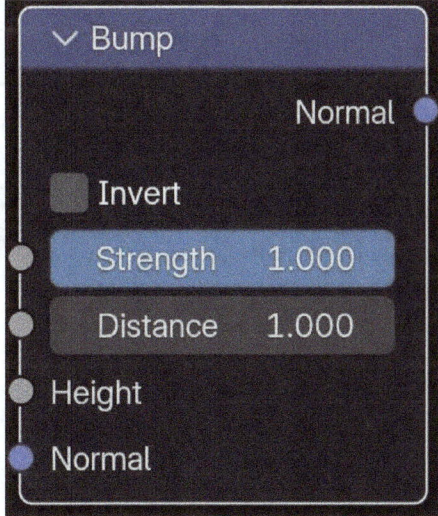

Figure 8.22 – The Bump node

To control this **Bump** node, we'll need a **ColorRamp** node connected to it. Let's add a
ColorRamp node and configure the following settings:

1. Select the first *black* handle and set its **Pos** value to 0.15.

2. For the second handle, change the **Pos** value to 0.5 and its **V** color value to 0.6.

Now, let's connect the last **Mix Color** node to the left-hand side of this **ColorRamp** node, and
connect the right-hand side of the **ColorRamp** node to the **Bump** node's **Height** slot, as
follows:

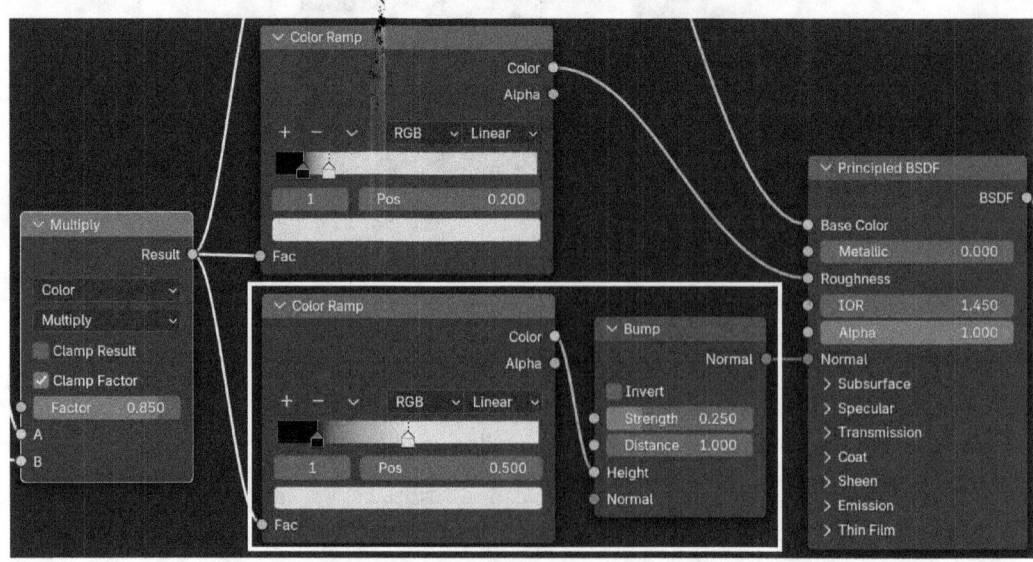

Figure 8.23 – Connecting ColorRamp to the Bump node

Make sure to connect the **Bump** node's right **Normal** slot to the **Normal** slot of **Principled
BSDF**, and reduce the **Strength** value of the **Bump** node to 0.25 to generate subtle bumps.
Now, if we go back to the 3D Viewport, this is how our material looks:

Figure 8.24 – Adding bumps to the mud material

Alright, we've added the bumps to our mud material. The next step would be to apply a displacement map for real geometry details.

However, it's important to note that this step is not necessary for our project. Displacement maps can significantly impact performance and rendering time because they modify the actual geometry of the surface.

For this project, sticking with bumps is a more efficient way to achieve the desired detail without overloading the system. But understanding how displacement works is still valuable for your knowledge and future projects where high-detail geometry is needed.

Adding displacement to the mud material

Displacement mapping allows a texture to manipulate the position of vertices on rendered geometry. Unlike normal or bump mapping, where the shading is distorted to give the illusion of bumps, displacement maps create real bumps.

To add displacement details, first, we need to switch the render engine to **Cycles**. You can do that by accessing **Render Properties** in the right-hand panel, as shown in *Figure 8.25*:

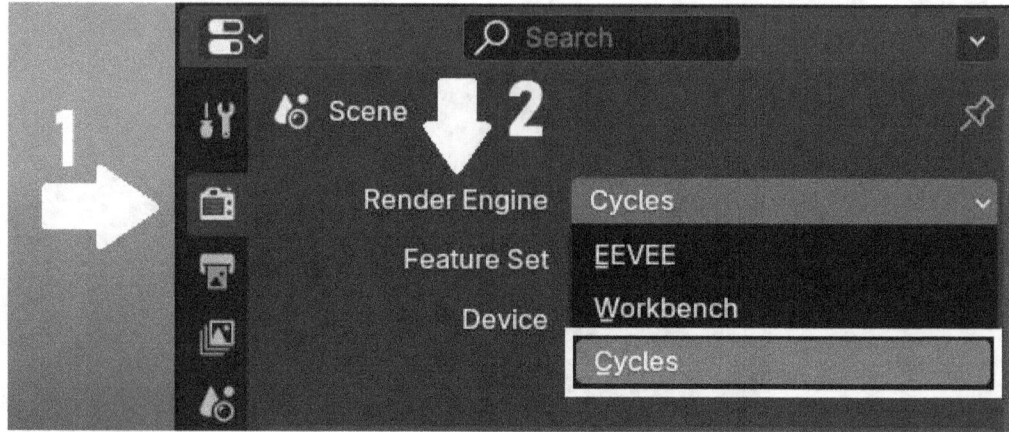

Figure 8.25 – Switching the render engine to Cycles

Next, with the sphere selected, go to **Material Properties** and scroll down to **Settings**. On the **Surface** tab, you'll find **Displacement**. Click on it and change it to **Displacement and Bump**, as follows:

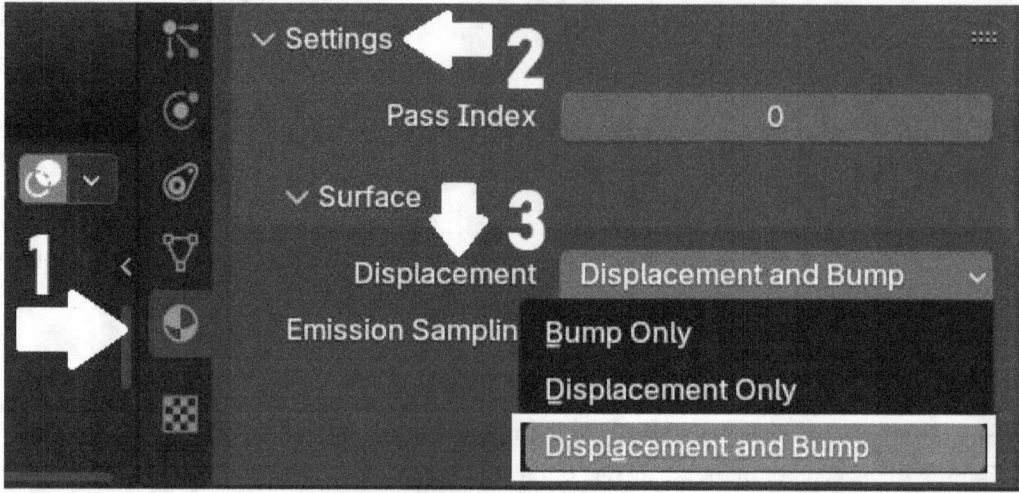

Figure 8.26 – Switching the Displacement type to Displacement and Bump

Now, let's go back to the **Mud** node setup and add a new node called **Displacement**:

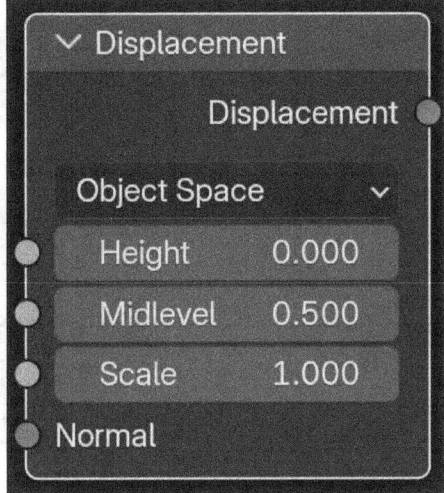

Figure 8.27 – The Displacement node

To control this **Displacement** node, we can reduce the **Scale** value of **Displacement** to 0.1. Then, connect the **MixColor (Multiply)** node to the **Height** slot of **Displacement**. Next, connect the **Displacement** slot to the **Displacement** slot of **Material Output**. The node setup is shown here:

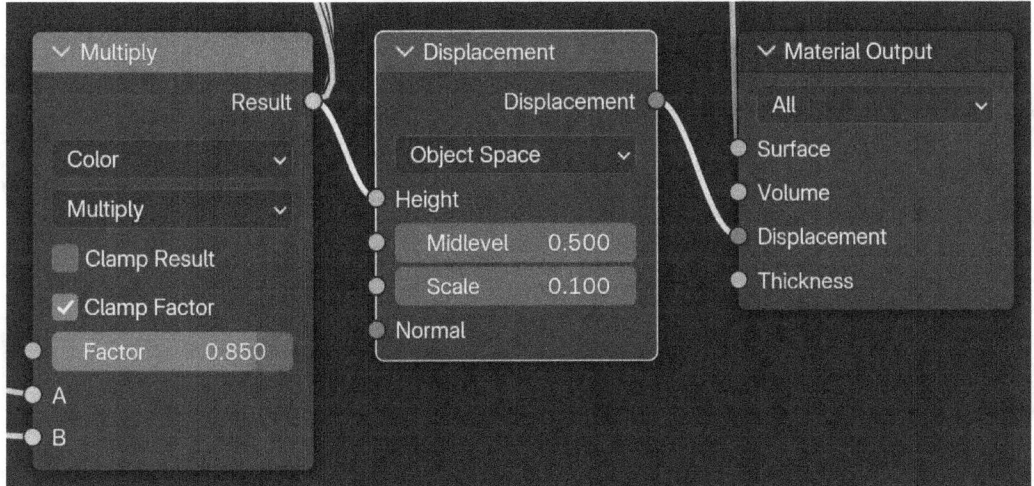

Figure 8.28 – Connecting MixColor (Multiply) to the Displacement node

Figure 8.29 shows the difference between the displacement scale of 1 (on the left of the figure) and 0.1 (on the right of the figure):

Figure 8.29 – Before (left) and after (right) reducing the Displacement Scale value to 0.1

Now, the displacement map of our mud material is working. In order to see it working, we need to switch to the **Rendered** mode, but before doing that, let's improve the lighting of our scene.

Setting good lighting in our scene

To change the lighting of our scene, we need to switch the **Shader Editor** to **World**.

At the top of the **Shader Editor**, we have the option to switch from the **Object** mode to the **World** mode, and the **World** mode is where we can adjust the lighting of our environment:

Figure 8.30 – Switching the Shader Editor mode from Object to World

By default, you will find two nodes: **Background** and **World Output**. Let's search for and add a new node called **Sky Texture** and connect it to the **Background** node, as shown in *Figure 8.31*:

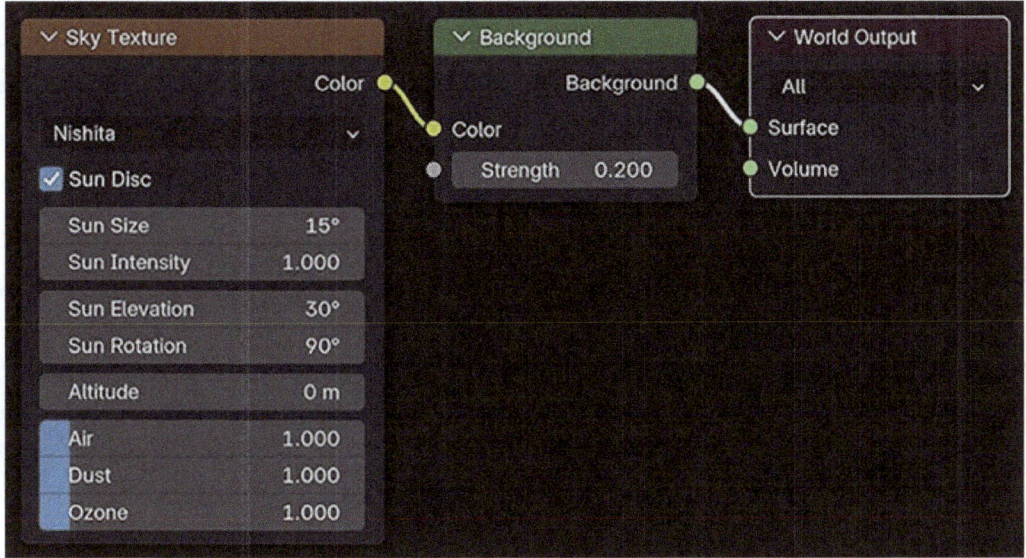

Figure 8.31 – Connecting Sky Texture to Background for lighting the scene

I applied some changes to **Sky Texture**:

- Increased **Sun Size** to 15 degrees
- Increased **Sun Elevation** to 30 degrees
- Increased **Sun Rotation** to 90 degrees

Now, let's go back to the 3D Viewport and switch the shading mode to **Rendered** by pressing *Z* and choosing **Rendered**. This is what the mud material will look like:

Figure 8.32 – The final result of the mud material

Basically, there we go! We created a nice-looking, realistic mud material using procedural texturing in Blender. It's time to use the mud material we created to texture the bottom section of the landscape.

For now, you can save this Blender file as `Procedural Mud Material` – we will be using this Blender file in the next chapter.

Summary

In this chapter, we went through the process of creating a realistic mud material using procedural texturing in Blender. We learned how to create water puddles by combining **Noise Texture** with a **ColorRamp** node, adding details, organizing our node setup by adding **Frame** nodes, adding color to the mud material, and adding reflection, bumps, and a displacement map. Finally, we applied nice lighting to render the mud on the sphere.

In the next chapter, we'll be creating an organic mask and using the mud material we created to texture the bottom section of our landscape.

Get this book's PDF version and more

Scan the QR code (or go to `packtpub.com/unlock`). Search for this book by name, confirm the edition, and then follow the steps on the page.

Note: Keep your invoice handy. Purchases made directly from Packt don't require an invoice.

9

Texturing Landscape with Mud Material

In this chapter, we will be texturing the landscape by mixing two different materials: the rocky snow and the mud we created in the previous chapters. To do that, we will be using a mask that separates the rocky snow from the mud in an organic, nice-looking way.

You will be comfortable with mixing two different materials on the same object while controlling where and to what degree you want the mixing to occur. Being able to mix different materials is a great skill that helps you generate unique materials and apply them to your objects.

In the second part of this chapter, you will learn how to optimize and organize your node setup by using groups. This is an important skill to acquire when working with complex material nodes. Node grouping will allow you to simplify a node tree by hiding away complexity.

You will learn how to pack all your nodes related to a specific material into a single group node that has only the essential parameters you need.

In this chapter, we'll be covering the following topics:

- Importing the **Mud** material
- Creating a texturing mask
- Texturing the landscape with mud and rocky snow

By the end of the chapter, you will be able to blend multiple materials on a single landscape using masks and organized node groups.

Technical requirements

This chapter requires a system capable of running **Blender version 5.0** or above (Windows, macOS, or Linux).

You can either use your own mud material or reuse the one we created in *Chapter 8*. If you prefer to use the provided version, please refer to this link: https://github.com/PacktPublishing/3D-Environment-Design-with-Blender-5-Second-Edition/tree/f0089c06132a9165773b4eb69f99a0610f9ad8ec/chapter-8.

Importing the Mud material

The first thing we need to do is import the mud material into the landscape scene. So let's go back to the landscape scene from *Chapter 7*. Note that in this scene, there is no mud material applied; only the rocky snow material (which was created in *Chapter 6*) is used on the landscape.

This is how the landscape looks so far with the rocky snow material applied:

Figure 9.1 – Final result of the landscape from Chapter 7

To import the mud material, we'll be using the **Append** feature. This allows us to reuse materials, objects, and other data loaded from another Blender file.

When bringing data from another Blender file, you have two options:

- **Append**: Creates a full, independent copy of the object or material inside your current file. You can edit it freely, and it will not affect the original file. This increases your file size but gives you total control.

- **Link**: Creates a reference to the original file. You cannot edit the object directly (unless you make a local override), but if you update the original file, it automatically updates in your scene. This is great for keeping file sizes low in large productions.

For this example, we use **Append** because we want a local copy of the material that we can tweak and apply freely without relying on external files.

Now, let's use the **Append** feature to import the mud material in the following steps:

1. At the top of the Blender scene, go to **File** and choose **Append...**:

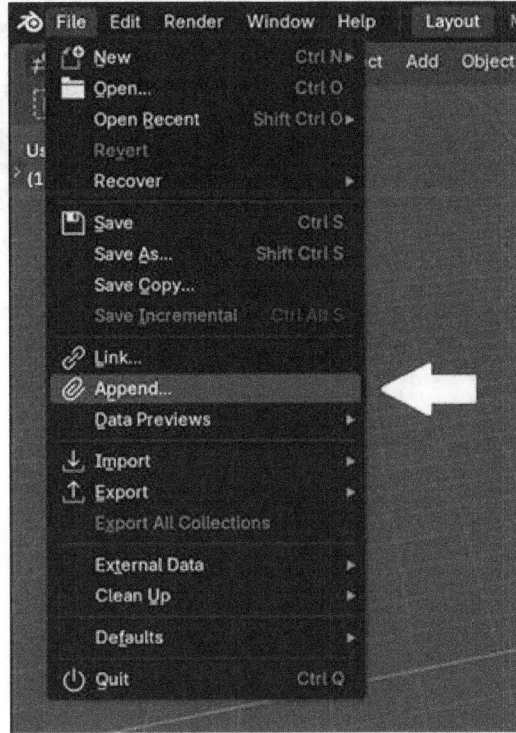

Figure 9.2 – Clicking on the Append… feature

2. A small window will pop up, allowing you to browse your files. Choose the Mud Material Blender file and click on **Append**.

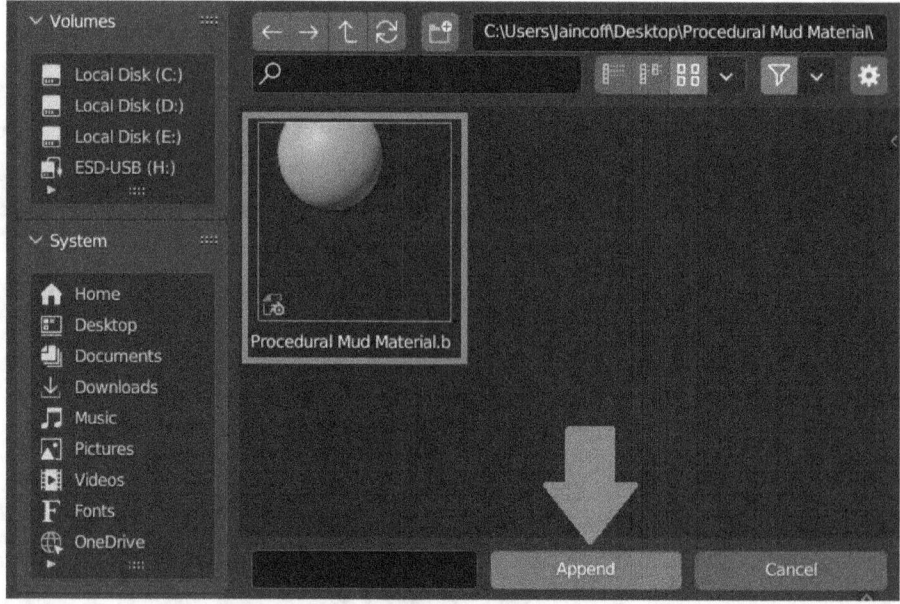

Figure 9.3 – Using Append to import the mud material

3. You will have access to multiple folders, and since what we need to import is a material, we need to choose the Material folder:

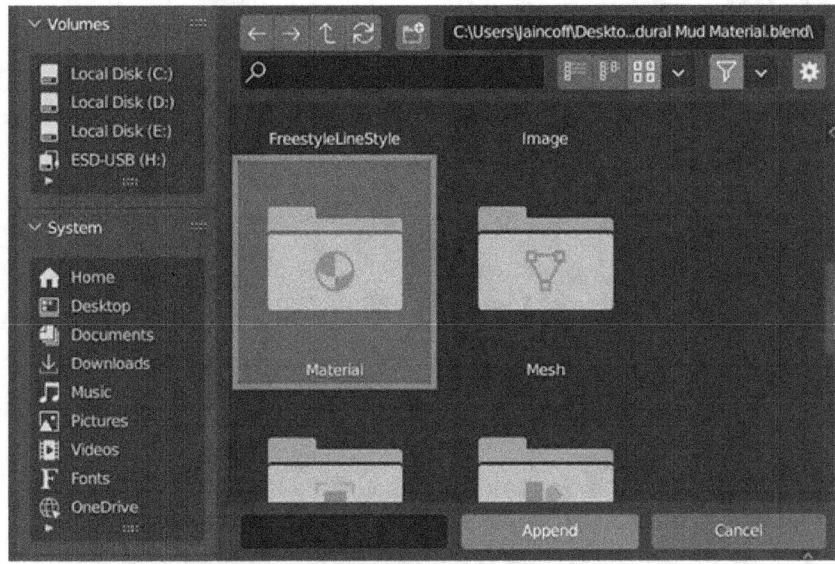

Figure 9.4 – Clicking on the Material folder to import the Mud material

Then, you will find the material we're looking for: **Mud**. Click on it and choose **Append**:

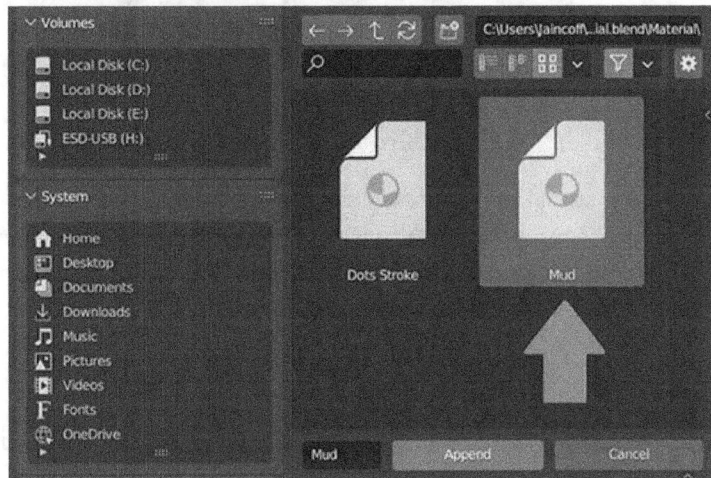

Figure 9.5 – Using Append to import the Mud material

And now the **Mud** material is part of our material library. Let's add the **Mud** material to the **Landscape** materials collection in the next steps:

1. Select the **Landscape** object.

2. Go to **Material Properties**.

3. Add a new material and choose **Mud**:

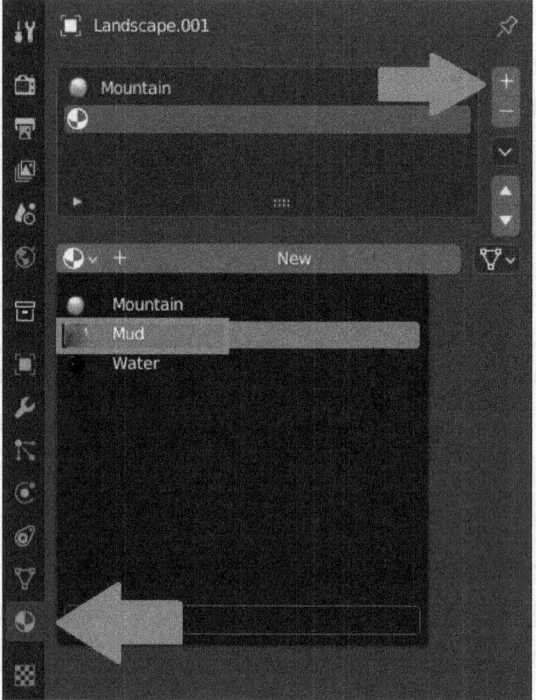

Figure 9.6 – Adding the Mud material to the landscape

Now, we have the **Mud** material as part of the **Landscape** materials – you won't see any change on the landscape because we haven't assigned the **Mud** material yet. Before assigning the **Mud** material to the **Landscape** object, we need to optimize and organize our **Mud** material to manage the nodes well and keep track of them.

Using groups to organize the Mud node setup

Grouping nodes can simplify a node tree by hiding away complexity. Sometimes when you are working on a material, the node tree gets bigger and bigger, which makes controlling the node a difficult task.

This is where node grouping comes in handy. It allows us to combine all the nodes related to a material into a single node that has only the essential parameters we need to customize our material.

To put this in perspective, this is our **Mud** material node setup:

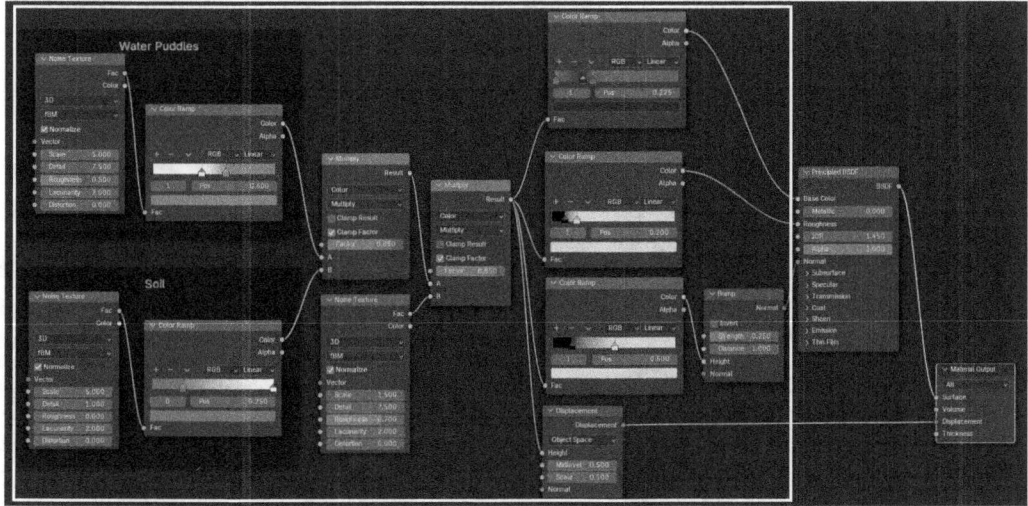

Figure 9.7 – The Mud material node setup

The mud node setup has 14 nodes, and it seems intimidatingly difficult to keep track of every setting. This is how it appears after grouping all the **Mud** nodes – a single node that shows only the parameters we need: the **Scale** value of **Water Puddles**, **Stones**, and **Mud Noise**:

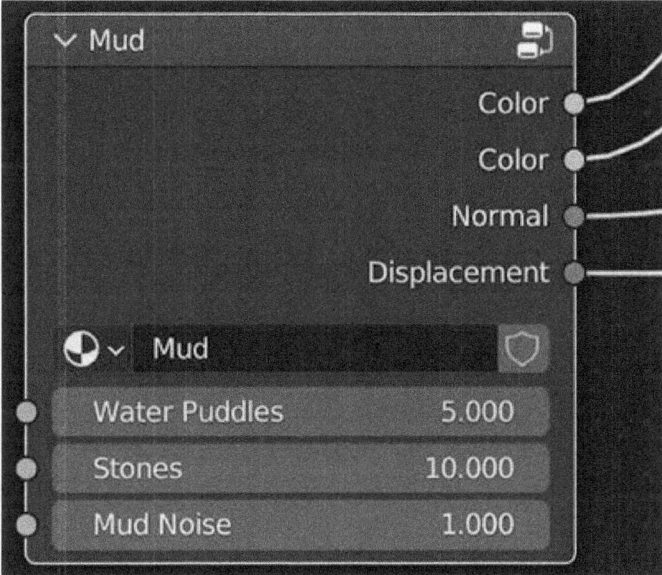

Figure 9.8 – Node group of the Mud material

To group the **Mud** nodes, let's select all the **Mud** material nodes except the **Principled BSDF** and **Material Output** nodes and press *Ctrl + G*, just like the *white* selection in *Figure 9.7*.

When a node group is created, new **Group Input** and **Group Output** nodes will be generated to represent the data flow into and out of the group. This is highlighted in *Figure 9.9* as follows:

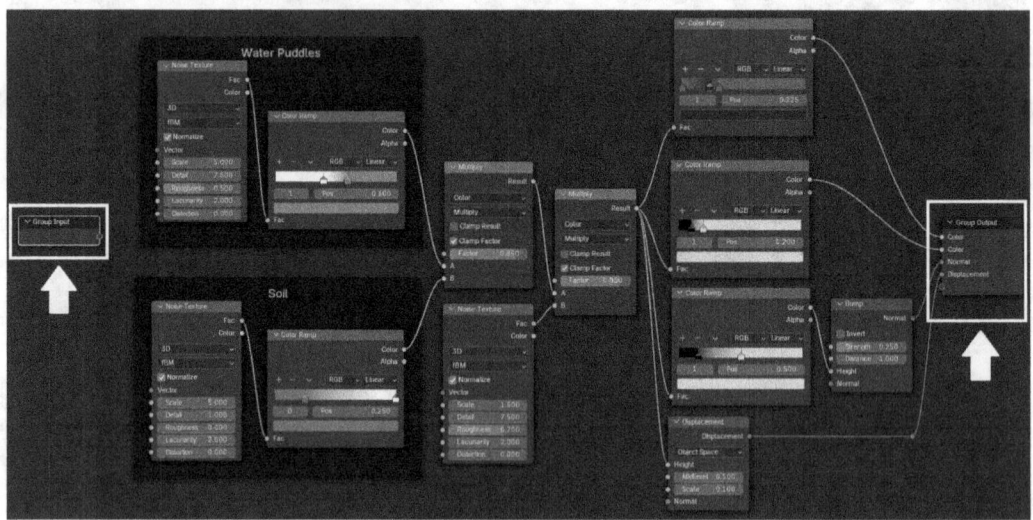

Figure 9.9 – Highlighting Group Input and Group Output

The first node that will appear on the left side of your node setup is **Group Input**. It will be disconnected from the rest.

Group Input is used to store information from the original node setup. You can use it to customize your node setup.

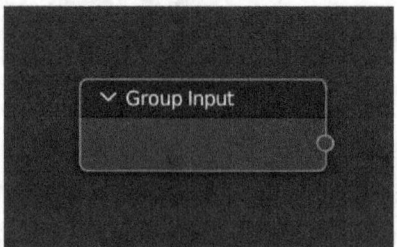

Figure 9.10 – The Group Input node

The second node that you will have when creating a group is **Group Output**. The purpose of the **Group Output** node is to display the result of our node tree. This node has the output slots that we filled in the **Principled BSDF** node, which are **Base Color**, **Roughness**, **Normal**, and **Displacement**:

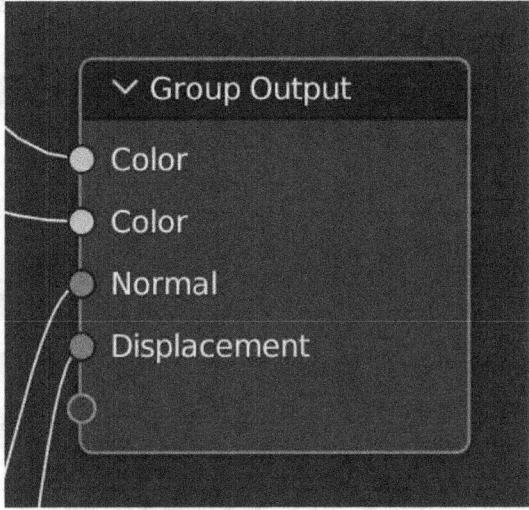

Figure 9.11 – The Group Output node

Now, to exit the node group, you can press *Tab* or press the *arrow* that you will find at the top of your Blender scene:

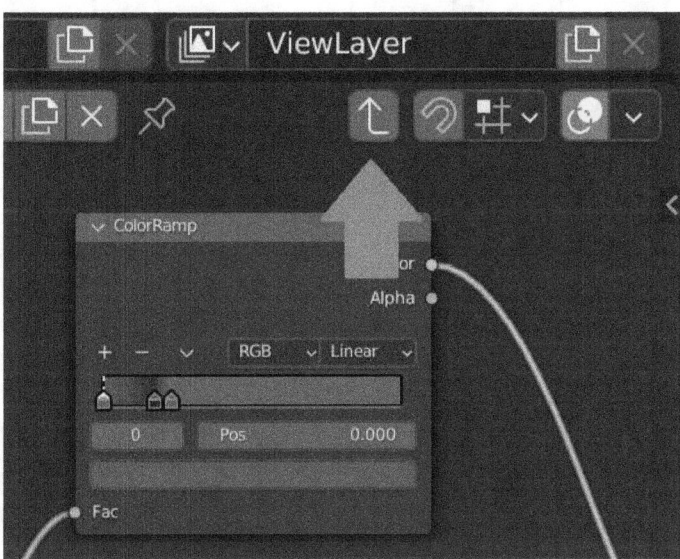

Figure 9.12 – Arrow sign to exit the node group

After exiting the group, we will see it as a single node. This way, we transformed the entire **Mud** node setup into a single node that could be easily manipulated.

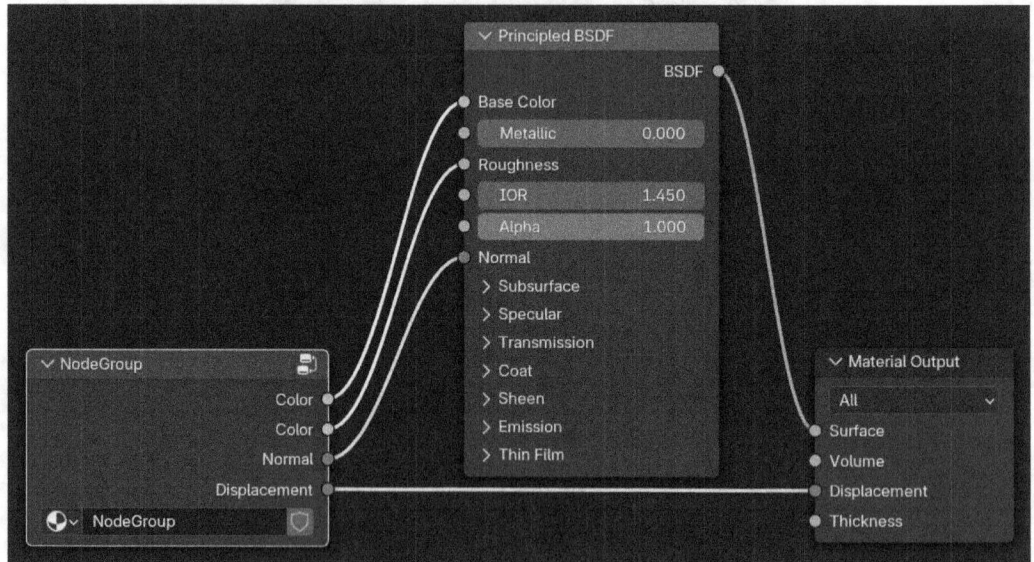

Figure 9.13 – Mud node group

Now, consider this: what if we want to change the **Mud** settings? We will need to extract the node setup again and tweak the nodes.

But what if we could just put the important values we needed in this node? This is what we will do now in the next section.

Adding custom settings to the node group

To add custom settings, we need to go back to the **Group Input** node. First, we need to edit the node group, select the node, right-click on it, and click on **Edit Group**:

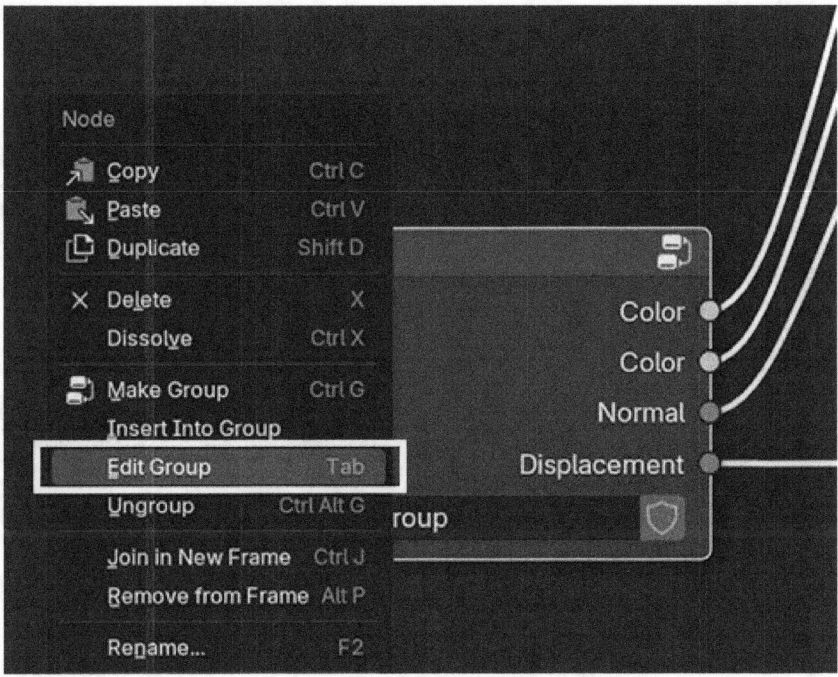

Figure 9.14 – Editing the Mud node group

In our mud example, if we want to pass a parameter related to the **Mud** material into the group, a socket must be added to **Group Input**. To do this, drag a connection from the hollow socket on the right side of the **Group Input** node to the desired input socket of the node requiring an input.

In the example here, we added a parameter to **Group Input** to control the **Scale** value of **Noise Texture**:

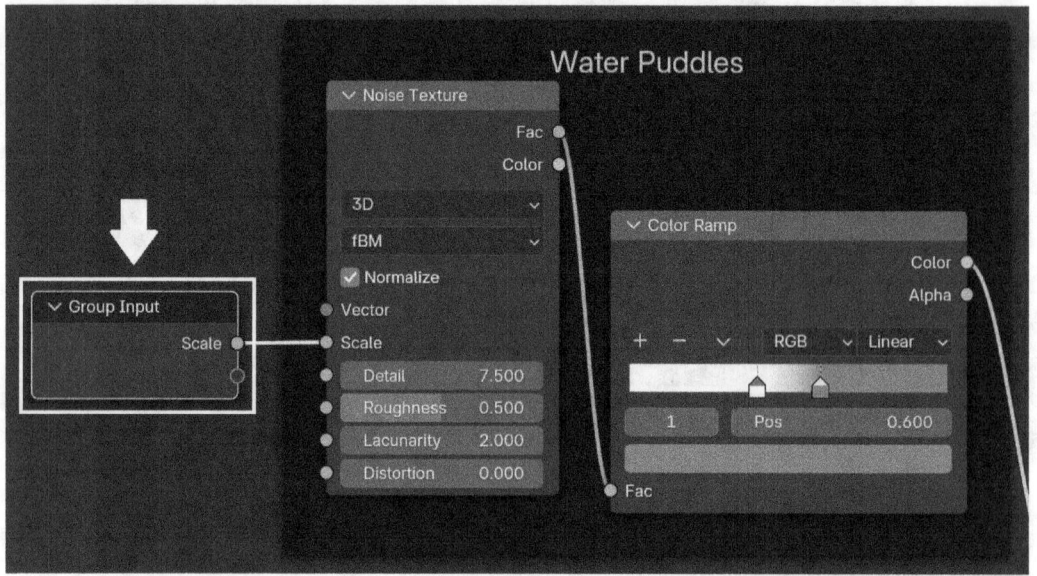

Figure 9.15 – Connecting Group Input to the Noise Texture Scale slot

If we select the **Mud** node group and press *N* to access the right panel, we will have access in **Properties** to **Inputs**.

If we press *N* to go to the right panel, we will find the **Group** tab. Here, we'll change the name of the slots listed under **Group Sockets** to make them easily identifiable:

- Change the **Group** name from **NodeGroup** to Mud Material
- Change the **Group Input** name **Scale** to Water Puddles
- Change the first and second **Color** input names to Mud Color and Mud Roughness, respectively

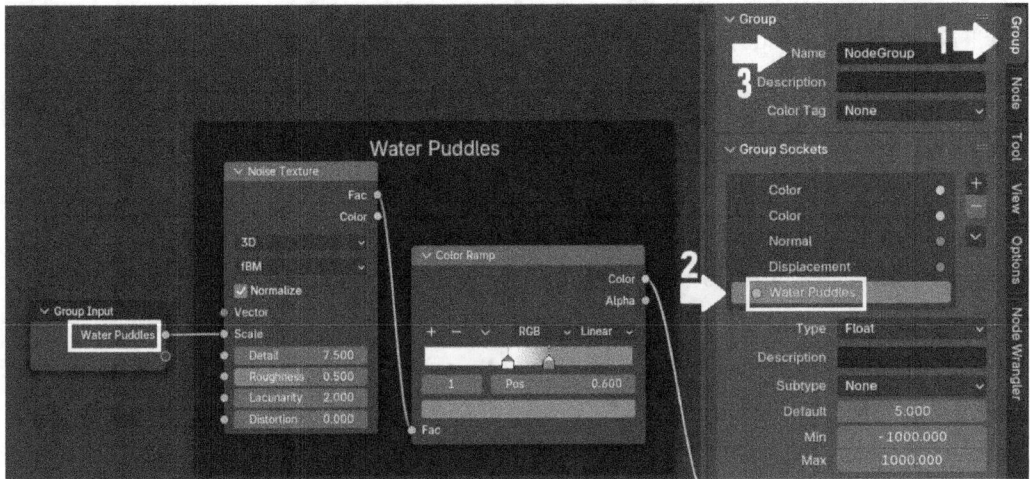

Figure 9.16 – Changing the name of the Mud group node

You can add more parameters to the **Mud** group, such as the number of **Soil** details and scale of **Mud Noise** textures. This way, the node group will have the necessary details you need to customize your **Mud** material:

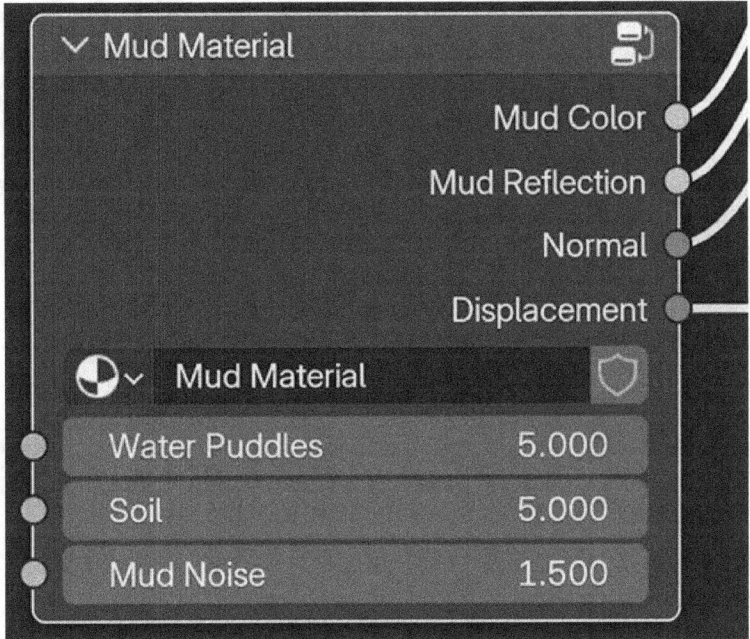

Figure 9.17 – Mud node group

Now that we have imported our **Mud** material and made it a single group node for easy access, it will be saved in the node group library. Now, it's time to create the mask that we need to texture our landscape.

Creating a texturing mask

In nature, snowy mountains melt upside down when they start to melt – meaning that the snow on the mountain top is the last part of the snow to melt. And as a result of the melting snow, mud is created at the bottom. We will replicate this by creating a mask that allows us to merge the rocky snow material and the mud naturally.

But first, let's understand the function of a mask. A **mask** is a grayscale (meaning black and white) texture that determines where and to what degree mixing occurs.

To create the mask, we will be using a node called **Separate XYZ**, and the best way to understand how this node works is by creating a simple example.

Let's follow these instructions:

1. Add a **Texture Coordinate** node.
2. Connect the **Texture Coordinate Generated** slot to a **Separate XYZ** node.
3. Connect **Z** of the **Separate XYZ** to a **ColorRamp** node.
4. Color the first handle of the **ColorRamp** node blue and the second handle red.
5. Connect the **Color** slot of the **ColorRamp** node to the **Principled BSDF** node's **Base Color** slot.

The **Separate XYZ** node separates the landscape mesh based on the colors we have in **ColorRamp**. If you use **Z** in **Separate XYZ**, we will have a vertical distribution of the colors following the **Z** axis. The same goes for other axes, such as **X** and **Y**.

In our case, we will need a vertical distribution of materials: snow on the top (red) and mud on the bottom (blue). So, we will keep using the **Z** axis in the **Separate XYZ** node.

Note that the *red* and *blue* handles are just for demonstrating how the **Separate XYZ** node works. This is what our mask looks like:

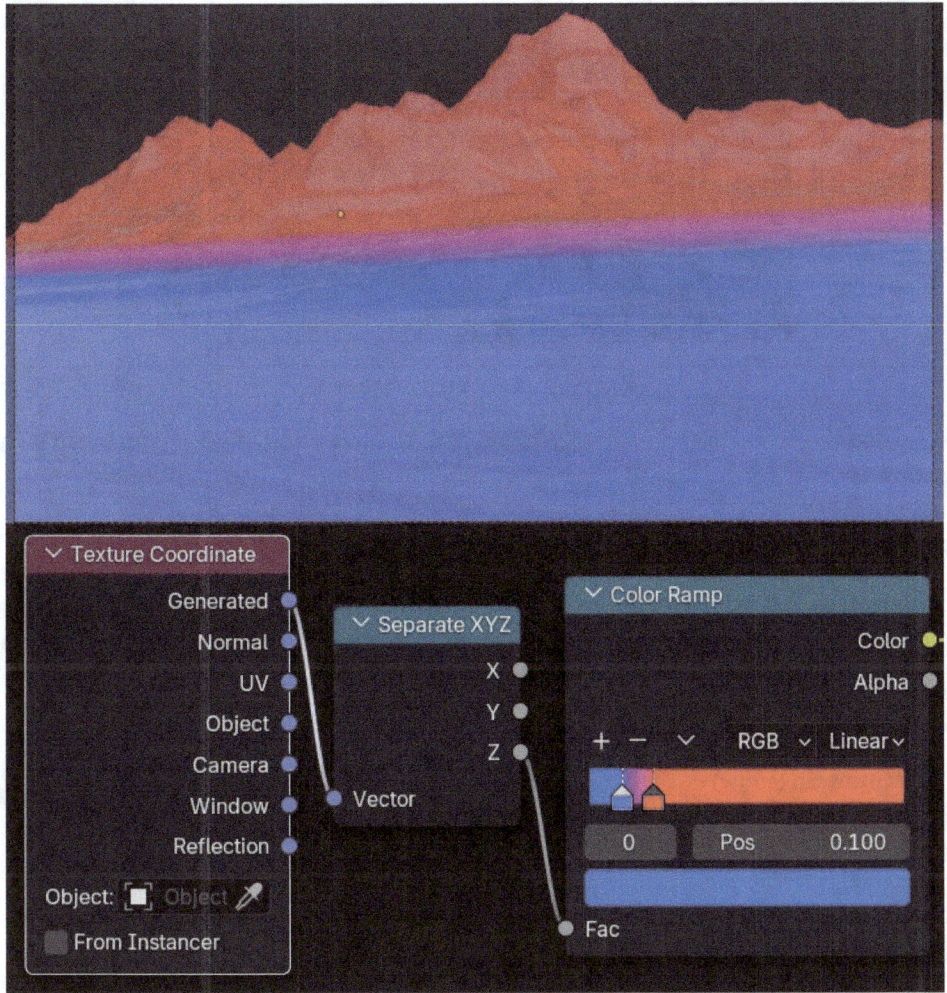

Figure 9.18 – Using the Separate XYZ node to texture the landscape with black, white, and red

Previously in this chapter, we defined a mask as a grayscale texture, which relies on the colors of black and white. To ensure that our mask functions correctly, we need to adjust the **ColorRamp** node by replacing the *red* and *blue* colors with *black* and *white*, restoring it to a proper grayscale format.

To keep our node setup organized, let's put our mask into a group and call the group Mask. Repeat the same steps we did before with the **Mud** material in the *Using groups to organize the Mud node setup* section.

This is the **Mud Mask** node we created:

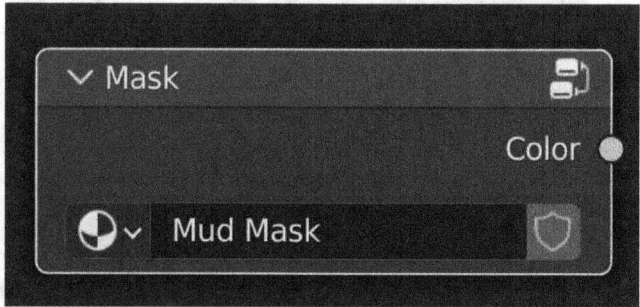

Figure 9.19 – Node group of the mask

Now, let's go ahead and use this mask to texture our landscape with mud and rocky snow in the next section.

Texturing the landscape with mud and rocky snow

Now, it's time to use the **Mud** material and the mask we created previously. But before doing that, let's put the **Landscape** material called **Mountain** into a group called **Mountain** (snow) by repeating the same steps we did with the **Mud** group material.

Now we have three node groups:

- **Mountain** (snow)
- **Mud Mask**
- **Mud Material**

Let's bring all the node groups we created; it is saved in Blender nodes now. Press *Shift + A* in **Shader Editor**, go to **Group**, and click on **Mud** and **Mud Mask**:

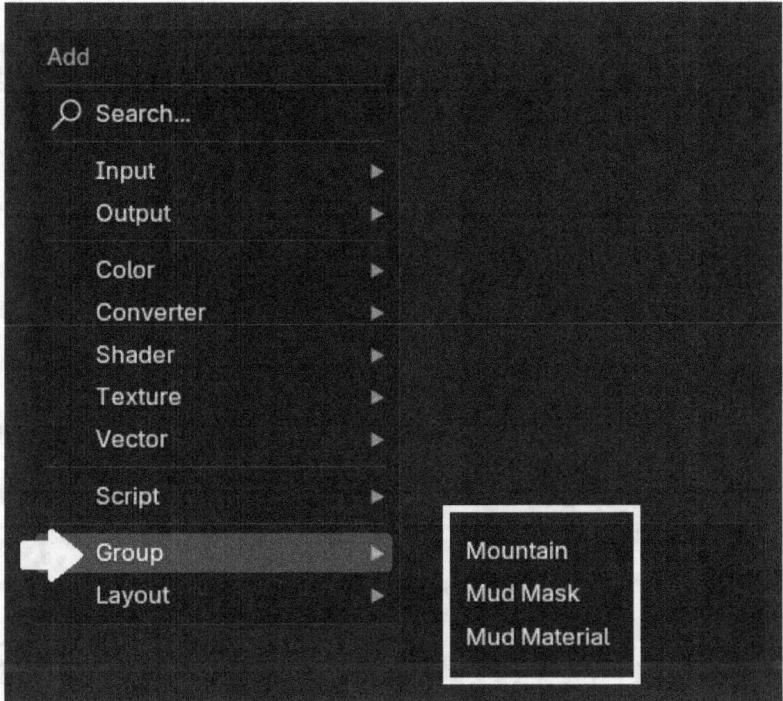

Figure 9.20 – Searching for Mud in Group

Here are all the groups we created. We have the **Mountain** group first, which is **Snow** and **Rock** combined, the second group is **Mud Mask**, and finally, we have the **Mud Material** group:

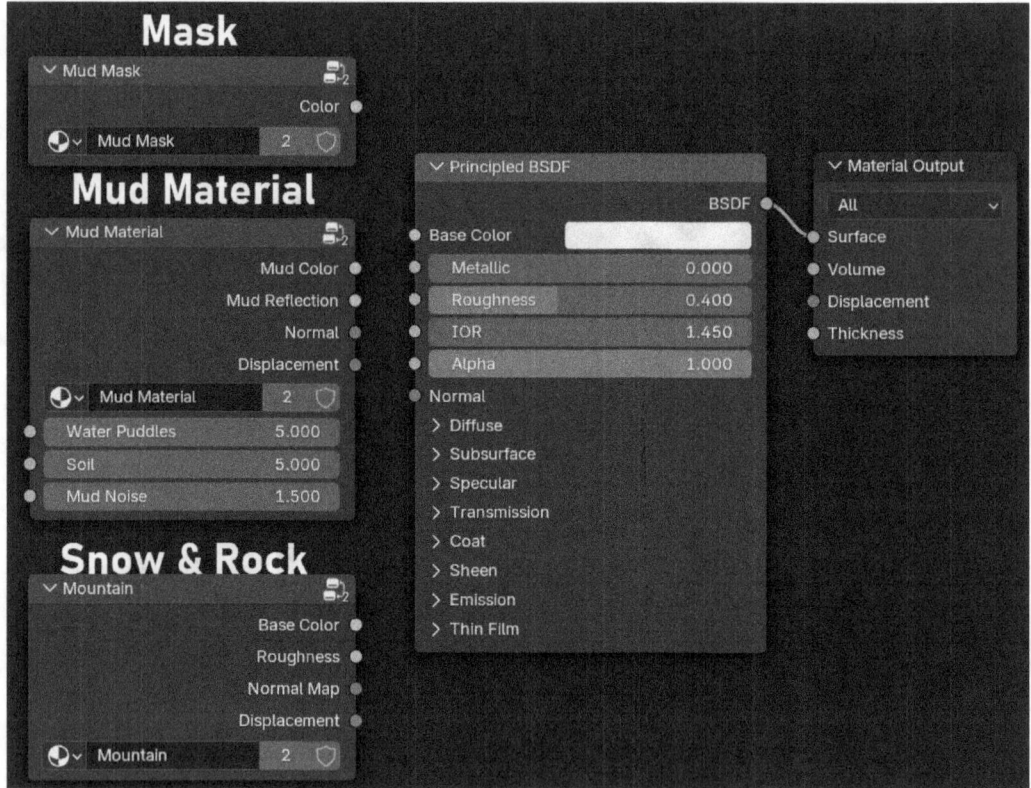

Figure 9.21 – Combining all the node groups

Now, let's start with mixing the **Base Color** slot:

1. Bring a **MixColor** node.

2. Connect the **Mud Mask Color** slot to the **Mix Color Factor**.

3. Connect the **Mud Material**'s **Mud Color** slot to **A** slot of the **Mix Color**.

4. Connect the **Mountain**'s **Base Color** to **B** slot of the **Mix Color**.

5. Connect the **MixColor** right **Color**'s slot to the **Principled BSDF** node's **Base Color** slot.

After mixing the **Mud Color** with the **Mountain Base Color** to define the **Base Color** of the **Principled BSDF**, this is how the node setup will appear:

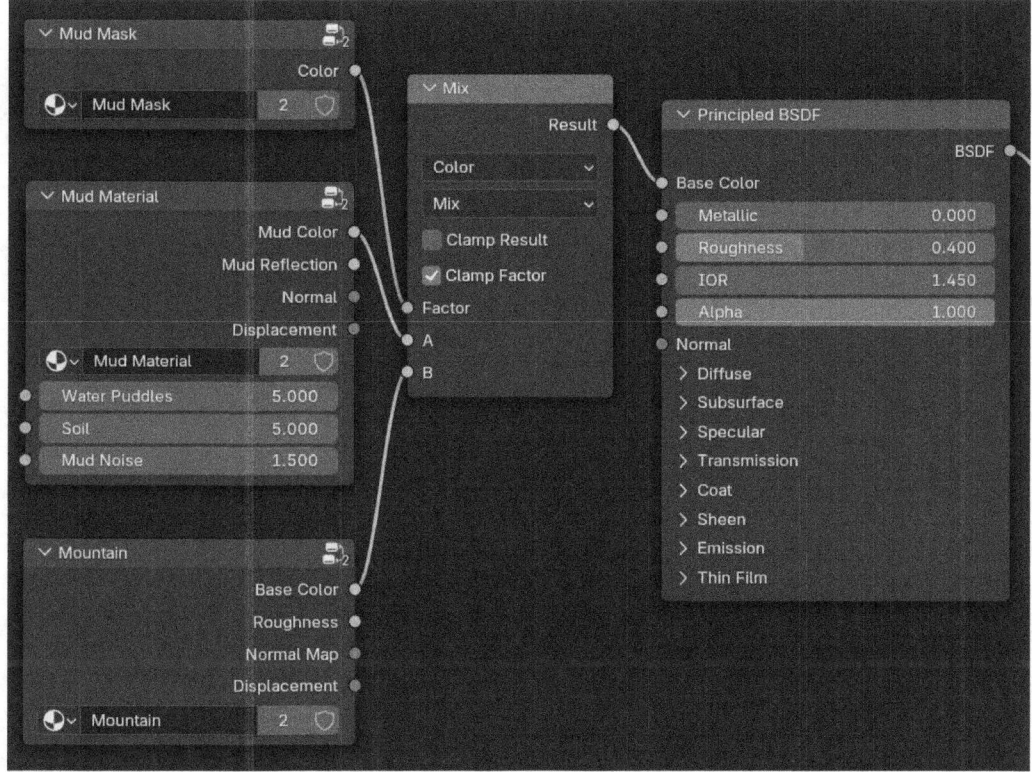

Figure 9.22 – Combining Mud Mask with the Mud and Mountain materials

Let's repeat the same connections for the remaining texturing channels: **Roughness**, **Normal**, and **Displacement**. Just as we mixed **Mud Color** with **Mountain Base Color** to define the **Base Color** settings of **Principled BSDF**, we now apply the same mixing logic to these channels so all material properties blend consistently.

Here are a few key points to consider:

- The **Mud Mask Color** slot is always connected to the **Factor** slot of the four **MixColor** nodes.

- The **Mud Reflection (Roughness)**, **Normal**, and **Displacement** slots need to be connected to the **A** slot of **MixColor**.

- The **Mountain Roughness**, **Normal Map**, and **Displacement** slots need to be connected to the **B** slot of **MixColor**.

This is the full node setup of mixing snow with mud using the **MixColor** node:

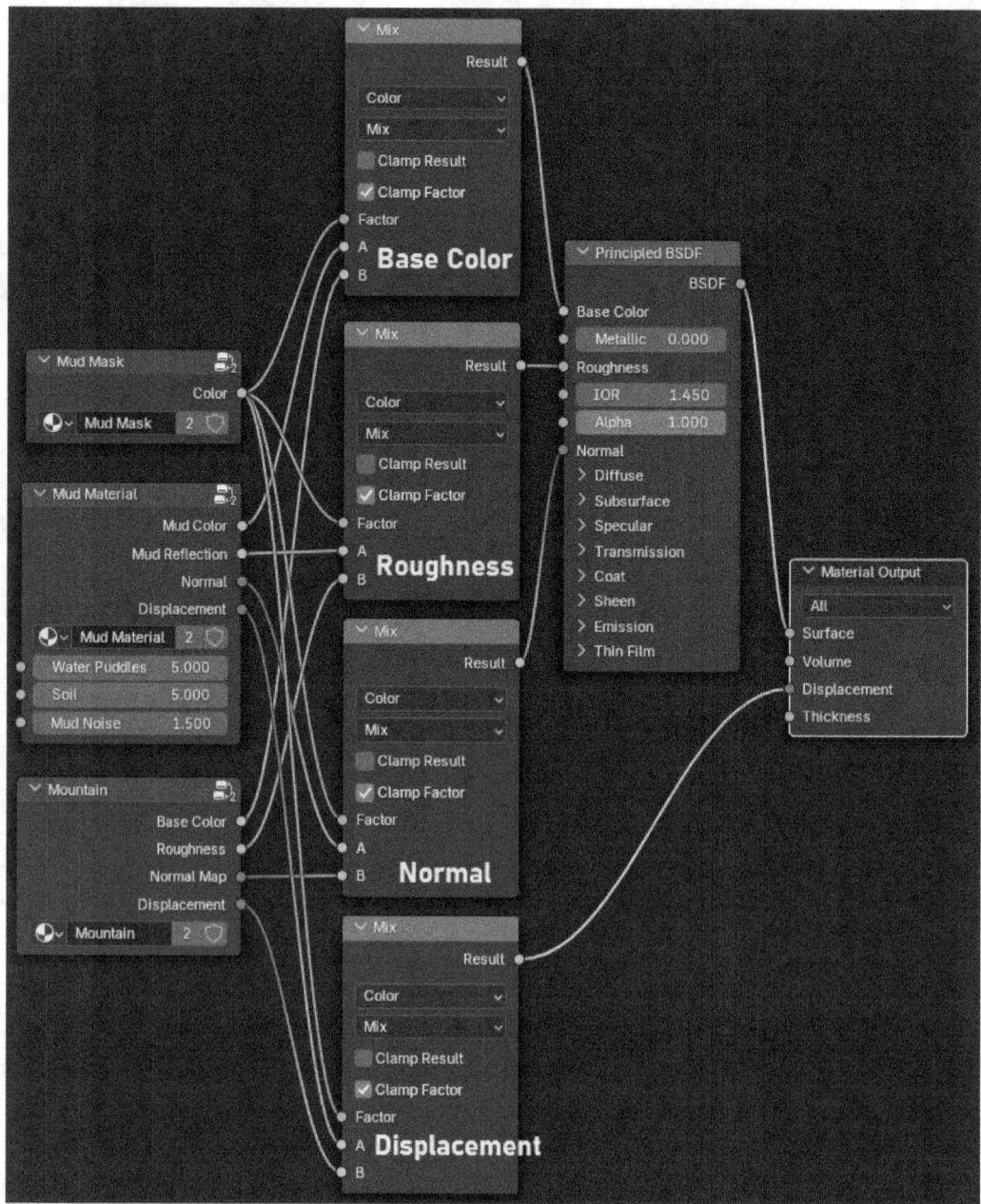

Figure 9.23 – Mixing Mud with Mountain using Mud Mask

And here we are: this is the result of the landscape when texturing it with the **Rocky Snow** and **Mud** material:

Figure 9.24 – Texturing the landscape with rocky snow and mud

The landscape looks alive with vivid colors. In the next chapter, we will add rocks and grass and improve the water shader to make it better fit the scene.

Summary

In this chapter, we learned how to texture the landscape by mixing two different materials, rocky snow and mud. We learned how to mix two different materials on the same object while controlling where and to what degree we want the mixing to occur by using masks.

Next, we learned how to optimize and organize our node setup by using groups, which allow us to simplify a node tree by hiding away complexity.

In the next chapter, you'll create realistic rock assets using an automated workflow, learning how to generate, texture, and optimize them for use in your landscape scene.

Get this book's PDF version and more

Scan the QR code (or go to packtpub.com/unlock). Search for this book by name, confirm the edition, and then follow the steps on the page.

Note: Keep your invoice handy. Purchases made directly from Packt don't require an invoice.

Part 3

Creating Natural Assets in Blender 5

In the third part of this book, we will focus on creating natural assets to fill our landscape and river environment. We will start with designing rocks, which are perfect for giving a realistic and natural feeling to our landscape environment. Then, we will learn how to create organic flowers based on real references. Finally, we will learn how to create trees that are optimized for large-scale environments.

This part of the book includes the following chapters:

- *Chapter 10, Creating Natural Assets: Rock*
- *Chapter 11, Creating Realistic Flowers in Blender*
- *Chapter 12, Creating Trees Ready for Large Environments*

10

Creating Natural Assets: Rock

In this chapter, we will be creating realistic rock assets using **Rock Generator**, a built-in Blender add-on. These rock assets are perfect for giving a realistic and natural feel to the landscape environment we're creating and can be used in multiple exterior nature visualizations.

While Geometry Nodes are the modern standard for procedural systems in Blender 5, we are utilizing the **Rock Generator** add-on for this specific workflow for two main reasons:

- **Speed**: The **Rock Generator** add-on generates unique and customizable rocks in seconds without the setup time of a complex node graph
- **Performance**: For large scenes or exports to engines such as Unreal, creating static meshes is often more efficient than maintaining *live* procedural data generated by Geometry Nodes

You will learn how to generate realistic rocks with one click. Also, you will be able to adjust the rocks' shape and add more detail to them.

Next, you'll learn how to unwrap and texture a rock. Here, you will learn the fastest way to set up **Physically Based Rendering** (**PBR**) materials in Blender. Finally, you'll learn how to optimize the rock geometry – you'll save 98% of rock geometry without sacrificing too much rock quality.

In this chapter, we'll be covering the following topics:

- Installing the **Rock Generator** add-on
- Creating rocks using the **Rock Generator** add-on
- Texturing the rock
- Setting up quick lighting for our scene
- Optimizing the rock geometry

The goal of this chapter is to teach you how to create complex organic rocks without doing any manual modeling. In environment design, time is your most valuable resource. By mastering this automated workflow, you can fill your landscapes with realistic detail in minutes rather than hours.

Technical requirements

This chapter requires a system capable of running **Blender version 5.0** or above (Windows, macOS, or Linux).

You can download the resources for this chapter from GitHub at `https://github.com/ PacktPublishing/3D-Environment-Design-with-Blender-5-Second-Edition/tree/ 391cdead4d8ea7bc9f973233238cfbd65b973f5f/chapter-10`.

Installing the Rock Generator add-on

The first step in creating rocks is to enable a pre-installed add-on called **Rock Generator**. It's a part of a larger add-on called **Add Mesh: Extra Objects**.

Follow these steps:

1. Let's jump into a new Blender scene. At the top, you'll find the **Edit** tab. Click on it and go to **Preferences...**, as shown in *Figure 10.1*:

Figure 10.1 – Clicking on Preferences... from the Edit menu

2. A new window will pop up. On the left side, click on **Get Extensions**.

3. You must click **Allow Online Access** to permit Blender to connect to the internet. This is required to browse, install, and update extensions directly from the online repository within the interface.

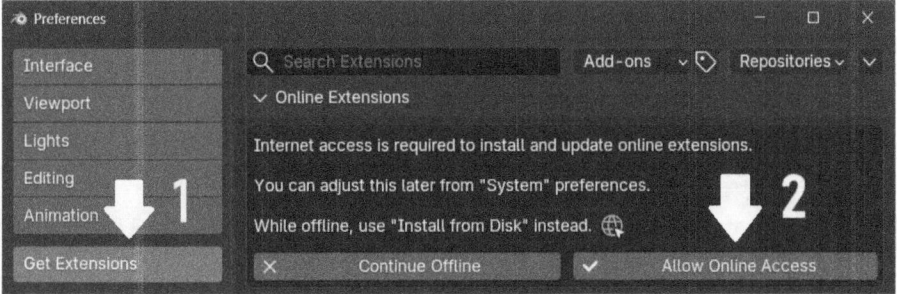

Figure 10.2 – Granting Blender permission to connect to the internet

Now that Blender has access to the online extensions platform, the next step is to search for the add-on we need.

4. In the *search extensions* bar at the top, search for Extra Mesh Objects.

5. The add-on will be shown in the search results. Click on the **Install** button on the right to enable the add-on, as shown in *Figure 10.3*:

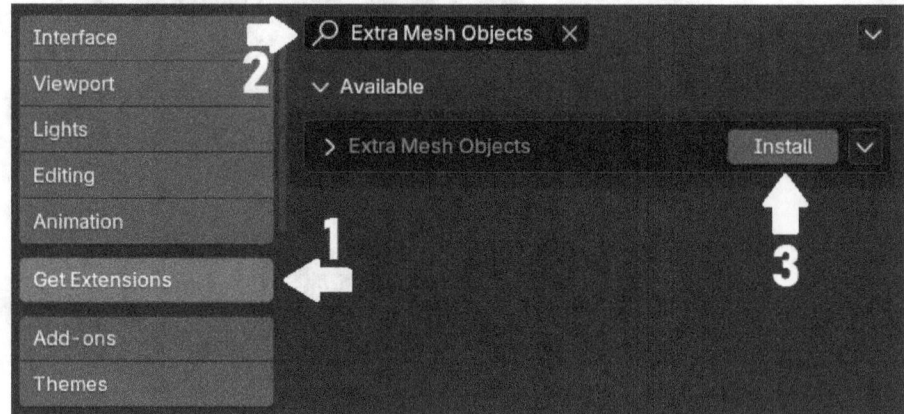

Figure 10.3 – Searching for the Extra Mesh Objects add-on

Basically, that's it; our **Rock Generator** add-on is installed. We can now use it to add rock objects to our scene.

Creating rocks using the Rock Generator add-on

In the 3D Viewport, press *Shift + A*, go to **Mesh**, and you will find **Rock Generator**. This add-on that we installed also comes with many tools, such as **Gears** and **Pipe Joints** (see *Figure 10.4*). However, for the scope of this chapter, we'll be focusing only on the rocks.

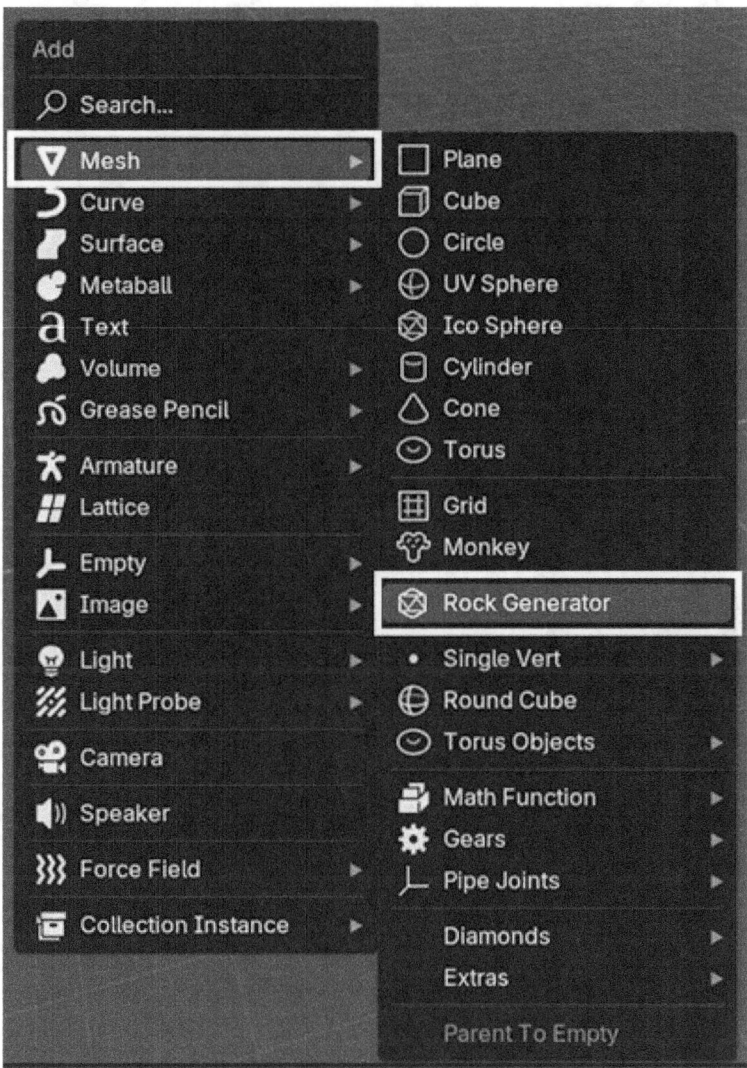

Figure 10.4 – Adding Rock Generator in the 3D Viewport

Let's get started with the steps to create and customize rocks:

1. Once you click on **Rock Generator**, a rock will appear in your scene. On the bottom left, you'll find a tab called **Add Rocks**. Click on it to start the customization of the rock:

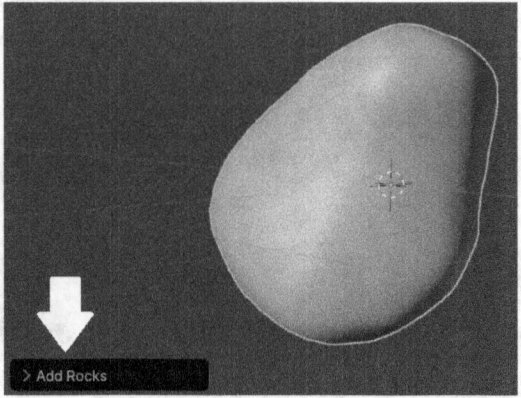

Figure 10.5 – Adding a Rock object

2. Click on the *left arrow* to expand the panel and access the **Rock Generator** settings.

3. The first thing to do is to disable the **Use a random seed** feature. This feature randomizes the shape of the rock automatically while you change the **Deformation** value (see *Figure 10.6*); it keeps generating different new shapes randomly. Personally, I find it frustrating.
   The default rock shape seems uninteresting, but you can easily create a variety of unique rocks by tweaking the following parameters:

   - **User Seed**: This value determines the base shape of your rock. Each time you change the seed, a new rock shape is generated. For example, I set **User Seed** to 7, which gave me an excellent starting point.

   - **Deformation**: This parameter changes the rock's structure, making the edges more pronounced and giving the shape more character. I set the **Deformation** value to 7.5 for a better result.

   - **Display Detail**: Increasing this value adds finer surface details to the rock, making it look more realistic. I recommend setting **Display Detail** to 3 for a well-detailed surface.

Change **Seed** when you need a completely different rock shape. Adjust **Deformation** when you like the rock shape but want to control how jagged or smooth the surface feels. *Figure 10.6* demonstrates this below.

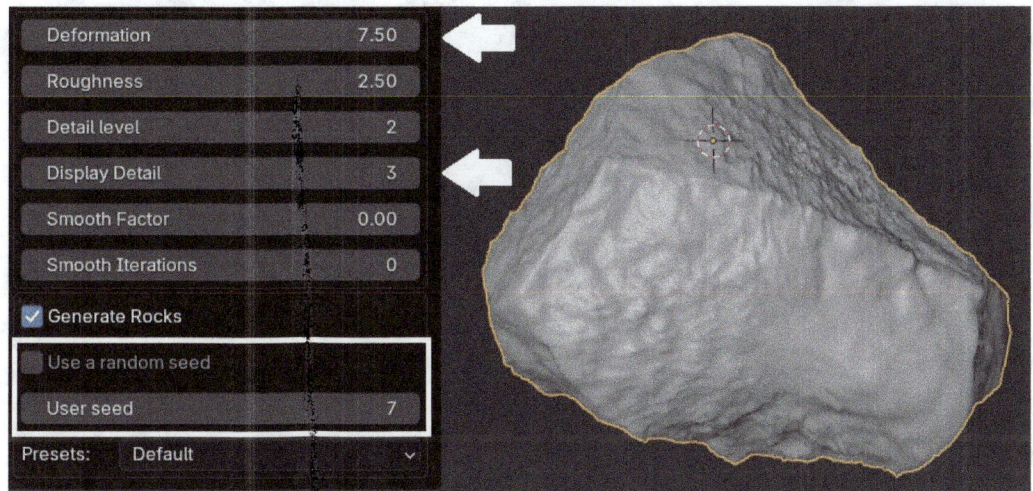

Figure 10.6 – Customizing the shape of the rock object

Under the hood, the **Rock Generator** add-on works by stacking multiple modifiers on the rock object, such as **Subdivision Surface** and **Displace**. We'll understand this better when we optimize the rock later in the chapter.

The shape of our rock is perfect now. Let's proceed with texturing it in the next section.

Texturing the rock

In order to texture the rock, we'll be using a rock PBR texture that you can download using this link:

```
https://github.com/PacktPublishing/3D-Environment-Design-with-Blender-5-Second-
Edition/blob/391cdead4d8ea7bc9f973233238cfbd65b973f5f/chapter-10/Rock-PBR-
Texture.zip
```

Let's get started with creating a material and assigning it to our rock.

Creating a rock material

To create the rock material, let's select the rock object and go to **Material Properties**, add a new material, and call it Rock.

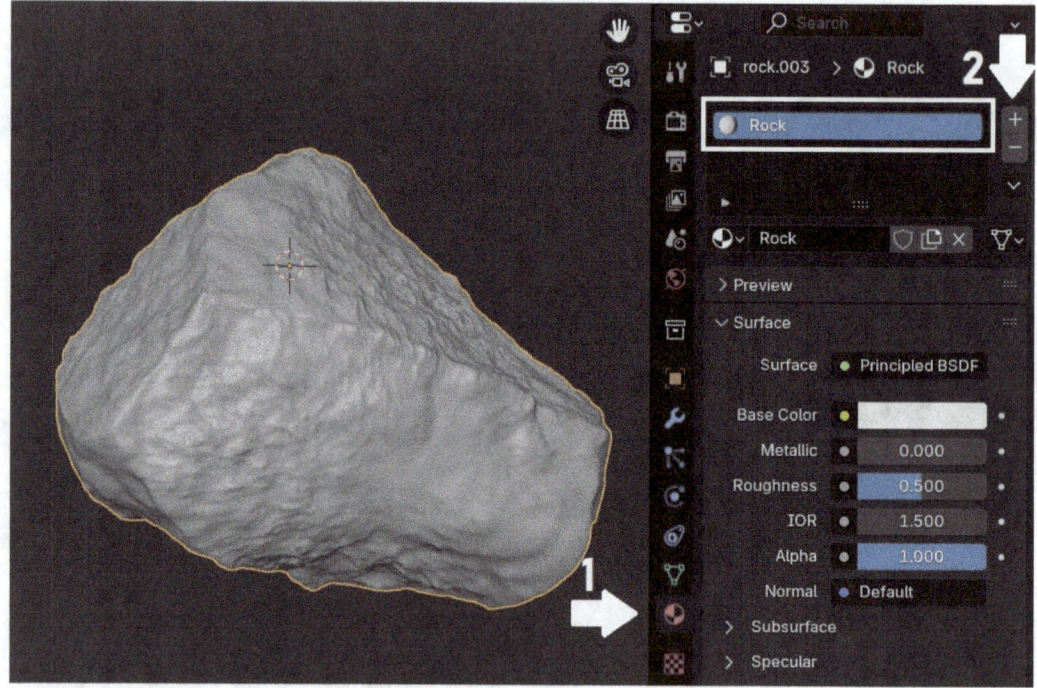

Figure 10.7 – Adding a Rock material to the rock object

In order to edit the **Rock** material, switch the bottom window of your Blender scene into the **Shader Editor**. By default, the rock material will have two nodes: **Principled BSDF** and **Material Output**.

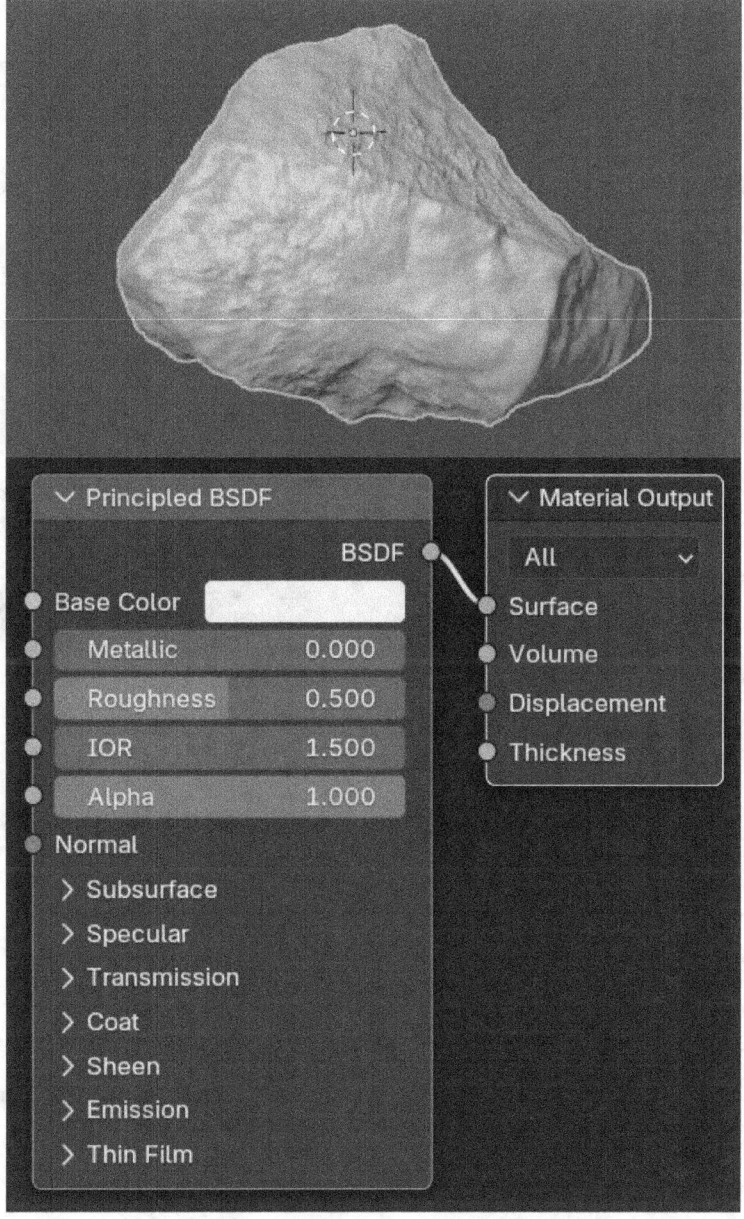

Figure 10.8 – The Principled BSDF node connected to Material Output

Our next move is to assign the rock textures to the rock object. To achieve this, we'll be using a trick that allows us to set up PBR materials with one click.

The fastest way to set up PBR materials in Blender

Creating materials using nodes is often one of the most daunting tasks for 3D artists. It's repetitive and time-consuming and can feel overwhelming. Thankfully, Blender includes a built-in add-on that simplifies working with nodes: **Node Wrangler**.

Node Wrangler is a powerful tool packed with features that make managing nodes much more efficient. In this section, we'll use it to quickly assign PBR textures, saving both time and effort.

Before we begin, let's ensure the add-on is installed and activated. You can do this by following the same steps we used to install **Rock Generator** in the *Installing the Rock Generator add-on* section at the beginning of the chapter.

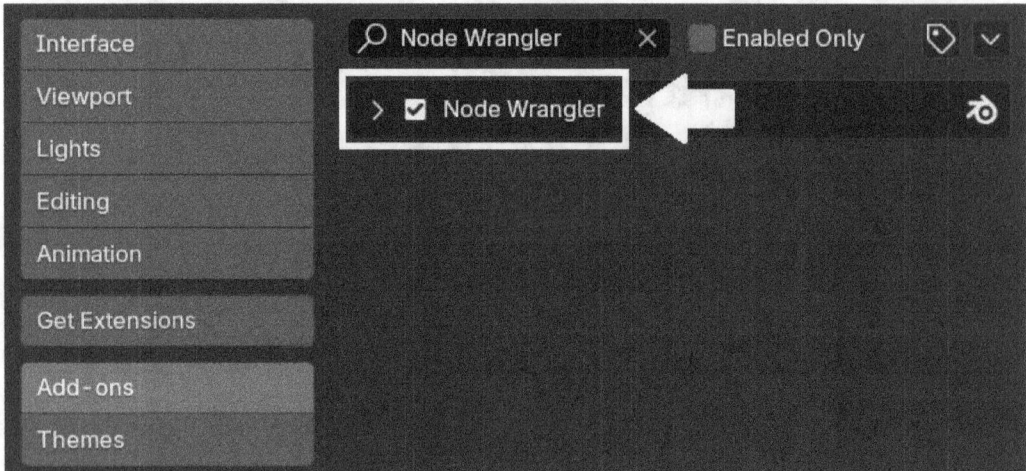

Figure 10.9 – Installing the Node Wrangler add-on

Once the add-on is installed, click the checkbox to enable it.

Now the Node Wrangler add-on is enabled, and we can use it to assign the rock textures to our rock object. To do this, let's go back to the **Shader Editor** and follow these steps:

1. Click on the **Principled BSDF** node to have it highlighted. This node will serve as the base for the PBR rock texture maps.

2. Press *Ctrl + Shift + T*, and a new file browser window will pop up.

3. Locate and select all the texture maps that you want to import from the rock folder you downloaded before, and click on the **Principled Texture Setup** button at the bottom.

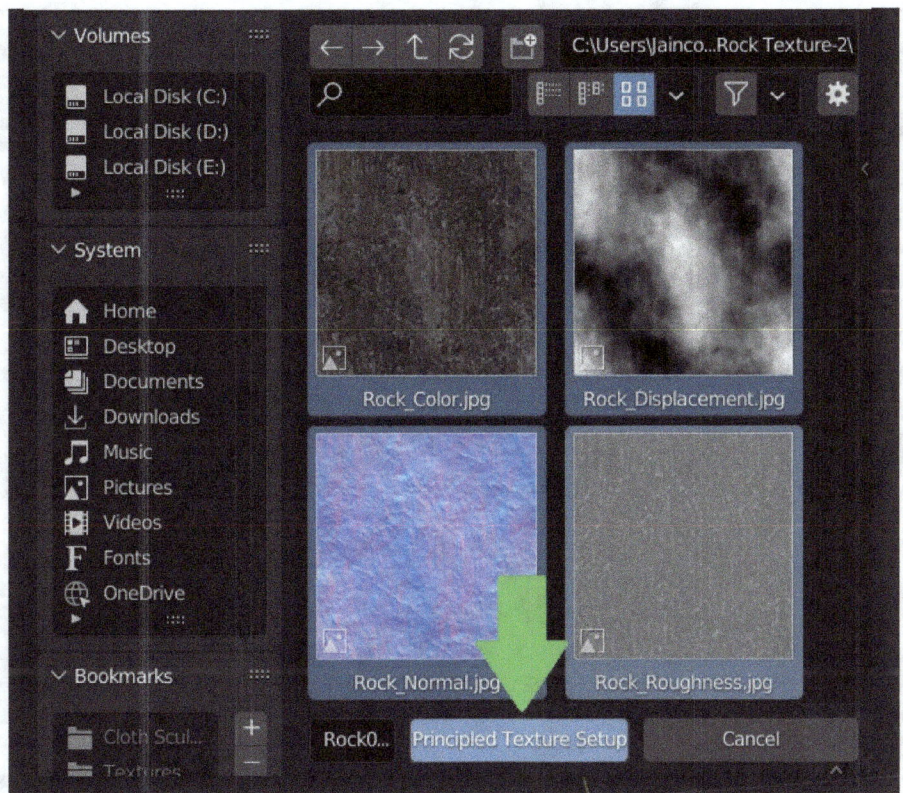

Figure 10.10 – Choosing the rock textures to be assigned to the Principled BSDF node

By using this combination of *Ctrl + Shift + T*, you will have all the textures assigned automatically as nodes to **Principled BSDF** with just one single click. You will also have the **Mapping** node on the left side, allowing you to adjust the scale and position of the rock texture.

To understand how the add-on works, it simply searched for keywords in the names of these textures. If the add-on finds the word *Color* in the name of a texture, it assigns that **Color** texture to **Principled BSDF Base Color**. This is why you need to make sure that the texture map names are clear.

This is the full node setup of the **Rock** material:

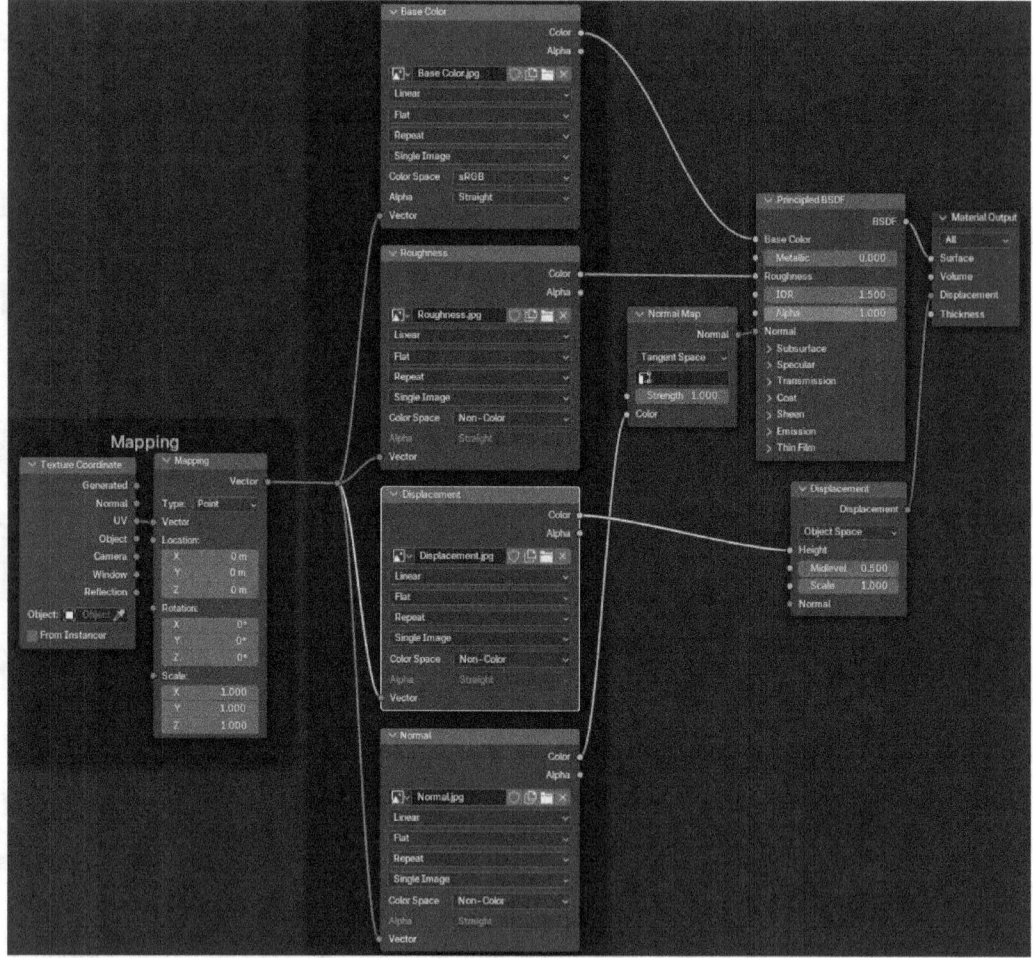

Figure 10.11 – Rock material node setup

In *Figure 10.11*, on the left, we have the **Texture Coordinate** node connected to the **Mapping** node. This allows us to control how the textures are positioned, scaled, and rotated on the object. By adjusting these nodes, we can precisely map the textures to fit the surface of the 3D model.

These nodes are then connected to the following textures:

- **Base Color**: It defines the primary color or diffuse texture of the material
- **Roughness**: It controls the shininess or roughness of the surface

- **Normal**: It adds surface details such as bumps and scratches without altering the geometry

- **Displacement**: It creates depth and geometry modifications for added realism

All these texture nodes feed into the **Principled BSDF** shader, which combines the material properties into a single node. Now, if we switch to **Material Preview** by pressing *Z* on the 3D Viewport, this is how our rock will appear:

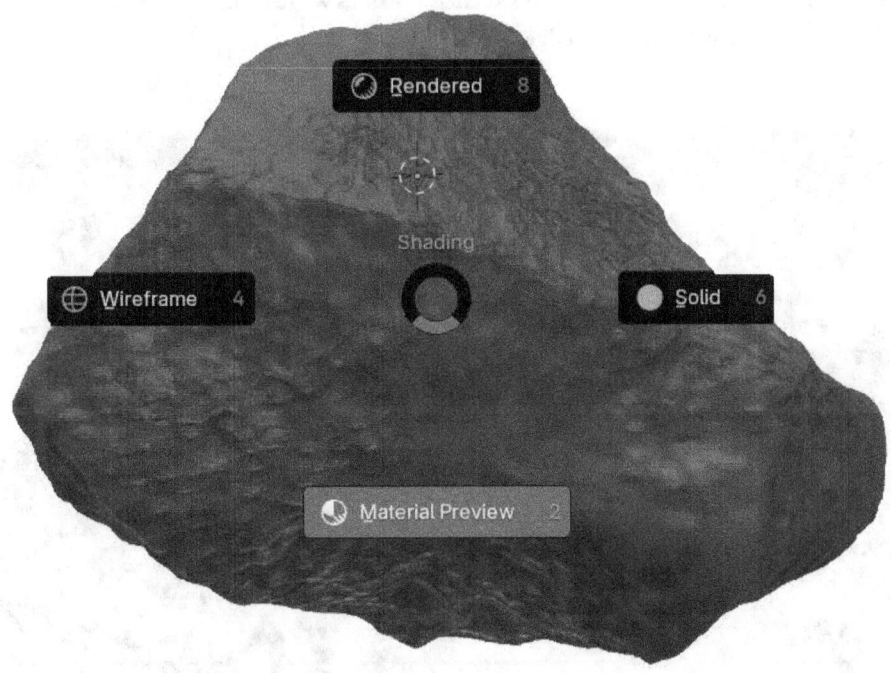

Figure 10.12 – Displaying the non-unwrapped rock in the Material Preview

We're not able to see the rock texture on our rock because the rock object is not unwrapped yet. Let's go ahead and unwrap our rock object.

Unwrapping the rock object

In order to unwrap our rock and have it ready to be textured, let's perform these steps (see *Figure 10.13*):

1. Select the rock object first.

2. Switch to **Edit Mode** by pressing *Tab*.

3. Press *U* and choose **Cube Projection** (as shown in *Figure 10.13*). Since rocks are naturally blocky 3D shapes, **Cube Projection** is the most efficient choice. It projects the

texture onto the object from six sides simultaneously (top, bottom, front, back, left, and right). This instantly creates an even UV map with minimal distortion, saving you the tedious work of manually marking seams.

> **Note**
>
> The **Cube Projection** unwrapping splits the UV map into separate islands, which can create visible seams where the rock texture edges meet. To minimize this, it is highly recommended to use seamless textures such as the ones we're using now. By using seamless textures, we hide these edges naturally.

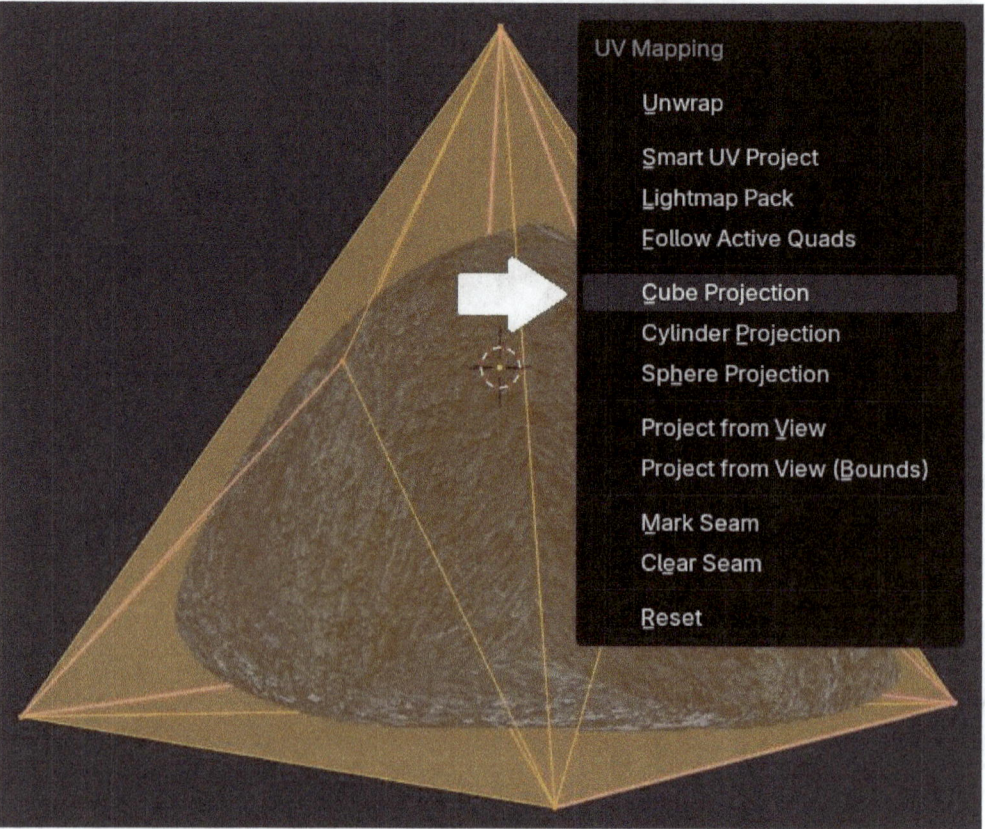

Figure 10.13 – Unwrapping the rock object

Now, if we switch to the Material Preview, our rock will be unwrapped and well textured, as shown in *Figure 10.14*:

Figure 10.14 – Displaying the unwrapped rock in the Material Preview

We need to see our rock in the **Rendered** mode to have a better idea of how it will appear in our final rendered scene. So, let's make a quick lighting setup in our scene.

Setting up quick lighting for our scene

To better evaluate the rock's shape and surface details, we'll set up a simple lighting environment. Let's set up a quick lighting setup for our scene. In the **Shader Editor**, I want you to switch the data type to **World**. Then, follow these steps:

1. Add a new **Sky Texture** node and connect it to the **Background** node, as shown in *Figure 10.15*:

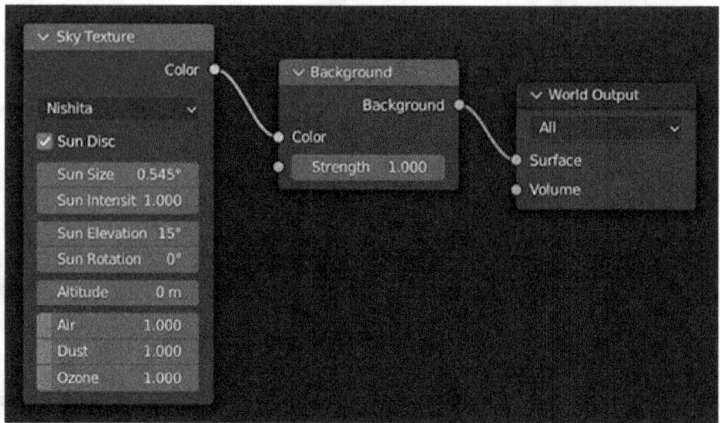

Figure 10.15 – Setting up the Sky Texture lighting node

To use **Sky Texture**, always make sure that you are on the Cycles rendering engine. We use Cycles because it is a ray-tracing engine, meaning it physically simulates how light bounces. This will make the rock look better. You can check that out by going to **Render Properties** in the left panel:

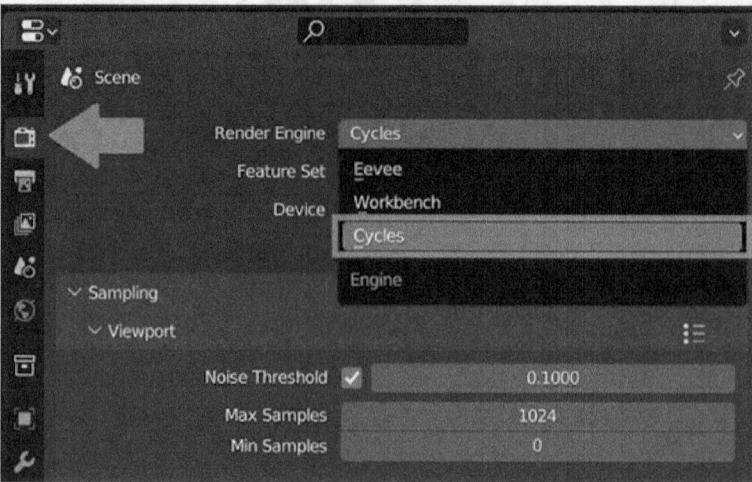

Figure 10.16 – Switching Render Engine to Cycles

2. Let's go ahead and switch the preview mode to **Rendered**. This is how our rock looks:

Figure 10.17 – Displaying the rock in the Rendered preview

The last step is to apply some optimization to our rock; it's heavy in geometry right now. We need to reduce the number of vertices that the rock holds because we'll be duplicating this rock tens of times in our landscape scene.

Optimizing the rock geometry

Before we can optimize the rock geometry, let's enable **Statistics** in **Show Overlays**, as shown in *Figure 10.18*:

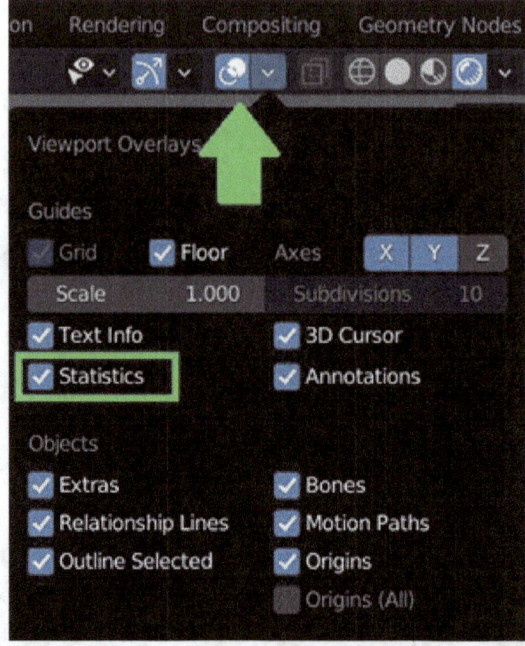

Figure 10.18 – Activating Statistics in Show Overlays

This way, when we select an object in our scene, its statistics will be displayed on the right side of the Blender interface. For example, in this case, I selected the rock object, and it shows that the model has over 49,000 vertices – a surprisingly high number for such a simple object!

Figure 10.19 – Displaying the rock object statistics

In order to reduce the number of vertices in our rock, let's go to **Modifier Properties**. You will find a bunch of modifiers added by **Rock Generator**. The first two modifiers are **Subdivision Surface** modifiers. Let's tweak these subdivision modifiers inside **Modifier Properties**:

1. Let's reduce the **Level Viewport** value of the first **Subdivision Surface** modifier to 1, as well as that of **Render**.

2. For the second **Subdivision Surface**, let's keep the **Levels Viewport** value at 2, as well as for **Render**.

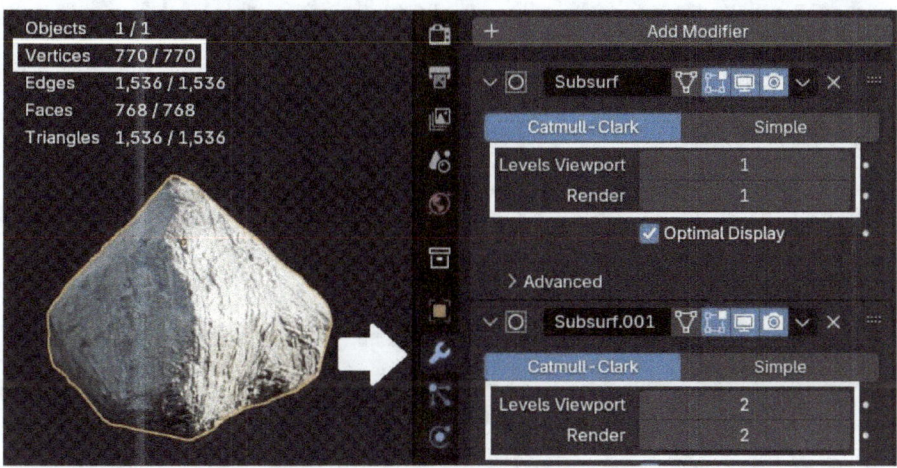

Figure 10.20 – Optimizing the rock object

Immediately, we dropped the number of vertices from **49.000** to **770** without sacrificing too much quality.

That's a huge drop. Imagine if we were required to duplicate our rock 50 times in the landscape scene. With our non-optimized rock, it would cost us around 2,450,000 vertices (49,000 * 50). That's almost 2.5 million vertices for rocks only. But with our optimized rock, it will cost us only 38,500 vertices (770 * 50).

The key takeaway here is that optimization creates a *performance budget* for your scene. By saving millions of vertices here, you ensure your computer has the resources left to handle thousands of trees, plants, and complex lighting effects later without slowing down.

Summary

In this chapter, we went through the process of creating realistic rock assets using the **Rock Generator** built-in Blender add-on. We learned how to generate and adjust the shape of rocks with one click.

Then, we learned how to unwrap and texture the rock using the **Node Wrangler** add-on. Finally, we optimized the rock geometry, reducing the vertex count from around 49,000 to just 770, which is a reduction of approximately 98%, without sacrificing too much rock quality.

In the next chapter, we'll be creating a new natural asset, which is flowers. Both rocks and flowers will be used to populate our landscape scene, making it look natural and realistic.

Get this book's PDF version and more

Scan the QR code (or go to packtpub.com/unlock). Search for this book by name, confirm the edition, and then follow the steps on the page.

Note: Keep your invoice handy. Purchases made directly from Packt don't require an invoice.

11

Creating Realistic Flowers in Blender

In this chapter, you will learn tips on how to create an organic-looking flower in Blender for our landscape environment scene. The flower that we'll be creating will be based on a real reference; the name of the flower is Buttercup.

We'll start by modeling the petals and the center. Then, we'll use the **Displace** modifier to add **Cloud** noise on the surface of the petals.

Next, we'll learn how to unwrap and texture the Buttercup flower. Finally, we'll diversify the flower branches, add the leaves using the alpha transparency trick, and give the flower a realistic scale measurement.

Creating your own flowers is a great skill to have. It allows you to fill your landscape scenes with unique details that look natural and organic. By understanding these steps, you won't just be able to make a Buttercup; you will be able to build any type of plant or flower you need for your future projects.

In this chapter, we'll be covering the following topics:

- Designing the petals of the Buttercup flower
- Modeling the petals of the Buttercup flower
- Modeling the stem of the Buttercup flower
- Texturing the Buttercup flower
- Creating the leaves of the Buttercup flower
- Sizing the Buttercup flower
- Final render of the Buttercup flower

By the end of this chapter, you will have a fully textured and realistic Buttercup flower. You will be ready to import it into our main landscape scene to add more detail to the environment.

Technical requirements

This chapter requires a system capable of running **Blender version 5.0** or above (Windows, macOS, or Linux).

You can download the resources for this chapter from GitHub at: `https://github.com/` `PacktPublishing/3D-Environment-Design-with-Blender-5-Second-Edition/tree/` `391cdead4d8ea7bc9f973233238cfbd65b973f5f/chapter-11`.

Let's get started by modeling the flower petals.

Designing the petals of the Buttercup flower

Let's start by creating the Buttercup flower's petals. Since this is a real flower, we must use a real reference to ensure the final result is accurate. We'll be using this image reference of the Buttercup flower:

Figure 11.1 – Buttercup flower petals

I'll put this image reference for download. In the GitHub repository of the book (see the *Technical requirements* section), you will find all the resources you need in this chapter.

After downloading this reference, press 7 on the 3D Viewport to go to the **Top Orthographic** view, and simply *drag and drop* this reference image into the 3D Viewport:

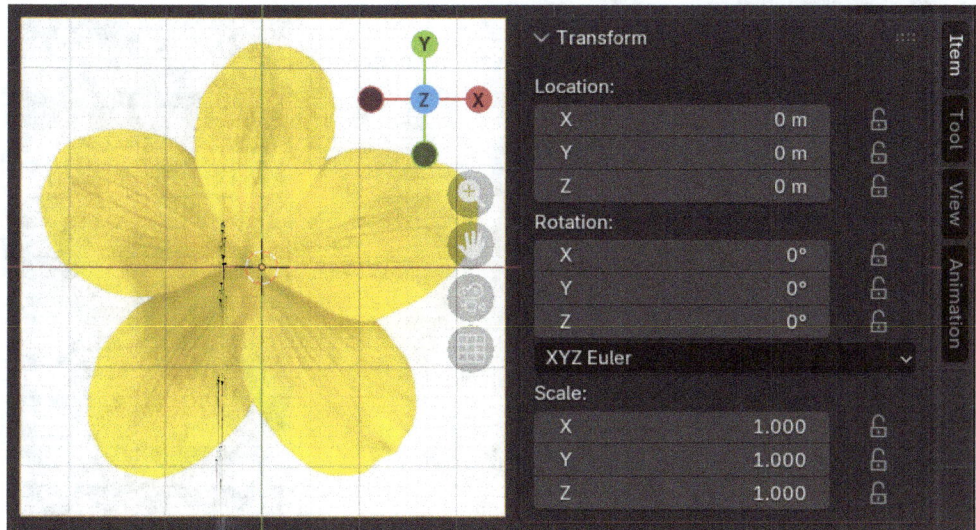

Figure 11.2 – Dragging the flower reference in the 3D Viewport

This way, we'll have the image reference laid down on the floor. Press *N* to access the **Transform** panel and make sure that the **Location** and **Rotation** values are set to 0 so that we can have the flower reference in the center of the grid.

Modeling the petals of the Buttercup flower

Let's start by creating a plane mesh and putting it on one of the petals in our reference.

In the **Edit Mode**, press *Ctrl + E* and choose **Subdivide**. This way, we'll subdivide our plane into *four* different small faces. We perform this step to have enough vertices on the edge of the plane to control.

Also, make sure to switch the preview mode to **Wireframe** by pressing *Z* in the 3D Viewport, so that we can see the flower reference and follow its petal edges.

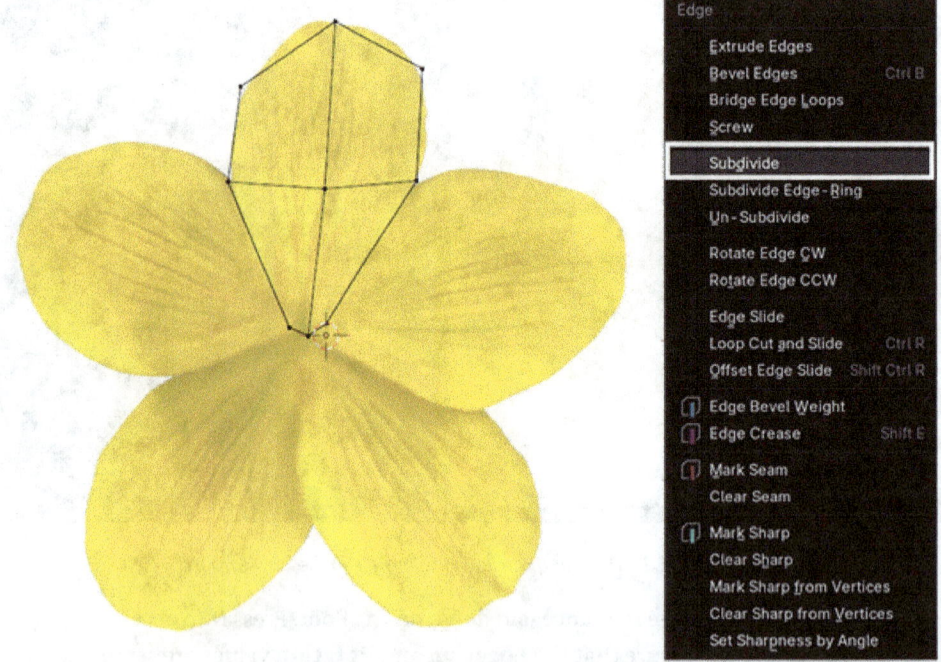

Figure 11.3 – Subdividing the plane using the Ctrl + E hotkey

Next, we'll need to add the **Subdivision Surface** modifier to the plane to make the petal smooth. This is shown in *Figure 11.4*, as follows:

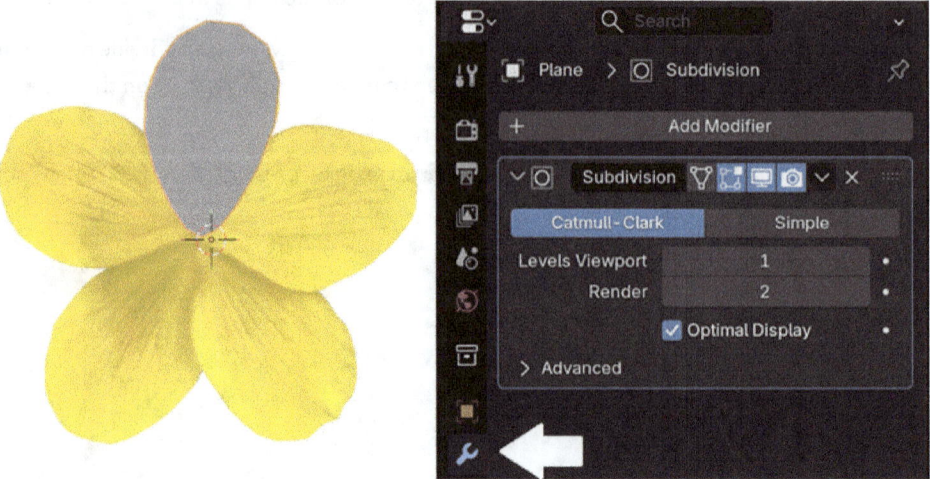

Figure 11.4 – Adding the Subdivision Surface modifier to the plane

Let's repeat the same alignment steps for the other petals. You can just duplicate the same plane, spin it, and put it on the next petal. Once you finish the alignment of the petal, our flower creation progress should look like this:

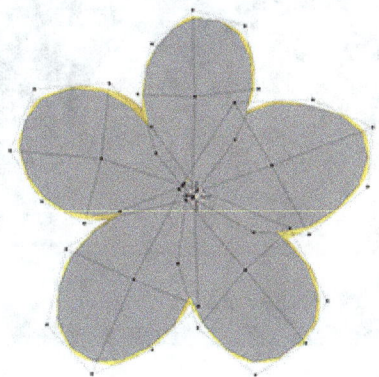

Figure 11.5 – Aligning planes with petals reference

Now we need to create the petals' curvature. So far, the petals are flat; we need to bend them upward. Let's select only the outer vertices of all five petals and lift them up until the curvature is created, as shown in *Figure 11.6*:

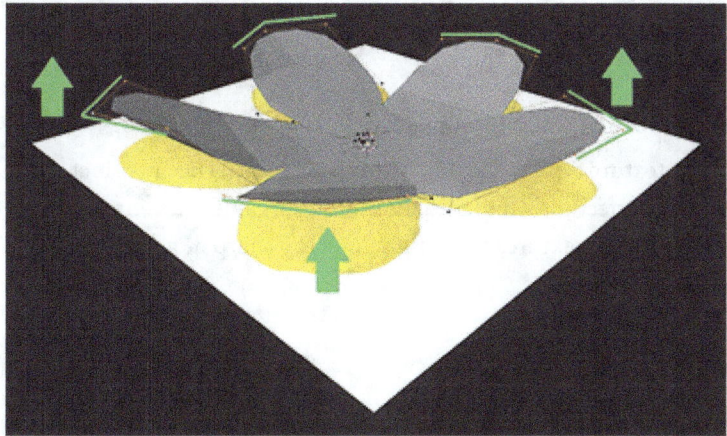

Figure 11.6 – Moving the petal edges of the flower up

To have a better idea of what Buttercup flower petals look like, let's take a look at a real image of this flower:

Figure 11.7 – Real reference of the Buttercup flower

(Credit: https://pixabay.com/photos/flower-buttercup-ranunculus-8030932/ by dendoktoor)

In *Figure 11.7*, you can see that the surface of the petals is not smooth; we need to add some noisy bumps on the surface. To accomplish that, we'll be using the **Displace** modifier. Follow these steps:

1. Select the petal object in the **Object Mode**.
2. Go to **Texture Properties**.
3. Click on **New** to add a new texture.
4. Set the new texture type to **Clouds**. We choose **Clouds** because it creates soft, random noise. This is perfect for simulating the subtle, organic unevenness found on real flower petals, unlike other textures that might look too sharp or geometric.

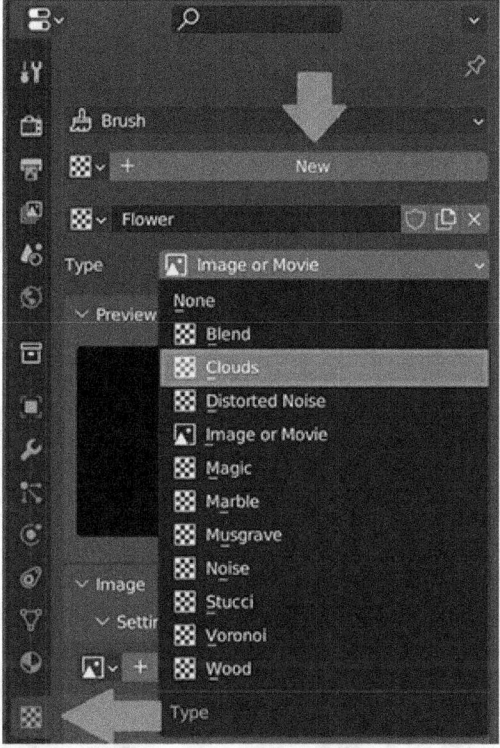

Figure 11.8 – Adding the Clouds texture

5. Go to **Modifier Properties** and search for the **Displace** modifier.

6. In the texture field highlighted in the *green* box, choose the **Flower** texture we created.

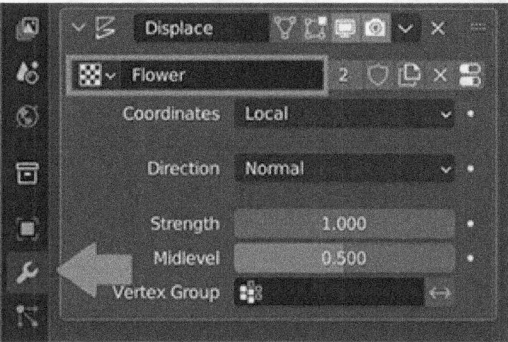

Figure 11.9 – Adding the Displace modifier to the flower

With the **Displace** modifier set to **Clouds**, the shape of the flower will look like this:

Figure 11.10 – Showing the flower with the Displace modifier applied

Notice that the petal edges look pointy and sharp. We can fix that by adding another **Subdivision Surface** modifier, similar to what we did in *Figure 11.4*. The new look of our petals is shown in *Figure 11.11*:

Figure 11.11 – Smoothing the flower petals by adding a Subdivision Surface modifier

Now that we have the flower petals, let's go ahead and create the stem of our Buttercup flower.

Modeling the stem of the Buttercup flower

The stem is the long, thin green part of a plant that rises above the soil and supports the flower.

Figure 11.12 – Reference of the Buttercup flower

(Credit: https://pixabay.com/photos/buttercup-sharp-buttercup-8101494/ by Nennieinszweidrei)

To create the flower stem, let's add a cube, jump into **Edit Mode**, and follow these steps:

1. Insert *four* horizontal edge loops.
2. Select each edge loop using *Alt + Left Mouse* and scale each edge loop as shown on the right side of the following figure.
3. Add a **Subdivision** modifier to this object to make it smooth.

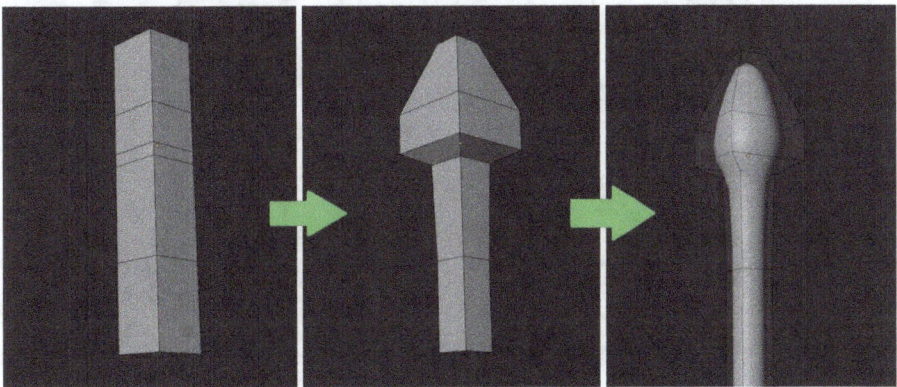

Figure 11.13 – Adding edge loops; scaling edge loops, and adding a Subdivision modifier (left to right)

4. Bring back the petals and place them in the center of our flower, as shown in *Figure 11.14*.

5. Let's work on the center of our flower by adding the small objects around the center:

    1. Add a plane.

    2. Scale it down exactly like the image on the left in *Figure 11.14*.

    3. Add the **Subdivision Surface** modifier to the plane.

    4. Duplicate it around the flower stem center.

Figure 11.14 – Flower seeds creation

This is how our flower looks so far in the **Solid** mode:

Figure 11.15 – Displaying the Buttercup flower in the Solid mode

Before we can duplicate our flower to make branches out of it, let's finish texturing it first, in the next section.

Texturing the Buttercup flower

Before we can proceed with texturing our flower, we need to make sure that all the petals of the flower are merged into one piece. To do that, you can press *Ctrl + J* to join them all into one unit.

Now, let's have a look at the steps for texturing the flower:

1. Select the petals, go to **Material Properties**, and add a new material. Let's call it `Flower-Petals`:

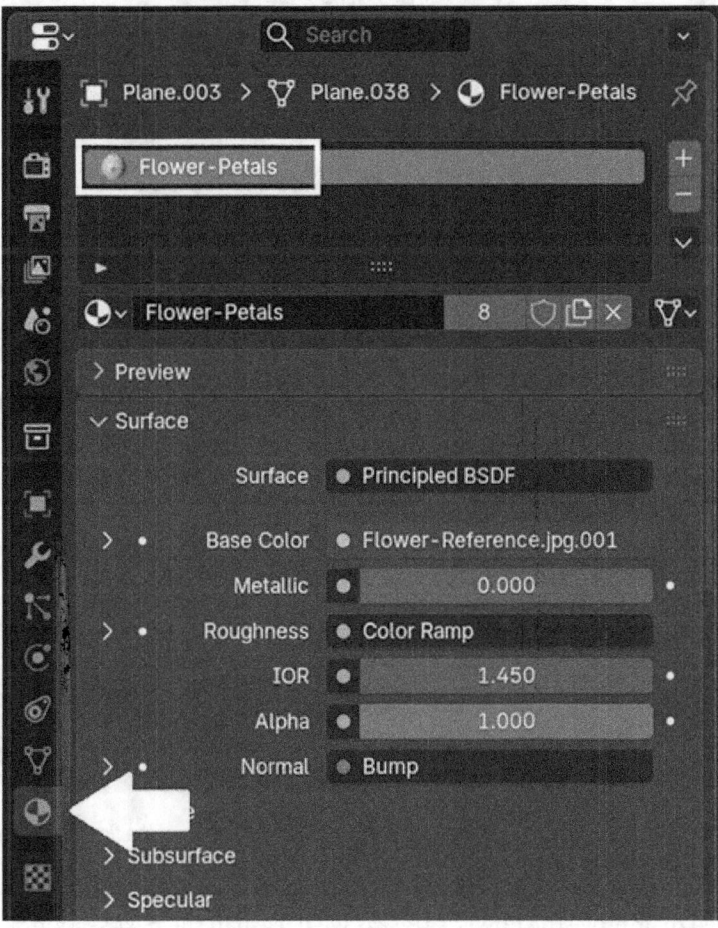

Figure 11.16 – Assigning the Flower-Petals material to the flower model

2. Switch the bottom window of your Blender scene into the **Shader Editor**.

3. Drag the image reference we used earlier in the **Shader Editor** and connect it to the **Base Color**.

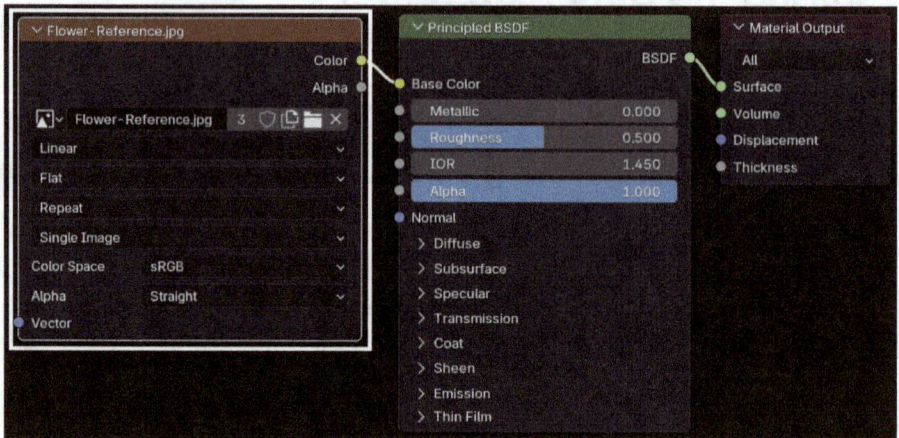

Figure 11.17 – Connecting the texture to the Base Color

4. Now, if we press Z and switch to the **Material Preview**, this is how our flower will look:

Figure 11.18 – Default unwrapping of the flower

You'll notice that our flower isn't properly textured because UVs aren't set up correctly. That's why we need to improve the flower's UVs, as we'll learn in the next section.

Unwrapping the Buttercup flower

We'll be unwrapping our flower by projecting the UVs from the top. To do that, let's perform these steps:

1. Press *7* in the 3D Viewport to go to the top.

2. Switch to the **Edit Mode**, press *U*, and choose **Project from View Bounds**.
   We use the **Project from View** unwrapping method because we modeled the petal directly on top of the reference image in the top view. This option creates a UV map that matches exactly what you see in the Viewport, ensuring the texture aligns perfectly with your mesh without needing complex manual adjustments.

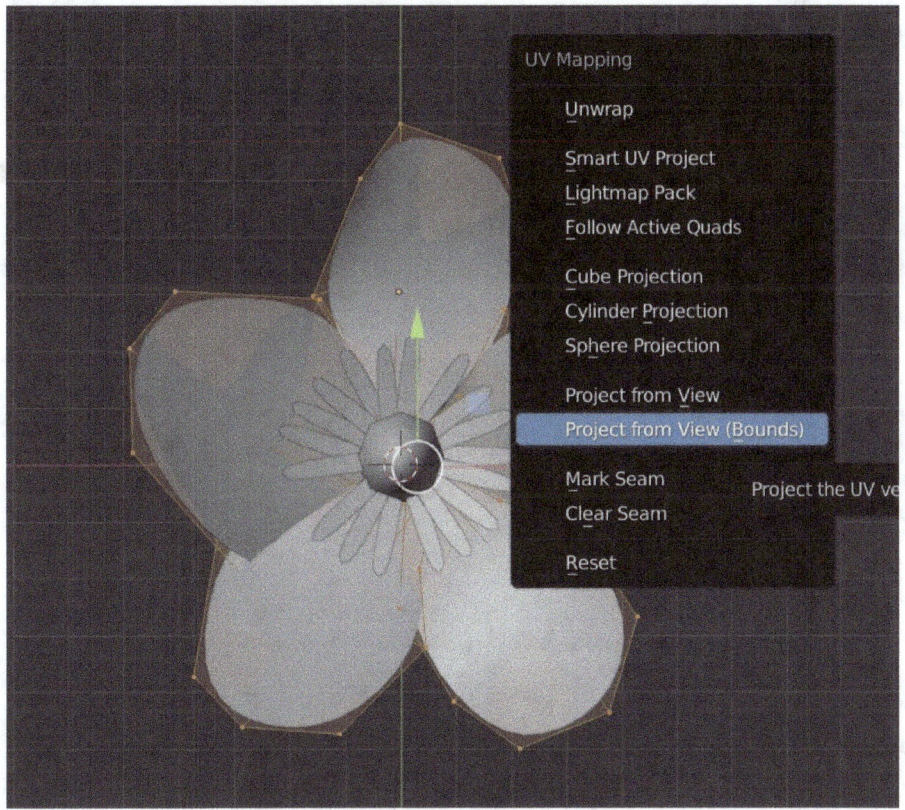

Figure 11.19 – Unwrapping the flower model

3. Switch from the **Shader Editor** to the **UV Editor** and start aligning the UVs with the reference petals. Do your best; it doesn't need to be 100% perfect.

Figure 11.20 – Tweaking the flower UVs

This is how our flower will look, better unwrapped but still lacking surface detail. So far, we've only worked on the **Base Color** of our flower. We need to work on the **Roughness** map as well as add the **Bump** node.

Figure 11.21 – Texturing the flower petals

Let's tweak the other material channels, so we'll head back to the **Shader Editor** and follow these steps:

1. Connect the **Flower-Reference** texture to a **ColorRamp** node.

2. Move the two **ColorRamp** handles close to each other.

3. Connect the right slot of the **ColorRamp** to the **Roughness** channel. This will give us a nice reflection on our flower petals.

4. Connect the **Flower-Reference** texture to a **Bump** node.

5. Set **Strength** on the **Bump** node to 0.150.

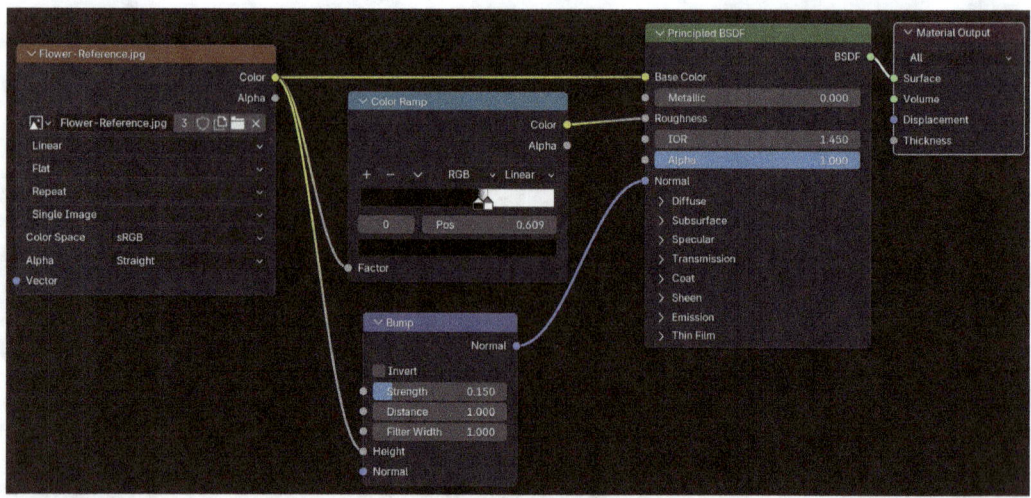

Figure 11.22 – Node setup of the flower material

This will make the flower petal reflective and bumpy.

Now, select all the small planes that make up the flower, and join them using *Ctrl + J*. Next, join the small combined planes with the petals. This ensures that the small petals share the same material and modifiers as applied to the main petals.

Figure 11.23 – Texturing the Buttercup flower

The flower petals are now complete and looking good. Next, we will focus on the lower part of the flower and create a realistic material for the stem.

Texturing the stem of the Buttercup flower

Let's create the second green material for the center stem. We need this because the stem has a different color and texture from the flower petals. By creating a specific material, we can make the stem look green and organic without changing the look of the flower head.

To begin the process, let's perform these steps:

1. Select the center stem and add a new material to it called Green　Stem.

2. In the **Shader Editor**, add a **Wave Texture** node. The **Wave Texture** node is perfect here because it creates long, linear patterns. This helps us simulate the natural vertical fibers and veins that run along the length of a real plant stem.

    1. Set **Scale** to 5.

    2. Set the **Distortion** amount to 15.

    3. Increase **Detail** to 7.8.

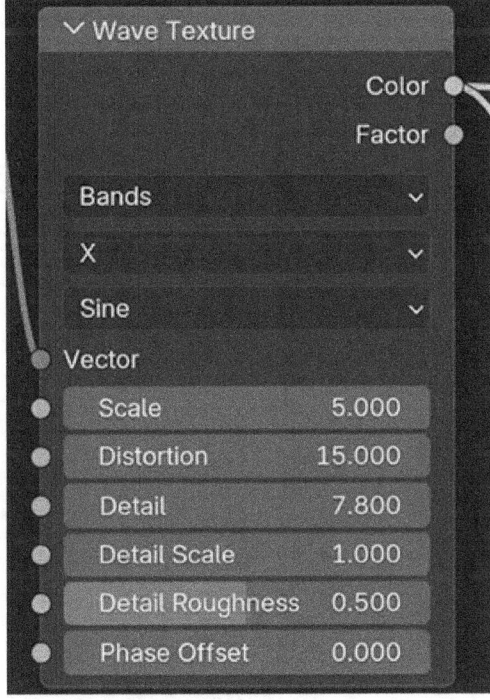

Figure 11.24 – Wave Texture node

3. Connect the **Wave Texture** node to a **ColorRamp** node.

4. Set the two handles in the **ColorRamp** node to *two different green colors* as shown in *Figure 11.25*.

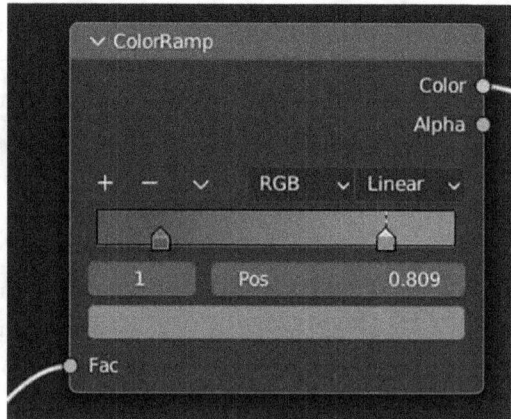

Figure 11.25 – ColorRamp node

Next, search for a **Bump** node, add it, and follow these steps.

1. Connect the **Wave Texture** node to the **Bump** node and connect the **Bump** node to the **Normal** slot of the **Principled BSDF** node, as shown in *Figure 11.26*.

2. Set the **Bump** node's **Strength** value to 0.25.

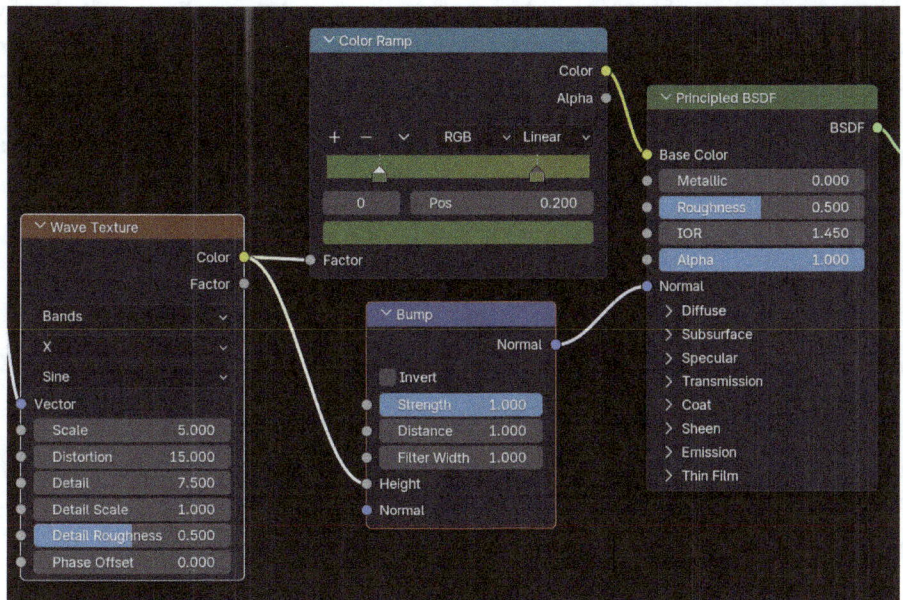

Figure 11.26 – Stem node setup material

With this setup, this is how our flower looks:

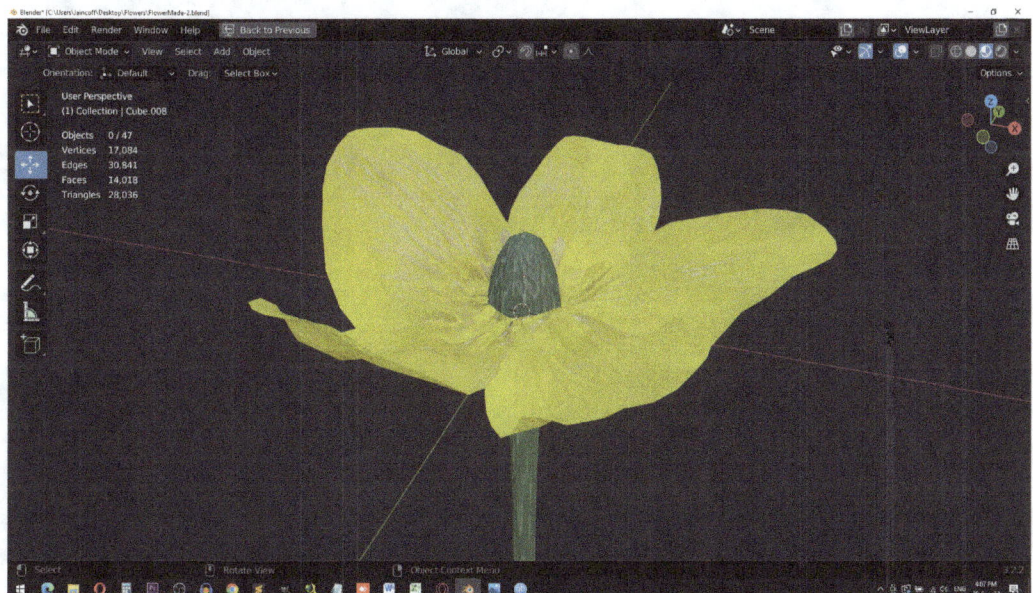

Figure 11.27 – Finishing the texturing of the Buttercup flower

Now we need to diversify our flower by branching it multiple times. You can do that by duplicating the first flower and putting it on the second. Make sure that the main stem is thicker than the secondary stem. This is demonstrated in *Figure 11.28*, as follows:

Figure 11.28 – Second-level branching of the Buttercup flower

After duplicating a few branches, this is how our flower will look:

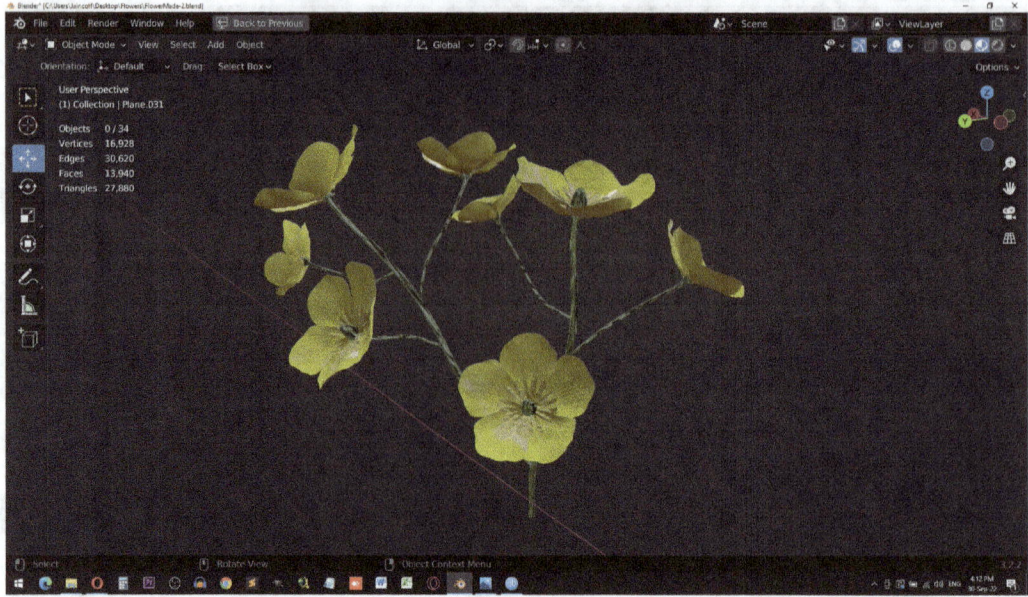

Figure 11.29 – Branching the Buttercup flower

Now that the flower branches are ready, the model is starting to look good. However, to make it look like a complete plant, we are still missing the green leaves at the bottom.

Creating the leaves of the Buttercup flower

The next step is to create the leaves of the Buttercup flower. Based on the following reference, we can see the shape of the leaves of the Buttercup flower:

Figure 11.30 – Image reference of Buttercup flower leaves

You can download this leaf image reference from this link: `https://github.com/PacktPublishing/3D-Environment-Design-with-Blender-5-Second-Edition/blob/391cdead4d8ea7bc9f973233238cfbd65b973f5f/chapter-11/Leaf-Texture.jpg`

Now, let's go ahead and create the leaves of the Buttercup flower.

Applying textures with alpha transparency

Before we start, let's understand what **alpha transparency** is. It is a way to make specific parts of an image invisible. This is the best method for creating leaves because leaves often have complex, jagged edges.

Modeling these shapes vertex by vertex would be very difficult and heavy for the computer. Instead, we use a simple plane and an image texture to define the shape, keeping our model lightweight and efficient.

To create the flower leaves using the alpha transparency trick, let's follow these steps:

1. Create a plane.

2. Assign to the plane a new material called Leaf.

Figure 11.31 – Assigning the Buttercup flower leaf texture to the plane

3. Drop the leaf image you downloaded into the **Shader Editor** and connect it to the **Base Color**.

4. Insert two edge loops on the *Y* axis and three edge loops on the *X* axis, and change the shape of the plane as follows:

Figure 11.32 – Changing the shape of the plane to fit the leaves

When rendering this plane, all we need to show is just the leaf; the other *white* spots must be transparent. This is where the **Alpha** slot in the **Principled BSDF** node comes into play. We need to create a *black and white* texture out of the leaf texture, where *white* will represent the green leaf and *black* will represent the leaf surroundings.

To achieve this, we'll create an alpha mask from the leaf texture using a **ColorRamp**. Follow these steps:

1. Let's connect the leaf texture to a **ColorRamp** node. The **ColorRamp** node will convert the leaf texture into a *black and white* texture (grayscale).

2. Bring the two *black* and *white* handles close to each other to sharpen the edges of the leaf.

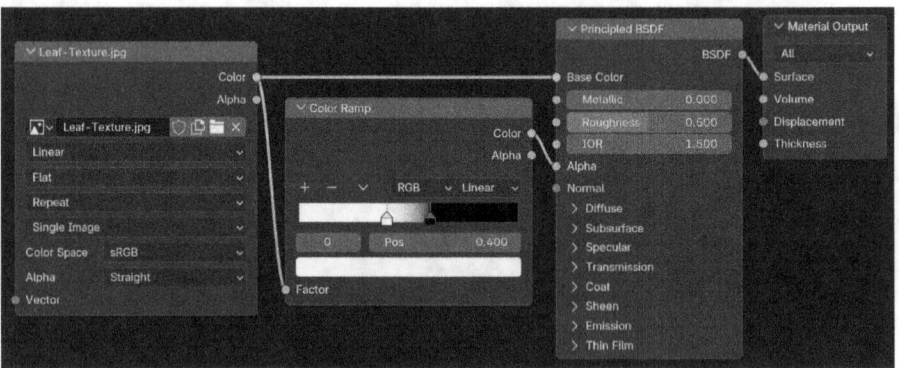

Figure 11.33 – Leaf node setup material

3. In case you want to see the **Alpha** channel we created, it basically looks like this:

Figure 11.34 – Black and white leaf mask

4. When connecting this texture to the **Principled BSDF Alpha** slot, Blender will only display what is *white* and make the *black* areas transparent when rendering, as shown in *Figure 11.35*:

Figure 11.35 – Making the leaf texture transparent on the edges

At this stage, you may notice that transparency behaves differently in the Viewport when using **EEVEE** in Blender 5.

Transparency in EEVEE in Blender 5

If you are using the **EEVEE** render engine in Blender 5 (specifically **EEVEE**), transparency is handled differently than in older versions. By default, **EEVEE** uses a **Dithered** method, which may look grainy in the Viewport.

To adjust it, follow these steps:

1. Go to the **Material Properties** tab.
2. Scroll down to the **Settings** panel.
3. Under **Surface**, look for **Render Method**.
4. You can switch this to **Blended** for smoother transparency or keep it as **Dithered**, depending on your performance needs.

For these leaves, the default settings usually work well, but ensure the **Transparent Shadows** checkbox is checked if you want light to pass through the leaves accurately.

With the transparency set up, we can now focus on refining the look of the leaves.

To make the leaves look better, be sure to work on the **Roughness** and add the **Bump** node to get better results, similar to what we did in *Figure 11.22* in the *Unwrapping the Buttercup flower* section.

Finally, put the leaves in different places of the flower stem, as shown in *Figure 11.36*:

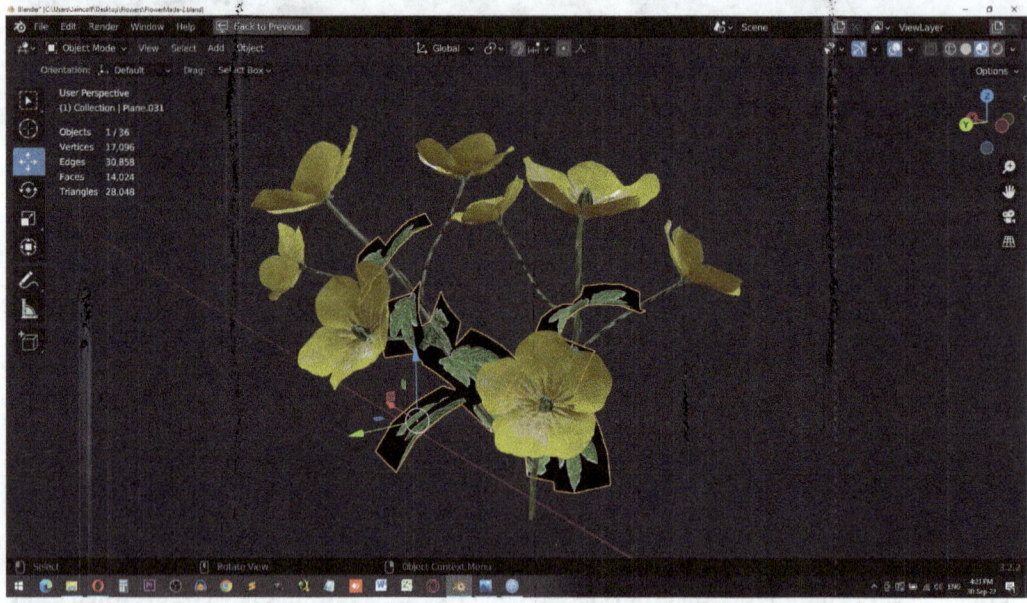

Figure 11.36 – Buttercup flower final result on Material Preview

Our Buttercup flower is now fully modeled and textured. However, before we can call it finished, we need to make sure its size matches real-world measurements so it fits perfectly into our scene.

Sizing the Buttercup flower

Our last step is to give the flower the right measurements. Based on Google research, Buttercup flowers reach 31 cm in height. So, any height between 20 cm and 30 cm will look reasonable.

In our example, the longest stem height is 0.27 m (27 cm). We can say that our flower branch size is reasonable. This is shown in *Figure 11.37*, as follows:

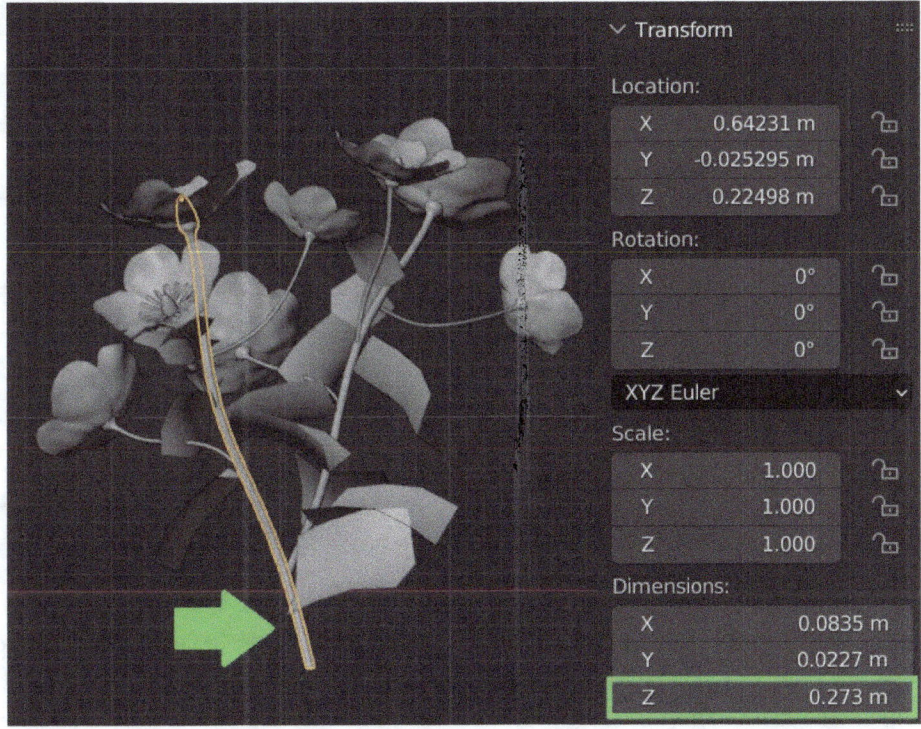

Figure 11.37 – Measuring the Buttercup flower main stem

In case you have a different size, you can press *N* to access the right **Transform** panel, select all the flower elements, and scale them up or down until they reach a realistic size.

Now that our flower is completed and well-sized, let's take a look at how our flower will look in the **Rendered** mode.

Final render of the Buttercup flower

We need to verify the result to make sure it looks good when importing into our landscape scene. This is how our Buttercup flower looks when rendered:

Figure 11.38 – Final render of the Buttercup flower

The final render shown here uses HDRI lighting, a camera with depth of field, and a focused composition. These are shown only for presentation purposes; we'll learn how to set up all of this in detail in the final chapter of this book.

Summary

In this chapter, we went through the creation of Buttercup flowers based on real references.

We started by modeling the petals and the center. We used the **Displace** modifier to add **Cloud** noise on the surface of the petals.

Next, we learned how to unwrap and texture the Buttercup flower. Finally, we diversified the flower branches and added the leaves using the alpha transparency trick.

In the next chapter, we will learn how to model a tree using Blender 5's **Sapling Tree Gen** add-on.

Get this book's PDF version and more

Scan the QR code (or go to packtpub.com/unlock). Search for this book by name, confirm the edition, and then follow the steps on the page.

UNLOCK NOW

Note: Keep your invoice handy. Purchases made directly from Packt don't require an invoice.

12

Creating Trees Ready for Large Environments

Trees are one of the most important visual elements in outdoor scenes. A well-made tree instantly sells scale, atmosphere, and realism, while a poorly optimized one can destroy performance.

In this chapter, we will create a spruce tree designed specifically for snowy environments. Spruce trees have a very recognizable structure: narrow tops, downward-facing branches, and dense foliage that can carry snow naturally. This makes them ideal for winter scenes, forests, and mountain landscapes.

Rather than modeling a tree manually, we will take advantage of Blender 5's **Sapling Tree Gen** add-on to generate a procedural base, then refine, optimize, and prepare it for use in large scenes where dozens—or even hundreds—of trees may be required. This is because trees are complex, organic shapes with thousands of branches and leaves. Trying to model this vertex by vertex is not only time-consuming but also very hard to get right. This **Sapling Tree Gen** add-on handles that organic complexity for us, making the process significantly easier and allowing us to generate realistic results in seconds.

In this chapter, we'll be covering the following topics:

- Why spruce trees work in snow scenes
- Using the **Sapling Tree Gen** add-on
- Generating the base tree
- Shaping the tree into a spruce
- Optimizing the tree for large scenes

- Creating branch-based leaves
- Texturing the tree trunk

By the end of this chapter, you will solve one of the hardest challenges in 3D: creating believable trees. Instead of struggling to model branches by hand, you will have a workflow to generate complex, organic trees in seconds.

Technical requirements

This chapter requires a system capable of running **Blender version 5.0** or above (Windows, macOS, or Linux).

You can download the resources for this chapter from GitHub at `https://github.com/ PacktPublishing/3D-Environment-Design-with-Blender-5-Second-Edition/tree/ 391cdead4d8ea7bc9f973233238cfbd65b973f5f/chapter-12`. The repo contains the following resources, which you need to complete the exercise in this chapter:

- Bark image texture
- Branch image texture

Why spruce trees work in snow scenes

As mentioned in the chapter introduction, we will be creating the spruce tree because it fits perfectly in our snow environment. Spruce trees naturally grow in cold climates. Their branches slope downward, preventing heavy snow buildup and allowing the tree to survive harsh conditions. Visually, this gives them a layered, conical shape that is very recognizable from a distance.

This structure also makes spruce trees perfect for the following types of environments:

- Snowy forests
- Mountains
- Winter cinematics
- Large outdoor scenes where repetition is unavoidable

Figure 12.1 shows a reference image of a spruce tree, highlighting its overall shape and branch structure:

Figure 12.1 – Reference image of spruce tree

(Credit: https://pixabay.com/photos/winter-forest-snow-winter-frost-7677111/ by Leonhard_Niederwimmer)

We will be using a built-in plugin in Blender 5 called **Sapling Tree Gen**. Our goal is not just to make *a tree*, but also to make a tree that can be duplicated many times without hurting performance.

Using the Sapling Tree Gen add-on

Blender 5 includes a powerful procedural tree generator called **Sapling Tree Gen**. It allows us to control the following aspects of a tree:

- Trunk thickness and taper
- Branch distribution

- Branch angles and rings
- Leaf placement and density

Since it is procedural, we can quickly generate variations later using the same base settings.

To begin, let's enable the **Sapling Tree Gen** add-on in the next section.

Enabling the Sapling Tree Gen add-on

The good news is that you don't need to download anything. The **Sapling Tree Gen** add-on comes pre-installed with Blender, but it is disabled by default. We just need to turn it on to start using it.

1. Go to **Edit | Preferences**.
2. Open the **Get Extensions** tab and click on **Allow Online Access**.

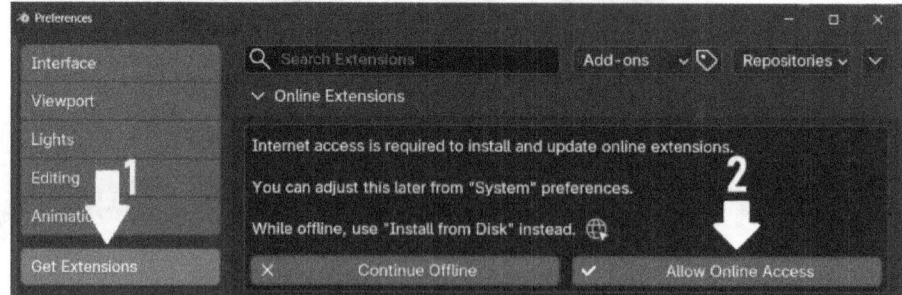

Figure 12.2 – Allow Online Access

3. Search for sapling tree gen.
4. Install the **Sapling Tree Gen** add-on.

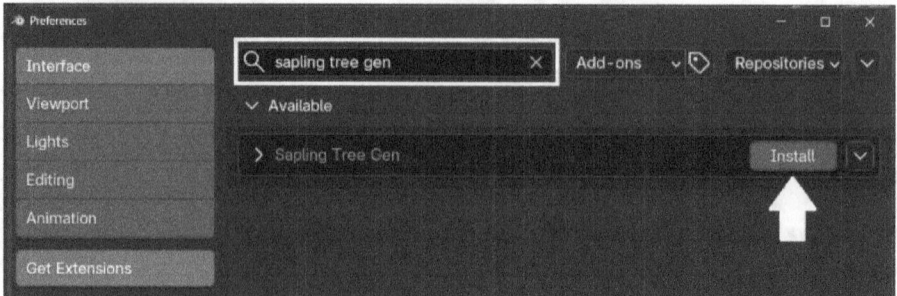

Figure 12.3 – Installing Sapling Tree Gen add-on

Once the add-on is enabled, the tree generator becomes available directly from the **Add** menu.

Now that the **Sapling Tree Gen** add-on is enabled, we'll move on to creating the base tree.

Generating the base tree

In the 3D Viewport, press *Shift + A* and go to **Curve**. Here, you will find **Sapling Tree Gen**; click on it.

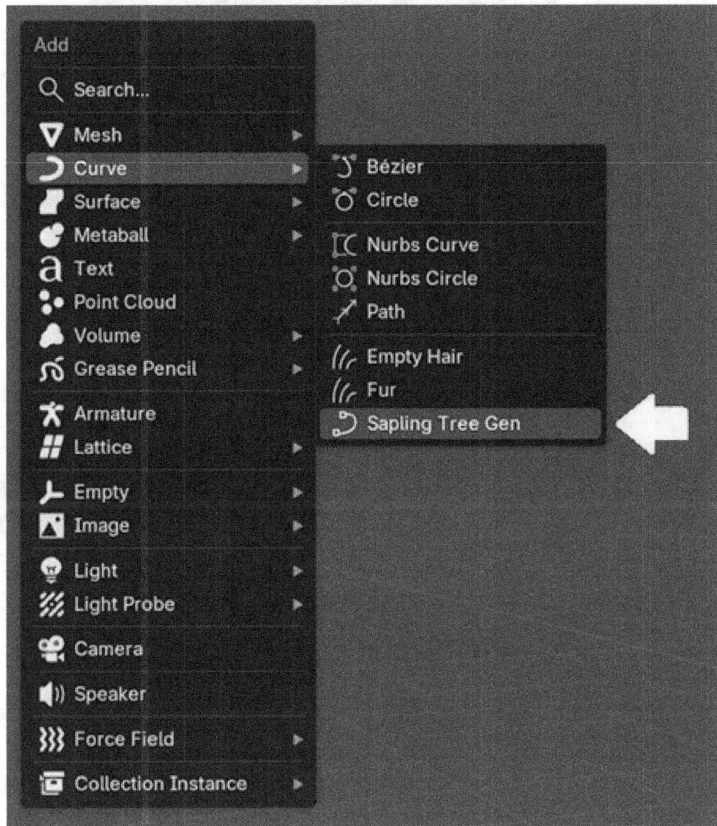

Figure 12.4 – Generating the tree base

The default tree will appear, along with a **Settings** panel in the lower-left corner of the Viewport.

Figure 12.5 – Sapling tree with default settings

Note

This **Settings** panel is temporary. If you click anywhere outside the Viewport before finishing your adjustments, it will disappear, and you'll need to add the tree again.

Now that you are aware of this limitation, let's proceed to the next step, where we will customize the parameters to create our spruce tree.

Shaping the tree into a spruce

With the default tree generated, we can now begin shaping it to match the characteristics of a spruce. *Figure 12.6* shows the default tree with a panel on the left side to adjust the generated tree:

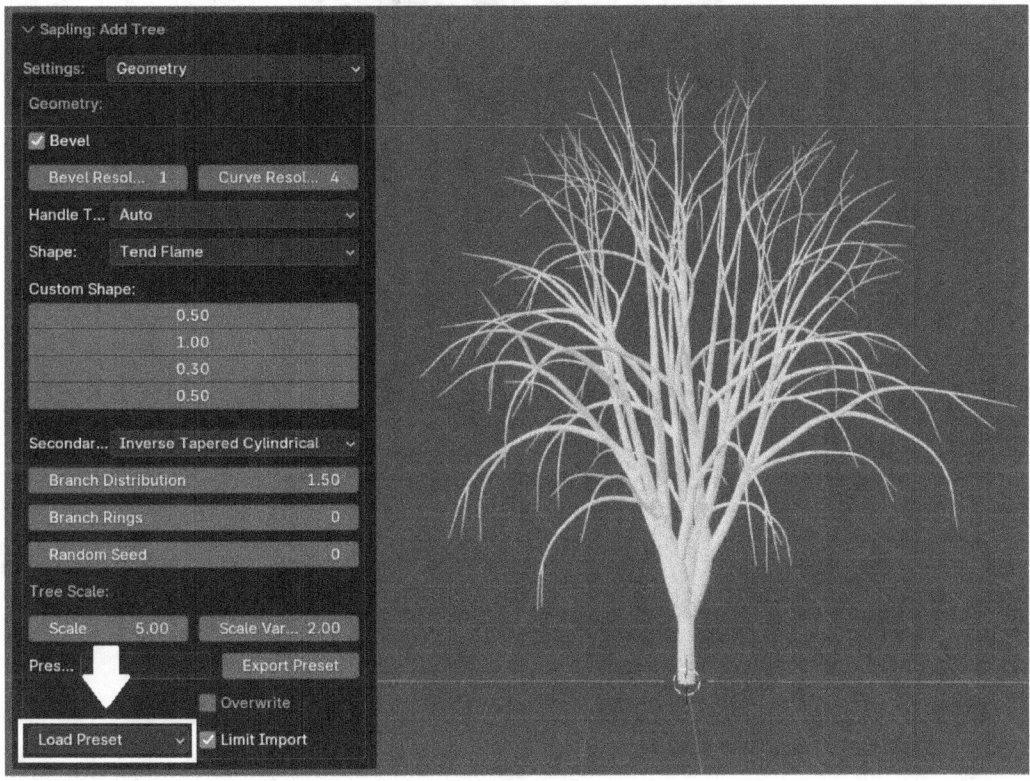

Figure 12.6 – Adjusting tree shape

In the **Settings** panel, firstly, change **Load Preset** to the **small_pine** preset. This way, our tree will look like a spruce tree, as shown in *Figure 12.7*:

Figure 12.7 – Shaping the tree into a spruce

The **small_pine** preset gives us the following:

- A narrow trunk
- Layered branch levels
- A silhouette close to a real spruce

From this point on, we will start refining the shape.

Adjusting Branch Distribution

For **Branch Distribution**, reduce this parameter from **1.60** to 1.00. This pushes the branches downward instead of upward, reinforcing the typical spruce look and making the tree feel heavier and more natural.

Next, we'll increase the number of branch layers to give the tree more visual density.

Increasing Branch Rings

For **Branch Rings**, we need to increase the parameter to 10 to have more rings and make the tree look full. More rings mean more branch layers, which does the following:

- Improves fullness
- Helps the tree be read better from medium and long distances
- Prevents the tree from looking flat or empty

Next, let's optimize the tree geometry.

Optimizing the tree for large scenes

By default, the **Sapling Tree Gen** add-on generates dense geometry. This is fine for a single tree, but impractical for large environments that require duplicating this tree multiple times.

Before moving forward, we must reduce geometry with a long-term scene mindset.

The mindset here is that we aren't just creating one tree; we are creating a forest. If this single tree is too heavy, duplicating it 1,000 times will make the scene unworkable. By reducing the geometry now, we ensure that we can scatter thousands of these trees later without slowing down the Viewport or crashing Blender.

By default, the resolution is set high for a close-up view. However, for a forest, we don't need that smoothness. Lowering the resolution allows us to strip away thousands of unnecessary faces while keeping the overall shape of the tree intact. So, let's tweak the resolution settings of our tree.

Adjusting resolution settings

We can significantly reduce geometry by lowering the curve resolution values:

- Set **Bevel Resolution** to 1.
- Set **Curve Resolution** to 1.

These adjustments reduce the number of vertices generated along the tree's curves while preserving its overall shape.

This is the impact of the adjustments in the resolution settings on the geometry:

- Original vertex count: **8,856**
- Optimized vertex count: **1,980**

This results in a *77% reduction* in geometry, while preserving the overall shape and silhouette of the tree:

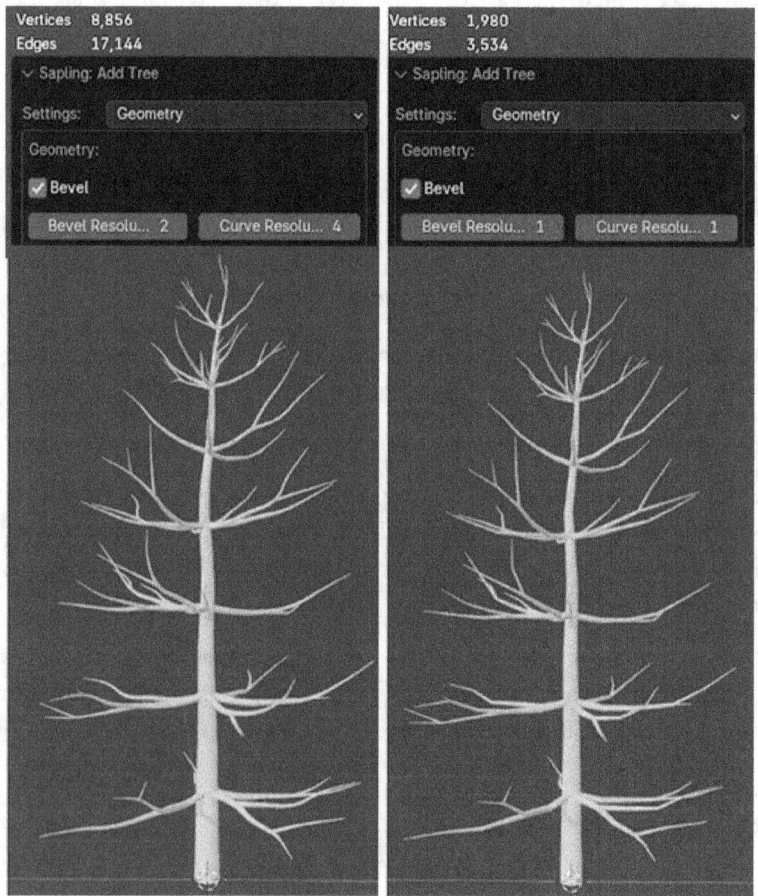

Figure 12.8 – Optimizing tree geometry

At this point, the tree is light enough to be duplicated dozens of times without performance issues, and you won't notice a big change in the shape of the tree.

In this section, we reduced the amount of geometry from **8,856** down to **1,980** vertices, which is a 77% reduction in geometry without losing detail. Now we're ready for the next step, which is adding leaves.

Creating branch-based leaves

Spruce trees do not use individual leaves. Instead, they rely on *needle clusters*, which are best represented using alpha-textured planes. Since modeling individual needles would create unmanageable and dense geometry, using images with alpha channels allows us to simulate this complex density with a simple texture, keeping the model lightweight and optimized for rendering.

Modeling the branch plane

We will now create the base geometry for the branch. This plane will serve as the canvas for the alpha texture, effectively holding the needle clusters and defining the branch's shape.

Follow these steps to begin modeling a branch plane:

1. Add a plane.

2. Enter **Edit Mode**.

3. Shape it to resemble a small branch cluster, similar to *Figure 12.9*. Use the same technique introduced earlier, in the *Creating the leaves of the Buttercup flower* section in *Chapter 11*. Add a plane, shape it to match the needle cluster, and UV unwrap it using the alpha channel.

4. Rename the object to Branch, as it will be referenced later by the **Sapling Tree Gen** add-on.

Refer to *Figure 12.9* to see how to shape the plane so it fits the needle cluster texture:

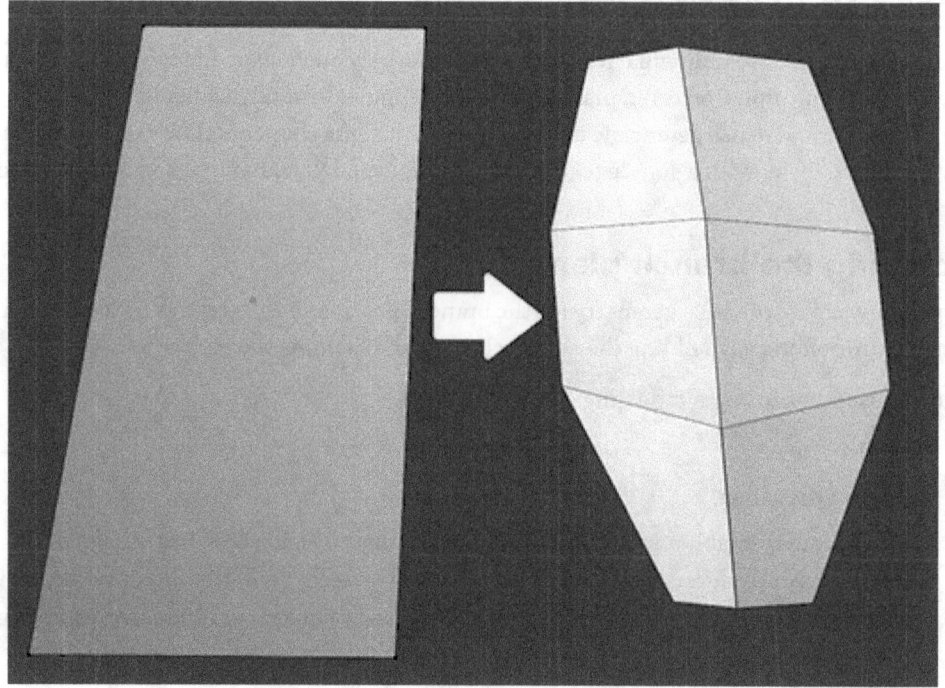

Figure 12.9 – Modeling branch mesh

With the branch plane modeled, we can now set up its material.

Texturing a tree branch

Now we will apply the material that turns our simple mesh into a realistic spruce branch. The goal of this section is to assign the needle texture and configure the alpha transparency, ensuring the cluster looks dense and natural.

1. Select **Branch** (the mesh plane we modeled in the preceding section).
2. Switch to **Shader Editor**.
3. Create a new material named Tree-Branch.

This material will allow us to assign the needle texture and define the transparency settings.

Now that the material slot is ready, let's proceed to the **Shader Editor** to set up the textures.

Setting up the Shader

In this section, we will configure the shader nodes to display the needle cluster texture. The main goal is to refine the transparency (alpha) settings to ensure the needles have crisp, defined edges without any visible background artifacts.

To achieve a clean cutout, we'll use a **ColorRamp** node to control the texture's alpha. Load the branch texture from the resources and make the following connections:

1. First, connect the **Color** output of the **Branch Image Texture** node to the **Base Color** input of the **Principled BSDF** node.

2. Next, connect the **Color** output of the **Branch Image Texture** node to the **Factor** input of a **ColorRamp** node.

3. Then, connect the **Color** output of the **ColorRamp** node to the **Alpha** input of the **Principled BSDF** node.

4. Finally, bring the *white* handle of the **ColorRamp** node close to the *black* handle. This tightens the contrast of the mask, which solves the issue of blurry edges and eliminates any *halo* artifacts around the needles.

This is the material setup in the **Shader Editor**:

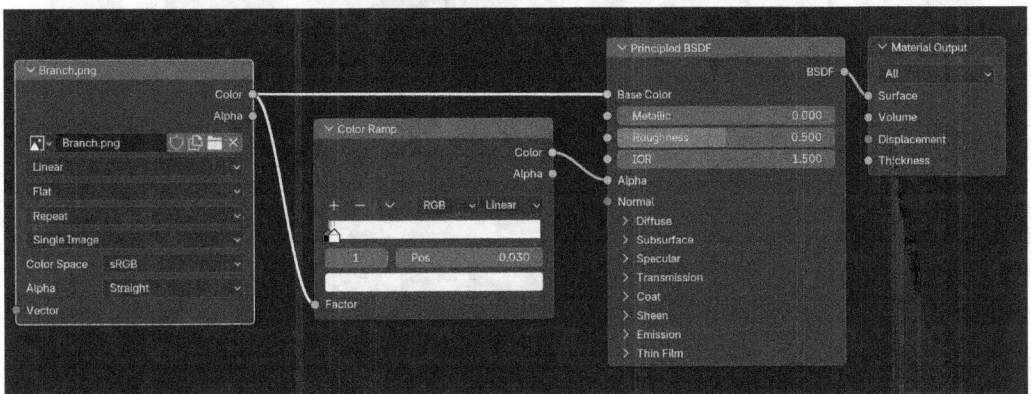

Figure 12.10 – Adding branch material

With the shader configured, the material is ready, but the image might look stretched or misaligned. To fix this, we need to unwrap the plane to match the texture coordinates.

UV unwrapping the branch

Now that the material is ready, we must tell Blender how to map the 2D texture onto our 3D plane. In this section, we will UV unwrap the mesh to align the image perfectly with the geometry, ensuring the needle cluster appears exactly where we intend.

To align the texture with the geometry, follow these steps:

1. Select the branch (that is, the mesh plane).

2. Enter **Edit Mode**.

3. Press *7* for **Top View**. This ensures the UV projection is perfectly flat and aligned with the texture, preventing distortion.

4. Press *U* for **Project from View (Bounds)**. This projects the UV map from your current view and scales it to the image boundaries, ensuring the texture covers the entire plane immediately.

5. Switch to **Material Preview** to confirm correct alignment, as shown in *Figure 12.11*.

Your branch should now appear as shown in *Figure 12.11*, with the texture correctly aligned to the geometry:

Figure 12.11 – Branch material preview

You now have a fully textured spruce branch cluster with accurate transparency, ready to be populated across the tree.

Setting the origin point to the stem

To ensure your branches attach and rotate naturally from their base rather than spinning around their center, you need to reposition the object's origin using the following steps:

1. Select your branch plane and press *Tab* to enter **Edit Mode**.

2. Select the single vertex in the bottom corner where the stem or leaf begins (this is where you want the rotation to happen).

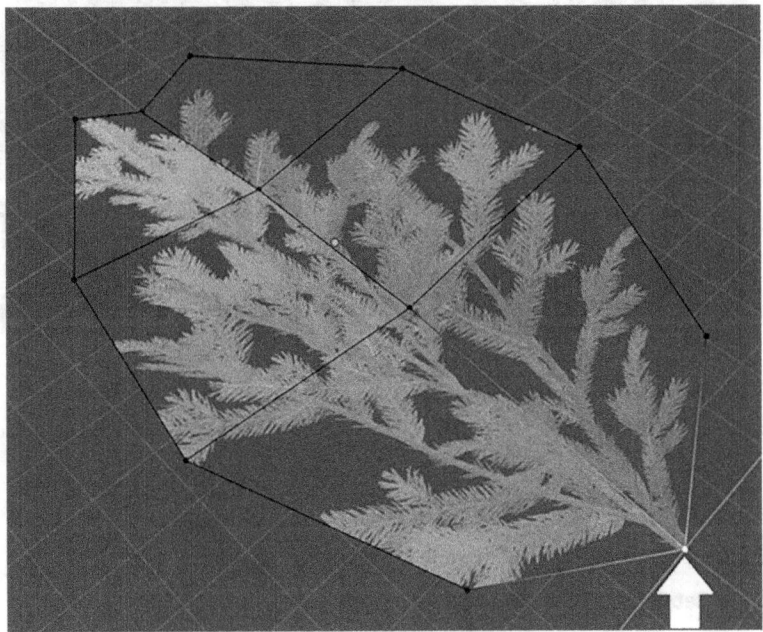

Figure 12.12 – Selecting the vertex in the bottom corner

3. Press *Shift* + *S* to open the **Snapping** menu.

4. Choose **Cursor to Selected**, as shown in *Figure 12.13*:

Figure 12.13 – Cursor to Selected

5. The *red-and-white* 3D cursor will snap exactly to that corner vertex (check the *white* circle in *Figure 12.13*).

6. Press *Tab* to exit back to **Object Mode**.

7. Right-click on the object to open the context menu.

8. Go to **Set Origin | Origin to 3D Cursor**.

The small *orange* dot (origin) will move from the center of the plane to the corner where you placed the 3D cursor:

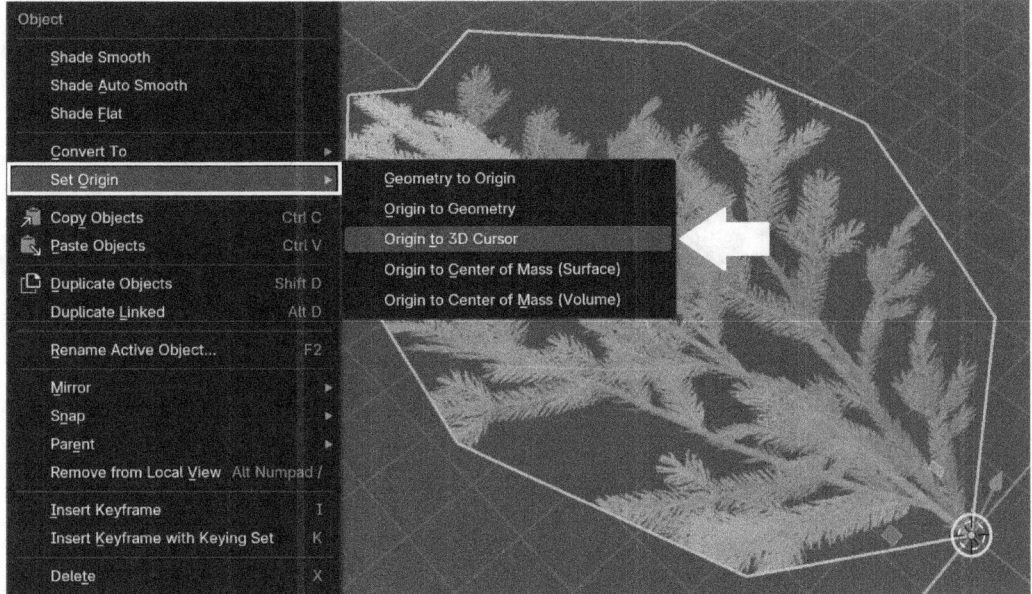

Figure 12.14 – Origin to 3D Cursor

Now, when you rotate or scale the branch, it will pivot from the stem rather than spinning around its center, making it much easier to place on a tree.

With the branch plane prepared, we can now attach it to the tree using **Sapling Tree Gen**'s leaf system.

Attaching branches to the tree

Back to the tree panel settings, we need to change **Settings** from **Geometry** to **Leaves**. Follow these steps:

1. Select the tree

2. In the **Sapling** settings, switch **Geometry** to **Leaves**.

3. Enable **Show Leaves**.

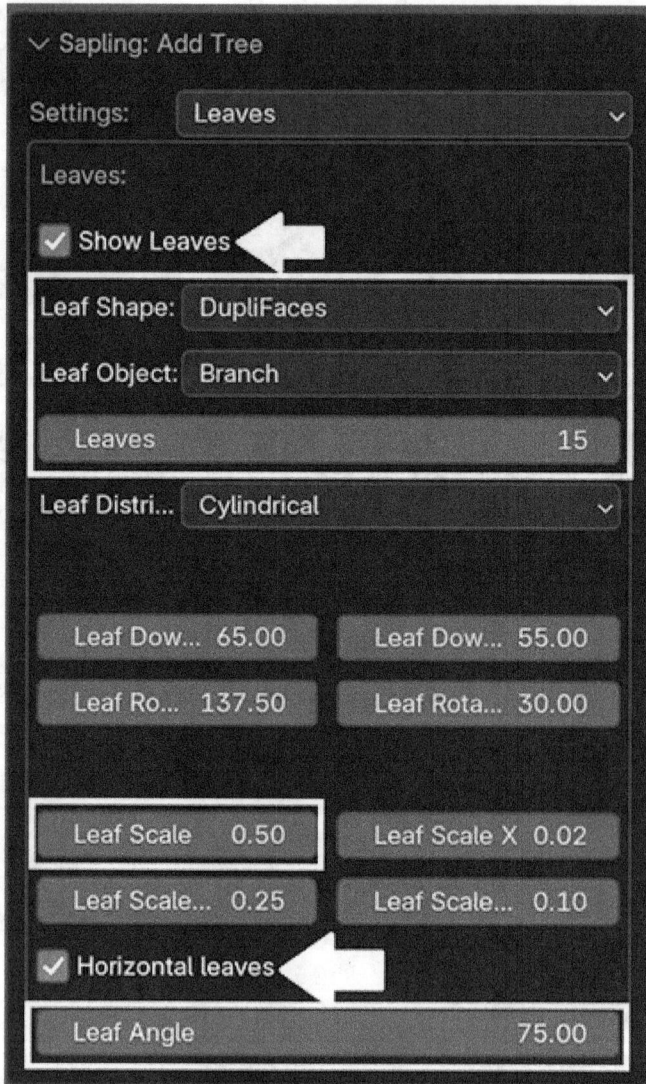

Figure 12.15 – Turning the Show Leaves option on

> **Note**
>
> If you lose access to the **Settings** panel, delete the generated tree and start over, as further adjustments are not possible without regenerating it.

4. Adjust the leaf parameters as follows:

   - **Leaf Shape**: **DupliFaces**
   - **Leaf Object**: **Branch**
   - **Leaves Number**: 15
   - **Leaf Scale**: 0.50
   - **Horizontal leaves**: enabled
   - **Leaf Angle**: 75.00

This is how the tree looks now, suitable for snowy environments.

Figure 12.16 – Adding tree branches

Now that the foliage is in place, we can move on to texturing the tree trunk.

Texturing the tree trunk

Now that the branches are complete, we will focus on the main trunk. In this section, we will set up the bark material and configure the mapping nodes to ensure the texture wraps correctly around the tree geometry.

We'll start by setting up a simple image-based material for the tree trunk:

1. Select the tree bark and add a new material in the **Shader Editor** called **Bark**.

2. Drag the Bark.png image texture into the **Shader Editor**.

3. Connect the **Bark** image texture's **Color** slot to the **Principled BSDF Base Color** slot.

To control this **Bark** material, let's add a **Texture Coordinate** node and a **Mapping** node:

1. Connect the **Texture Coordinate** node's **UV** slot to the **Vector** slot of the **Mapping** node.

2. In the **Mapping** node, set the **Z** angle to **90** degrees.

Figure 12.17 – Texturing tree bark

Now our tree is ready for use. This is how the tree will look:

Figure 12.18 – Generated spruce tree final result

The spruce tree is now as follows:

- Procedurally generated
- Optimized for duplication
- Suitable for snow scenes
- Ready for variation and placement

This completes the tree asset creation process. You now have a high-performance spruce tree that is required for large-scale environment design.

Summary

In this chapter, we created a spruce tree suitable for snowy environments using Blender 5's **Sapling Tree Gen** add-on. We started by generating a procedural base tree and shaping it to match real spruce characteristics by adjusting branch distribution and branch rings.

Next, we optimized the tree geometry to make it efficient for large scenes without sacrificing visual quality. We then modeled and textured branch-based leaves using alpha transparency and attached them to the tree through the **Sapling Tree Gen** add-on.

Finally, we applied a bark material to the tree trunk and aligned the texture correctly. The resulting tree is optimized, reusable, and ready to be duplicated across the environment.

In the next chapter, we will use scattering techniques to place assets naturally throughout the landscape.

Get this book's PDF version and more

Scan the QR code (or go to packtpub.com/unlock). Search for this book by name, confirm the edition, and then follow the steps on the page.

UNLOCK NOW

Note: Keep your invoice handy. Purchases made directly from Packt don't require an invoice.

Part 4

Rendering Epic Landscape Shots in Blender 5

In the last part of this book, we'll learn how to use Geometry Nodes to scatter all the natural assets we created. Then, we will finalize and apply some improvements and final touches to the landscape and river environments. Finally, we will learn about rendering and compositing to create epic 3D environment shots.

This part of the book includes the following chapters:

- *Chapter 13, Using Geometry Nodes to Scatter Objects in Blender*
- *Chapter 14, Finalizing the Landscape and River Scenes – Lighting, Rendering, and Compositing*

13

Using Geometry Nodes to Scatter Objects in Blender

Scattering is a foundational skill in all 3D environment design. When building environments, manually placing thousands of objects by hand is simply impossible. Scattering systems automate this massive task, allowing you to populate huge scenes in minutes while keeping the placement, scale, and rotation looking completely organic.

In this chapter, we will use the **Geometry Nodes** in Blender to scatter flowers, trees, and rocks throughout our landscape environment. You were introduced to Geometry Nodes in *Chapter 4*, where we used the system to create natural, lifelike plants and scatter them in our scene.

Even though we are repeating the same Geometry Nodes technique you learned in *Chapter 4*, consider this the *boss level*. Instead of just scattering a single plant, we will step up the complexity by layering multiple different assets: trees, flowers, and rocks, all at the same time.

In this chapter, we will first understand why Geometry Nodes have replaced the old Particle System. Next, we will learn how to build a simple *scattering machine* to place objects in specific areas, randomize their scale and rotation, and control their density using weight painting. Finally, we will learn why this method is far more efficient for your computer's memory.

Gaining proficiency in this workflow is essential for environment design, as it replaces the settings of the old Particle System with a flexible, node-based workflow used in professional studios.

In this chapter, we'll cover the following topics:

- Why should Geometry Nodes be used for scattering objects?
- Importing rock and flower assets into the landscape environment
- Using Geometry Nodes to scatter rocks and flowers

- Scattering flowers and rocks in different vertex groups using the **Join Geometry** node
- Adding trees to the river scene

The goal of this chapter is to give you the skills to populate your large landscapes with thousands of assets in minutes, creating organic, living scenes with minimal effort.

Technical requirements

This chapter requires a system capable of running **Blender version 5.0** or above (Windows, macOS, or Linux).

You can download the resources for this chapter from GitHub at: `https://github.com/PacktPublishing/3D-Environment-Design-with-Blender-5-Second-Edition/tree/82092b8342cf7390f47db151ecc34e47fb8d671a/chapter-13`.

Why should Geometry Nodes be used for scattering objects?

As discussed in *Chapter 4*, Geometry Nodes is Blender's modern system for procedurally generating and modifying geometry. Unlike the old **Particle System**, which was a pre-made list of settings you could only tweak slightly, Geometry Nodes allows you to build your own logic.

I want you to consider this situation: your project is to build a 3D garden in Blender. You have created all the assets in your garden: plants, flowers, rocks, and stones. Now, it's time to scatter all these assets across different areas of your garden, but there are some tips to keep in mind:

- The size of plants should be different. As you know, in nature, it's almost impossible to find two plants of 100 percent the same size. The same thing goes for the orientation of plants: each plant must have a different rotation angle at all angles, *X*, *Y*, and *Z*.
- The plants should be scattered randomly; there shouldn't be an obvious pattern.

Here is a good example of using Geometry Nodes to scatter plants:

Figure 13.1 – Good example of Geometry Nodes used to scatter plants organically

Now, let's use Geometry Nodes to scatter rocks, trees, and flowers across our landscape and river scenes, but first, we need to import the assets into the scene.

Importing rock and flower assets into the landscape environment

The first thing we need to do is import the rock, tree, and flower objects into the landscape scene, so let's go back to the landscape scene from *Chapter 9*. In this scene, we have the landscape textured with rocky snow and mud, as shown in *Figure 13.2*:

Figure 13.2 – Final result of the landscape scene from Chapter 9

Now, let's import the rock object into our landscape scene.

Importing the rock object

To import the rock object that we created in *Chapter 10*, let's perform the following actions:

1. Go to **File** and click on **Append**.

Figure 13.3 – Choosing Append from the File menu

2. Choose the Rocks.blend Blender file and click on it.

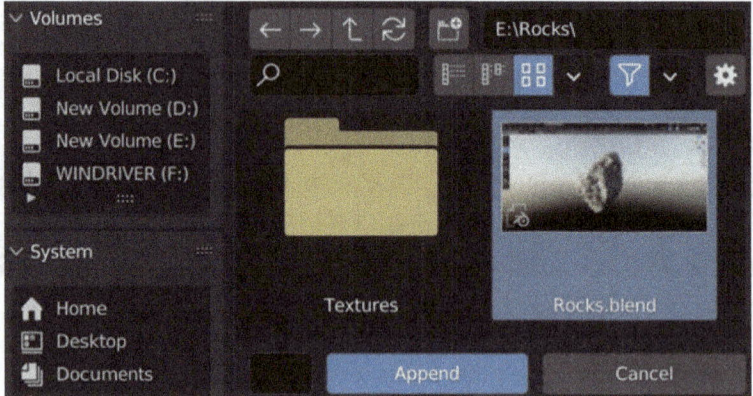

Figure 13.4 – Clicking on the Rocks Blender file

3. Click on the Object folder.

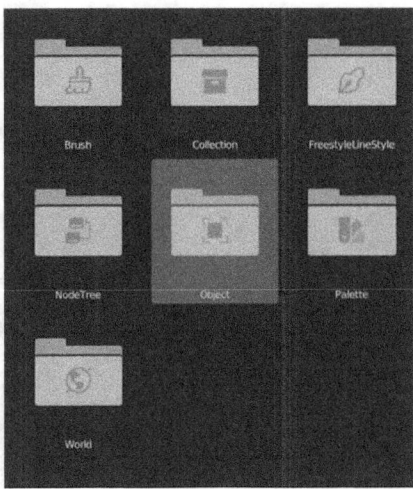

Figure 13.5 – Choosing Object folder

4. Double-click on the Rock object.

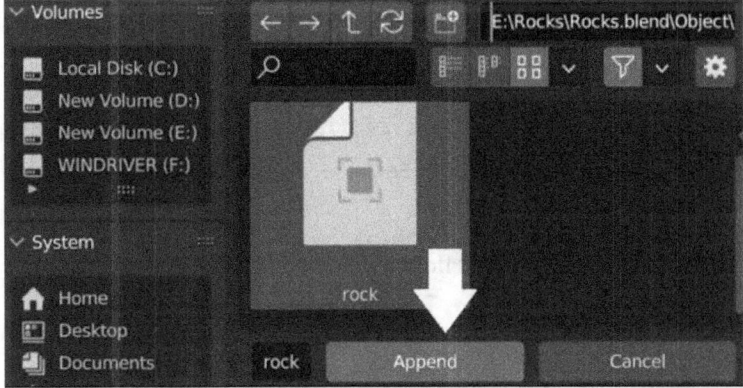

Figure 13.6 – Choosing the rock object to be appended

And basically, you'll have the rock in your scene, as shown in *Figure 13.7*:

Figure 13.7 – Rock object appended into the scene

The next step is to append the flowers to our scene. Repeat the same steps with this flower library, which you can download here: https://github.com/PacktPublishing/3D-Environment-Design-with-Blender-5-Second-Edition/blob/main/chapter-13/Flowers.blend.

Now that we have both the rock and flowers, let's proceed with scattering them in our landscape environment.

Using Geometry Nodes to scatter rocks and flowers

To use Geometry Nodes to scatter rocks, follow these steps:

1. Select the landscape object.
2. Switch to the **Geometry Nodes** tab.
3. Click on **New** to create a new **Geometry Node** modifier.

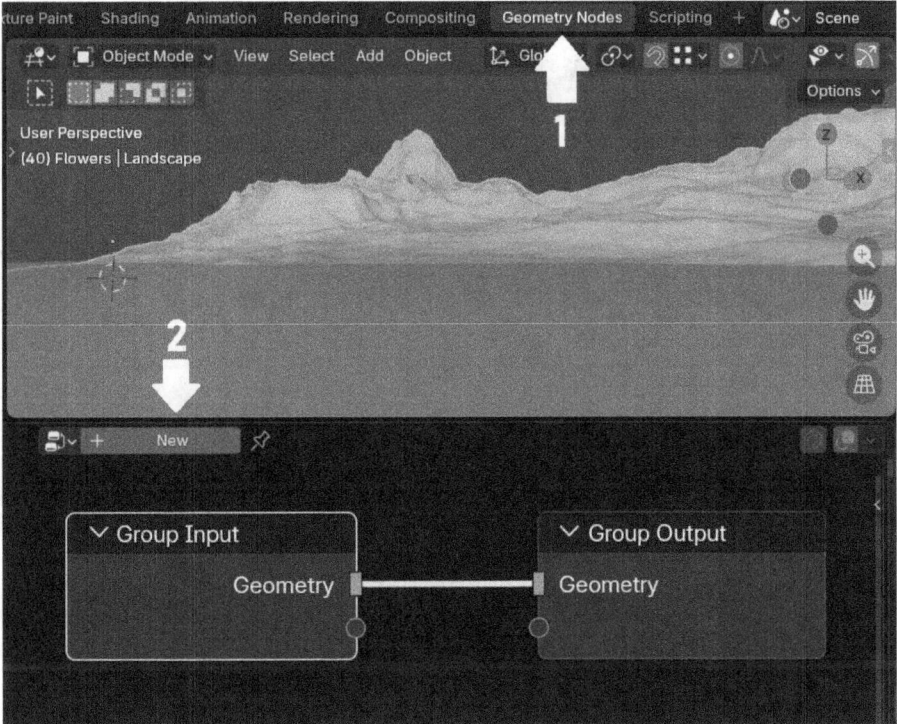

Figure 13.8 – Switching to the Geometry Nodes tab

Next, we need to add the **Scatter on Surface** node and drop it between the **Group Input** and **Group Output** nodes. We will follow the same steps we used in *Chapter 4* to scatter plants. You can refer back to the section titled *Using Geometry Nodes to scatter plants and leaves in our scene*, in *Chapter 4*, specifically around *Figure 4.37*. As you can see in *Figure 13.8*, we are starting with the same setup that we had in *Figure 4.37* in that chapter.

Note that when we use Geometry Nodes to scatter objects, Blender doesn't actually duplicate the heavy 3D mesh 10,000 times. Instead, it creates *instances*. Think of instances as lightweight ghost copies that just point back to the original object data. This uses a tiny fraction of your computer's memory, allowing you to build massive, dense forests that the old Particle System simply couldn't handle.

> **Note**
>
> Our landscape environment is very large. To avoid Viewport lag or potentially crashing
> Blender, make sure you reduce the **Density** on the **Scatter** node to a really low value
> (like 0.01) *before* connecting it. Once you assign the weight map that limits where the
> assets spawn, you can safely increase the **Density** value.

Creating separate vertex groups for assets

Back in *Chapter 4*, we only had one plant collection. Here, we have two different asset types
that we want to scatter in very specific locations:

- **Flowers (Collection)**: These should grow next to the water, but not directly touch the
  water.
- **Rocks (Object)**: These will be scattered along the cliffs and water edges. It is perfectly
  fine if the rocks intersect with the water.

To achieve this, we need to create two separate vertex groups to act as maps. Let's have a look
at the steps to do this:

1. Select the landscape and go to the **Object Data Properties** tab (**green triangle** icon).
2. Under **Vertex Groups**, click the **plus** (**+**) button twice to add two groups.
3. Name them Rocks and Flowers.

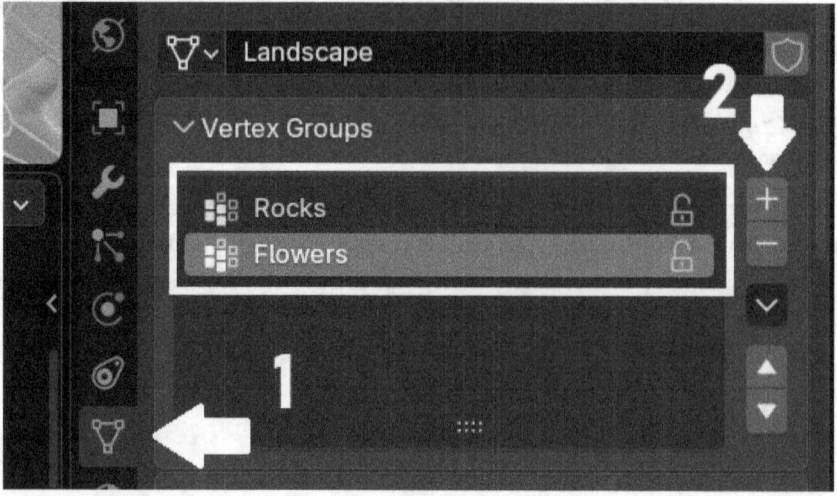

Figure 13.9 – Adding the Rocks and Flowers Vertex Groups

Now, to control the placement more precisely, we'll use **Weight Paint**, which we'll study in the next section.

Using Weight Paint to distribute flowers and rocks

Weight Paint is a brush that allows us to create a heatmap on an object with vertices. The heatmap is a cold-to-hot color gradient: *blue* (*cold*) refers to no distribution of objects, while *red* (*hot*) means 100% distribution of objects in the *red* area.

This is an example of a heatmap:

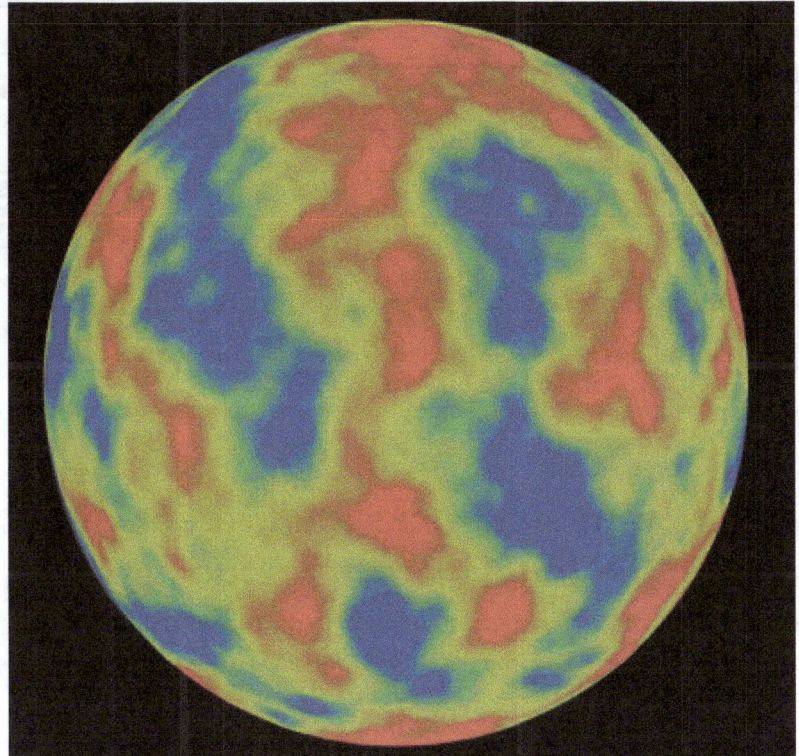

Figure 13.10 – Example of a heatmap

Now, follow these steps (see *Figure 13.11*):

1. Make sure your landscape is selected.

2. In the **Properties** panel, select the **Flowers** vertex group you just created.

3. Switch your Viewport from **Object Mode** to **Weight Paint** mode.

4. Using your brush, paint the areas where you want the flowers to grow, keeping them away from the direct water line.

5. Next, select the **Rocks** vertex group from the list, and paint the areas around the cliffs and water edges.

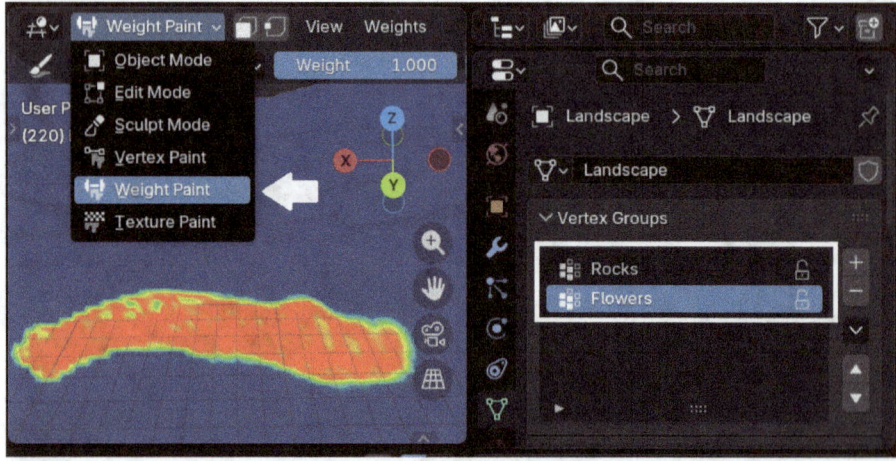

Figure 13.11 – Weight painting the landscape

Now that we've defined where each asset should appear, let's bring everything into Geometry Nodes and scatter both rocks and flowers on the same landscape.

Scattering flowers and rocks in different vertex groups using the Join Geometry node

Now that we have our maps, we need to bring them into the **Geometry Node Editor**. Because we are scattering two different assets on the same ground, we will use a **Join Geometry** node. Follow these steps:

1. In the **Geometry Node Editor**, add two **Scatter on Surface** nodes. Set one to your **Rocks** object and the other to your **Flowers** collection (ensuring **Pick Instance** is checked for the collection).

2. Connect the **Geometry** output from the single **Group Input** node into *both* **Scatter on Surface** nodes. This ensures both scatters calculate based on the clean, original ground.

3. Add a **Named Attribute** node (set to **Float**). Type Rocks in the name field, and plug its output into the **Distribution Mask** input of your **Rocks Scatter on Surface** node. Repeat this with a second **Named Attribute** node for your **Flowers**.

4. Add a **Join Geometry** node right before your **Group Output**.

5. Plug the outputs of *both* **Scatter on Surface** nodes, plus a line from the original **Group Input** (so your ground stays visible), into this **Join Geometry** node.

6. Make sure to use the **Randomize** features in the **Scatter on Surface** nodes to vary the scale and rotation, similar to what we did in *Chapter 4*.

The node setup should look like the following:

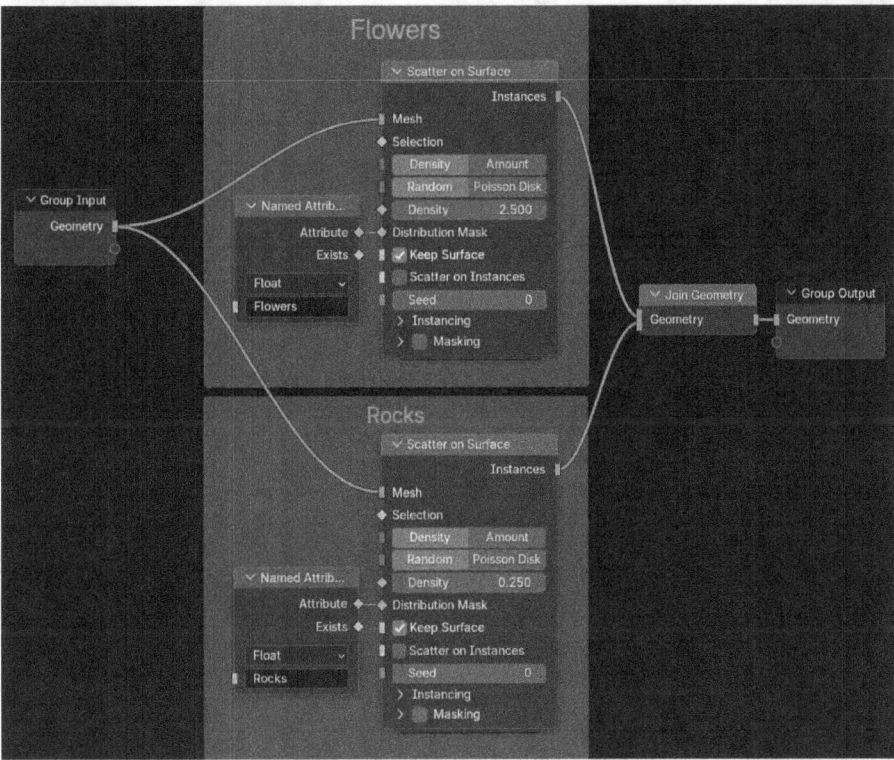

Figure 13.12 – Using Join Geometry to scatter flowers and rocks in parallel

This is how the rocks and flowers will look once they are scattered naturally across the environment:

Figure 13.13 – Displaying rocks and flowers in the landscape environment

Next, let's work on our second environment: the river scene.

Adding trees to the river scene

We can use the same workflow applied earlier in this chapter for scattering rocks and flowers, but this time adapted for trees. Reusing this method keeps the scene consistent and gives you precise control over where trees, flowers, and rocks appear.

As demonstrated earlier in the chapter, we can apply the same steps for adding rocks and flowers to the river scene that we created in *Chapter 6*.

Figure 13.14 shows the river scene with rocks and flowers scattered; all we need to add are trees:

Figure 13.14 – Rocks and flowers scattered across the river scene

Before we begin the process, let's add a third **Vertex Group** in your **Object Data Properties** and name it Trees.

Figure 13.15 – Adding the third "Trees" Vertex Group

Let's weight paint the tree areas, just as we did for the flowers in *Figure 13.11*, by following these steps:

1. Make sure your river object is selected.

2. In the **Properties** panel, select the **Trees** vertex group you just created.

3. Switch your Viewport from **Object Mode** to **Weight Paint** mode.

4. Using your brush, paint the areas where you want the trees to grow, keeping them away from the direct water line.

Now, to scatter the trees in the **Trees** Vertex Group, switch to the **Geometry Nodes** tab and execute the following steps:

1. Select the river object first.

2. This time, we will use *three* **Scatter on Surface** nodes.

3. Combine all three of them, along with the original ground, using a single **Join Geometry** node right before the output, as shown in *Figure 13.16*.

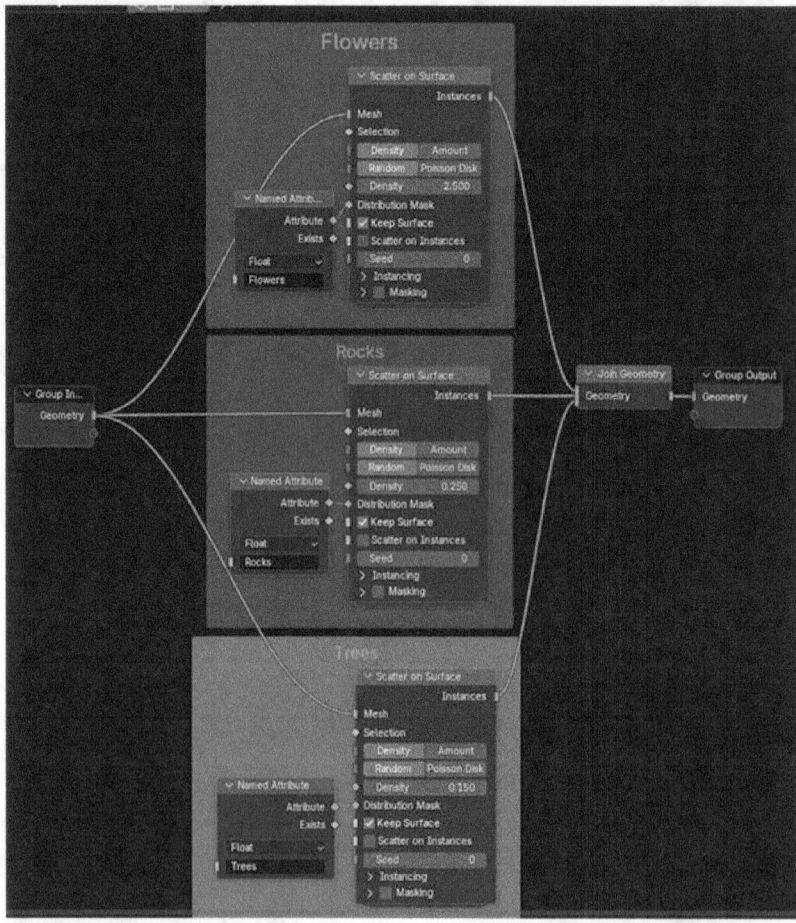

Figure 13.16 – The final Geometry Nodes tree setup for the river scene

This is how the river scene looks with all the assets (rocks, trees, and flowers) scattered across the river:

Figure 13.17 – Scattering trees in river scene

Here is the final river scene rendered in the 3D Viewport:

Figure 13.18 – Final result of the scattered flowers, trees, and rocks in the river scene

There we go, our scene has all the essential elements to it!

Summary

In this chapter, we modernized our workflow for scattering objects by using Geometry Nodes instead of the Particle System. We learned how to build a flexible scattering system using the **Scatter on Surface** node, which makes it super easy to place our assets across the environments we created.

By using the **Join Geometry** node, we successfully combined multiple scattered assets, like rocks, flowers, and trees.

To control exactly where these objects appear, we used Weight Painting. We also used the random features within our scatter nodes to change the scale and rotation of our assets, giving us that natural, organic look. The **Scatter on Surface** node we used is not only faster and much better for your computer's memory, but it also gives you the power to build massive environments that would be impossible with the old tools. In the next chapter, we will focus on rendering and compositing our final scene.

Get this book's PDF version and more

Scan the QR code (or go to packtpub.com/unlock). Search for this book by name, confirm the edition, and then follow the steps on the page.

Note: Keep your invoice handy. Purchases made directly from Packt don't require an invoice.

14

Finalizing the Landscape and River Scenes — Lighting, Rendering, and Compositing

Now that you've created your landscape scene, you'll want to try rendering it. In this chapter, you'll learn how to aim your camera, render a scene, and apply some compositing tricks.

First, we will make some adjustments to the landscape shape, including improving the water material to make it better fit our landscape theme, and then set up some realistic lighting using an HDRI map and jump into rendering and compositing.

Finalizing these details is what transforms a raw 3D scene into a professional, polished artwork.

In this chapter, we'll be covering the following topics:

- Adjusting the landscape shape
- Improving the **Water** material
- Setting realistic lighting in our scene
- Rendering the scene
- Compositing the scene

The goal of this chapter is to guide you through the critical *finish line* of production—lighting, framing, and post-processing—so you can showcase your environment at its absolute best.

Technical requirements

This chapter requires a system capable of running **Blender version 5.0** or above (Windows, macOS, or Linux).

You can download the resources for this chapter from GitHub at https://github.com/ PacktPublishing/3D-Environment-Design-with-Blender-5-Second-Edition/tree/ f0089c06132a9165773b4eb69f99a0610f9ad8ec/chapter-14.

Visit this link to check out the video of the code being run: https://packt.link/gKM1O

Adjusting the landscape shape

In order to produce some excellent rendered images, it would be great if we could expand our landscape environment to fill in the empty areas in the background, as shown in *Figure 14.1*:

Figure 14.1 – Landscape scene with empty space in the background

To fill out the empty space highlighted in the preceding figure, let's create a secondary landscape object (refer to *Chapter 6*). Be sure to tweak the settings to generate a unique shape, preventing the background from looking like a repetitive copy of the foreground.

One setting that should stay constant is **Noise Type**. Set the new landscape **Noise Type** option to **Slick Rock** so that it will be compatible with our first landscape:

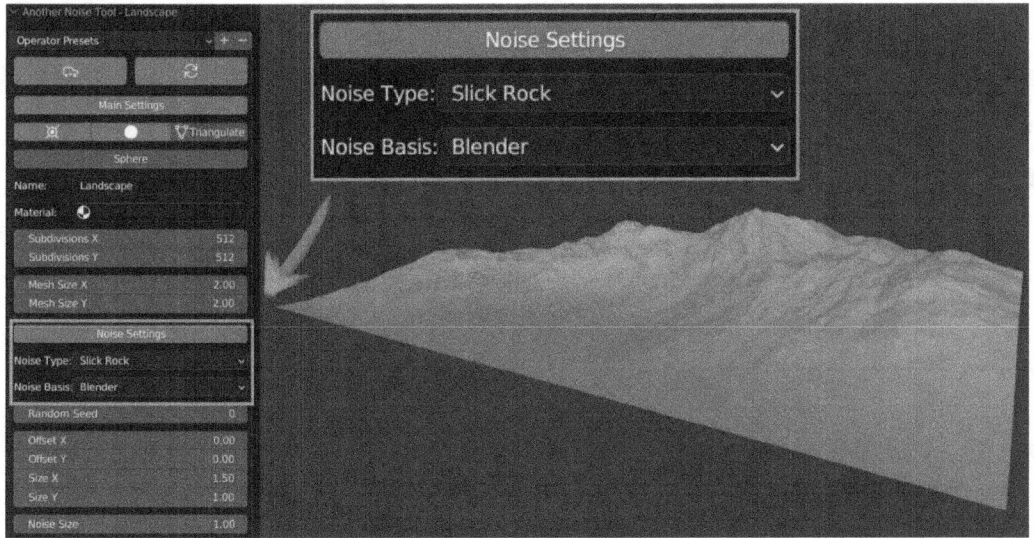

Figure 14.2 – Changing Noise Type to Slick Rock and Noise Basis to Blender

Next, move it forward and spin it around on the Z axis, as shown in *Figure 14.3*:

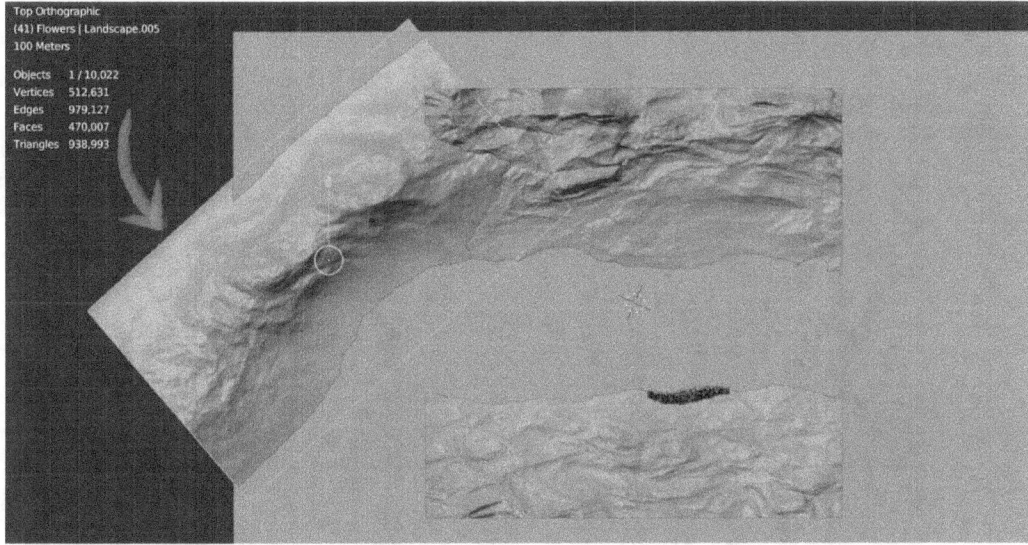

Figure 14.3 – Duplicating the landscape to fill in the empty space in the back

Now, we can see that our environment looks complete and pleasing to the eye.

Figure 14.4 – The landscape scene with more details in the back

However, our new landscape doesn't have a material assigned. So let's texture it in the next section.

Assigning the Mountain material to the new landscape

To maintain visual consistency, let's apply the **Mountain** material from the first landscape to the new one. Let's follow these steps:

1. Select the new landscape.

2. Go to **Material Properties**, which you will find empty.

3. Click on the **Materials** library and choose the **Mountain** material.

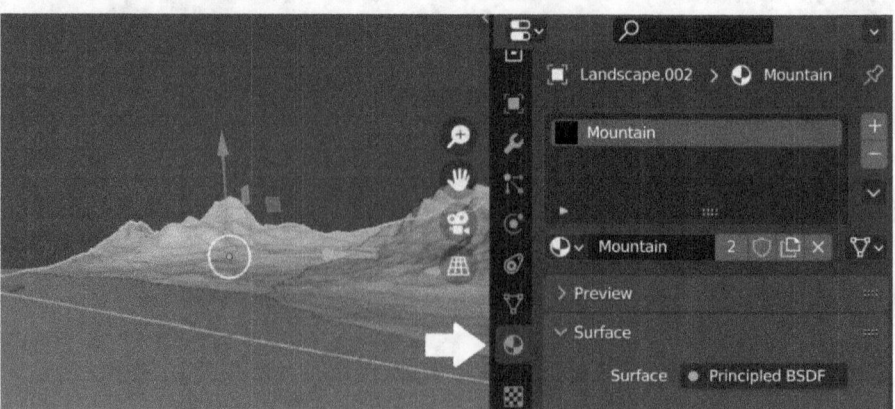

Figure 14.5 – Assigning the Mountain material to the second landscape

Now, our second landscape will look like the first one:

Figure 14.6 – Texturing the second landscape

This is the first change we apply to our landscape environment; now, the background of our landscape scene will be filled in and look more realistic. Next, let's tweak the **Water** material.

Improving the Water material

So far, the color of the water is *bluish* and doesn't look very realistic. The ground is muddy, and since the water is reflective, it should have a muddy color too, so we need to apply some tweaks to the **Water** material.

Figure 14.7 – The landscape scene progress from Chapter 9

To tweak the **Water** material, we first need to make a change to the **ColorRamp** node:

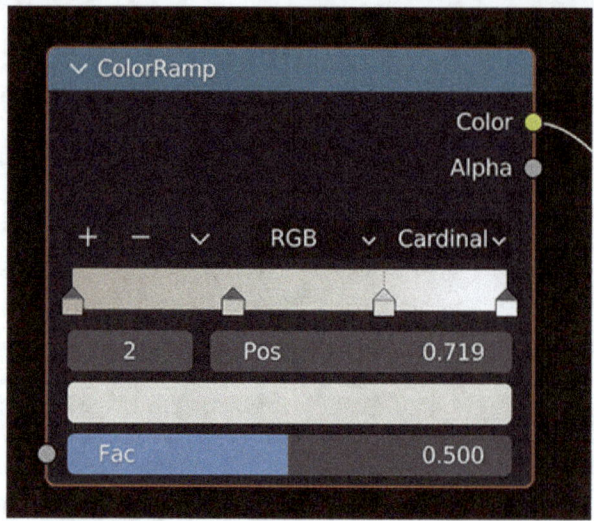

Figure 14.8 – Tweaking the ColorRamp node

Let's give the first *three handles* a creamy color that grades from *dark* to *light creamy*. The last handle color is purely *white*.

The second change is to the **Mix Shader** node. Set the **Fac** amount to 0.1 so that we can have only 10% of water transparency (in the **Transparent BSDF** node).

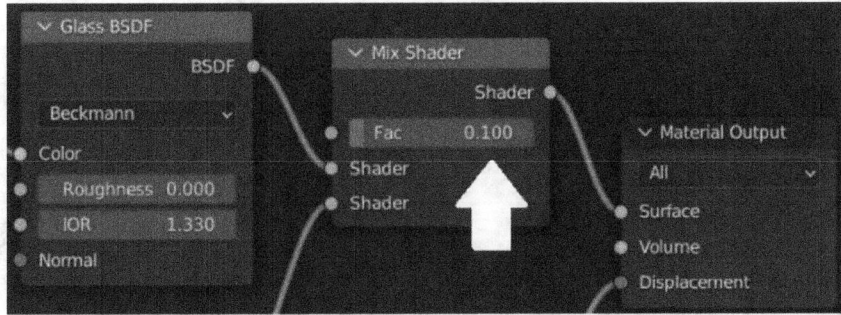

Figure 14.9 – Reducing the Mix Shader Fac value to 0.1

Here's the full node setup of the **Water** material that was created earlier in *Chapter 7*:

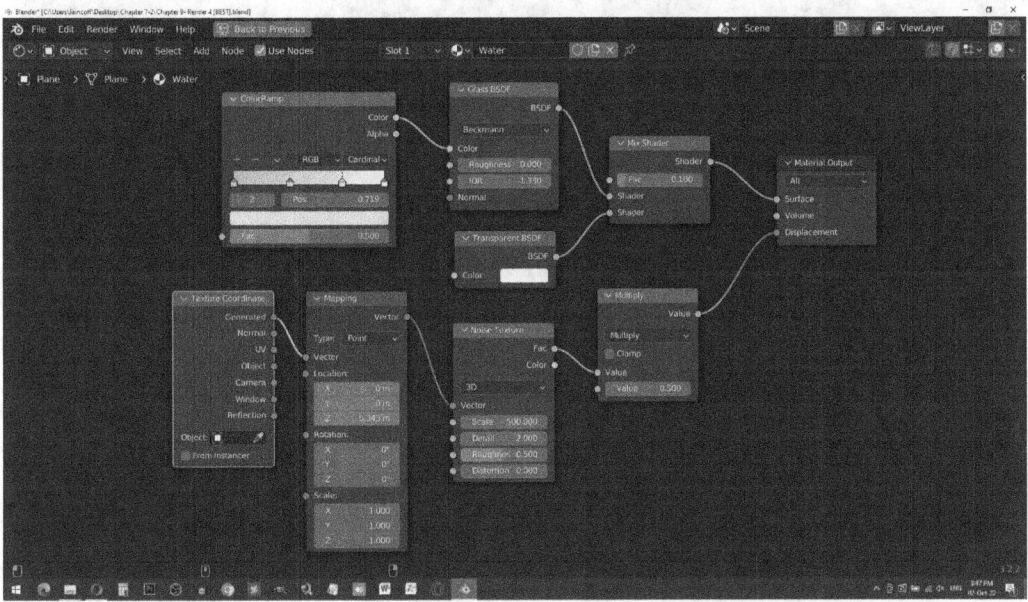

Figure 14.10 – New node setup of the Water material

These are the changes we applied to the water; it looks like this now in the **Rendered Preview** mode:

Figure 14.11 – Rendering the new Water material

The water blended better with the muddy color of the landscape and now looks more realistic than before. Now, let's set up realistic lighting in our scene by using HDRI maps.

Setting realistic lighting in our scene

To set up realistic lighting in our scene, we'll be using an HDRI map. **HDRI maps** are one of the most efficient and quickest ways to light your 3D scene and achieve realistic results in Blender. HDRI maps are usually a 360-degree panoramic image of real-world lighting that contains accurate lighting detail.

Let's get started on using an HDRI map in our scene. *Figure 14.12* shows the HDRI map we'll be using; it has a nice sun reflection. We can use it to emit light onto our landscape scene to achieve accurate lighting, resulting in more realistic 3D renders.

Figure 14.12 – HDRI map used to lighten the scene

You can download the HDRI map using this link: `https://github.com/PacktPublishing/3D-Environment-Design-with-Blender-5-Second-Edition/blob/f0089c06132a9165773b4eb69f99a0610f9ad8ec/chapter-14/HDRI.hdr`.

You can refer to the *Setting up an HDRI environment background for our scene* section in *Chapter 5* to learn how to assign and tweak HDRI maps in Blender.

Rendering the scene

One of the most important aspects to learn when becoming a 3D artist is how to create professional-looking renders of the scenes you create. A *professional render* goes beyond just high-quality textures; it relies on deliberate composition, lighting, and framing to guide the viewer's eye and tell a story. To capture that perfect frame and establish the scene's composition, you first need to add a camera.

Adding a camera to the landscape scene

Adding a camera to your scene is simple. Press *Shift + A* in the 3D Viewport, scroll down, and you will find the **Camera** object. When you add the **Camera** object, it will appear in your scene as follows:

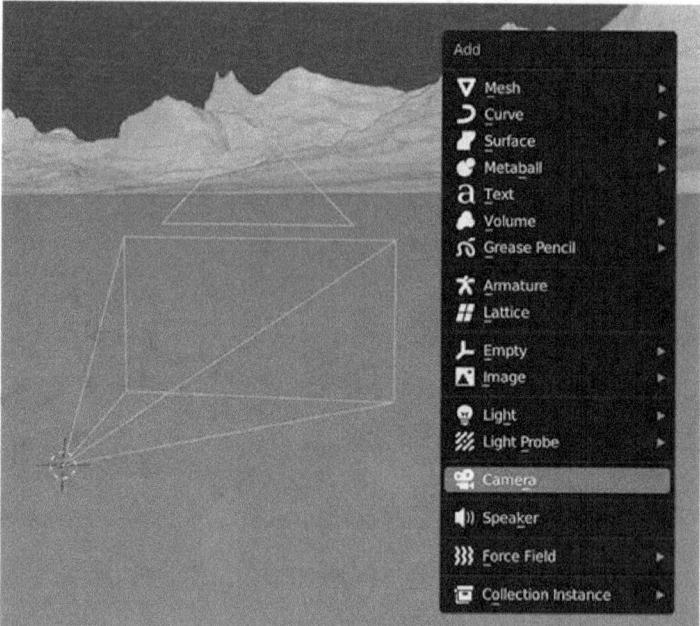

Figure 14.13 – Adding a Camera object to the scene

Next, we need to correctly position our camera for rendering. So, let's find the best shot by navigating to a point in our 3D Viewport that includes everything: the landscape, water, flowers, and rocks. This is shown in *Figure 14.14* as follows:

Figure 14.14 – Picking the best shot to position the camera

Now, we want the camera to be pointing at this scene. To put it in this position, we need to press *Ctrl + Alt + 0*.

Alternatively, you can go to the **Viewport** menu and select **View** | **Align View** | **Align Active Camera to View**.

You'll notice that the camera is now pointing at your current view. You will see the following frame:

Figure 14.15 – Pointing the camera to the current view

What's inside the frame is what's going to be included in the rendered image.

If you want to exit the camera view or return to it, you can press the *0* hotkey on the numpad.

Before moving on to the render settings, let's also add and position a camera for the river scene.

Adding a camera to the river scene

Let's repeat the same steps as provided in the *Adding a camera to the landscape scene* section to add a camera and position it like this:

Figure 14.16 – Adding a camera to the river scene

Before giving our scene a render, let's tweak the rendering settings in the **Render Properties** tab, starting with the render engine.

Changing the render engine

In order to achieve maximum realism, we need to use the **Cycles** render engine. Let's first switch to **Render Properties** and set the render engine to **Cycles**. **Cycles** is a physically-based path tracer, meaning it accurately simulates how light bounces and interacts with materials, which is essential for achieving true photorealism in nature scenes.

> **Note**
>
> Please refer to the *Differences between the three render engines of Blender* section in *Chapter 5* to understand the difference between the render engines in Blender.

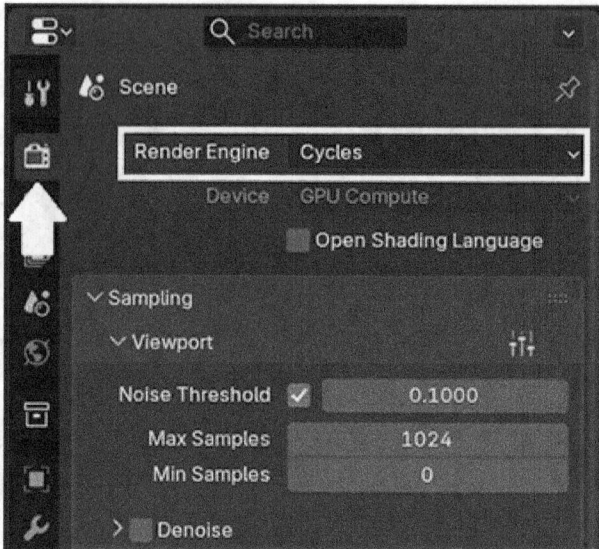

Figure 14.17 – Switching the render engine to Cycles

Under the **Render Engine** setting, we have the **Device** option. If **Device** is set to **CPU**, change it to **GPU Compute**. This will significantly improve your render times and make the Viewport more responsive, especially if you have a strong GPU card.

Next, let's tweak the next rendering setting, which is the sample amount.

What is the right number of samples to use?

Sampling refers to the samples, which are the noise that appears as your scene is rendering. You will see it soon when we render our landscape scene.

Blender gives us three ways to control the rendering samples:

- **Max Samples**: Blender will stop the rendering process once that number of samples is reached.
- **Min Samples**: Blender should always exceed the **Min Samples** value when rendering.
- **Time Limit**: Here, you can set a timer. For example, if you set it to 5 minutes, this means that Blender will keep rendering the image until the time limit of 5 minutes is reached. The number of samples rendered will be based on how powerful your setup is. Faster computers will render with more samples.

The more samples you use, the clearer your render image will be – but also, the more time it will take to be rendered.

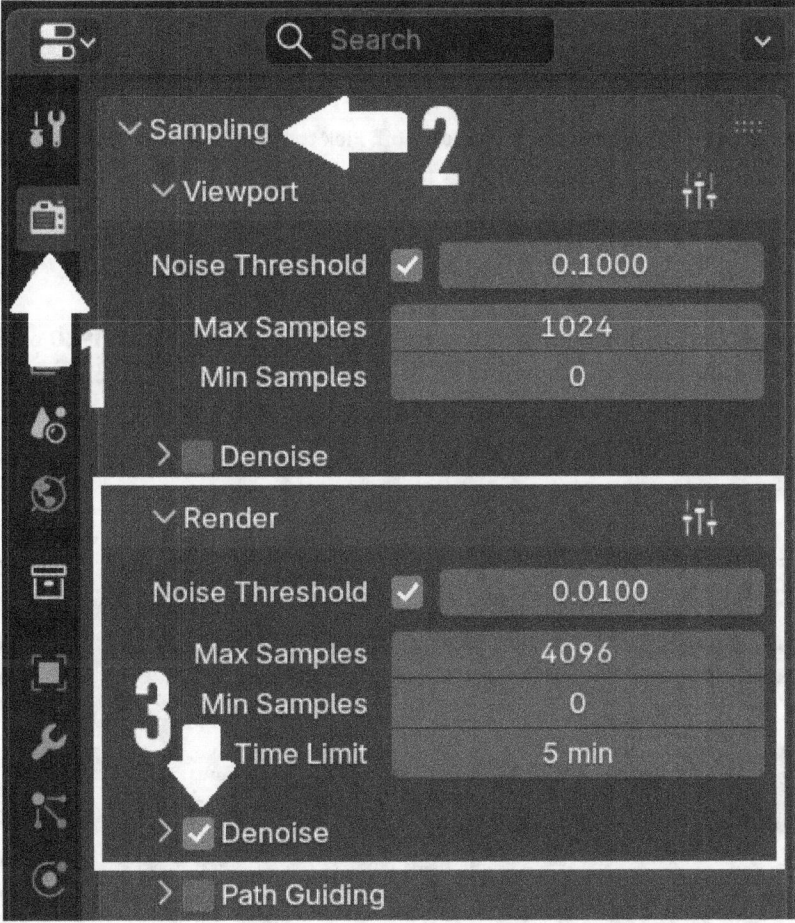

Figure 14.18 – Changing the Render Sampling settings

In our case, let's set the **Render** tab **Time Limit** value to 5 minutes. The time limit is a more precise way to control the render time, especially when rendering large animations. A 30-second 24-frames-per-second animation rendered at 5 minutes per render will take exactly 60 hours of rendering (30 * 24 * 5 = 3,600 minutes = 60 hours).

Also, make sure that the **Denoise** box is checked so that we can have a clear final render without noise.

> **Note**
>
> Be careful: **denoising** can sometimes smooth out important fine details or textures, making the image look *waxy*. It is a good approach to perform two test renders: one with **Denoise** on and another with **Denoise** off. Pick the version that looks best for your specific scene.

Changing the render image resolution

You can control the render image size, for example, the default settings are **1920** pixels on **X** and **1080** pixels on **Y**, meaning that this is a 2K render image quality. You can increase it up to 4K by duplicating the 100% value to 200%, or 50% for 1K quality.

For the **River** render resolution, I set it to 3000 px on **X** and 3700 px on **Y**:

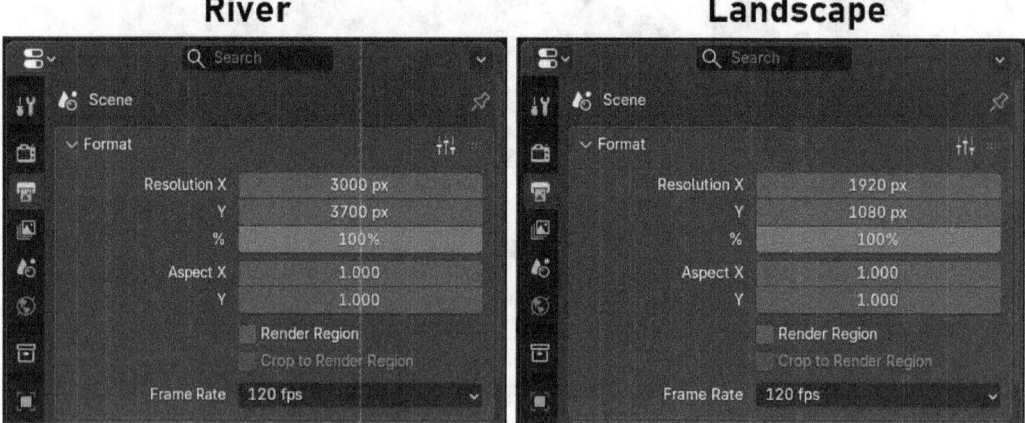

Figure 14.19 – Changing the Render image resolution for the landscape

With the camera positioned and the render settings configured, we're now ready to render the landscape scene.

Rendering the landscape scene

Let's go ahead and give our scene a render by going to the **Render** tab at the top of the Blender UI, as shown in *Figure 14.20*. You can also use the *F12* hotkey to access the **Render** tab.

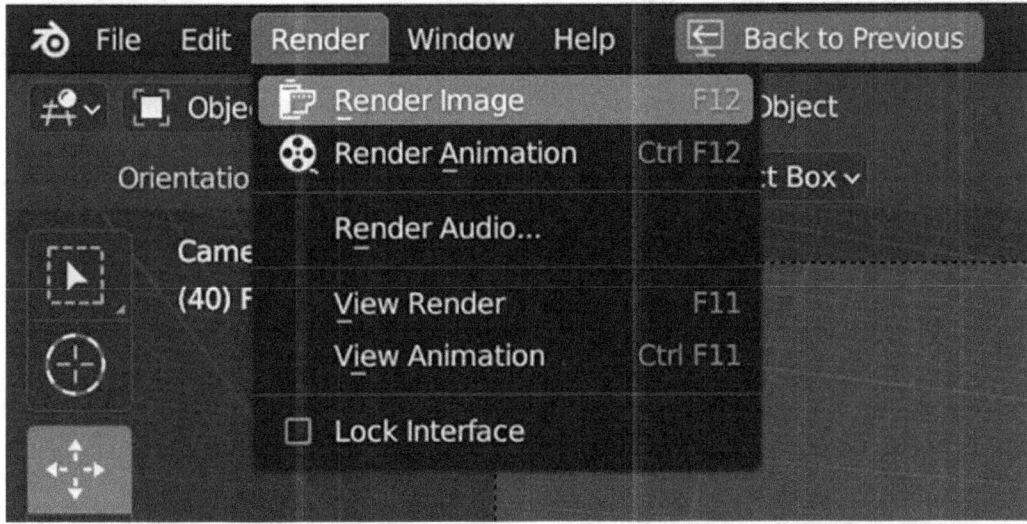

Figure 14.20 – Rendering the scene from the camera view

Immediately, a new window will pop up, showing your render getting clearer and clearer. Once finished, you will have your render completed.

Then you can go to **Image** and click on **Save As an Image** (see *Figure 14.21*). Locate the destination where you want to save your image.

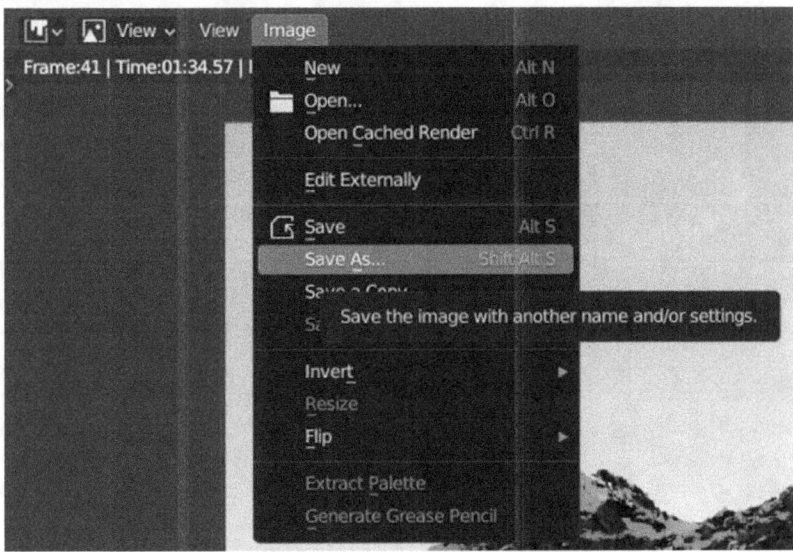

Figure 14.21 – Saving the render image

This way, you'll be saving the render as an image on your computer. *Figure 14.22* shows the rendered saved image of the project:

Figure 14.22 – Rendered saved image of our project

Figure 14.23 shows the river render as follows:

Figure 14.23 – Rendered saved image of our river

Now that we have our scene rendered, the next step is to work on the compositing to make it stand out.

Compositing the scene

Compositing allows us to enhance the final render by adding post-processing effects that make the image more believable. Using compositing, we can change the overall mood of the scene. For example, we can give it a cold, bluish atmosphere or a warm, sunny feeling.

> **Note**
>
> Before switching to the **Compositing** workspace, make sure the scene has already been rendered. Without a render, there will be no image input available in the Compositor.

At the top of the Blender interface, you will find several workspace tabs. To begin compositing, follow these steps:

1. Switch to the **Compositing** tab.

2. Once in the **Compositing** space, add a new compositing group.

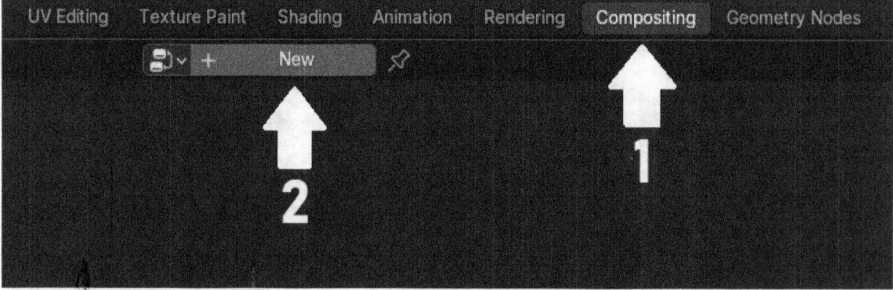

Figure 14.24 – Switching to the Compositing tab in Blender

By default, you will see three nodes, as shown in *Figure 14.25*:

- **Render Layers**
- **Viewer**
- **Group Output**

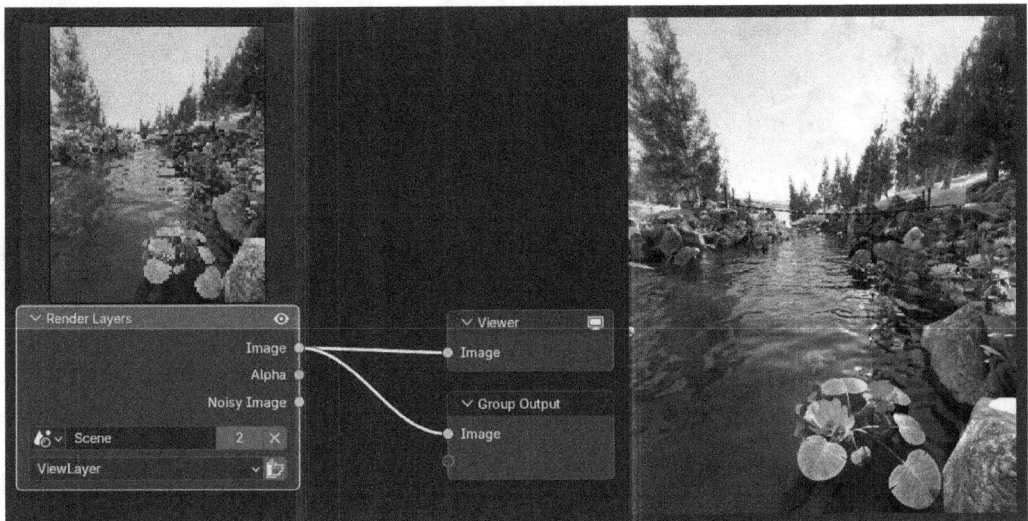

Figure 14.25 – The Render Layers, Viewer, and Group Output nodes

The rendered image will appear in the background. To navigate the background image, use the following keys:

- *V*: Zoom out
- *Alt + V*: Zoom in
- *Alt + Middle mouse button*: Pan

Let's start with the first compositing effect, which is **Color Balance**.

Using the Color Balance node

The **Color Balance** node adjusts the color and values of our render. We can change the overall mood of our render by adjusting the color balance.

Now, let's use the **Color Balance** node to adjust the color mood of the render:

1. Press *Shift + A* and add a **Color Balance** node.
2. Move it between the **Render Layers** node and the **Composite/Viewer** nodes.

Figure 14.26 – Adding the Color Balance node in our compositing setup

Now let's change the color of the last circle, **Gain**, to *blue*. This way, we'll have a cold, blue feeling in our scene:

1. Set **Hue** to 0.6.

2. Set **Saturation** to 0.2.

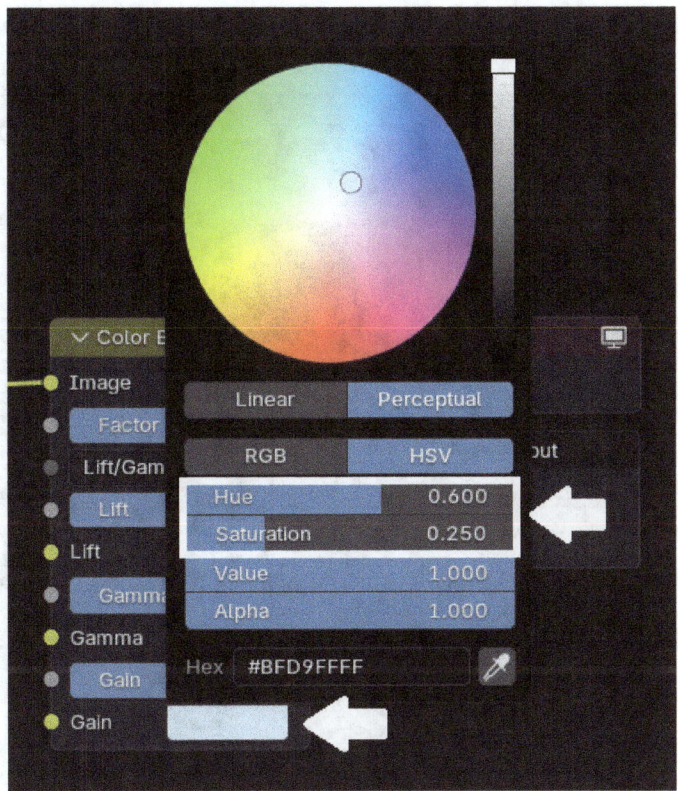

Figure 14.27 – Tweaking Color Balance for a cold, blue look

This is our render with this cold, blue effect:

Figure 14.28 – Changing the overall color of our render to bluish

On the other hand, if we changed the color of **Color Balance** to *red*, we'd be giving our scene a warm feeling:

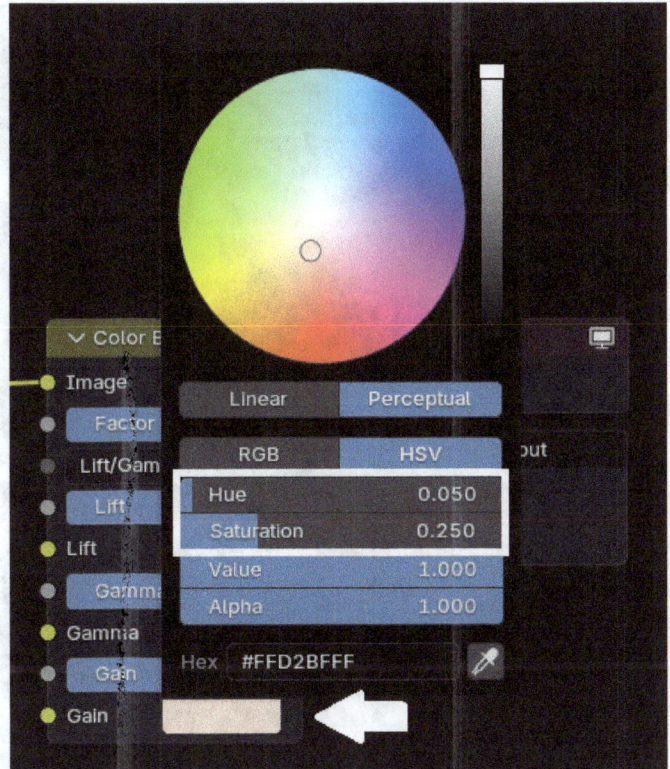

Figure 14.29 – Tweaking Color Balance for warm color grading

To create a warm atmosphere, follow these steps:

1. Set **Hue** to 0.05.

2. Keep the **Saturation** value at 0.25.

This is our render with the warm, red effect:

Figure 14.30 – Giving our render a warm feeling

Small color changes in the **Color Balance** node can significantly affect the mood and emotional tone of the environment.

Adding sun beams

Sun beams help emphasize the sunlight's direction and add realism to outdoor scenes. To apply this to our scene, follow these steps:

1. Press *Shift + A*.

2. Add the **Glare** node. The **Glare** node is used to add lens flares, for glows around exposed parts of an image, such as the sun or bright lights.

3. Change the mode from **Streaks** to **Sun Beams**.

You will notice an **X** marker on the background image. Move this marker manually to the position of the sun:

Figure 14.31 – Adding Sun Beams to the river render in compositing

Use the following recommended settings to fine-tune the sun beams to achieve a softer, more natural sunlight look.

4. Change **Quality** from **Medium** to **High**.

5. Expand the **Highlights** tab to see more settings:

   1. Set **Threshold** to 5.

   2. Check the **Clamp** option.

   3. Reduce the **Strength** value to 0.25.

6. Change the **Tint** value, which is the color of the sun beams, to a warm sunny color.

Figure 14.32 shows the result as follows:

Figure 14.32 – Tweaking Sun Beams to the river render in compositing

Let's add the second composting effect to our render, which is the **Glare** node.

Adding Glare to the render

We will now use the **Glare** node to add post-processing highlights. This enhances the brightest pixels in the scene, adding streaks or fog to simulate a real camera lens looking at the sun.

Follow these steps to add and adjust the **Glare** node in the compositing setup:

1. To add the **Glare** node, press *Shift + A* and add a **Glare** node.
2. Move the node between the **Render Layers** and **Color Balance** nodes.

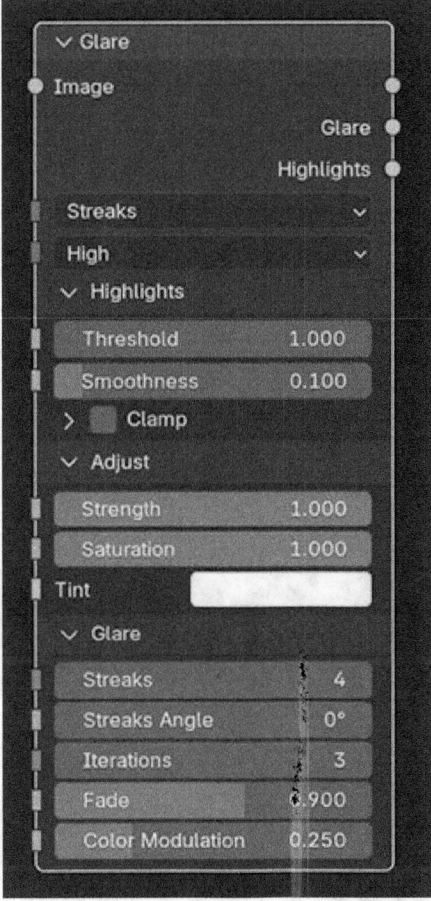

Figure 14.33 – The Glare compositing node set to Streaks

Immediately, you will see the nice stars on your render. We can make the following tweaks:

- Increase **Threshold** to 5
- Reduce **Strength** to only 0.5
- Increase **Streaks** to 6 instead of **4**
- Add one iteration, and set the **Iterations** to 4
- Set **Fade** to 0.85

You will see streak effects as follows:

Figure 14.34 – Glare compositing applied to the river render

The same setup can be applied to the landscape environment to achieve consistent lighting effects, as shown in *Figure 14.35*:

Figure 14.35 – Applying the Glare node to the rendered image in compositing

With **Color Balance**, **Sun Beams**, and **Glare** combined, the render gains depth, atmosphere, and a more cinematic appearance.

And there you have it! This is the final result of our landscape environment render.

Summary

In this chapter, we used Blender's **Compositor** feature to enhance our final renders. We adjusted color mood using the **Color Balance** node, added directional light effects with **Sun Beams**, and enhanced highlights using the **Glare** node. These compositing techniques help push a render closer to a photorealistic result without changing the 3D scene itself.

Congratulations on completing this journey! You now possess the skills to turn a blank Viewport into a living, breathing landscape. Remember that every expert was once a beginner who didn't quit. Keep practicing, stay curious, and enjoy the endless creative freedom that 3D art offers.

Get this book's PDF version and more

Scan the QR code (or go to packtpub.com/unlock). Search for this book by name, confirm the edition, and then follow the steps on the page.

Note: Keep your invoice handy. Purchases made directly from Packt don't require an invoice.

15

Unlock Your Exclusive Benefits

Your copy of this book includes the following exclusive benefits:

DRM-Free PDF Version

Download DRM-free PDF and ePub copies of this book.

7-Day Packt Library Access

Get 7-day unlimited access to 8,000+ books and videos. No credit card required.

Available for first-time Packt+ trial users only.

Next-Gen Reader Access

Read this book on Packt Reader with progress sync, dark mode and note-taking.

Follow the guide below to unlock them. The process takes only a few minutes and needs to be completed once.

Unlock this Book's Free Benefits in 3 Easy Steps

Step 1

Keep your purchase invoice ready for *Step 3*. If you have a physical copy, scan it using your phone and save it as a PDF, JPG, or PNG.

For more help on finding your invoice, visit `https://www.packtpub.com/en-us/unlock?step=1`.

 Note

> If you bought this book directly from Packt, no invoice is required. After *Step 2*, you can access your exclusive content right away.

Step 2

Scan the QR code or go to `packtpub.com/unlock`.

On the page that opens (similar to *Figure 15.1* on desktop), search for this book by name and select the correct edition.

Unlock Your Book's Free Benefits

Bought a Packt book from Amazon or one of our channel partners? Unlock your free benefits in 3 easy steps.

Find Your Book   Sign Up or Sign In   Upload Purchase Proof

Need Help?

Search for your book here

✦ **1. Find Your Book**   ∧

🔍 Search by title or ISBN

👥 **2. Sign up (Free) or Sign In**   ∨

☁ **3. Upload Purchase Proof**   ∨

Figure 15.1: Packt unlock landing page on desktop

Step 3

After selecting your book, sign in to your Packt account or create one for free. Then upload your invoice (PDF, PNG, or JPG, up to 10 MB). Follow the on-screen instructions to finish the process.

Need Help

If you get stuck and need help, visit `https://www.packtpub.com/unlock-benefits/help` for a detailed FAQ on how to find your invoices and more. This QR code will take you to the help page.

> **Note**
>
> If you are still facing issues, reach out to `customercare@packt.com`.

packtpub.com

Subscribe to our online digital library for full access to over 7,000 books and videos, as well as industry leading tools to help you plan your personal development and advance your career. For more information, please visit our website.

Why subscribe?

- Spend less time learning and more time coding with practical eBooks and Videos from over 4,000 industry professionals
- Improve your learning with Skill Plans built especially for you
- Get a free eBook or video every month
- Fully searchable for easy access to vital information
- Copy and paste, print, and bookmark content

At www.packtpub.com, you can also read a collection of free technical articles, sign up for a range of free newsletters, and receive exclusive discounts and offers on Packt books and eBooks.

Other Books You May Enjoy

If you enjoyed this book, you may be interested in these other books by Packt:

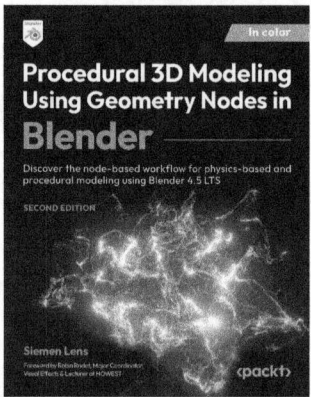

Procedural 3D Modeling Using Geometry Nodes in Blender, Second Edition

Siemen Lens

ISBN: 9781836203018

- Discover the different node inputs and outputs that Geometry Nodes have to offer
- Get to grips with the flow of the Geometry Nodes system
- Work with Geometry Nodes use cases through fun projects that advance with each chapter
- Link Geometry and Material node editors using Named Attributes
- Explore the flow of the Simulation Zone in Blender 4.5 LTS
- Create both simple and complex physics simulations mathematically
- Understand mathematical terms such as velocity, forces, collisions, and vectors
- Work with variables in your Geometry Nodes-based workflow

Blender for Beginners Part 1, Third Edition

3D Tudor (Neil Ian Bettison), Vanessa Haralambous

ISBN: 9781837631094

- Customize Blender for speed by clearing workspaces, overlays, the Status Bar, and Outliner filters
- Model with precision using Extrude, Inset, Bevel, Loop Cut, Knife, Spin, Slide, Shear, and Rip
- Produce shading-friendly topology with bridges, fills, smoothing, Auto Smooth, and sharps
- Shape faster with curves, modifiers, lattices, and constraints and stay non-destructive
- Keep meshes clean with selections, transforms, normals, naming, and file organization
- Build principled PBR materials with Node Wrangler and Ambient Occlusion helpers

Packt is searching for authors like you

If you're interested in becoming an author for Packt, please visit authors.packt.com and apply today. We have worked with thousands of developers and tech professionals, just like you, to help them share their insight with the global tech community. You can make a general application, apply for a specific hot topic that we are recruiting an author for, or submit your own idea.

Share your thoughts

Now you've finished *3D Environment Design with Blender 5, Second Edition*, we'd love to hear your thoughts! Scan the QR code below to go straight to the Amazon review page for this book and share your feedback or leave a review on the site that you purchased it from.

https://packt.link/r/1-836-20329-2

Your review is important to us and the tech community and will help us make sure we're delivering excellent quality content.

Index